There Is

John D. Caputo, *series editor*

PERSPECTIVES IN
CONTINENTAL
PHILOSOPHY

CLAUDE ROMANO

There Is

The Event and the Finitude of Appearing

TRANSLATED BY MICHAEL B. SMITH

FORDHAM UNIVERSITY PRESS
New York ▪ 2016

There Is was first published in French under the title *Il y a* by Presses Universitaires de France, © 2003 Presses Universitaires de France.

Cet ouvrage, publié dans le cadre du programme d'aide à la publication, bénéficie du soutien du Ministère des Affaires Etrangères et du Service Culturel de l'Ambassade de France représenté aux États-Unis.

This work received support from the French Ministry of Foreign Affairs and the Cultural Services of the French Embassy in the United States through their publishing assistance program.

Visit us online at www.fordhampress.com.

Library of Congress Cataloging-in-Publication Data

Romano, Claude, 1967–
[Il y a. English]
There is : the event and the finitude of appearing / Claude Romano ; translated by Michael B. Smith. — First edition.
pages cm. — (Perspectives in Continental philosophy)
Includes bibliographical references.
ISBN 978-0-8232-6714-9 (cloth : alk. paper) — ISBN 978-0-8232-6715-6 (pbk.)
1. Events (Philosophy) 2. Phenomenology. I. Title.
B2433.R663I413 2016
142'.7—dc23

2015006061

Printed in the United States of America

18 17 16 5 4 3 2 1

First edition

For Melanie

"Il y a un vaisseau qui a emporté ma bien-aimée.
Il y a dans le ciel six saucisses et la nuit venant on dirait des asticots dont naîtraient les étoiles
[. . .] Il y a mille petits sapins brisés par les éclats d'obus autour de moi."

—Guillaume Apollinaire, "Il y a"

Contents

Preface

Does phenomenology have to be presented as a transcendental discipline? By "transcendental," I do not mean in this case *every* attempt to question phenomena with respect to their presumed conditions of possibility. To reject out of hand the possibility of a transcendental questioning would, in a sense, mean giving up philosophy altogether. Therefore the problem does not involve the validity of a certain type of questioning (and a certain type of argumentation) but rather the more precise meaning the word "transcendental" has taken on since Kant, that of the *subjective* conditions of possibility, or yet again, that of a *de jure* priority of the subject in relation to the object. This both ontological and epistemological priority is indissociable from the initial formulation of the task of phenomenology. In Husserl's view, phenomenology as a descriptive science must take *appearing* as the *de jure* source in order to inquire into the meaning of that appearing. But what does it mean to inquire into that meaning? It means to trace back what appears to subjective functions. All phenomena are phenomena *for* a consciousness, which means that consciousness, interpreted as a transcendental instance [*instance*], is the condition of possibility of the phenomenalization of phenomena. This is how we must take the word "constitution." Constitution is not the real production of phenomena by the pure ego, but the necessary and *unilateral* dependence of what appears vis-à-vis its modes of appearing, that is, the lived experiences (*Erlebnisse*) in which it announces itself and that *confer* its meaning on it. This is an absolute priority of consciousness, a "being that is prior in itself,"[1] that precedes and makes possible the natural being of the world. By virtue of this primacy, the world takes on an objective direction of development and at the same time becomes the correlate of a *Sinngebung*: "The Objective world, the world that exists for me, that always has and always will exist for me, the only world that ever can exist for me—this world, with all its Objects, as I have said, derives its whole sense and its existential status, which it has for me, from me myself [*aus mir selbst*], *from me as the transcendental Ego*, the Ego who comes to the fore only with the transcendental-phenomenological epochē."[2] Is this orientation of phenomenology necessary? Inevitable, even? To inquire into the appearing of everything that appears—does this necessarily entail tracing what appears to a "phenomenon" understood as a phenomenon *of consciousness* that, although intentional, establishes a relation of dependence and conditionality between the world and the pure ego?

Heidegger was the first to formulate questions such as these at the very beginning of his career. But he responded in *Sein und Zeit* by adopting, to a large extent, the transcendental approach. In maintaining that Being-in-the-world cannot be elucidated by having recourse to an entity of the same mode of being as itself, but only by appealing a being whose being includes an understanding of being, that is, to a being that exists and is in the world, Heidegger rejects the a-cosmic aspect of the Husserlian transcendental ego, but he continues to make *Dasein* and its transcendence the condition of possibility for the appearing of the world. He transforms Husserlian transcendentalism from within without breaking away from it entirely. It is true that *Dasein* is only the clearing [*Lichtung*] of the manifestation of beings because it is, more genuinely, the very site of the truth of Being. With this limitation, however (the limitation of an idealism ontologically reinterpreted as the dependency of being upon subsisting and at-hand beings from the point of view of the understanding of Being qua determination of existence),[3] Heidegger is able to maintain that "idealism affords the only correct possibility for a philosophical problematic."[4] And he designates the leading back of the Being of beings in general to the Being of the subject "ontologically well understood,"[5] or rather to the understanding of Being as the ontological determination of existence, as "phenomenological reduction."[6]

It is true that Heidegger himself judged the "hermeneutically transcendental" approach of *Sein und Zeit* (as he calls it in his *Nietzsche*) harshly. Thus he opened up entirely new paths within phenomenology. Still, it is not sure that these paths necessarily have to simply coincide with his own itinerary (see chapters 1 and 2). Indeed, what obstacle is there, from the point of view of phenomenology, to adopting a perspective of the transcendental style? Among the following chapters, there are many that attempt to answer this question not by means of a general argument, but on the basis of "the things themselves," following the guiding thread of particular phenomena: for example, in examining the phenomenological status of the body in perception and in questioning the soundness of the Husserlian distinction between flesh (*Leib*) and body (*Körper*). This distinction rests mainly on transcendental presuppositions—including in such authors as Merleau-Ponty, who sketched out a critique of the transcendental approach. It is because in such authors flesh is conceived from the outset as a-cosmic that it can, in a sense, become pan-cosmic, that it can extend to the entire cosmos, as we see in *The Visible and the Invisible*, and that it can thus lead to replacing an egological idealism with a carnal one (see Chapter 5). In other words, here flesh can only stand out as a possible guiding thread of phenomenology if phenomenology continues to be conceived of as a method whose goal it is to trace the process of appearing back to its constituting sources in a "subject"—"carnal" no doubt, but prior to the world and preordained for it. Now the "conditions of possibility" of perception—are they not of such a nature that they require *the belonging of the "subject" to the world qua body?* This assertion does not necessarily lead us back to a form of naturalism—and still less one of positivism—that would be diametrically opposed to the transcendental approach. In this respect, it is not without interest to examine an initiative like that of Gibson, who, rejecting both naturalist reductionism and its idealist counterpart, asserts that "perception" makes sense neither at the level of a physiological description of organs nor at the level of an a-cosmic consciousness (or flesh), but only at the level of the primordial encounter between a live individual and a life-milieu, itself highly structured, interspersed with suggestions for action ("affordances") and vital meanings. In short, he asserts that perception is an *intrinsically relational* phenomenon, or, as he says, an "ecological" one (see Chapter 6).

In reading the following texts, a second series of problems, more circumscribed but no less crucial, bearing on the relationship between phenomenology and logic will be encountered. Indeed, if phenomenology cannot claim to say anything about phenomena without specifying the meaning of its own *logos*, we must consider the extent to which the phenomenological *logos* must meet the requirements that the contemporary logic issuing from Frege imposes—or wants to impose—on it. Does that logic, the novelty of which went largely unnoticed by Husserl, Heidegger, and later phenomenology provide the norm, so to speak, for what may have the status of a *logos* of phenomena? This question, obviously of considerable importance, is approached in these pages essentially from a critical perspective through an *Auseinandersetzung* with a certain analytic tradition, more specifically the one stemming from the logical positivism of Carnap and the Vienna Circle. The sensitive point of the controversy concerns the possibility of speaking meaningfully of "beings" or of "nothingness." Through this question, of course, it is more broadly the problem of the status of logic within philosophy that is posed (see Chapter 7).

Finally, a third order of problems, present throughout this journey, bears on metaphysics in the sense that term has taken on since Nietzsche—that of a unitary historical formation of Western thought taken as a whole. The question of metaphysics understood in this sense seems to me to be at the heart of any philosophical approach worthy of the name. And this is, first of all, because philosophy, qua *Western* philosophy, certainly does not represent the whole of thought, of meditative or "philosophical" thought in a much broader sense—no more than "European humanity," as Husserl put it (and regardless of what meaning is attributed to it) is the whole of humanity or can be held up as the *telos* or supreme norm of humanity. For while there is no Greek or Indian mathematics, there is indeed a Greek or Indian thought, just as there is a Persian, a Chinese, an Arab, an African, and a Japanese thought. No dialogue would ever be possible between them and therefore no philosophical effort of rationality, without a prior delimitation of their respective presuppositions—and therefore, to start with, of those orienting our own approach once we venture to do "philosophy."

In this respect, a critique of the hermeneutic philosophy of the last century is in order. Despite the brilliant, path-breaking initiative of Heidegger, hermeneutics has turned away almost entirely before the path that seemed to be opening up before it. Thus turning away from the problem of metaphysics, explicitly for some of them (Gadamer),[7] in a less clearly stated way for others (Paul Ricoeur or Charles Taylor), the representatives of philosophical hermeneutics have taken this step largely to the detriment of their own coherence. To understand better is not just to understand "otherwise": it is to try to thematize the limitations of one's own understanding. In this respect the "dialogue that we are," as Gadamer calls it (quoting Hölderlin), does not stop at the shores of the Mediterranean. To understand ourselves is essentially to understand our own limitations, that is, to strive to understand the wherewithal of our self-understanding, which generally remains hidden from our understanding. Understanding does not have what keeps it from understanding itself—its "limits," or its "presuppositions"—as an incidental object, but rather as its primary and ultimately sole object.

To guide us in such an undertaking, we have at our disposal the foundational works of Nietzsche and Heidegger. I indicate in one of the following studies (Chapter 3) that Bergson's contribution on this question is far from negligible. Furthermore, in it I advance the thesis that if the question of metaphysics has meaning and real importance, the research should be able to be developed to a large extent independently of the particular presuppositions of its initiators (which obviously does not mean independently of *all* philosophical presuppositions), namely, in Nietzsche's case, the attempt to overturn Platonism and Christianity in order to allow the advent of a humanity "beyond good and evil," or, in Heidegger's case, the project of surmounting the forgetful nihilism into which the history of Being draws us, and which has as its most extreme consequence the essence of modern technology. We need not adopt Heidegger's conception of the history of Being to be able to recognize that the question of the delimitation of metaphysics has meaning, nor that it is, more than ever, an unavoidable task. I propose, in this respect, that a distinction be made between the question of the *delimitation* of metaphysics (qua task that still lies, to a great extent, before us) and the question of its *closure* (which assumes that with Heidegger we have reached the ultimate basis of its characterization and, in sum, the last word on that undertaking). The question of the unity of metaphysics is and remains a question—an *open* question that, by definition, cannot become the property of one sole individual.

This task, it must be added, is *philosophical* through and through. This point would be superfluous were it not for the fact that today we see the formation of a historical trend that has contributed works of the first order, but interprets the question of metaphysics in a narrow and ultimately reductive sense. Metaphysics, understood as onto-theology, began roughly with Duns Scotus and ended with Kant. The concept of "onto-theo-logy" that is pressed into service to shore up this thesis is thus not Heidegger's, but rather Kant's.[8] The important thing is to know at what moment theology tends to become a "special" discipline, subordinate to a general "ontology"; that is, at what moment, owing to a reinterpretation of Being as a transcendental concept and the abandonment of the Thomist device of analogy, God enters as a mere exemplum under the extension of *ens in quantum ens*. In short, the important thing is to understand the new cartography of metaphysics emanating from the Scotist turn toward univocity and on which modern metaphysics as a whole depends. On the pretext of making the concept of onto-theology, and with it the Heideggerian inquiry into the unity of metaphysics, more historically "rigorous," we run the risk of diminishing the acuity of that concept by opening it up to a simple homonymy. Is the problem of metaphysics only that of the status of God and theology in their relation to the nascent "ontology"? We must recall what Heidegger pointed out on this matter: "In order to recognize the fundamentally onto-theological character of metaphysics, we do not need to orient ourselves toward the purely scholastic concept of metaphysics. On the contrary, the scholastic concept is merely a doctrinal formulation of the essence of metaphysics thought metaphysically. *The names ontology and theology as they are used here do not possess the identical senses they have in the scholastic concept of metaphysics.*"[9] Thus the "scholastic" approach to the problem of metaphysics—which Heidegger here rejects in advance—has the weakness of cutting the research off from its living, properly philosophical sources: for the delimitation of metaphysics only makes sense by the *invention* of pathway out of it, that is, as the counterpart to a *positive* conceptual elaboration. In philosophy, even history cannot proceed solely historically; otherwise it risks losing sight of the very questions that give it life.

The formulation of these various problems allows us to make our way toward what constitutes the core of this work and gives it its title. *There Is* explores not only questions that *Event and World* and *Event and Time* did not treat thematically; it attempts to go a step further with respect to those two works. It is no longer a question of setting out from the event to inquire into its phenomenological meaning and to question existence itself—its structures and status. Now what is at stake is the more radical inquiry into the very appearing of the event, that is, of specifying what it means for it to "come about," "happen," or "occur." Now, to try to describe this taking-place phenomenologically presupposes first of all a break with the conception of change passed down to us by Aristotle—the only conception, in fact, that has been the object of a true analysis within metaphysics. To "come about," for an event, is not to "change" in the same sense as that which, in another respect, also *remains* through time may be said to "change"; it is not, as in the Aristotelian expression, to become something by something from something; it is neither to modify itself nor to modify its temporal situation; it is even less to occur as a modification of the "world," itself considered as being a last "substratum": for, with the occurrence of the event there also necessarily occurs a transformation of the world; the critical upheaval of the event does not leave its context unchanged, but rather shows it in a new light. The world and the event suddenly burst forth together; they are cosmogenetically one in that mutation of the appearing. One cannot attempt to describe this sort of change without resorting to paradoxical expressions: "change without anything having changed" (Bergson), change from nothing to something, absolute change [*changement du tout au tout*]. In order to try to conceptualize such a change—which I propose to call "there is," in order to distinguish it from the one thematized by Aristotle—we must, then, accept the possibility of speaking in a certain sense of an occurrence out of the blue, of a "passage" from nothing to something. Is a "phenomenology" of nothing possible? It must be, if the nothing is closely connected to the event and articulates its appearing, if the "there-isn't" is inseparable from any there-is as such (Chapter 7).

The "there is," that immobile mutation, so to speak, since it lacks any substratum that could be said to "change," this "change," if you will, by which the event does not change into something else but changes into itself, advenes or supervenes, is therefore at the center of this research. The question of the there-is is the very question of the appearing as it is posed to any phenomenology. To move back from the event that appears to the very appearing of the event is clearly not to seek something else behind the event, but rather to question the phenomenological meaning of supervening and thus, in relating it to nothingness, to interrogate what is at stake for all true phenomenology (and is its *ultimate* stake): the phenomenological meaning of the world as such.

Through these laconic indications it becomes possible to see how the question of the there-is allows me to articulate the three series of problems distinguished above: (1) the question of transcendentalism; (2) the logico-phenomenological question of nothingness; and (3) the question of the delimitation of metaphysics. A phenomenology of the event excludes the event's being subjected to something like prior conditions of possibility. The event does not take place in an "opening" that conditions its meaning through and through; the event is not possible before occurring for the person to whom it happens. Here there is not, on the one hand, the appearing of the world as transcendental horizon, and on the other, what appears there, the appearing being as such, the event; what is characteristic of the event qua phenomenon is rather that it does not let itself be closed up in the alternative of appearing and that which appears, of Being and beings, or even of givenness and the given.[10] Its phenomenological "syntax" is different. The opening of appearing, in this case, takes place at the same level as that which appears, and *as* that appearing itself: the event, by transforming the meaning of the situation on the basis of which I am to understand it, opens the world dimensionally by opening dimensionally to itself. Even if it presupposes that I can interpret it on the basis of the whole of my experience, my situation, my history, these prerequisites are nothing other than a necessary—and nowise sufficient—condition for grasping its meaning, because to understand it is to understand how it transforms that situation, that experience, that history; how it appears irreducible to all prior understanding and is itself the opener and initiator of its own meaning. Thus, to describe the there-is of the event is also and always to describe my own finitude and the finitude of the world in which it appears. The question of nothingness and that of the world are one and the same question, as that of finitude. The world and the event are suspended in nothingness; they co-articulate the finitude of appearing. What metaphysics leaves—among other things—unconceptualized is not therefore just the there-is in its difference from all other change and in its wake temporality inasmuch as it is irreducible to every interpretative approach in terms of inner-temporality (see Chapter 3) but also and primarily nothingness as such.[11] The thinking of nothingness, on the other hand, does not necessarily lead back to the (Heideggerian) thinking of Being, but distinguishes itself from it in principle (see Chapter 8).

I wish to thank those who, in various capacities—directors of publications, organizers of seminars and colloquia—have elicited these texts, published them in an earlier version, or authorized their inclusion in this volume[12]: Jad and Nicole Hatem, Jean-François Lavigne, François Makowski, Jean-Luc Nancy, Guy Petitdemange, Mario Ruggenini, Bernard Stevens, Jacques Taminiaux, and Marlène Zarader. I also extend my thanks to the exacting readers from whose remarks I have benefited: François Calori, Dominique Pradelle, François Roustang, Martin Rueff, Bernard Stevens, Yves-Marie Visetti, and of course Jean-Luc Marion.

PART I

Event and Metaphysics

1

Some Sources and Prolongations of "Evential Hermeneutics"

In a passage from *Below the Volcano*, shortly before the tragic denouement, Malcolm Lowry writes, "but there is always a door left open in the mind . . . for the entrance and the reception of the unprecedented, the fearful acceptance of the thunderbolt that never falls on oneself, for the lightning that always hits the next street, for the disaster that so rarely strikes at the disastrous likely hour, and it was through this mental door that Yvonne . . . now perceived that something was menacingly wrong."[1] If I had to try to sum up some six hundred–odd pages of analysis in a few words, I would say that my two books[2] have no other goal than to attempt to describe that "door left open in the mind," as Malcolm Lowry calls it, and that isn't perhaps exactly "a door in the mind," but, more profoundly, the mind as such, the very humanity of man. Why his humanity? Isn't it more accurate to define the human being by the possession of language, by life in society, by technological productivity, by the exercise of scientific thought? But perhaps we will understand neither the "social" constitution of man nor the essence of his technology nor the ingenuity of his rational thought (we will not even understand what "to understand" means) if we do not take into consideration—and even, if we do not *set out from* that which only apparently belongs to a totally different order, to the radical unpredictability of what happens, and happens for no apparent reason—if we do not set out from that unprecedented, unheard-of that Malcolm Lowry, like Nietzsche and like Heraclitus before him, thought of in the form of the lightning bolt.

Event and Tragedy

It is not entirely by chance that I began with a quote from a novel. For philosophy, doesn't the event in its unrepeatable and indomitable singularity remain "forever *apeiron*," as Husserl insists, since "phenomenology can recognize with objective validity only essences and essential relations"?[3] As we will progressively see, this is far from being the case. In this task, literature can serve philosophy's ends better than philosophy itself can. And as a matter of fact—not "literature," which is a late invention, but something that surely cannot be designated by that term (and even less by "theatre"): tragedy. For if there is a "literary" form in which the event is the main thing, showing all things in its light, it is surely that one. Hence it can furnish us with an indirect ontology of the event.

It is man confronted with the immense, the gripping, the overpowering, and the enigmatic that constitutes the tragic theme par excellence. The heroes, in triumph or defeat, moving before our eyes—these exemplary specimens of humanity ceaselessly remind us by their wanderings and their sufferings that the measure of the human cannot be found in itself, but resides in what exceeds its measure: the superhuman, the divine. Now it is first through the shock of the unforeseeable, in the metamorphosis of the familiar, that the superhuman is revealed at the same time it escapes us. The event is what creates between human ends and the divine omnipresence the gulf of a gaping contradiction; and yet it is only through that crisis and that confrontation that the possibility of understanding himself is opened to man. This is why the unexpected, in the tragedy, always bears the stamp of its divine origin. There is no tragedy without an exceptional crisis that destroys the established order, overturning the situation in which the characters are caught up and introducing a radical break between a before and an after. It is the murderous insanity of Ajax and his absurd mass slaughter that bring dishonor on him and make him the laughingstock of the Argives; it is the plague that rages in Thebes and the oracle ordering the discovery of Laius's killer to rid the city of its curse. Only the critical impact of the event, its decisive and decisional power, places the hero before an alternative and gives birth to the drama as such: Ajax's desire to commit suicide, a desire in which two conceptions of honor stand in conflict: the implacable quest of Oedipus, his impassioned search for a guilty party. Henceforth everything the characters do will be in response to that crisis inscribed within them. This means that the action of the characters is completely in the power of *tukhē*, all human initiatives only revealing more and more the power and depth of its reign. *Tukhē*, a term we would be wrong to translate too quickly as "chance," since it is a necessary chance. Twice in *Ajax* we find the expression *tēs anagkaias tukhēs* (v. 485, 803). This necessary chance, this meeting from which there is no escape and that decides everything else—life and death—this is what the event is. Though itself gratuitous, unfounded, it is that which itself founds a destiny. The tragic existence unfolds completely beneath its power. Thus, Ajax exclaims, "there is nothing which man should not expect: the dread power of oath is conquered, as is unyielding will" (v. 648). And, similarly, it is not only because he is a foundling that Oedipus—the tragic figure par excellence—says he is "the son of *Tukhē* (*paida tēs tukhēs*)" (v. 1080): through this expression the obscurity of *all* birth is alluded to in an exemplary way, that is, the human condition. For the tragic event always has a hidden facet, a part remaining in the shadows; it is constitutionally elusive, even though man thinks he has grasped it; the more we think we have taken its meaning by surprise, the more it steals away. This is why the oracles are misleading. In giving us the illusion that they have mastered the unexpected, they hide it still more deeply from us, since we cannot try to decipher its meaning otherwise than by the yardstick of our own expectations, our own hopes, and since the event never occurs except against all expectations. "Before he sees it happening," the play *Ajax* concludes, "no one can foretell the future, or what his fate will be."

Yet the event, even though remaining shrouded in darkness, even though surpassing the measure of man's expectations and understanding, is precisely what reveals man to himself and initiates him to his own humanity. For man is only man as he relates to the event, that is, to the immense, the frightening, the enigmatic. In the crisis brought about by the event, the hero is exposed, in a sense, outside himself—brought to light—thrown into the limelight; and at the same time, precisely because he remains a man, that is, finite, he remains in the dark to himself and all the more so in that his truth is thrown into his face, so to speak. Thus, as Karl Reinhardt remarked profoundly, the mainspring of the tragedy, particularly in Sophocles, is the confrontation, within man, of lucidity and illusion, of the truth and the lie, of unveiling and veiling. What is tragic is the enigma man is for himself. Thus Oedipus, the decipherer of enigmas, proves incapable of deciphering his own enigma. His truth, the sign of his finitude, that is to say of his submission to the law of *tukhē*, remains all the more hidden for his passionate attempt to discover it. Thus tragic time is a time that reveals and conceals, that conceals the more it reveals, because it is the time of the event. "All things the long and countless years first draw from darkness, and then bury from light" (φύει τ' ἄδηλα καὶ φανέντα κρύπτεται)."[4] It is true, of course, that behind or "below" this time, a different or a beyond time shows through, from behind this turbulence of premonitions and anguish—a distant, pacific time, the time of the gods and that of the chorus. But even there, error and dissimulation are never entirely eliminated, because the chorus also hopes and trembles. The fragile understanding that transpires through these trials—immortalized by the *tô pathei mathos* of *Agamemnon*—has, of course, a meaning that is quite other than psychological: it is not knowledge of oneself, but knowledge of the human as such, that is, man's understanding and taking upon himself of his own finitude. What the hero understands, as the chorus of *Antigone* reminds us, is that he is an incomprehensible monster. And he can only understand this by the experience through which he is transformed and that renders him unrecognizable to himself. "It is when a person is alienated from himself by his fate," writes Reinhardt, "that he first understands himself for the being that he is."[5] Madness, abduction, ecstasy—these are but the scenic, palpable expression of that estrangement through an experience. It is in becoming estranged from himself that man can face his own strangeness. This is why the mainspring of Greek tragedy, masterfully exemplified by *Oedipus Rex*, is the constant tension between what man can recognize as his and what remains for him forever enigmatic, the unresolved tension between understanding and bafflement. This is the essential point of tragic anthropology: it is also its point of rupture with modern tragedy. Not that the latter has no knowledge of the event. The echo of this radical indecision of the world beneath the sway of the surprising is also found in Racine, at the beginning of *Phèdre*, for example.

> That happy time no longer is. All has changed its look
> Since to these shores the gods have sent
> The Daughter of Minos and Pasiphae.[6]

But henceforth it is as if that echo has been muted, not, indeed, in its poetic beauty, but because the anthropology underlying tragedy has changed. Tragedy has become the locus in which a certain freedom and a certain providence clash—a certain will and a certain *fatum*, a certain interiority and a certain exteriority. In order to express it, a new literary form, that of poetic introspection, had to be invented. It is only of this tragedy that one can say, with Schelling, that it was "the contest between human freedom and the power of the objective world in which the mortal must succumb *necessarily* if that power is absolutely superior, if it is fate. And yet he must be *punished* for succumbing because he did not succumb *without a struggle*." That punishment, Schelling added, "was the honor due to freedom."[7] Greek tragedy, on the contrary, knows nothing of that alternative: it does not oppose freedom to necessity, it does not think according to that distinction. This is why it also describes in the greatest detail the dramatic aspect of the event—its temporality of the "too late." For this expression, which recurs so frequently in the chanted laments of the chorus and by which Creon defines himself—he is "the one who takes notice too late" (ὀψιμαθής)—belongs to the very temporality of the event, which, transcending as it does our powers (including that of understanding), has no meaning other than an "open" one, a meaning constantly in abeyance, appealing to an ever possible reinterpretation. "If Creon comes 'too late,' as Reinhardt insists, it is not because things developed faster than could be expected. . . . He comes too late because he is a man, and, as such, finite."[8] This is also why ancient tragedy is less concerned with divvying up, in an initiative, the human and the divine contribution: rather it reveals between these aspects of action a collusion, a coalescence and, as it were, an indistinction. Between man and the gods, it always celebrates frightening betrothals. For the initiative of men eludes them for the most part. At the very moment when Oedipus believes he is going forward with open eyes and chooses to pursue his investigation to the end, he does not know the true significance of his choice: "In his purely human dimensions the agent is not the sufficient cause and reason for his actions: On the contrary, it is his action, recoiling upon him as the gods have, in their sovereignty, ordered, that reveals him to himself, showing him the true nature of what he is and what he does."[9] It is this turning around, by which man discovers that he is not the measure of his acts, that Aristotle thematizes under the name *peripeteia*, that is, a reversal of action to its opposite (τὸ ἐναντίον τῶν πραττομένων μεταβολή) and that defines, in his view, on a par with discovery, the specificity of the tragic genre.[10] This term, "*peripeteia*," has nothing to do with its modern French homonym "*péripétie*" [incident]; in many respects it is even the negation of it. Here no will, let alone any freedom, makes the agent an *author* of his acts; at most he is their coauthor, together with *Tukhē*. The formula of the tragic *praxis* is, therefore, that of *Agamemnon*: "passion conspiring with divine *Tukhē*."[11]

There can be no question, obviously, of our reverting to tragic anthropology. But through it, something is said about the event—its relation to being-man, its relation to human understanding and *praxis*—that goes far beyond the circumstances of the emergence of this anthropology, its mythological or theological background. The proof of this is that tragedy has continued to survive the tragic genre. In the twentieth century, as André Malraux has noted,[12] Faulkner is the tragic novelist par excellence. In a well-known essay, Sartre expressed surprise, indignation even, that Faulkner did not know what freedom was. But Faulkner is a tragic writer, and as for Sartre's thought, it knows nothing of what the event is. And therefore it does not know real freedom either—the freedom that is conferred to men, and that is not that demiurgic, infinite power of which Sartre believes himself to be the proprietor. But with that subtlety that is peculiar to him, and that he always maintains even in the midst of error, Sartre nonetheless expressed the essential thing: the true subject of Faulkner's poetics is temporality. But what temporality? "Faulkner's present is irrational in its essence; it is the event, monstrous and incomprehensible, which comes upon us like a thief—comes upon us and disappears. Beyond this present, there is nothing, since the future does not exist. . . . The present was not first a future possibility. . . . No: to be present is to appear without reason, and to sink in."[13] Here we have tragic time reduced to its skeleton, so to speak, its structure of *after-the-fact*, of "too late," which Sartre describes even better when he spells out what he means by "sinking in" ["*enfoncement*"]: "I use this word, for lack of a better one, to indicate a kind of arrested motion of this misshapen monster." But is this just "Faulkner's metaphysics"? Precisely because the event is unforeseeable, unthinkable, and because that is a characteristic of its essence, its temporalization can only be that of the after-the-fact. The event reveals itself to me as such only when it has already taken place, that is, too late to be avoided, too late for me to back away. Thus, in passing, it does not just disappear, and Sartre has to correct his own description by bringing to light—remarkably well—the "mobility" by virtue of which the event changes into itself: "Its metamorphosis can submerge it at the bottom of our memory or leave it on the surface. Only its own density and the dramatic meaning of our lives can determine its level."[14] And because our existence itself only arises through the event of our birth, that is, because it is structured by possibles that it did not make possible, imbued with a meaning that it cannot entirely decipher and that makes it forever an enigma, that after-the-fact dimension also structures the temporality of our existence. This does not mean, as Sartre thinks, that the after-the-fact dimension blocks off the future of our existence, but on the contrary that it restores the future to our existence in the only possible form: that of an eventuality transcending all projects. But the philosophers, with the possible exception of Hannah Arendt, have oddly ignored birth. They would have it that man began absolutely, and that he began, if possible, with freedom. Faulkner opposes that illusion with his tragic lucidity. Speaking of time, that "mausoleum of all hope and desire," he has one of his characters say, "Because no battle is ever won he said. They are not even fought. The field only reveals to man is own folly and despair, and the victory is an illusion of philosophers and fools."[15]

The Event in Philosophy: Aristotle

But philosophy as a whole, beginning with Plato, has been constituted by turning away from tragic thought. Not *all* philosophy. Aristotle, given his ongoing critical dialogue with Plato, and especially the influence of Greek tragedy on his thought, is the Greek thinker of the event par excellence. Aristotle, not the Stoics! And this is true despite the fact that it is the Stoics who developed an explicit doctrine of the event, conceiving of it as an incorporeal *lekton*, that is, as a something (*ti*) that isn't—only bodies are—but supervenes as a supplement to being. With Aristotle we find ourselves in the opposite situation: the event, conceived of as an accident (*sumbebēkos*), has no more than a problematic status in the teaching of being qua being, and is very close to non-being, since what is primordially is *ousia*. Nevertheless, Aristotle thought the event with a rare depth, precisely *because* he thought, in close proximity to tragic thought, human finitude.

Through what expressions is the event expressed in his thought? The first one to come to mind is *to gignomenon*[16]: that which happens, goes on, the process or fact. This word will designate frequently the event in general, in Alexander of Aphrodisias, for example.[17] But in Aristotle *to gignomenon* concerns all that becomes, beginning with the processes of nature, and is not applied primarily to the domain of human life. Following a suggestion by Carlo Diano, it could be argued that it is rather the word *tukhē* that *eventus* translates,[18] the very word used by the tragedians. This term is the substantivized form of the aorist *etukhen*, from the verb *tunkhanō*: to be encountered, to be found, to befall, or to occur. Moreover, the circumstance that this word comes from an aorist form takes on a certain importance with respect to its event-related meaning. Indeed, as Carlo Diano emphasizes, *tukhē* "designates the fact in its momentary happening. . . . this distinguishes it [*tukhē*] from *moira*, which has its verb in the prefect (*heimartai*), and implies . . . the idea of a predetermined necessity."[19] Indeed, the aorist is distinguished from the perfect by its processual character (it is indefinite, *aoristos*, in the sense of not being enclosed within ascribable limits); it expresses, according to Gustave Guillaume, "an action that unfolds in the past in the form of an action *taking place*"[20] as contrasted with that action *having* taken place, immobilized, crystallized; "the aorist depicts the verb in progress, moving toward a goal"[21]; the perfect, on the contrary, has the aspect of a state that has been reached, a result. It describes the event not in its coming, but in its completion, as accomplished, finished: it designates "a form of present obtained late in the past."[22] Incidentally, we can see another indication that the Latin *eventus* partially translates the Greek *tukhē* in the evolution of this last term in post-Aristotelian philosophy: *to tunkhanon*, still another term derived from the verb *tunkhanō*, designates the event for the Stoics.[23]

But what is *tukhē*? Aristotle's response is strictly phenomenological. Unlike the Stoics and the Epicurians, who, after him, would set necessity (*heimarmenē*) in opposition to chance (*tukhē*) as two ultimate cosmological principles, Aristotle does not seek any principle *behind* phenomena or any ultimate reason for things. It is only with a concern to "save the phenomena" that he has recourse to the popular notion of *tukhē*. This is why the definitions he gives for it, however various they may be, only appear to be contradictory. At times he seems to see in *tukhē* simply ignorance of the true causes of what happens[24]; at other times, the fortuitous event—or the event, without qualification—is defined as the exceptional, in contrast with the uniform (the natural) and as what derives from causes, but "indefinite and undetermined (*apeirōn kai aoristōn*)."[25] As Aubenque notes, "the indefinite and the undetermined never refer, in [Aristotle's] work, nor indeed in Greek philosophy in general, to the correlate of our ignorance (which is expressed as ἄδηλος) but rather as objective properties of things"[26]: the indeterminate for us is also indeterminate in itself. But must we really decide between the two? Doesn't Aristotle's hesitation reveal the phenomenological character of his method? The fact is that there are no "objective properties" for Aristotle, because there are no "subjective" ones either. To him, *tukhē* is certainly real, and it is on that sole condition that it can be known. *Tukhē* is that limitation that the contingency of the world imposes on our search for causes, and it is the reason that search loses its way in the indeterminate. *Tukhē* is, then, *inseparably* a determination of the world and of our knowledge. This is why Aristotle does not set in opposition the undetermined and the unknowable, what is in itself and what is for us: the *tukhē* is "of the domain of the indeterminate (*aoristou*) and impenetrable for man (*adēlos anthrōpōi*)."[27] In this sentence, the *kai* [translated as "and" in the preceding sentence] means "that is to say." *Tukhē* is not simply an appearance behind which a real concatenation of causes is concealed. Nor is it a principle located beyond phenomena. This is why, on the one hand, we must not entirely reject the objection according to which there are no facts due to chance: that assertion, in itself, is not absurd.[28] But on the other hand, we must avoid transforming *tukhē* into a new principle of explanation: it is not "a cause in an absolute sense (*aition ōs d'aplōs*)," but only an accidental cause (*aition ōs sumbebēkos*).[29] The way in which Aristotle tries to approach it and grasp its essential characteristics is phenomenological and immanent.

This is shown in a well-known text from *Metaphysics*. It could be maintained, by virtue of the necessary concatenation of causes, that a man who will die a violent death necessarily had to die in that way: he will die a violent death if he goes out, he will go out if he is thirsty, he will be thirsty if he has eaten spicy food, etc. We can go back from the future event to its cause, and to the cause of this cause until the present moment, which is determined. Does this mean that future events are therefore determined? Aristotle rejects that consequence. "He who is alive must die—for some stage of the process has been reached already; for example, the contraries are present in the same body—but whether by disease or violence is not yet determined; it depends upon whether so-and-so happens. Clearly, then, the series goes back to some starting point, which does not go back to something else. This, therefore, will be the starting-point of what is produced by *tukhē* (ὁπότερ' ἔτυχεν), and the cause of its generation is nothing else (αἴτιον . . . ἄλλο οὐθέν)."[30] Here *tukhē* is the principle of what in principle eludes all assignable cause, given that the search for causes must be pursued infinitely, the principle of the lack of any *ultimate* principle, or yet again, the cause of what has no other (determinable) cause than itself. As Carlo Diano emphasizes in reference to this same passage, Aristotle's entire reasoning here comes down to a kind of tautology: it is "in homage to the phenomena," he writes, that Aristotle "interrupts the series in the tautology of the ὁπότερ' ἔτυχεν, which is the tautology to which we resort whenever we say of an event, and hence of a *tukhē*, that it is due to *tukhē*."[31] This is what already takes place in Chapter 9 of *De Interpretatione*, in which Aristotle refuses to assign a truth-value to the singular propositions referring to the future, because this truth-value will not be assignable until the event has taken place: it is not necessary that there will or will not be a naval battle tomorrow, but it will be necessary for there to have been such a battle if it takes place; and it will be necessary for there not to have been such a battle if it does not take place: it will take place if it takes place, and if it doesn't it won't.

But the Aristotelian analysis of the event does not stop with that tautology. There is a "that's the way it is" only for someone who can imagine that things could have turned out otherwise; there is an event, that is, a transformation of the meaning of a life, only for someone who, in general, can give his or her life a meaning, that is, for an agent oriented toward goals within a practical situation. Therefore we must distinguish between two forms of chance: a chance that runs through nature, and is but the fluctuating limit with which the world foils our causal explanation; and a chance that concerns us, since it disrupts our own goals and forces us to review them. A blind chance, and a chance that involves us personally (*qui nous regarde*). On the one hand, Aristotle speaks of an *automaton*, and restricts it to natural entities, animals and children, excluding man; on the other, he speaks of *tukhē* proper, which he proceeds to define as follows: a "cause by accident (*aition kata subebēkos*) occurring in things that, being toward some end, are also in the realm of decision."[32] Indeed, in order for there to be *tukhē* in this sense, that is, good or bad luck, fortunate or unfortunate outcomes, there must be finality (*hou heneka*). But this finality alone is not enough: for example, a lost horse who finds his way back to the stable by mere chance (*automaton*), that is, without assignable cause, does in fact act in a final way; and yet, Aristotle clarifies, it is only metaphorically, from our point of view, that we can say that he was lucky, since, not having deliberated on his situation, not having made a decision, the horse cannot *understand* his good luck. Therefore *tukhē* only involves the living on two conditions: he must be an agent capable of making a decision (*proairesis*) and equipped with thought (*dianoia*), since the latter makes the former possible. In short, even if Aristotle doesn't spell it out here, he must be an agent endowed with a practical intellect (*nous praktikos*). "*Tukhē* and event (*to apo tukhēs*) are in everything involving luck, and practical activity in general."[33] The event is always what has meaning, what can be considered as good or bad, lucky or unlucky. It presupposes, on the part of the one to whom it happens, an understanding of the situation in which it takes place, and the ability to modify his own goals in keeping with that situation. The relation between *tukhē* and decision appears here to be complex: there is *tukhē* only because there has been decision, but, conversely, all *tukhē* is *tukhē* in view of a decision. This is well exemplified by the case of a man who goes to the market and meets his debtor and thus, by chance, gets his loan paid back.[34] It is because at the beginning of that action of going to the market a decision took place that in turn presupposed an understanding of the situation and a deliberation on what would be a good thing to do, that luck can occur: then it is as if the lender had gone to the market on purpose to collect on his loan. Luck manifests a "teleology of the as if,"[35] as Wolfgang Wieland calls it. Everything happens as if the event manifested a *telos* precisely at the point where a *telos* is lacking, since it is to a different goal that the first action was directed. But on the other hand, even though Aristotle hardly emphasizes that aspect of the question in his *Physics*, luck is only luck if I seize the *kairos*, the occasion, by means of another decision: if I *decide*, in meeting my debtor, to get reimbursed. Luck is luck, and event event, only for a being capable of understanding them and making up his mind to seize the possibilities they open up for him.

This distinction on the part of Aristotle is crucial: it permits the differentiation between what I have elsewhere called fact and event. The event belongs not to the neutral domain of facts and their causes, but to that of meaning, that is, to a domain in which the understanding of a situation by an agent comes into play. This understanding, in turn, is practical through and through: it is inseparable from the agent's self-assigned goals, from his action on things and therefore also from the meaning these things take on for him. This understanding, this practical knowledge—Aristotle uses the term *phronēsis* to designate it. Now, not only does one who decides always decide in such a way that an understanding of the situation is implied in his decision, but, additionally, he always decides in such a way that he himself is concerned in person, by what he decides on. *Phronēsis* is "knowledge of the things that concern us (*ta peri auton eidenai*)"[36] or yet again "knowledge [of what is good] for oneself (*to auto eidenai*),"[37] so that the "self," selfhood, is structurally implied in it. As Rémi Brague points out, *phronēsis* is "the faculty of making decisions [in keeping with the situation] in the domain of contingent realities that can be accomplished by oneself and that are directed toward what is good for this same *self*."[38] All action is both action to be accomplished *by* me and *for the sake of* myself. This is why, as Aristotle stresses on the subject of the difference between actions taken willingly and those taken unwillingly, no one, unless he is mad, can ignore himself when taking action.[39] We can understand better, consequently, the assertion that *tukhē* is possible only for man. It is only in the sphere of human praxis, in which there is both the understanding of a situation and decision, that the phenomenon of *selfhood* becomes fully manifest. The specific characteristic of the event—as opposed to the simple fact, which properly speaking befalls no one—is to always happen to someone personally, so that he must make a personal decision about who it is he will be. The event thereby reveals itself as being an occasion for change. For the occasion (*kairos*) is never, no more than the event, without decision: "The agents themselves have to consider what is suited to the circumstances on each occasion."[40] The occasion is neither simply a factual state nor something that the agent creates himself, but rather what is born of the juncture of action and situation, what articulates them, so to speak, with one another. It is only when man makes a decision amid events he does not master, but "meets with," that is, amid circumstances delineating a situation, that there may be occasions for him as well. Thus it is that, in the wake of the tragedians, Aristotle always sees the finitude of human action as immersed in a conjuncture eluding any total mastery by the agent himself.

It is true that in a sense Aristotle opposes a certain tragic conception of action, as expressed in Euripides's *Medea*, for example.[41] This conception, in Aristotle's view, would lead to seeing in the passions a true coercion on the agent, alienating his actions from him and thus destroying all moral responsibility. Even when we act under the sway of passion, Aristotle counters, it is willingly that we let ourselves go. One of the indications of this is that we take pleasure in becoming intoxicated with anger. At the same time, the assertion that the agent acts intentionally (*hekōn*) does not lead Aristotle to say that there exists in the agent a principle of action that depends on himself alone. In his view, to say that virtue and vice are *eph'hēmin*, that they depend on us, is just to say that the principle of action resides in the agent himself. It is to insist on the spontaneity that makes the agent the *aitia*, that is, inseparably the cause and the one being responsible for his act. It is not in the least to set in opposition, as will the Stoics after him, an inner free will (*autexousion*) that is exclusively under the power of the agent, an unconditional initiative that depends on him alone, on the one hand, and a necessity (*heimarmenē*) imposed on him from without, on the other. It is in this sense that Aristotle remains closest to the tragedians. For him, the assertion that when a man acts—with the exception of cases in which he is under physical restraint and cases in which, ignorant of the circumstances of his act, he is mistaken about what he is doing—he possesses "in himself" (*autos*) the principle of his action does not mean that he is, by himself, the principle of his acts: that *autos*, on the contrary, "refers to the human individual taken as a whole, conceived of as the manifold of dispositions forming his particular character, *his ēthos*."[42] In sum, Aristotle not only conceives of the practical self as what is involved in all *phronēsis*, but he also envisages the *singularity* of the agent (his *ēthos*),[43] as constituted through a history: and therefore—to put it in anachronistic terms—he conceptualizes the radical historicity of the agent himself, underlying his action. That history that has made us what we are before any initiative on our part is what has formed our *ēthos* to the point of our not being on an even playing field, even with respect to the acquisition of human excellence (*aretē*). "It is therefore not of small moment whether we are trained from childhood in one set of habits or another; on the contrary it is of very great, or rather of supreme, importance."[44] Thus Aristotle reserves a place at the very heart of the distinction *hekōn/akōn* for the social and historical conditions in which the action unfolds. The intentionally performed act is definitely spontaneous, in the sense that its cause, here, is immanent to the agent himself; but this does not amount to saying that the agent is the only cause of his acts, since he is not the only cause, nor even the principal cause of his *ēthos*, which in turn makes him who he is and makes him act as he does. This is not to say, either, that he is not responsible for his acts: it is just that the idea of "responsibility" here in no way presupposes the subsequent idea of "free will." To be responsible is to be called to take upon oneself an action whose consequences and previous history escape one to a great extent, which was already the meaning of tragic responsibility: it was in claiming his responsibility for what he had done, while being neither the starting point *in an absolute sense* nor the author of it, that the tragic hero takes over the burden of his action, the responsibility for it. So Oedipus when he declares, "I have excluded myself."[45] His guilt is not that of a subject who is the source and master of his acts, but that of a man who accepts bearing his suffering as a burden: "my plague can rest on no other mortal."[46]

Because he saw the historicity of the agent and the event-oriented nature of human life, Aristotle never broke entirely with the tragic conception of life. This is why he always maintained the fragility of human excellence, exposed as it is to the reversals of *tukhē*.[47] As opposed to the Greek historians, Thucydides in particular, who contrasts human nature, *anthropinē physis*, with the religious power of *Tukhē*, as being "two . . . radically heterogeneous orders of reality,"[48] Aristotle, in a manner similar to that of the tragedians, continues to think of them as two complementary and inseparable poles. This is probably one of the meanings that can be attributed to his position favoring poetry over history—the famous assertion in his *Poetics* that the former is "more philosophical" than the latter.

From Fundamental Ontology to Evential Hermeneutics

These digressions devoted to Greek tragedy and Aristotle are only apparently off-topic. They have made it possible for us to enter directly into the heart of the matter. Not that Aristotle or the tragedians are the sole possible source of a phenomenology of the event; but they do make up one of its privileged sources. How is the event to be conceptualized? And in what way does that conceptualization pertain to hermeneutics? How are we to construe the expression "evential hermeneutics"? "Evential" as opposed to "evental," refers in both my books to the difference between fact and event already implicitly present in Aristotle, as I have attempted to show. The fact happens to no one, or to just anyone. It eludes complete explanation because the contingency of the world imposes a *de facto* limit on our causal explanations. The event, on the other hand, possesses that dimension of referentiality and of address according to which it is always an event *for* someone. Furthermore, there is no event outside a context of praxis. It is the event that upsets the hierarchy of the agent's objectives, the configuration of his possibilities, the way in which he understands them, and himself in light of them, that is, his world as such. Not only does the event always concern the *meaning* of the existence that it disrupts and modifies, but it always involves the *selfhood* of the one to whom it happens. By contrast with the fact, it is not what can *in fact* be explained more or less completely, but what belongs *in principle* to an order of meaning prior to that of causal explanation.

As for "hermeneutics," it is the method that lays the most stress on the question of the finitude of human understanding, and more precisely on the intrinsically temporal and historical nature of the activity of understanding itself, on understanding qua *praxis*. It is no accident that Gadamer, the main representative of philosophical hermeneutics after Heidegger, always pointedly invoked the Aristotelian concept of *phronēsis* to describe the activity of the interpreter and work of history (*Wirkungsgeschichte*) underlying it. Like Aristotle's *phronēsis*, understanding always involves something singular: a text, a work of art, an event, the words of an interlocutor within a dialogue. Like *phronēsis*, understanding always relates at once to what is to be understood, the situation of the interpreter, and the interpreter himself: to understand is also to understand ourselves through what we understand and through our way of understanding it. These various traits make up the pragmatic and historically conditioned nature of all interpretation. "The Aristotelian project of developing a practical science," writes Gadamer, "represents, it seems to me, the only scientific-theoretical model according to which the scholarly disciplines that are based on 'understanding' can be developed and thought through. . . . Aristotle has made it clear that practical reason and practical insight are not teachable as science is, but must be exercised in praxis, and this is only possible because of an inner link with the *ethos*."[49] It is not possible here to enter into further detail on the implications of this close connection between practical knowledge and hermeneutics for the characterization of hermeneutics itself. In any case, it leads to a reconsideration of the relation between philosophy and the positive sciences (and their methodology) in light of that assertion that "the model provided to us by practical philosophy . . . must be put in place of these 'theories.' "[50]

But the philosopher par excellence who thought out the finite nature of understanding and was also the first to have exhumed the Aristotelian concept of *phronēsis*, giving it fundamental ontological meaning within an analytic of *Dasein*, is Heidegger. One would therefore expect to find in the existential analytic an explicit treatment of the event in its relation to human existence. This expectation, as we shall see, may well prove unfounded.

As henceforth becomes apparent from an analysis of the courses immediately preceding *Sein und Zeit*, in which the conceptualization of fundamental ontology gradually takes shape, Heidegger derived from a profoundly original reading of Aristotle, particularly from Book 6 of *Nicomachean Ethics*, some of the motifs that oriented his thought. We find in a footnote to §43 of *Sein und Zeit* the acknowledgment of that debt, which is in fact twofold: "The way in which 'care' is viewed in the foregoing existential analytic of Dasein, is one which has grown upon the author in connection with his attempts to Interpret the Augustinian (that is, Helleno-Christian) anthropology with regard to the foundational principles reached in the ontology of Aristotle."[51] The *foundations* here are supplied by Aristotle, and the purpose is that of an *ontological* rereading of Christian anthropology. That dependence is henceforth documented by the publication of the main courses and writings of this period and by excellent historical studies[52]; I have no intent to revisit them in detail. My purpose is rather to attempt to develop the following question: In the phenomenological recasting of Aristotle leading to the elaboration of fundamental ontology, is there still a place for *tukhē*? What I mean is, not a contingent place—as Heidegger does indeed encounter this concept *in passing*, in his 1941–42 course on Plato's *Sophist*,[53] for example—but a necessary and central place within ontological conceptualization.

It seems to me that the answer to that question must be no. In reading Book 6 of *Nicomachean Ethics* in his course on *The Sophist*, Heidegger implicitly sets up a parallel among three of the modalities of *alētheuein* (the disclosure of beings, qua ontological determination of human life, that is, of life endowed with *logos*), namely *epistēmē*, *poiēsis*, and *phronēsis*, and the three modes of being of *Dasein*, namely simple, noncircumspective (*umsichtsfreie*), contemplative looking at (*Hinsehen*),[54] making possible the discovery of beings in the mode of Being-subsistent (*Vorhandenheit*); the circumspective preoccupation as giving access to beings in their usability, qua Being-within-reach (*Zuhandenheit*); and last, resoluteness (*Entschlossenheit*) insofar as it enables *Dasein*'s facing itself and leads it back to its mode of being: existence. If we keep this parallel in mind, it is already significant to note that the reference to *tukhē* never comes up in Heidegger's commentary regarding *phronēsis* itself, that is, regarding the nontheoretical, entirely practical understanding thanks to which *Dasein* relates to its own Being qua to-be about which it has to decide in each situation, but solely regarding *poiēsis*, which corresponds, in the existential analytic, to the everyday, inauthentic (*uneigentiliche*) modality of its existence.

This would, of course, be only a very external indication, if it were not confirmed by an internal reading of *Sein und Zeit*. What is the status of the event (*Ereignis, Geschehnis, Vorkommnis*) within the ontology of *Dasein*? I have treated this problem in more detail elsewhere[55]; so I will limit myself to a succinct response. The event, as soon as it comes up in *Sein und*

Zeit, is traced back to an inauthentic modality of *Dasein*, that is, to an ontological dissimulation of its existence. Hence event is conceived of as being only relevant to a categorial ontology incommensurate with existential ontology. In sum, whenever it is thematized, the event is invested with a mode of being that is *incompatible* with that of existence. *Dasein* is defined ontologically without any relation to events; furthermore, its ontological constitution *precludes* our being able to define it as a being to which something can happen. This becomes clear in particular in the analysis of being-toward-death, in which only *Dasein* in deterioration (*Verfallen*) understands the *existentiale* of dying (*Sterben*), that is, of "thrown Being towards its ownmost potentiality-for-Being, which is non-relational and not to be outstripped"[56] (in other words, anxiety before the possibility of no longer being in the world, before the "possibility of its impossibility") as mere demise (*Ableben*), that is, understands dying as a mere event (*Ereignis*) to come. It is the They, Heidegger says, that perverts the ontological meaning of Being-toward-death by understanding the end of *Dasein* as "a well-known event (*Ereignis*) occurring within-the-world"[57] and consequently by concealing its character as a possibility. It is the They *and it alone* that, in order to escape the vertigo of anxiety, "concerns itself with transforming this anxiety into fear in the face of an oncoming event (*Ereignis*)"[58]; it is this same They that, by giving a primacy to the death of others, transforms the being-certain (*Gewißsein*) that belongs to resoluteness into a mere empirical certainty (*empirische Gewißheit*), that of an "event of public occurrence (*Ereignis*)"[59] that concerns everyone, that is, basically, no one.

In these passages, Heidegger is not satisfied with furnishing an elucidation of the phenomenon of death, keeping it as far as possible from all reality, hence from any event, but *more generally*, he states a thesis that concern *the status of the event itself* in the economy of fundamental ontology. By defining it by within-the-worldness (*Innerweltlichkeit*), by attributing to it the mode of being of reality (*Wirklichkeit*) as opposed to existence, Heidegger deprives the event of all existential status, or, which amounts to the same thing, strips existence itself of all evential status: the event henceforth can belong only to a categorial ontology, an ontology of *Vorhandenheit*. It is possible to find confirmation of this in the passages devoted to "the attestation by *Dasein* of an authentic potentiality-of-being" (§54–§60) and in those on the phenomenon of historicality (§72–§77). In the former, Heidegger says that the call of conscience does not resonate as an event and "gives no information about world-events (*Weltereignisse*)"[60]—only the They can understand it this way, that is, misunderstand it. As for the existential constitution of historicality, it must not be understood on the basis of a "changing appearing and disappearing of events (*Begebenheiten*)," nor even on the basis of "man as the 'subject' of events (*Ereignisse*)"[61]: such determinations never pertain to anything but an ordinary understanding of history.

If that "reduction" of the event in order to have access to the ontological meaning of the Being of *Dasein* is not contingent, if it is necessarily and structurally part of the conceptualization of *Sein und Zeit*, what could the reasons for this be? What prevented Heidegger from conferring a place to the Aristotelian *tukhē* within the new ontological conceptualization inaugurated by *Sein und Zeit*? It seems to me that the answer to this question must be sought in three main directions.

First, the question refers us to what Heidegger has himself called the "formality" necessary for all ontology, that is, to a subtle form of essentialism that remains present in *Sein und Zeit* despite a certain critique of Husserlian apriorism.[62] A good illustration of this is contained in the following assertion: "If I say of *Dasein* that its basic constitution is Being-in-the-world, I am then first of all asserting something that belongs to its essence (*Wesen*), and I thereby disregard whether the being of such a nature factually (*faktisch*) exists or not."[63] But the "fact" that *Dasein* comes into existence only by the *event* of a birth—is this merely of the order of the fact for that existence? Does it not condition *Dasein*'s *meaning* through and through—that is, the understanding we have of it—and, along with that understanding, the very meaning of our finitude? In other words, the "fact," for that existence, of having to befall us in fact by the event of a birth—does this not belong on principle to what must henceforth be called the "evential" constitution of that existence? Or yet again, must not *Dasein* be determined *in its Being* by one event at least, in order to be what it is: *Dasein*? It becomes clear that the absence of an analytic of birth in *Sein und Zeit*, even though such an analytic seems fully required by the characterization of the historicality of *Dasein* as that which "*stretches along between* birth and death,"[64] must be more than a simple omission.

Second—and this second trait is inseparable from the first—the impossibility of a thinking of the event derives here from the permanence of a certain transcendental style of thought, despite Heidegger's break with classical transcendentalism. If Heidegger, on the one hand, opposes the Cartesian and Husserlian formulation of the problem of the reality of the outside world by asserting that the meaning of the Being of the world cannot be elucidated by recourse to a being having the same mode of being, but only by reference to a being that is ontologically Being-in-the-world, on the other hand, through the "ontic privilege" of *Dasein* that is to be ontological, the latter keeps a quasi-transcendental posture: there can be beings only for a *Dasein* inasmuch as *Dasein* is determined in its Being by the understanding of Being. Thanks to its transcendence, Being-in-the-world is the *condition of possibility* for the appearing of all beings. It is itself the ontological openness (*Erschlossenheit*) making possible all ontic discoveredness (*Entdecktheit*); it is itself "truth" in the first and originary sense. This is what might be called, taking some license, the "latent transcendentalism" of fundamental ontology—a transcendentalism progressively abandoned with the *Kehre.* A fair number of concepts that will concern me here belong to this "ontological transcendentalism," such as "world," "facticity," and "thrownness" (*Geworfenheit*). In this respect the following question must be asked to Heidegger: Must not the world befall or happen to *Dasein* in an inaugural event (even though constitutively lost)? Furthermore, do not *all* events affect the existential foundations [*assises*] of the world, so that the world itself is at stake and in suspense in its critical transformation? As for the concept of "facticity" (*Faktizität*), it is worth keeping in mind that it was the invention of Fichte—that is, it also originally belongs to the context of transcendental philosophy.[65] It is true that for Heidegger facticity is not primarily the characteristic of what is given to me ready-made, already there; it is not the factuality (*Tatsächlichkeit*) of Fichte—or even of Sartre; it is not what an unconditional freedom finds as already there in front of it; it designates a characteristic of existence itself qua care. However, the permanence of the conceptuality of facticity in Heidegger is what precludes a thinking of the *eventialness* of existence as such. Facticity is nothing but the obverse of project, and of *Dasein* as world-forming; *Dasein,* by its radical autonomy and self-sufficiency, remains the origin of the world. The same is true of *Geworfenheit.* Here again, the question must be asked: Can thrownness designate an ontologico-formal determination that would be neutral with respect to the factual existence of *Dasein,* and is it not rather enrooted in the event of *Dasein*'s coming into the world? Last, as has been pointed out on more than one occasion, particularly by Hans Jonas, this "latent transcendentalism" also leads to a derivation of life from the Being of *Dasein,* and thus, it should be added, to a true exclusion of life from the horizon of *existential* analytic. Let us recall that this exclusion goes back, in reality, to the thinker who inaugurated the "transcendental motif," as Husserl called it—that is, to Descartes. It is Descartes who reinterpreted Augustine's *cogito ergo sum,* which was also a *cogito ergo vivo,*[66] severing it from any reference to life, and therefore to the body and animality. A similar break is found, *mutatis mutandis,* in the ontology of *Dasein.*

Finally, a third reason—perhaps the main one—for that "forgetfulness of the event" in *Sein und Zeit* seems to me to be the following: By reinterpreting Aristotle's *phronēsis* in its relation to *poiēsis* and *episteme*, Heidegger submits it to a profound reorientation: it is no longer just the "foundations set by Aristotle's ontology" that determine the meaning of the reappropriation of Christian anthropology, but *at least as much* Christian anthropology—and more precisely, as we shall see, *a particular* Christian anthropology more marked by Kierkegaard than Heidegger would be ready to acknowledge—that sheds light on the interpretation of Aristotle's ontology. Through *phronēsis*, as we have seen, man necessarily maintains a certain relation to himself, for it is for his own sake that he acts, or yet again, it is for the sake of his life (*zōē*) as a good life (*eu zēn*). "In the case of φρόνησις", Heidegger writes, "the object of the deliberation is ζωή itself; the τέλος has the same ontological character as φρόνησις."[67] What Heidegger says seems to be slightly different, but actually is very far from what Aristotle says. For the Stagirite, the object of *phronēsis* is the contingent as such, "the things that can be otherwise than they are,"[68] and its end (*telos*) is *good action* (*eupraxia*) or "things good or bad for man (*ta anthrōpoi agatha kai kaka*)."[69] In short, *phronēsis* and *proairesis* always refer to an *action* to be carried out for the sake of a good life, and not to the agent himself and his life, which are not, as such, things about which there could be a decision. But Heidegger understands "*praxis*" here in an entirely different sense than Aristotle: he understands it in a sense he considers "originary," as synonymous with existence itself: "The object of φρόνησις is πρᾶχis," Heidegger specifies, "the ζωή of man, human *Dasein* itself."[70] To say that *phronēsis*, as a mode of disclosure (*aletheuein*), has *praxis* itself as its object and goal amounts to saying, in Heidegger's interpretation, that existence concerns itself with itself as the object for an originary *praxis*. Thereby the decision no longer bears upon the means necessary to attain the good life, living well (*eu zēn*), or happiness, but upon life *qua life*, that is, upon the meaning of life as such. *Eudemonia* becomes *Eigentlichkeit*. The decision is no longer decision about this or that, but absolute decision, bringing us face to face with an absolute alternative, the alternative between being oneself and not being oneself, or yet again, the decision between the transparency of *Dasein* for itself and its self-dissimulation in a life that is alienated by concern with beings that pertains to *poiēsis*.[71] "The deliberation of φρόνησις," Heidegger writes, "is ruled by the either-or. . . . With φρόνησις . . . there is no more or less, no 'this as well as that,' but only the seriousness of the definite decision, success or failure, either-or."[72] The reader will easily remark the influence of Kierkegaard: Aristotle's *phronēsis*, recast in light of the Kierkegaardian "either-or," means henceforth the possibility of an absolute decision, that is to say, a decision that is not about a particular option, but for or against decision itself[73]—a decision, as Kierkegaard would add, that tears us away from the esthetic stage and brings us into the dimension of ethics, and then, by a new "leap," that is to say, by a further decision,[74] into that of religion. What is involved here is a "choosing to make this choice,"[75] as Heidegger puts it, which is a tearing away from non-choice, from the indecision of inauthenticity, and is called in *Sein und Zeit* "resoluteness": *Entschlossenheit.* Furthermore, Heidegger does not hesitate to interpret *bouleuesthai* and *boulē*—that is, according to the usual translations, the act of deliberating and deliberation—as modes of actualization of *phronēsis*, as being identical with resolution itself: "βουλή is the resoluteness, the being-resolved."[76] This resoluteness is the condition of possibility of the "transparency of action" (to be understood as "of existence"), that is, of the "truth of existence" or of its authenticity. "The βουλεύεσθαι of the φρόνησις involves the Being of *Dasein* itself . . . that is, the right and proper way to be *Dasein.*"[77] Now resoluteness, in *Sein und Zeit*—and also, incidentally, the Kierkegaardian absolute choice—is necessarily connected to conscience (*Gewissen*). This is why Heidegger can easily conclude that *phronēsis* is to be understood, in its ontological sense, as the equivalent of conscience: "But it is nevertheless clear from the context that we would not be going too far in our interpretation by saying that here Aristotle has come upon the phenomenon of conscience (*Gewissen*). Φρόνησις is nothing other than conscience set into motion, making an action transparent."[78] Therefore *kairos* will have to be understood no longer in the sense of the opportune moment, but rather in the Johannine sense of the "instant."[79] By means of this "radicalization" and especially of this pattern of shifts and transfers to which he subjects Aristotle's text, Heidegger is henceforth able to hear in the self-referential nature of *phronēsis* an echo of the Kierkegaardian definition of existence. The existent, Kierkegaard claims, is he who possesses an infinite interest in his own existence. Eliminating "infinite" we get the definition of *Dasein* as the being "ontologically distinguished by the fact that, in its very Being, this Being is an issue for it," that is, whose being is determined by *mineness* (*Jemeinigkeit*).

The point here is not to tax Heidegger with historical inaccuracy: it is a fact that his interpretation is violent, but this *deliberate* gap is first of all what gives it its strength—and its seductive power. It is rather a question of taking note of the fact that, once existence is submitted to an *absolute* alternative, that of authenticity or inauthenticity, once it is suspended, so to speak, to an *absolute* event that decides on its fate absolutely (for resoluteness, Heidegger will say, has already anticipated all possible events, thus withdrawing *Dasein* from the realm of surprise),[80] there is no longer any role for *tukhē*. Resolute *Dasein* is free of "chance," "luck," the "incidentals" (*Zufälligkeiten*),[81] that is, the events of the world (*Weltgegebenheiten*); its existence "can no longer be *outstripped* [*überholt*] by anything"[82]; it has become through and through transparent in the instant (*Augenblick*). There can be no other true event in that existence than resoluteness itself.

Conclusions

I have attempted to carry out, as it were, an "indirect" phenomenology of the event in its relation to existence—or better yet, with the adventure as a historical and evential modality of actualization of that existence—not by trying to summarize phenomenological descriptions, an undertaking that seems to me, if not impossible, at least sterile and disappointing, but by emphasizing a few milestones that have guided me along the way. I hope I have succeeded in showing the legitimacy and relevance of the concept "event" in interpreting this adventure afresh as openness to what befalls us, and in describing its temporality. It is here, in a sense, that it all begins, and that this text ends.

To conclude on a less "negative" note, I would like to make a final remark. For Aristotle, *tukhē*, and contingency as well, are first and foremost determinations of the world itself. Contingency, the characteristic of things that can be otherwise than they are, is fundamentally rooted in the presence of matter, as the indeterminate power of opposites,[83] which introduces into sublunary movements an irregularity and unpredictability differentiating them for the uniformity of the movements of the heavenly bodies. Here we are far removed from the medieval and modern concept of contingency, such as formulated especially by Duns Scotus. Indeed, in his case, contingency is in the world only because it is first and fundamentally in the free will of God. It is defined as the modality of that of which the opposite can take place at the very moment in which that thing or event is actualized: "*Non voco hic contingens quodcumque non-necessarium vel non-sempiternitum, sed cujus oppositum posset fieri quando illud fit; ideo dixi 'aliquid contingenter causatur,' et non 'aliquid est contingens.'*"[84] Contingency is a characteristic, not of things, but of their causation in and by divine freedom. Indeed, it belongs to will itself, as free will, to be the power of opposites, not successively, but at the same moment, so that, when the will has posed an act, it could, at the same moment, have posed the opposite act. Without going into the details of this Scotist doctrine of contingency, which has had considerable influence on Modern thought, we can make the following remark: by making contingency the very structure of the world, independently of any creative freedom, Aristotle appears to us today more modern than the Moderns. This modernity, which we found earlier in the confrontation of Aristotle to hermeneutics, should now be sought in his relation to contemporary science. Biology in particular relies on a concept of contingency that is not unrelated to that of the Stagirite: it is a *statistical* indeterminacy within a cloud of probabilities. This indeterminacy is linked with the process of becoming itself. Biology rediscovered contingency as it progressively abandoned the idea of a world ordered by the divine will, and as it came to accept, through evolutionary theory, the irreducible historicity of living beings, that is, as history was elevated by it, in the words of François Jacob, "to the rank of major cause."[85]

This rediscovery deeply modifies the relationship between human initiatives and the contingency of the world. There is contingency in the world, but this contingency no longer derives from a freedom belonging to divine or human action. Thus Aristotle would not say that it is because I am free—in the sense of being able to determine myself as it were "randomly," *etukhē poiein*[86]—that there is contingency in the world, as the modern tenants of free will and their existentialist heirs would do, but conversely, that it is because there is contingency and *tukhē* in the world that there is also room in it for human initiative. Only a few centuries after Aristotle's death, his disciple Alexander of Aphrodisias, probably inspired by the Stoic idea of *autexousion*, developed the idea of a freedom of choice (*exousia tēs aireseōs*),[87] conceiving of it as a kind of inner chance.[88] On his view, there is a non-being that, when it is present in the causes outside ourselves, gives rise to fortune and chance (*tukhē*, *automaton*) and, when it is inside us, makes it so that there are things that are in our power (*eph'hēmin*), and the opposites of which are equally possible. But, as a matter of fact, Aristotle does not think in these terms. For him it is, as it were, because events and contingency are present outside us that they can be present inside us as well. As Aubenque emphasizes, it is *tukh*ē, and it alone, that "frees man, while at the same time making his existence precarious and jeopardized."[89]

In order to understand this, we need no less than a veritable revolution in our way of thinking, that is, a break from our philosophical Modernity: an abandoning of the separation of body and soul such as has been passed down to us from Descartes, of the scission between subject and object, and at the same time a renewed conception of action that no longer sets in opposition the contingency of acts and the determinism of nature. We must be able to conceive of human life as intrinsically bound to the world, as a life-in-the-world, following Hans Jonas. To be sure, biology tries to explain certain *facts* positively; evential hermeneutics, on the other hand, tries to give a phenomenological account of how the adventure comes about and is phenomenalized: these two disciplines are not situated at the same level. But they are not mutually exclusive. On the contrary, it is the analysis of the evential nature of the human adventure that forces us to reintroduce into the field of philosophy both a thinking of life—without which the relation of the human being to the history of his species would in a sense be destroyed—and a cosmology that idealism and transcendentalism had progressively expelled from it.

It is because man is, among living beings, the one whose genetic program, according to Ernst Mayr's expression, is the most "open," that is, the least restrictive in the regulation of the various aspects of his behavior, the most open to the unexpected and undecided, that man is also, among living beings, the most free: "it gives him a certain freedom of response," as François Jacob writes.[90] This ability to respond, this "responsivity" to the contingent qua contingent, is what defines freedom. It is also what confers a history on the living human being. Here, biology and paleontology join hands. What makes man's singularity, as Leroi-Gourhan has put it forcefully, is that he places the main part of his technical and symbolic innovations outside himself, in the social organism, in a trans-individual memory passed on from generation to generation: "The whole of our evolution has been oriented toward placing outside ourselves what in the rest of the animal world is achieved *inside* by species adaptation."[91] This is how culture is born. There is no reason, in this respect, to set in opposition nature and culture, but, on the other hand, it is only if we understand the essence of man as consisting in his specific "openness" to events, that we can truly attempt to think the two of them together. It is because man is, biologically, of all living beings, the one whose behavior is the most "open," and therefore also the one whose life is the most precarious and exposed to the unforeseeable, that he possesses both a culture and a freedom. This freedom is *outside him*, in his history, in that depository of signs and archives that are those of his collective memory—a memory of the immemorial, that alone can make of his birth, once for all, a *human* one.

2

Possibility and Event

The question of time was never addressed by Heidegger,[1] as he himself specifically recognizes, except in the restricted and rigorously determined perspective of a *different questioning*—whose relevance and necessity are the object of the sustained justificatory effort of *Sein und Zeit*—oriented toward *Being as such*: "But all this forgets that we are not inquiring into time in any old way, nor are we inquiring into the experience of time, but we are inquiring into time *because*, and *in so far as*, Being is understood from time, in the light of time. The *particular way* we are inquiring into time is already prescribed *by the question of Being*, that is by what we already know about this question, quite apart from its connection with time."[2] This assertion of Heidegger is crucial in several respects: on the one hand, because it ascribes a (necessarily limited) "scope" to the questions brought to bear in *Sein und Zeit*, and seems to leave open the possibility of a different problematic, no longer envisaging time within the horizon of the question of being[3]; on the other, because if, as Heidegger asserts elsewhere, "formality" (*Formalität*) is inseparable from any ontological characterization,[4] the analysis of ecstatic temporality, approached from the point of view of an ontological questioning, cannot escape a certain *formalism*.

From this twofold observation, two orders of questions follow. The first is *internal* to the work of Heidegger itself: This limitation of the question about time itself to a problematic that is ontological through and through—is it not in contradiction with the constantly stated project of "interpreting temporality in itself"[5] or of "speaking of time temporally"?[6] The second goes beyond his work itself: Is it not required, in order to successfully carry out the task that Heidegger himself sketched out, to remove time entirely from the framework of the question of Being? Which would come down to *deformalizing* time in one fell swoop? To think time temporally, to respond to Heidegger's concern, would then be to try to think how temporality *temporalizes itself*, to try to think of the very springing forth of ecstatic temporality in the contrasted unity of its ecstasies? What about such a project? Is it not required by the very conceptuality of *Sein und Zeit* itself, at the point where this work reaches, perhaps, its outer limits: the relation between event and possibility?

The Reduction of the Event and the Bringing to Light of the Originary Phenomenological Meaning of Possibility

Why take as our starting point these two notions: possibility and event? What role do these two concepts play in fundamental ontology that gives them a methodological primacy for trying to answer the questions raised above? This role can be better defined if we attempt to follow the progressive elaboration of the concept of ecstatic temporality at the beginning of the 1920s, setting out from the analyses that Heidegger devotes to the temporality of the originary Christian life. The overall principle of those analyses could be formulated as follows: The elucidation of the originary phenomenological meaning of the temporality of Christian life rests on a *de-worlding* of the eschatological event and—through the bringing to light of the modalities according to which that event is *lived*, that is, "experienced" in advance in the present in the form of hope—in a *reduction* of that event, qua phenomenon of the world, to the "how" (*Wie*) of its appearing in and for the factical experience of life, in short, in the *subordination* of that event to its *possibility* for the Christian, insofar as that possibility conditions the transformation of his factical life itself in its entirety.

Indeed, in 1920–21, Heidegger taught a course in Freiburg entitled "Introduction to the Phenomenology of Religion," the second part of which was devoted to clarifying original Christianity, taking his orientation from Paul's two Epistles to the Thessalonians.[7] The purpose of the course was to shed light on "the factical experience of life" proper to original Christianity—the concept of "life" escaping by principle all naturalism and all biologism[8]—as it transpires within a conceptualization that has not yet been corrupted by the introduction of elements coming from Greek philosophy, and as it can be described through a number of phenomenological features that supplied a first, rather coherent sketch of the future analytic of *Dasein*. (1) In all factical experience of life an experience of the world is essentially co-implied: "'life' and 'world' are not two separate self-subsistent Objects. . . . World is the basic category of the content-sense in the phenomenon, life"[9]; (2) Factical life is defined essentially as *Bekümmerung*, concern,[10] a concept that anticipates the ontologico-existential concept of care (*Sorge*); (3) This life tends to conceal itself from itself, to cover itself, to self-dissimulate; it is characterized by the phenomenon that Heidegger, in these years, calls ruinance (*Ruinanz*) and sometimes even, already, "inclination to degradation (*Verfallensgeneigtheit*)"[11] and that prefigures the *Verfallen* of *Sein und Zeit*; (4) All these characteristics must be isolated and brought out phenomenologically at the level of factical life and consequently require a pre-understanding (*Vorgriff*) of that life rooted in that life itself.[12] It is on the basis of these insights into the phenomenological concept of life that a properly *philosophical* interpretation becomes possible—an interpretation that concentrates more specifically on the problem of the temporality of factical life in originary Christianity.

The essential question of a "phenomenology of religion" can be none other than the following: *In what mode of givenness* does God let himself be summoned before the life of the Christian? This "mode of givenness," Heidegger replies, is first of all temporal: "Christian religiosity lives temporality as such."[13] Conversely, "the meaning of temporality [of Christian life] determines itself out of [its] fundamental relationship to God."[14] The center of Christian life is indeed the eschatological problem of the return of Christ at the end of time, or his *parousia*. This παρουσία must not be understood here originarily as presence (*Anwesenheit*) in keeping with the current Greek meaning of the term, but as "the appearing again of the already appeared Messiah."[15] The Christian relates to this return of Christ in glory through hope (ἐλπίς). But what is the phenomenological structure of hope? Does hope (*Hoffnung*) reduce to the expectation (*Erwartung*) of something objectively accessible and graspable? Not at all. Heidegger makes an express distinction between the meaning of Christian eschatology, as it emerges in the Pauline Epistles, and the one that regulated Jewish thought before it. While in Judaism the *eskhaton* is constituted by the impending coming of the Messiah qua future event (*Ereignis*), the structure of Christian hope is different, since it is not only an expectation (*Erwartung*) of a future event, but also of the divine *parousia* as a *return* of God in his glory—a *second* coming, which consequently only has meaning in relation to a first coming, that of Christ in the flesh who became man. The Christian experience of time is thus suspended between an "already" and a "not yet" that gives it its distinctive structure. But this "already" refers not only to a past event, nor this "not yet" only to a future one; this tension between "already" and "not yet" is rather constitutive of the temporality of the Christian in that the latter is *already* justified—on the condition of having faith: "Therefore being [already] justified by faith, we have peace with God through our Lord Jesus Christ"[16]—but in which that justification remains *yet to come*, which makes Christian existence a *hope* of salvation: "For we through the Spirit wait for the hope of righteousness by faith."[17] Because the *eskhaton* of the return of the Messiah is not an objectively apprehensible event that could arise from a successive, linear time, the temporality of the experience of factical life requires a phenomenological interpretation going beyond the ordinary and *objective* concept of time. Thus, Heidegger emphasizes that the concepts through which Paul grasps the temporal phenomenon are not taken from the objective measurement of time but from the inner structuration of the factical experience of life itself. This is the case, in particular, when Paul asserts, speaking of the Thessalonians, that "he experiences their having-become (γενηθῆναι)."[18] The having-become, *das Gewordensein*, refers here to a dimension constitutive of the factical life that the Christian does not cease experiencing as long as he experiences that factical life, and not to a mere past event that he would somehow leave "behind him": "Having-become is not, in life, [just] any event [*Vorkommnis*] you like. Rather, it is incessantly co-experienced, and indeed such that their [the Thessalonians'] Being now is their having-become. Their having-become is their Being now."[19] Such a "past," therefore, does not refer to past—and passed—events; it is not understandable by the measure of a time conceived of as an unfolding of lived experiences (*Ablauf von Erlebnissen*)[20]; it points in the direction of what *Sein und Zeit* will call "having-been" (*Gewesenheit*),[21] that is, toward an ecstasy of time that originarily determines the instant (*Augenblick*) and the to-come (*Zu-kunft*) and is temporalized co-originally with them. It is therefore only as "having-become" that the "already" can structure originary Christian life and give it its eschatological structure. And, similarly, the "not yet" that belongs to that life cannot be interpreted phenomenologically on the basis of the expectation of a future event: the originary phenomenological meaning of the future is inseparable from the elucidation of hope. This is what Chapter 5 of the Epistle to the Thessalonians reveals, which is the nodal point of Heidegger's entire commentary, since it is there alone that the temporal structure of the Christian experience is laid bare in the sharpest outline in its totality. The question Paul's interlocutors ask him is about the moment at which the *parousia* will come about, or, as Heidegger says, the question of its "when": Is the return of the

Messiah imminent? Do we still have a long time to wait? Paul responds by disqualifying that question and replacing it with the problem of the *how* of factical life itself. "But of the times [*khronoi*, which Heidegger restores to the singular, with *Zeit*] and the seasons [*kairoi*, which Heidegger translates, also in the singular, with *Augenblick*], brethren, ye have no need that I write unto you. For yourselves know perfectly that the day of the Lord so cometh as a thief in the night. For when they shall say, Peace and safety; then sudden destruction cometh upon them, as travail upon a woman with child; and they shall not escape. But ye, brethren, are not in darkness, that that day should overtake you as a thief. Ye are all the children of light, and the children of the day: we are not of the night, nor of darkness. Therefore let us not sleep, as [do] others; but let us watch and be sober."[22] In this passage, Paul leads the question of the "when" of the end of days to that of the different modalities of living (*zwei verschiedene Weisen des Lebens*)[23]: the important thing is not *when* the *parousia* of Christ will take place—since the Son Himself does not know the day or hour—but rather *in what disposition* the Christian must be to be open to that *parousia*; what is important is to be "awake" in order not to be surprised by Him who will come like a thief in the night. The two differentiated modalities of living foreshadow here the existential distinction between authenticity and inauthenticity, as is attested by Heidegger's commentary on this passage: "Those who find rest and security in this world are those who cling to this world because it provides peace and security . . . their expectation [*Erwarten*] is absorbed by what life brings to them. Because they live in this expectation, the ruin [*Verderben*] hits them in such a way that they cannot flee from it. They cannot save themselves, because they do not have themselves [*sie sich selbst nicht haben*], because they have forgotten their own self [*das eigene Selbst*], because they do not have themselves in the clarity of authentic knowledge [*eigentlichen Wissens*]."[24] Therefore those who await the *eskhaton* of the end of days as a simple event to come, those who would like to know the day or hour, are thereby stricken with ruin; they exist only in deterioration, as *Sein und Zeit* will say; they are absorbed by the world with which they are concerned, and they understand themselves (that is, they misunderstand themselves) on the basis of this world; they live in the forgetfulness of their authentic Self, far from themselves, "in darkness." Their waiting is entirely "for this world," and this is why they think of the *parousia* of Christ as a mere future event, which would take place along with other events *in* the world, and thus be interpreted temporally as a present to come. They think they can merely expect that event as having to happen "someday," and even "speculate" (*speculieren*) on the moment he will come—while, as Heidegger points out, "the when (*das Wann*) [of that event] is in no way objectively graspable"[25]—because they understand temporality itself as an objective chronology, as a succession of nows, according to a concept of "time" that Heidegger will later qualify as "ordinary."

Their brothers, those who do not live in darkness, those who are the "children of light" and who live in full light, do not evade the fundamental insecurity (*Unsicherheit*) of "the day or hour" and consequently of their own life: for, as Heidegger stresses, "there is no security for Christian life; the constant insecurity is also characteristic for what is fundamentally significant (*Grundbedeutendheiten*) in factical life"[26]; they are, as Paul invites them to be, less concerned about the *when* than the *how* of their lives. They relate therefore to the Second Coming of Christ not in the manner of expectation (*Erwartung*) of an event to come, but in that of being-awake (*wachsam sein*) for a possibility of each instant that looms over them with its imminence. The "imminence" of the possible is not to be understood here as a mere "impending future," a present that will soon be actualized, that is to say, apprehended according to a successive and objectively graspable temporality; it must be understood as a possibility that is *only* possible and the very possibility of which constitutes its essential "reality." If they can remain awake in this way, in the instant, in view of a possibility that is only possible, this, says Heidegger, is because they possess a preliminary knowledge—"for yourselves know perfectly [οἴδατε]"—by virtue of what they *already* are, a knowledge that is therefore rooted in their ownmost having-become (*Gewordensein*). Thus, the instant (*Augenblick*) of the awakening, in its fundamental and frightening insecurity—a prefiguration of the *Unheimlichkeit* of *Sein und Zeit*, discovered in anxiety as the basis of selfhood—is the result of the anticipation of a possibility (the coming of Christ as *second* coming) that is open to the Christian by virtue of what he *already* is, that is, by virtue of a preliminary understanding of himself. *The instant resulting from the hope of a possibility of every moment qua return toward the ownmost having become*: such is, grasped in its formal structure, the temporality of the factical experience of life in originary Christianity. Only he who, remaining wakeful in the instant in anticipation of an imminent possibility, relates to his having-become in an authentic self-knowledge—only he *is truly in possession of himself*; and, thus acceding to his authentic Self (*eigene Selbst*) before God, he can consequently be saved.

What can this Heideggerian reading of Paul's Epistle to the Thessalonians teach us about the genesis of *Sein und Zeit*, and more specifically about the elaboration of the concept of "authentic temporality"? Is this point of departure merely fortuitous? Is it not decisive, to some extent, with respect to the destiny of the work, in conformity with the aphorism Heidegger likes to quote: "Provenance is always future"?[27] Indeed, on what does Heidegger's entire interpretation of Paul rest? We can sketch out this response: on the suppression of an ambiguity that remains constantly present in the Pauline Epistles and that ultimately decides the meaning of eschatology itself. Bultmann summarizes this ambiguity when he writes, "Though Paul still expects the end of the old world to come as a cosmic drama that will unfold with the imminent *parousia* of Christ (I Thess. 4:16; I Cor. 15:23, 51ff), that can only be the completion and confirmation of the eschatological occurrence that has now already begun."[28] An event that is already present (he who has faith is *already* justified) and yet *still to come*: it is in this very tension that the whole structuration of Christian theology resides.[29] Now Heidegger highlights only one of the aspects of that eschatology in his interpretation, and, on the other hand, he *reduces* (in the phenomenological sense of the term) any conception of the end of the world as a "cosmic drama" that would come about at a certain given moment of time conceived of as a succession of nows. What gives the temporality of factical experience of Christian life its authentic structure is not the expectation of an event in the world, but the wakefulness of the Christian before the imminence of a possibility-at-every-moment. We find here the *analogon* of a phenomenological reduction, even though Heidegger does not use the term, insofar as the reduction is the method making it possible to lead what appears back to its mode of appearing, and for every phenomenon to pass from its *Was* to its *Wie.* Now, only such a modification of the look makes it possible to accede, through the bracketing of the *parousia* as a future worldly event, to the phenomenon of hope in its Christian meaning-content, qua modality of experience of factical life, and consequently to its temporality—a reduction that makes it possible therefore to recognize the originary phenomenological meaning of possibility as it determines and wholly penetrates factical life (as will, later, the existence of *Dasein*). Consequently we see the point on which Heidegger's interpretation of Paul inevitably stumbles: the impossibility of a *complete* reduction of event to possibility. From the Pauline point of view, the *parousia* of Christ cannot be understood *exclusively* as a possibility; it must be thinkable *also* as an event to come. The path toward *Sein und Zeit* seems therefore already mapped out: since the reduction of the eschatological event and its subordination to possibility cannot be completed setting out from Christian thought, since there always remains, in that perspective, a residuum after the phenomenological reduction, a literally irreducible nucleus of factual positivity, Heidegger will have to change course, and horizon, so to speak, and adopt from the start the viewpoint of a methodological atheism.[30] In what, more precisely, does this *radicalization* of the temporal problematic that constitutes at the same time a *reduction* (radical, this time) of the event consist? It resides in a substitution of decisive significance: the instantaneous wakefulness as hope for the return of Christ is replaced by Being-towards-death qua authentic resoluteness within the transparent (*durchsichtig*) instant or moment of vision (*Augenblick*); presence before God is replaced by the mortality of *Dasein* qua possibility of its Being, possibility of its impossibility. For only the reduction of the event brings out possibility as possibility: this is what will be confirmed by the analyses of *Sein und Zeit* devoted to the *existentiale* of dying (*Sterben*).

From these well-known analyses I cannot, in the restricted framework of this inquiry, provide more than a summary and schematic characterization, more often than not referring the reader to the texts themselves. The entire modus operandi of *Sein und Zeit*, in the chapter devoted to Being-towards-death (§46ff), consists once more in a *reduction* of *the event* of death in order to bring fully to light the existential phenomenon of the *mortality* of *Dasein*, as a signal, unrealizable, and in this sense also insuperable potentiality of Being-in-the-world. The result of the preliminary interpretation of *Dasein*, carried out from the point of view of everydayness, had been the highlighting of the *Being* of the exemplary being as care. But if care (*Sorge*) is as structure in each case *total*, which articulates inseparably the three ontological characteristics of existence, that is, being-ahead-of-itself (existentiality), Being-already-in-the-world (facticity) and Being-alongside beings (deterioration), what ensures the *totality* of that structure? Only the phenomenon of Being-towards-death, on the condition of being interpreted *originarily*, can bring us an answer to this question about the totality of the structural whole of *Dasein*. In understanding at first the meaning of this totality as "conclusion" or "fulfillment," (*Abgeschlossenheit, Vollendung*) however, the analyses of *Sein und Zeit* end up in an impasse; for these concepts are only suitable for subsistent (*vorhanden*) realities. "The fruit ripens" means, ontologically, "the fruit reaches its fulfillment" (*vollendet*), it attains its own completeness; all its potentialities are realized with its coming-at-an-end in maturity. But is it the same way with man? Of course, with death, *Dasein* "has run its course," but has it reached any fulfillment in the sense of all its own potentialities having been realized, like a puzzle that is finished when I put the last piece in? No: because *Dasein*, when it dies, has not completed its specific possibilities: rather they have been *taken away* from it. The existential meaning of dying is not understandable in the way the "end" of a subsistent being is grasped; "the 'ending' which we have in view when we speak of death, does not signify *Dasein*'s Being-at-an-end [*Zu-Ende-Sein*], but a *Being towards-the-end* [*Sein zum Ende*] of this entity."[31]

But what does such a "Being-towards-the-end" mean existentially? Not, surely, the expectation (*Erwartung*) of an event still to come, experienceable in the world; for death, as the end of experience, makes the experience of the end impossible. This impossibility of experiencing death as an innerworldly event is not the result of a limitation of my faculty of knowledge, but the consequence of the ontological structuration of the being that I am. Death as such is unexperienceable because at the very moment *Dasein experiences* the loss of its Being-in-the-world, it is no longer even determinable as *Dasein*; it "eludes in principle any possibility of getting experienced at all."[32] We can say of *Dasein* what Jack London says of his hero on the threshold of death, feeling the worry of a forever impossible knowledge: "And at the instant he knew [what death was] he ceased to know."[33] Thus, "by its transition to no-longer-being-there [*Nichtmehrdasein*], *Dasein* gets lifted right out of the possibility of experiencing this transition and of understanding it as something experienced."[34]

The "detour" through the "objectively accessible" experience of the death of others cannot any more afford us an answer to the question of the *totality* of the structural whole of *Dasein* as care. The phenomenon of the death of others leads to the same aporias as that of my own death: far from furnishing an " 'objective' givenness of death"[35] qua innerworldly event, it confirms the fundamental unexperienceability of such a "phenomenon": "We do not experience the dying of others in a genuine sense; we are at best always just 'there alongside.' "[36] If, in everydayness, the deteriorated *Dasein* merges entirely with the They in which "everyone is the other, and no one is himself," if, in the common identifying with the world, "one is what one busies oneself with" and each *Dasein* can, within certain limits, *be* the other *Dasein*, the phenomenon of death, on the contrary, suspends this possibility of the They and is withdrawn by essence all delegation: "*No one can take the Other's dying away from him.*"[37] At most one can die *for* the other, that is, sacrifice oneself for him, without *taking his place* in what constitutes an unwavering possibility of his Being: his essential mortality. Death is a possibility that each *Dasein* must assume in the first person without any possibility substitution: it is ontologically constituted by the mineness (*Jemeinigkeit*) as a fundamental characteristic of *Dasein*'s Being.

However, the major presupposition of all these analyses, a presupposition never questioned by Heidegger and of which it is appropriate to explore the consequences, is that every event as such can *be experienced* in the sense in which a *given occurrence* is experienced, that is to say, can be empirically and objectively accessible. For, from the unquestionably unexperienceable character of the death of others ("dying is not a given occurrence [*keine Begebenheit*], it is a phenomenon to be understood existentially, and it is to be understood in a distinctive sense which must still be more closely delimited"),[38] Heidegger will conclude that that death is not an event. But is every event as such a "given occurrence"? Are experience and "experienceability" the only measure of the event in its eventness? Isn't an event precisely the unexperienceable—by the standards of an empiricist concept of "experience"[39]—and this, precisely, insofar as it is an *event*? Or, putting it differently, can every event be conceived of as a mere "fact of experience (*Erfahrungstatsache*)"?[40] For the moment, whatever the case may be concerning the answers to these questions, the result of the above analyses is to remove the phenomenon of death from any understanding of death in terms of an event.

Dying, in the existential sense, means a way of being of *Dasein*, which consequently is rooted in the structure of care: first, death is a *potentiality-for-Being* that *Dasein* in each case must take over; it concerns *Dasein*'s *potentiality-for-Being*-in-the-world (existentiality), since the latter is the ultimate possibility of no longer being (or, better, of no longer *having any potentiality-for-Being*) in the world. Second, *Dasein* has to take over this signal possibility of its existence insofar as it is always already *thrown* into it. *Dasein* is destined to death from the moment it is born: "*Sobald ein Mensch zum Leben kommt, sogleich ist er alt genug zu sterben.*"[41] This second moment of the existential concept of death is that of facticity: "Thus the existential conception of 'dying' is made clear as thrown Being towards its ownmost potentiality-for-Being, which is non-relational and not to be outstripped."[42] Now, anxiety had been manifested, in the first part of *Sein und Zeit*, as that *Grundstimmung*, that fundamental and signal mood of *Dasein*, which made possible a phenomenal givenness of that being in its entirety, and prepared the ground for the determination of its Being as care. Anxiety gathers within itself the two structural moments of existence and facticity: anxiety carries, as does all *Stimmung*, two essential characteristics, the "in the face of which" (*das Wovor*) and the "for which" (*das Worum*): "that in the face of which we have anxiety is thrown Being-in-the-world; that for which we have anxiety is our potentiality-for-Being-in-the-world."[43] But since "being thrown into the world" means, more fundamentally, being thrown into death (into the possibility of no longer [having the potentiality for] being-in-the-world), and since potentiality-for-Being means taking on this possibility which is nonrelational and not to be outstripped, the possibility of my own impossibility, the existential concept of *dying*, is strictly identical with the phenomenon of anxiety grasped in its existential meaning-content: "Being-towards-death is essentially anxiety."[44] Dying (*sterben*), for *Dasein*, does not have the meaning of a factical demise (*Ableben*), but means existentially being thrown in a signal possibility of its Being and to be anxious about that possibility as long as it "lives": "*Der Tod ist eine Weise zu sein, die das Dasein übernimmt, sobald es ist.*"[45] The assumption of this ultimate and not to be outstripped potentiality-for-Being into which *Dasen* is thrown is only possible in anxiety, and this is why all factical being-anxious is fundamentally a being-anxious *toward* death.

But just as anxiety is most often "covered over" in the carelessness of the They, similarly the existential phenomenon of Being-towards-death, qua rooted in care, includes a third moment: deterioration. What is primordial in the everyday understanding of death is not the *potentiality-for-being* into which every *Dasein* is thrown as long as it exists, but the innerworldly *event* of death: the They "'knows' death as a constantly occurring event, as a 'case of death.' Someone or another 'dies,' be it a neighbor or a stranger. People unknown to us 'die' daily and hourly. 'Death' is encountered as a well-known event occurring within-the-world (*bekanntes innerweltlich vorkommendes Ereignis*)."[46] He who dies is not the Self isolated through anxiety, but the anonymous and indeterminate They. Everydayness is *reassuring*: it "does not let the courage of being anxious about death come out," it turns *Dasein* away from that not to be outstripped possibility of itself (its mortality) to present it with death as an event that is future and, for that very reason, *not yet present*. While in the anxiety of death, *Dasein* is transported before itself in that it is entrusted to its not-to-be-outstripped possibility, the They, on the contrary "concerns itself with transforming this anxiety into fear in the face of an oncoming event [*Ereignis*]."[47] Anxiety, made ambiguous, will be taken for cowardice. Thus, in the ordinary understanding of death, there is a primacy of the event (*Ereignis*) over possibility. And this primacy must be reversed, in order to remove death from its ordinary understanding and to gain access to the existential phenomenon of dying *in its authenticity* (*Eigentlichkeit*).

In Being-towards-death as an existential phenomenon, death, as we have seen, is *Dasein*'s "*ownmost, non-relational, and . . . not-to-be outstripped*" possibility.[48] But what makes the authenticity of that possibility? Or, to put it differently, What is it that confers on this ownmost possibility the phenomenological privilege it possesses—as long as it is not covered over by the everyday understanding of the They—for the sake of bringing to light the phenomenon of authenticity? First, death is a possibility that *Dasein* can only have or, rather *be* itself irreplaceably: death suffers no delegation, procuration, or dismissal. Second, death is the ownmost (the most authentic) possibility because it reveals a signal meaning of possibility that distinguishes it sharply from all "possibilities" in the sense in which the They speaks of them in general. Indeed, what characterizes the possibilities offered to preoccupation (*Besorgen*) is the following phenomenal feature: "Being out for something possible, there is a tendency to *annihilate the possibility* of the possible by making it available to us."[49] This is what happens when *They* expect death: the expectation (*Erwarten*) "is not only an occasional looking away from the possible to its possible actualization, but essentially a *waiting for that actualization*."[50] The They covers over the possibility of death by actualizing it in advance. But the possibility of death gives no support to actualization—for "to actualize" that signal possibility of *Dasein* that death is would mean nothing other than a provocation of demise, and thereby Being-in-the-world would remove the very the ground necessary for a being existing *toward death*; that is to say, it would annihilate all "reality" *at the same time* as all "possibility." Absolutely unavailable, death can never be grasped as a subsistent "reality." While the possible is generally understood as the complement of the real, the possibility of death, radically unrealizable, is the opposite of a potential being: for actuality is the actualization of potentiality, but the event of death deprives the mortal of the potentiality for dying that makes him such. If, for Leibniz, the reality of the possible increases in proportion to its propensity for being actualized, here it is the *possibility* of the possible that increases in proportion to its unavailability. Death, as possibility withdrawn from all actualization, is therefore a possibility that is nothing but possibility. Death is also what reveals thereby the properly existential meaning of possibility. "On the other hand, if Being-towards-death has to disclose understandingly the possibility which we have characterized, and if it is to disclose it *as a possibility*, then in such Being-towards-death, this possibility must not be weakened: it must be understood *as a possibility*, it must be cultivated *as possibility*, and we must *put up with* it *as a possibility* in the way we comport ourselves towards it."[51]

It is perhaps permissible to ask: What is a possibility that is *nothing but* possibility and that cannot be actualized as such? What is a possibility that is, strictly speaking, the possibility of *nothing*—of no event? Even if this possibility is understood as the possibility of its own annihilation *qua* possibility, can this "annihilation," in turn, be understood otherwise than as an event that is to come? Does Heidegger not strip death of its sting by defining it solely as a way to be (*Weise zu sein*) in which *Dasein* is engaged and by identifying it ontologically with anxiety? Could anxiety break out if death did not always *also* announce itself to me as a future event? Can "dying" in the existential sense be wholly dissociated from the *event* of demise in such a way that not only the two phenomena stand in opposition, but the latter is *derived* from the former? Does the phrase "*Dasein* can demise only as long as it is dying"[52] truly indicate a relation of foundation, and does it not inevitably call for its converse? Is it not *because* I have access to the demise of others—and through theirs, to my own—that I can *also* be anxious, in my Being, for that Being itself?

However it may be with these questions, the analyses of dying as opposed to undergoing demise result in a distinction between two modes of certainty that are irreducible to one another: on the one hand, the certainty (*Gewißheit*) of the They, an "empirical certainty" that death, seen as a public event, will occur in the world: "*One* experiences daily the 'dying' of others. Death is an undeniable 'fact of experience'"[53]; on the other hand, the being-certain (*Gewißsein*) that belongs to *Dasein* alone, insofar as it is resolute, isolated by anxiety and brought back from deterioration toward its ownmost possibility, a certainty that is no longer about a fact, nor commensurate with an alleged "experience" that *Dasein* would have of the death of others, but the certainty of a possibility at every moment. This certainty is "higher" than that of the They, because it leaves death its character of possibility. On the contrary, the assurance that death as an innerworldly event will occur "someday" but provisionally not yet, consists in covering over *Dasein*'s ownmost possibility: "Death is deferred to 'sometime later,' and this is done by invoking the so-called 'general opinion.' Thus the 'They' covers over what is peculiar in death's certainty—*that it is possible at every moment* [*daß er jeden Augenblick möglich ist*]. Along with the certainty of death goes the *indefiniteness* of its 'when' [*die* Unbestimmtheit *seines Wann*]. Everyday Being-towards-death evades this indefiniteness by conferring definiteness upon it."[54] It is easy to take note of the connection between these analyses and those of factical life in originary Christianity. Only the anxious certainty that relates to death as to *Dasein*'s ownmost possibility is reconcilable with the radical indetermination of the "when" of death. This certainty is all the more certain, that is to say, it covers over even less the imminent character of that death, in that it leaves more indeterminate "the day or hour."

The anticipation of death, then, has as little to do with the morbid anticipation of a coming event as with the carelessness that flees from it in "diversion (*divertissement*)." For the possibility of death toward which *Dasein* is projected "offers no support for becoming intent on something, for 'picturing' to oneself the actuality which is possible, and so forgetting its possibility." *Authentic* Being-towards-death "as anticipation of possibility . . . first *makes* this possibility *possible*, and sets it free as possibility."[55] Therefore it is *Dasein* and it alone that, by the anticipation of the possibility of death, "*makes* this possibility *possible*"—which indeed does not mean that it *creates* that possibility—and restores it to its possibility beyond all "actualization." Thus, the anticipation of the not-to-be-outstripped possibility that *Dasein* itself *is* "discloses also all the possibilities which lie ahead of that possibility," including "the possibility of taking the *whole* of Dasein in advance in an existentiell manner; that is to say, it includes the possibility of existing as a *whole potentiality-for-Being*."[56]

We are therefore in possession of the answer to the question raised at the beginning, that of *Dasein*'s *whole potentiality-for-Being*. The categorial concept of outstanding (*Ausstand*), from which the analysis of Being-towards-death set out, in which *Dasein*'s "ahead-of-itself" presented itself as "not yet," revealed itself to the genuinely existential consideration as *Being-towards-the-end*, which is something that "in the depths of its Being, every *Dasein* is."[57] The "wholeness" of which it is question is not the addition of subsistent parts, since the analysis of Being-towards-death brought out that *Dasein is its possibilities against a background of impossibility*: death. But death can only be this signal possibility of *Dasein* because the latter *is*, at bottom, possibility; death is the possibility that I am, and consequently my Being as a mortal is entirely within the possibility of my death; I will not die someday, I am dying at every moment with all my Being (*de tout mon être*). It is therefore a characterization of possibility as exceeding all actualization—and thereby all *event*—that constitutes the core of Heidegger's analyses.

The Meaning of Time and the Aporias of Birth

This existential interpretation of Being-towards-death and the phenomenological reduction of events that goes along with it, because they bring out the eminent meaning of possibility qua *possibility of the impossibility of Dasein* (the very repetition of the word "possibility" in this phrase indicating that death is a possibility that must be understood only *as possibility* and stands farthest from all actualization), condition, therefore, the whole analysis of ecstatic temporality. The direction/meaning (*sens*) of time, in its authentic temporalization, is the future; but the ontological-existential meaning of the future only discloses itself in the anticipatory resoluteness toward death: the relation to the authentic future is not expectation (*Erwartung*) of a future event, but *Dasein*'s *coming to itself* from the not-to-be-outstripped possibility that it *is* itself: "Anticipatory resoluteness, when taken formally and existentially . . . is *Being towards* one's ownmost, distinctive potentiality-for-Being. This sort of thing is possible only in that *Dasein can indeed* come towards itself in its ownmost possibility, and that it can put up with this possibility as a possibility in thus letting itself come towards itself—in other words, that it exists. This letting-itself *come-towards*-itself in that distinctive possibility which it puts up with, is the primordial phenomenon of the *future as coming towards.*"[58] The "future" understood existentially as the *direction/meaning* (sens) of authentic temporality is therefore not a present that is not yet "actualized" and that someday *will be*, but "*die Kunft, in der das Dasein in seinem eigenstem Seinkönnen auf sich zukommt,*" the coming in which *Dasein* comes back to itself in its ownmost potentiality-for-Being. Similarly, it is only out of authentic Being-towards-the-end that *Dasein* can return to its having-been and take it over as such. Through this movement of coming back toward oneself, *Dasein* is the one it has been, or, more precisely, it is having-been (*gewesen ist*). As Heidegger writes in a phrase that is practically impossible to translate: "*eigentlich zukünftig* ist *das Dasein eigentlich* Gewesen"[59]: "authentically coming-towards-itself *is* the *Dasein* authentically *having-been.*" This coming back to itself by which *Dasein* takes over its ownmost having-been is what Heidegger calls *repetition* (*Wiederholung*).[60] By returning toward its ownmost being-in-debt from the anticipatory resoluteness of death, *Dasein* can become authentically and totally "transparent" (*durchsichtig*) for itself in the instant or moment of vision (*Augenblick*).[61] Therefore, resoluteness, in that it makes the potentiality-for-Being of the exemplary being authentically and totally transparent in its understanding-towards-death, makes it possible for "the whole of *Dasein* [to be] completely 'given.'"[62] This givenness of *Dasein* as a whole in the gathering together of its ecstasies is accomplished in the instant: "It [i.e., the instant: *Augenblick*] is the mode of resolute existence in which the *Dasein*, as being-in-the-world, holds and keeps its world in view [*im Blick hält und behält*]."[63] Only a resolute *Dasein* can attain the fullness of the instant in which temporality is wholly gathered in the cohesion of its ecstasies—an instant that does not "pass away," does not flow, in the manner of the inner-temporal now, but designates an ecstatic phenomenon, the pure ecstatic phenomenon of the authentic being-present-at . . . , and receives a synoptic status in conformity with its etymology (*Augen-Blick*). Authentic temporality, understood by Heidegger from the phenomenon of Being-towards-death, consists, therefore, in "instantaneous-repetitive-anticipation."

What shall we say, therefore, of the *first event*, the precursory and inaugural event that makes all the others possible—the phenomenon of birth? Can birth receive a properly existential status in the framework set forth by Heideggerian conceptualization? If the analysis of ecstatic temporality had been achieved, as early as 1921, through the reduction of the eschatological event and its leading back to the possibility of an instantaneous wakefulness, which is nothing but another name for hope, if that reduction of the event is confirmed and radicalized in *Sein und Zeit* in the form of a leading back of death qua demise to dying, that is to say, to anxious Being-towards-death as potentiality-for-being for the possible impossibility of existence, what shall we say, then, of that other event—birth—which opens time as such for *Dasein*, of that other "end" of existence? It is no accident that Heidegger, addressing this problem at the beginning of Chapter 5 of Section 2 of *Sein und Zeit*, "Temporality and Historicality," returns once more to the question of *Dasein*'s potentiality-for-being-a-whole: "If we look back on the preceding discussion of the ontological meaning of everydayness, *a serious reservation arises.* Have we indeed brought the whole of *Dasein*, as regards its authentically *Being*-a-whole [Ganz*sein*], into the fore-having of our existential analysis?"[64] The justification for this scruple is to be found in the observation that if the question of Being-towards-the-end has indeed been answered, death is "just *one* of the ends by which *Dasein*'s totality is closed round. The other 'end,' however, is the 'beginning,' the 'birth.'"[65] Leaving aside the phenomenon of birth, the earlier orientation of the analytic remained 'one-sided': for "only that entity which is 'between' birth and death presents the whole which we have been seeking."[66] The interpretation of *Dasein* with respect to its potentiality-for-being-a-whole requires a twofold completion, not only by the inclusion of an analytic of "being-towards-the-beginning," but also by the determination of the existential meaning of this "between": "Not only has Being-towards-the-beginning remained unnoticed; but so too, and above all, has the way in which *Dasein stretches along between* birth and death."[67] But what is the logic of this "and above all"? Indeed, we would expect the analysis of this "stretching between" itself to follow from a prior interpretation of Being-towards-the-beginning. Now, this is not the case. The analytic of birth is simply omitted from *Sein und Zeit*. So of the two questions left unexamined, only the second gets a true elaboration in the chapter devoted to historicality. But this second question—that of the "between"—is itself only intelligible on the condition of having already answered the first question, which Heidegger does not do. What justifies this omission of an analytic of birth—which had in fact been announced—in Heidegger's *Hauptwerk*? And before considering this, is it really a matter of an *omission*? If such were the case, the reasons for it should be sought in the existential conceptualization itself.

In order to convince ourselves of the necessity of an analytics of birth in the economy of *Sein und Zeit*, we must take an initial argument into account. It could be that the phenomenon of birth is beyond the domain of a properly existenti*al* ontology and that birth, like other *existentiales*,[68] comes under an existenti*ell* anthropology. Could it not be maintained that birth, since it plays no directive role in the undertaking of fundamental ontology, can be omitted without compromising the project of *Sein und Zeit*? This argument, however, raises an objection of principle: If the Being of *Dasein* is formally determined as care, and if, as Heidegger writes, "As care, *Dasein is* the 'between' [birth and death],"[69] the result is that birth, as an ontological structure, belongs to its Being in an essential way. Furthermore, there is an obvious existential connection between death and birth: "Understood existentially, birth [*Geburt*] is not and never is something past in the sense of something no longer subsistent [*Vorhanden*]; and death is just as far from having the kind of Being of something still outstanding, not yet subsistent but coming along. Factical Dasein exists as born; and, as born, it is already dying, in the sense of Being-towards-death."[70] We must not misunderstand the meaning of this connection here: the connection is not, in conformity to the meaning of ecstatic temporality that we have just been brought to light, the subsisting relation between two *events* occurring "in" time, itself understood as "a series of lived experiences"; for the "dying" of which it is a question here is not the *event* of death, but existential dying, the resolute and ready-for-anxiety anticipation underlying all Selfhood. According to such a dying, *Dasein* doesn't have its death before it, as an innerworldly event; it is dying at every moment with all its Being. Therefore, to assert that *Dasein* dies as being born is not to advance a commonplace tautology, but rather to include natality itself, as distinct from the *event* of birth, in the ontological content of the Selfhood of *Dasein*. This naturally precludes the consigning of this phenomenon to the field of an existentiell anthropology only subordinated to fundamental ontology.[71]

But a second argument could be offered to justify this absence in *Sein und Zeit* of an analytic of birth (or natality): If this phenomenon is not the object of a thematic ontological interpretation, it is simply because it is already "included," so to speak, in the existential phenomenon of Being-towards-death; and consequently the natality of *Dasein*, as distinct from any innerworldly event, must get its meaning, in the formality (*Formalität*)[72] of its ontological characterization, from authentic Being-towards-the-end. Indeed, the existential concept of dying is characterized as "thrown Being towards [*Dasein*'s] ownmost potentiality-for-Being, which is non-relational and not to be outstripped"[73]; it already includes the moment of *Geworfenheit* in its definition. *Dasein* is not only mortal in the sense of a factical demise; it is delivered over to its death, *thrown* into it. Birth is existentially nothing but this deliverance, this consignment of *Dasein* to its death. The *existentiale* that first makes it possible to think *Dasein*'s birth is therefore

Geworfenheit itself. This thrownness becomes originarily manifest in mood (*Stimmung*): because it is always already thrown in the There of Being-in-the-world, *Dasein* immediately feels its being as a "weight," a "burden," from which, as long as it exists, it cannot free itself. The They-self, however, has a tendency to dodge the "*facticity of its being delivered over*,"[74] thrownness as such, just as it flees the inexorable imminence of death. This is why this burden, consisting for each *Dasein* in its existence, and making its facticity manifest to it, is most often covered over in everyday existence. On the other hand, it is eminently revealed by anxiety: in this *Grundstimmung* there appears a certain "abandonment [*Überlassenheit*] of *Dasein* to itself"[75] inseparable from the phenomenon of birth, and that would justify to some extent the translation of *Geworfenheit* by the heavily connotated word "dereliction."

To these ontological determinations of self-deliverance, of thrownness, of facticity, and of abandonment that might belong, without a doubt, to an analytic of birth, we must add the phenomenon that Heidegger dubs "finding-oneself-in-a-state" (*Befindlichkeit*). Moods constitute modes of that originary self-discovery by *Dasein* as thrown into the midst of beings: "An entity of the character of *Dasein* is its "there" in such a way that, whether explicitly or not, it finds itself [*sich befindet*] in its thrownness. . . . As an entity which has been delivered over to its Being, it remains also delivered over to the fact that it must always have found itself—but found itself in a way of finding which arises not so much from a direct seeking as rather from a fleeing."[76] For everyday *Dasein* only turns toward that charge and that weight of its own existence to which it is assigned by its facticity in order to better turn away from them and flee them more certainly. Only the mood of anxiety, which brings *Dasein* back to its deterioration, does not dodge the abandonment of existence and thus constitutes a "disclosure which is quite distinctive": "that which we have anxiety about is our potentiality-for-Being-in-the-world."[77] In this eminent mood, *Dasein* is transported "before the nothingness of Being-in-the-world," that is, inseparably *thrown into Being and delivered over to its death.* In making manifest the internal link between birth and death, or, as Heidegger puts it, "thrownness into death," the *Grundstimmung* already also reveals the co-belonging of Being and nothingness, later highlighted in "What Is Metaphysics?"

The analytic of death is therefore inextricably an analytic of birth, and *vice versa.* By being born, *Dasein* is not only thrown into the world, but in one and the same movement delivered over to its death. Conversely, only a being that is born in the depths of its Being can be called by this very fact a "mortal." For to die, existentially, does not mean to be exposed to the *event* of death, but, as I have already stressed, "thrown Being towards [one's] ownmost potentiality-for-Being, which is non-relational and not to be outstripped"; that is, to be exposed in its Being to anxiety. Hence the analogies between the phenomena of the beginning and of the end from the point of view of an existential interpretation become manifest: (1) Just as the existential interpretation of death is prior to all biology and ontology of life, similarly the possibility of all bio-ontic analysis of birth must be excluded; therefore the phenomenon of birth cannot be approached, as has been the case since Aristotle, on the basis of the concept of generation (γένεσις); (2) Just as the hermeneutics of Being-towards-death is by principle distinct from any "metaphysics of death" or any speculation on the "beyond," the immortality of the soul, so no faith or certainty relative to the origin or the destination of *Dasein* removes from *Geworfenheit* its character, that of "the inexorability of an enigma"[78]; (3) Last, and this is in my view the most important, just as "dying is no given occurrence, but a phenomenon to be understood existentially," similarly, birth is never a simple fact having occurred in the past that *Dasein* could, in a sense, leave behind itself, but rather accompanies *Dasein* as long as it exists, and is subject to anxiety. "Factical *Dasein* exists as born; and, as born, it is already dying, in the sense of Being-towards-death. As long as *Dasein* factically exists, both the 'ends' and their 'between' *are*, and they *are* in the only way which is possible on the basis of *Dasein*'s Being as *care*."[79]

Consequently, only authentic existence truly has access to birth (as an ontological structure), since it does not dodge death. It is in the anticipation in which *Dasein* attains for the first time its possible authenticity and wholeness that it can relate authentically to its birth, to take charge of it and take it over as such. Therefore, it is probably in the passages devoted to being-in-debt (*Schuldigsein*) that the delineations of an analysis of birth appear. *Dasein* is not in debt in the sense of a factical indebtedness, but it can contract such an indebtedness only because it is in debt in the depths of its Being. In the ontological concept of debt an ontological negation is included: the exemplary being did *not* itself posit its own foundation; it is rather thrown into it: "As being, *Dasein* is something that has been thrown; it has been brought into its 'there,' but *not* of its own accord. As being, it has taken the definite form of a potentiality-for-Being which belongs to itself, and yet has *not* given itself to itself."[80] To the extent that it did not posit its own foundation, and that it did not give birth to itself, *Dasein* never exists except starting from its foundation, without ever being able to free itself from it; it "never gets back behind its thrownness," Heidegger writes, but neither does it find that thrownness "behind it" like an event that has factually taken place. *Dasein is* its thrown foundation, the nullity of its Being. "It itself, being a basis [*Grund-seiend*], is a nullity of itself."[81] *Dasein* is never in possession of its ownmost Being and, as a result, must constantly appropriate it. Its Being does *not* come from a project of its own, but conversely it is only on the basis of this nullity of its Being, of this originary Being-released (*Entlassenheit*)[82] that it can regain its ground and be this ground in the project of its potentiality-for-Being. This is why the ground "is never anything but the basis for an entity whose Being has to take over Being-a-basis (*Grundsein*)."[83] The existential determination of the debt qua being-the-ground-for a nullity means, therefore, that *Dasein*, while not having itself posited its ground, *is* nevertheless its ground in the making possible of its ontological project. The nullity of its being can thus be *assumed* by the resolute *Dasein*: "When *Dasein* is resolute, it takes over authentically in its existence the fact that it is the null basis of its own nullity,"[84] because, as opposed to the They-self, it no longer dodges its ownmost, non-relational, and not to be outstripped possibility. The nullity that lies in the depths of its existence—due to the fact that *Dasein* has not given itself its ground—thus manifests itself, in anticipated resoluteness, as identical to the nullity that resides in the ownmost possibility of *no longer* being in the world. Here, therefore, the intimate bond between birth and death appears once again, "We have conceived death existentially as what we have characterized as the possibility of the impossibility of existence—that is to say, as the utter nullity of *Dasein*. Death is not 'added on' to *Dasein* at its 'end'; but *Dasein*, as care, is the thrown (that is, null) basis for its death."[85] It is only anticipation, therefore, that makes Being-in-debt manifest, so that *Dasein* remains in debt even in the not-to-be-outstripped possibility of its death. The two moments of death and debt are not only inseparable, but additionally "equiprimordial."[86] The nullity of existence, in other words, its thrown ground, can thus be "*taken up* (*aufgenommen*) *into existence*"[87] by the resolute *Dasein* that understands for the first time its potentiality-for-Being in debt authentically and totally. If nullity can be thus "taken up" into authentic existence—or, according to Martineau's paraphrase "accepted, integrated, and taken over,"[88]—then this possibility must also apply to birth. "[*Dasein*'s] 'birth' is caught up [*eingeholt*] into its existence in coming back from the possibility of death (the possibility which is not to be outstripped), if only so that this existence may accept the thrownness of its own 'there' in a way which is more free from illusion."[89] But is such a "taking up" of birth into resolute existence possible? What, existentially, is the meaning of this possibility of *Dasein*'s to "catch up" into its existence birth, death, and their "between"?[90] Have we not arrived at this point at the outer limits of Heidegger's conceptualization?

What of the possibility that *Sein und Zeit* attributes to *Dasein* to relate authentically to its birth in the anticipatory resoluteness toward its death, and to "catch up" into existence its beginning as a moment of its potentiality-for-Being-a-whole? Does birth allow itself to be "integrated" so easily into authentic temporality, and does it not rather threaten the latter from within, preventing all "totalization" of *Dasein*?

The clarification of the meaning of authentic temporality allowed us to distinguish the ecstatic phenomenon of the having-been (*Gewesenheit*) from the "past" (*Vergangenheit*) in the ordinary sense. *Dasein* never becomes "past" in the sense of a subsistent being that *no longer* is, but exists rather as "having-been-there." It is because it is never a past to itself in the sense of a non-present subsisting being that it can authentically relate to its having-been and *take over* this "past" in the project of a future. The same is rigorously true of birth; but what can "to take over one's birth" mean? Is not birth, precisely qua birth, that which is impossible to take over, if "to take over" means to take responsibility for, to take upon oneself, to not leave in forgetfulness? What exactly is this "oneself" that could take upon itself being born? Such a taking responsibility for would, moreover, presuppose it is *I*, in the existential sense, who am born. Now, I can assert only one thing: "I was born [*je suis né*]," in the twofold sense of the past tense and the passive, or rather "there has been a birth." Birth is primarily that event that befalls me impersonally, even before I can take over its burden of being, an event that makes all my possibilities possible, and therefore that I cannot inherit as a factical possibility that is mine, since it is rather what lies at the basis of all possibility of inheritance. Birth, qua impersonal event, and event impossible to take over, radically transcends my thrownness and hence also my ownmost potentiality-for-Being. It is not an inherited possibility that I could take over, but that through which I inherit myself and all my possibilities, situated, therefore, *on the hither side* of them.

There is more. If birth can be "caught up into existence" and taken over authentically, if it is fundamentally no different in this respect than any other possibility inherited by *Dasein*, it follows necessarily that that possibility, taken over in resoluteness, must also be open to a possible "repetition" in the properly existential sense, which, as we know, does not simply mean a "restitution" of the past, but on the contrary, a "release"[91] with respect to it. The authentic having-been, in which birth appears "included," is defined essentially by this possibility of repetition. But then what does a "repetition" of birth mean? Is not birth, among all my "inherited" possibilities (actually itself never inherited, since it founds the possibility of all inheritance), the only one that cannot, strictly speaking, be "repeated"?

And this, for a twofold reason: not only—and this goes without saying—because it is part of the meaning of birth, precisely qua event, to happen *only once*, to be unique and consequently unrepeatable, to be the condition of possibility for all repetition, but also—since to "repeat" an inherited possibility is by the same token to be "released" from it—because there I can never be "*released*" from my birth, because every pro-ject presupposes it and can only go forth into the future by tearing itself free from this "thrownness (*jet*)" preceding all pro-ject. In other words, as Heidegger acknowledges, every project is in itself essentially "null," a thrown project, and nothing else.[92]

In truth, if birth cannot be "taken over," nor "repeated" by *Dasein*, if it consequently goes beyond the framework of ecstatic temporality, it is for a reason of principle: "taking over" means to take charge of a possibility qua possibility to come in the project of an *authentic* potentiality-for-Being; now, my birth cannot be authentically taken over, because it is what is essentially *inauthentic*: "*one* is born into oneself" without ever being able to take one's own birth upon oneself; to be sure, "I am the one who is born," but this very assertion, I can only utter it in the first person because others first took it over and pronounced it in my name: *I* am never born in the existential sense, because that would amount to making of the undergone event of birth purely and simply a modality of my potentiality-for-Being, while I can never receive my Being—and the potentiality-for-Being that is inseparable from it—except *from others*. Being born is never being born alone. Being itself is always entrusted to me and conferred on me as a *gift*. For *Dasein*, Being is the *event* of this gift, which necessarily goes beyond its own potentiality-for-Being, consequently surpassing all power of appropriation. At the ground of every resolute existence lies something that was given to it before it could appropriate it, and that as a consequence precedes and grounds the distinction between authenticity and inauthenticity. Not only a nullity running all the way through existence in project, for that nullity still belongs to the ontological constitution of *Dasein*, whose inauthenticity (*Uneigentlichkeit*) merely means the factical being-covered-over, qualified as "deterioration" and ontological fallenness, of a necessarily primary, originary, irreducible authenticity. On the contrary, if birth is only thinkable according to the scheme of heteronomy,[93] if Being is given to me by the other even before I can appropriate it, and, by thus surpassing all my powers of appropriation, also transcends all the projects that define my potentiality-for-Being-a-whole, then Selfhood, as an ontological structure, can no longer be considered originary. Authentic temporality is only authentic on the condition of standing out against the background of a past "anterior" to all having-been. Birth opens existence to a past "older" than any past *of mine* and to possibilities *other* than those that I project, because the Being given before and in excess to all appropriation is not initially and originarily *mine*. It is only *mine* by becoming so, but it only becomes so by temporalizing itself before any project of mine, differing therefore from itself since the beginning, and making of this appropriation itself an infinite task. Existence opens up from a ground that it does not itself temporalize but that connects it with a "time" older than its time, and that only allows it to temporalize itself. *Dasein* can only take possession of its own Being and thereby reach its existential authenticity because it is already, before all authenticity and appropriation, entrusted to itself and exposed to the still anonymous alterity of a gift that surpasses it and makes of its very Being an enigma—an "enigma" that is deeper, in a sense, than the one envisaged by Heidegger. In birth, and before all ownership of its existence and authenticity, but also before all positing of a true alterity, since the latter derives from the former, *Dasein* is wholly exposed to a gift that it can neither appropriate nor understand, but that irrupts into its most intimate existence and thus makes possible its intimacy with itself. To be oneself is henceforth no longer to project oneself toward a self-contained potentiality-for-Being within the closure upon itself of mortal existence, but rather to deepen the enigma of a meaning that, because it comes always from outside of finite *Dasein*, opens up its existence to a task that is never completed with death.[94]

Insofar as birth can be neither "taken over" nor "repeated," it exceeds the framework of authentic temporality, and, far from allowing the searched "totalization" of *Dasein*, *it rather threatens this "totality and disrupts it."* Indeed, birth beckons toward a past older than any "having-been," and, as such, impossible to take over. It opens the past of *Dasein* to a more-than-past, prior in principle and in fact to any "repetition." This past-anterior, prior to my past and my projects, since I am not contemporary with the event of my advent in being, is at the same time an *immemorial* past—not because it was "lived through" and then forgotten, but because it is prior to all memory and all forgetting, which presuppose a possible relation to Being through which Selfhood is conquered, and therefore also a power of speech through which that Selfhood proffers itself by means of the verb "to be." Immemorial, birth escapes for an additional reason the *existentiales* elaborated in *Sein und Zeit*. For in this work, forgetting always goes along with a fall, a loss of oneself, a failing that only concerns *Dasein* in deterioration. Forgetting, to be sure, is defined as "a 'positive' ecstatical mode of one's having-been,"[95] and not as a privative mode of memory. True, it is only against the background of such an originary forgetting that both memory and its opposite, the factical non-preservation of a particular recollection, "forgetting" in its derivative sense, are possible. But it remains nonetheless true that this originary forgetting is only such from the perspective of derived (inauthentic) temporality: what is "originary" and "positive" from the point of view of derived (inauthentic) temporality can therefore appear only as negative and derived from the vantage point of originary (authentic) temporality. Furthermore, if inauthenticity is but "dissimulation," there is no forgetting that cannot be fully overcome, nor any obscurity that cannot be dissipated in the transparence of authentic existence. But if the forgetting of birth is a forgetting from which there is no awakening, a primary, in-itself, and founding forgetting, we must conclude either that birth does not affect *Dasein* in its authentic temporalization, which would go against Heidegger's most constant declarations, or, on the other hand, that the distinction between the two temporalities, "the *awaiting which forgets and makes present*" and the "instantaneous-repetitive-anticipation,"[96] cannot be maintained beneath the constraint of the phenomenon of birth—a phenomenon that is prior to the divisions it introduces.

By contrast with Being-in-debt (which is open in resoluteness from the anticipation into the authentic future), birth is not to be conceived of as a "groundless ground" (which is still a ground, however, since, though delivered over *Dasein*, it can be *taken over* by it), but as a "bottomlessness" (*Ungrund*), according to Shelling's expression, which is radically inassimilable, non-repeatable, unable to be caught up into existence, ultimately im-memorial in an originary sense, and finally irreducible to the division between authenticity and inauthenticity that determines the conceptuality of *Sein und Zeit* through and through. To conceive of birth itself—outside any ontological formality—as an *event*, to think of events and existence as inseparable, to grant an *evential* meaning to existence itself: is this not therefore the condition for a true *deformalization of time* that transforms radically the ontological conceptuality, giving access to a *different temporality*, more originary than the one described by Heidegger?

The Springing Forth of Events and the Renewed Meaning of Possibility and Existence

Let us recapitulate the fundamental characteristics of the event (*Ereignis*, *Geschenis*, or *Vorkommnis*) as they emerge from the analyses of *Sein und Zeit*: (1) The event pertains essentially, for Heidegger, to *actuality* (*Wirklichkeit*) and not to possibility: it occurs in the world the way a fact (*Tatsache*) or a state of affairs (*Sachverhalt*) does. Its factuality (*Tatsächlichkeit*) contrasts by principle with facticity (*Faktizität*) as an ontological characteristic of *Dasein*—a facticity that takes on meaning only in the light of existence as potentiality-for-Being; (2) All *Ereignis* is essentially *Weltereignis*,[97] event of and in the world, innerworldly event. Now, only an entity pertaining to a categorial ontology can be considered, in the fullness of its phenomenal determinations, as *innerworldly*. Events are therefore stripped from all existential meaning; (3) Given these first two characteristics, the actuality of events can receive only the ontological meaning of *Vorhandenheit*; (4) Events, qua "innerworldly," are necessarily experienceable. Everything that is unexperienceable—the death of other people, for example—is therefore not an event.

Is this interpretation of events, considered in its overall features, legitimate? Is it phenomenologically *originary*? Can we, *must* we, accept this surreptitious *reduction* of events to mere innerworldly facts (*Tatsachen*) that are in addition actual and experienceable, and as a consequence the subordination of events to an ontology of *Vorhandenheit* incommensurate with that of *Dasein*—a reduction that is at the same time the condition for the bringing out of the originary ontological meaning of possibility as a determination of existence? But on what conditions do we have the right to question the phenomenological legitimacy of this reduction of the event to the fact? Only on the condition of being able to shed light on, and elaborate conceptually on, a more originary meaning of events, which—removing the latter from their fourfold characterization by Heidegger—would thereby escape such a reduction. Events, taken now in a different sense—irreducible to facts, prior to existence qua finite potentiality-for-Being—would on the contrary be presupposed by such existence, as being formative of it. Far from event being conceivable as an "*existentiale*" of *Dasein, an originary thinking of event would lead to the highlighting of an "evential" meaning of existence as such.*

What is an event? How is an event phenomenalized for the one it affects? Does this phenomenalization not lead to calling into question the fourfold determination that Heidegger gives of this phenomenon in *Sein und Zeit*?

1. Events, considered in their full phenomenological radicality, are never reducible to their actualization in a state of affairs having the ontological characteristic of *Vorhandenheit*. As literally *eventum*, that which happens, an event presents something irremediably in excess with respect to its actualization, with respect to all *factum*, that is, etymologically, to the "already done," the completed, the achieved. This characteristic of excess possessed by the events resides in the load of possibilities they hold in reserve, making them into something that disrupts the worlds, individual entities, and persons, delivering them to a bottomless dimension that belabors existence and stands on the hither side of all self-possibilization.

As such, events do not pertain to *actuality* (with the mode of being corresponding to it, *Vorhandenheit*), but to possibility, indeed to the possibility of making possible, to *possibilization*. As distinct from the fact (*Tatsache*), which simply occurs in an accomplished and definitive present, an event is what lies in reserve in every fact and every actualization, giving it its load of possibilities and hence its future, what re-transfigures the world introducing in it an excess of meaning that transcends all understanding (*Verstehen*) understood as finite project of a potentiality-for-Being. An event, therefore, is only thinkable as such—that is, in its evential character—in its relation to possibility, since it is that which *reconfigures in each instance the possibilities of existence*, introducing a wide gap in the self-closure of possibilities, since *after* the springing forth of an event, things will never be as they were *before*; it will no longer be the same world, with its open possibilities, since the event's very upsurge, by opening up new possibilities and correlatively closing out others, upends what is still to be called, after the terminology of *Sein und Zeit*, "the world." If indeed the world is "*das Ganze der wesenhaften inneren Möglichkeiten des Daseins*,"[98] then we must assert, against Heidegger, that it is not *first* my freedom that projects a world beyond entities and possibilizes all my possibilities configured into a world by my resolute project toward death,[99] but that it is the event, understood more radically in its relation to possibility, that, by its very upsurge, reconfigures all my possibilities before any project *of mine* and is world-forming for the "entity" that I am.

2. As a consequence the relationships between the world, understood existentially, and the event, understood in its most radical sense (a sense that remained unnoticed by Heidegger) are reversed: the possibility of making possible, *the possibilization* that makes a world beyond all entities reign, is not the characteristic of an autarkic freedom belonging to *Dasein*, but a feature of events in which all freedom is rooted; by reconfiguring my possibilities more originarily than any project of an authentic potentiality-for-Being does, events *reconfigure my world by their upsurge and manifest this world as such*. The *Ereignis/Weltereignis* equivalence, established by Heidegger, shatters at this point beneath the pressure of the phenomena. A "world" can hold sway for *Dasein* only *out of* events in which its possibilities originate. An illness, a bereavement, an encounter, if they are in each case true events, do not leave the world unchanged, but introduce a gap, a break, the opening of a rip, a gaping hole into which the former world *collapses*,[100] and with it selfhood as the project of a potentiality-for-Being. Selfhood is here exposed to the risk of either sinking away entirely, or integrating the event not within the former world—which would amount to denying its significance, to freezing existence itself in a

more and more fragile "world," a world having lost its grip on the present and on my true possibilities (a forerunner to madness, in which the event wins out over existence, and the existent, incapable integrating the event into his existence, sinks into the pseudo world of delirium)[101]—but with a world transfigured by the very experience that the event requires me (and no one else) to undergo.

But to define the event as that which *reconfigures* the essential possibilities of the existent in their reciprocal relation and articulation—this also comes down to thinking the phenomenological meaning of "possibility" differently. Here, "to reconfigure" means not only to redistribute, to reorder possibilities otherwise that would be given to *Dasein* from elsewhere, but also to open up radically new ones, and correlatively close down old ones—that is, in each instance, to *possibilize them*. The possibility of the possible, since it originates in the event, is therefore literally its *eventuality*. Such "possibilities" are no longer rooted in the *formal* ontological constitution of *Dasein*, which would make possible their factical emergence. They only open up and announce themselves starting with the event. The event not only opens up for *Dasein* factical possibilities situated *on the hither side* of its ontological possibilization; it confers an evential meaning on possibility that can no longer be understood in light of the Being of the exemplary entity.

In *Sein und Zeit*, it is clearly asserted that "possibility" does not designate, for *Dasein*, the opposite of "actuality" in the sense of empty (logical) possibilities that Being-in-the-world might accept or reject, become involved in or back away from, but that existence is basically *potentiality-for-Being*. This potentiality-for-Being, qua *finite* potentiality-for-Being, is what manifests itself in the anticipated resoluteness toward death, inasmuch as it opens up for *Dasein* all its factical possibilities and convokes it to the situation in which it has in each case to choose itself.[102] Such a "potentiality-for-Being" therefore does not designate, for *Dasein*, a manifold of contingent external possibilities; it is at the very foundation of its selfhood. All possibility, in this respect, is fundamentally *mine*, since it belongs to a being whose ontological constitution is determined by mineness (*Jemeinigkeit*). But what about the "possibility" of the possible, if what reconfigures my possibilities is the *impersonal* event? What about the very meaning of "possibility," if the reconfiguration of the world as it emerges in and out of the event conditions my potentiality-for-Being through and through, by opening it up to possibilities that are not mine at the outset, but that, being impersonal, or rather prepersonal, fall to me before any possibility of my choosing them, appropriating them, and existing them first-personally? Here, "possibilities" are no longer what is open by the free projection of a finite potentiality-for-Being, but *what comes to me without coming from me* in the ordeal undergone through the event (a joyful gift or a violence suffered, but in each case *something endured*, that is to say, imbued with impossibility, and revealing a fundamental unpower as lying at the bottom of existence),[103] which challenges me to be reborn, to be myself otherwise, that is to say, to come toward myself from the alterity with respect to myself that the event, anonymously, caused to emerge.

3. Events are essentially impersonal; this is one of their main phenomenological characteristics. It is true that events always befall *someone*; they happen to me, brooking no substitute, to me who experience them, and this is why they call for my responsibility and, by upending my possibilities, oblige me to transform myself: "I become [myself] only insofar as something happens, and something happens [to me] only insofar as I become."[104] But while the event always befalls *someone*, it still retains, in its own phenomenological tenor, an essential *anonymity* different from that of the "They," as deteriorated mode of selfhood. An event is *singular*, *unique*, and consequently, necessarily *unrepeatable*, and yet, even in its extreme "individuation," it remains no less *anonymous*. As Deleuze says, "it is the *'they'* [*le* On] of impersonal and pre-individual singularities, the 'they' of the pure event wherein *it* dies in the same way that it rains."[105] There is but one thing I can say about the event: *it* happens to me. This impersonal "it" marks the derived character of mineness (*Jemeinigkeit*) in relation to the originary anonymity that permeates existence and restores it to a store of possibilities that there is no question of *taking over*, but to which it is delivered without return, in the absolute impossibility of exerting any "mastery" over them.

In this sense, death is an event, and probably even an event par excellence. It is true that in the case of death we can never say that it has happened, in the sense of a *present* occurrence, since the moment it is present I lose all capacity for being there and experiencing it. And yet the possibility of death, and its ultimate certainty, signify an *eventuality* standing in the background of all other eventualities: the last eventuality of all my eventualities. Death is closest to us—so close that we don't even see it—"close to death, we no longer see death" (Rilke)—not only in the suspended imminence of an at-every-moment possibility, but as what comes to us without coming from us, ad-venes (*evenit*) to us in the impersonal mode of the event, since when I believe I have it in my grasp, it is death that grasps me, and by releasing me from myself it delivers me over to the ungraspable. This silent death that always accompanies us through our whole lives is an event that can happen in one unique occurrence, but only on the condition it happens "many times," as Proust says[106]—and more precisely, on the condition of taking place in every other event in which what is involved is a transformation of myself and the world, a fundamental *stirb und werde*—and therefore on the condition of haunting existence as a "possibility" that is radically impossible to take over or to take responsibility for—*in the same way as time is.* Death, as long as I exist, has not yet *happened* (as innerworldly *fact*), but it never ceases to *ad-vene* (*advenir*), coming to me from a future that is radically future, without any possible matching with my present, that I cannot anticipate because, as Blanchot writes, "in it *I* do not die, I have fallen from the power to die. In it *they* die; they do not cease, and they do not finish dying."[107] Death unfolds in the space separating the fact from the event, since its continual occurrence can never actualize it, since its evential character transcends by essence all possible actualization. An event par excellence, which never ceases happening to me without ever being accomplished as an actualized fact, and which, when it really takes place, no longer happens *to me*, since it deposes the "I" itself. A death exceeding all potentiality-for-Being, all resoluteness, and all possible totalizing of existence over itself. Thus understood, such a death no longer means this signal possibility closing my resolute existence back onto itself, but rather, what opens it from the outside and confers a meaning on it that it did not itself project—*a meaning* open to a resumption by others, and that consequently transcends the horizon of my finitude.

4. By its impersonal nature, *the event therefore transcends Being defined by my mineness.* This obliges us to reconsider the "relations" between selfhood and the event on a completely different basis from the one offered by *Sein und Zeit.* Indeed, in Heidegger's *Hauptwerk*, selfhood is entirely approached in light of its relation to Being, as *Dasein*'s comprehensive potentiality-for-Being in view of its ownmost possibilities, in the anticipative resoluteness of death, and *Self-constancy*, "steadiness that has been stretched along"[108] that has caught up into itself its two "ends," death and birth, and can no longer be "*outstripped* by anything,"[109] since what is announced in it is the closing in on itself of existence and of its *meaning* as *existentiale* of *Dasein*. But with events and the reconfiguration of possibilities that they bring about, it is a radically different sense that emerges in existence, irreducible to my comprehensive potentiality-for-Being in view of the totality of my ontological possibilities. An event has no meaning that could be grasped and apprehended on the basis of understanding as an *existentiale*; it is the origin of its own meaning as it declares itself in existence before any comprehensive potentiality-for-Being towards death.

This is why an event breaks *Dasein*'s "steadiness that has been stretched along," introducing a radical split between past and future. In and through events, selfhood itself, as a relation of understanding to Being, is altered in its principle. Selfhood can only grasp itself, henceforth, through this break, this hiatus that challenges existence to be reborn and to understand itself otherwise by carrying out new world-projections rooted in an anonymous reconfiguration of its possibilities. In this respect, the event cannot be understood as a *fact* first occurring unproblematically within the world that, in a second moment, "would alter my lived experiences" and transform me myself; for the event *is nothing other* than this transformation of the world and of existence—a transformation sometimes as silent and discreet as the fact is noisy and gaudy—that can only be grasped *after the fact (après coup)*, when, the former world having fallen away, I am challenged to renew myself and to espouse this otherness incommensurate with my possibilities. This radical transformation of Being-in-the-world (of its moods and understanding of oneself and of others) is not the *causal consequence* of the event, for the *significance* of the latter cannot be approached in the naturalistic terms of cause and effect: the conditionality of the event is not of the order of an "effect" that follows mechanically from its happening, independently of its relation to the person to whom it happens. An event belongs rather to the order of an upheaval of meaning that brings into play, in an originary way, the selfhood of the one to whom it happens. An event takes place only when I am able to confront its overwhelming ordeal, when selfhood—as a relation to the eventuality more actual than any actuality of what is beyond the measure of my projects and my expectations—has not given way to a pure alterity, sunken into the unreality of delirium or madness; and at the same time, the event signifies this transformation itself, the mourning of the loss of who we were. More originary than the relation to Being by which mineness falls to *Dasein* (a relation that always signifies the relation of the entity that I am to *my* Being or to Being as *mine*) the experience of an event is a relation to something impersonal that I can appropriate only by integrating it to a new world-projection, but that, at the very moment I integrate it, *has already changed me*, in such a way that I will never be the same: prior, consequently, to self-constancy by which *Dasein* defines itself in its authenticity.

Indeed, the trait of Heidegger's conceptualization that is the most clearly opposed to a sustained inquiry into the event is the opposition between *Dasein*'s two modes of being: authentic and inauthentic. That opposition, let us note, conveys the deep impression left by Kierkegaard, and more generally by Christian thought—Paul, of course, but also

Augustine—in methodologically "atheist" fundamental ontology. For Kierkegaard, as was already the case with Paul, human existence, conceived entirely from the perspective of conversion, can face no other alternative than that of being-for-God (in faith and justification), on the one hand, and that of being-against-God (in fall and sin), on the other. Furthermore, conversion having taken place *once*, Christian existence is already justified in its entirety—that is, pardoned—and it *must* continuously be so despite its subsequent relapses; we find the same structure in Heidegger's authenticity, which "has already anticipated every possible moment [*Augenblick*] that may arise from it"[110] and made itself "transparent" in the instant, no longer being able to be "impugned" by the inauthenticity of the "They."[111] *Dasein* is therefore facing one single alternative: to be oneself or to be the they-self, *Eigentlichkeit* or *Uneigentlichkeit*. Thereby is ruled out the possibility of a *becoming-other by and through the experience of events* qua upheavals of the world, qua reconfigurations of all its essential possibilities. All otherness with respect to oneself is ascribed by Heidegger to *Dasein*'s inauthentic mode of being; all change of the Self is only approached in light of a successive and derivative temporality, stemming from the phenomenological occultation of authentic, originary temporality.

Does not therefore the selfhood of *Dasein*, approached ontologico-existentially as "self-constancy" (*Selbst-ständigkeit*)[112] *reproduce* the scheme of the permanence of substance in relation to its changing predicates, a scheme undoubtedly belonging to a categorial ontology from which the purpose of existential analytic was precisely to set us free? It is true that, as opposed to the permanence of the "subject" of metaphysics, which is of a piece with an ontology of *Vorhandenheit*, the existential stability of *Dasein* excludes both the alleged immutability or invariance of a substrate and a continuous change of its qualities: that stability is located decisively on the hither side of the permanence/change alternative that ascribes its horizon to traditional ontology. And yet the hallmark of the traditional metaphysical analysis of the permanence of the "subject" lies in its tendency to consider the unchanging substrate *apart* from its changing predicates—in other words, to demote all alterity to the level of qualities adhering to the substrate, without this affecting the substrate in its identity itself. Heidegger, who breaks radically with this kind of analysis, does not succeed in solving all its difficulties. No alterity, no originary difference from itself disturbs *Dasein*'s "autonomy"; all alterity, understood as a radical lack of selfhood, is shunted off to the side of the "they-self" that is but the shadow cast by the Self and its factical "covering." Being-in-the-world has no need, strictly speaking, to *become* itself in the undergone experience of events, since it already is itself in the "maintained," supremely transparent moment of vision in which it chooses itself and that seals its fate forever. Selfhood does not signify the ability to face what happens to us and to advene to us as "other" through this experience; the temporality of *Dasein* remains formal and empty, empty and formal like the moment in which nothing passes away or arises, since, as Heidegger writes, "in the moment [*Augenblick*], nothing can occur"[113]—and consequently no event. Now, there is no true temporality without difference with respect to oneself and *originary* alterity. Only temporality that would temporalize itself starting from events could welcome this alterity to oneself constitutive of one whom we can no longer designate as "*Dasein*," an alterity without which a thought of time is probably impossible.

It is in the evential of despair,[114] that is, in the radical impossibility of integrating the event into a new world-projection, that the event's impersonal nature comes out most acutely—since, with despair, existence in its entirety sinks into a bottomless impersonality. Despair is not only the collapse of my possibilities, "the impossibility of my possibilities,"[115] but the incapacity of appropriating the event and integrating it into a new world-projection, and therefore also the impossibility of transforming oneself through it. Despair is not to be understood merely as a privation of hope. Rather it designates the collapse of selfhood in its evential sense. The existent, annihilated by the event, can no longer "regain itself" or exist in the first person. Everything sinks into a kind of anonymous vigil, in which I am without being there, in an impersonal stupor in which suffering, at its highest point, has become painless. The inability to integrate the event into a world-projection, the falling back on the hither side of selfhood, go hand in hand with a radical disinterest in the world (disinterest that is to be thought of in its strong sense, as the absence of all for-one's-own-sake: in such a collapsed "world," *Dasein*'s Being is no longer an issue for it) and an absolute *detachment* from it. When we are sad, at least we are attached to our sadness; there is something of ourselves in it, something against which we can struggle, something to which we can let ourselves go, and not that vigil without anyone there that sets in during true moments of despair—and that literally means the inability to be sad. *It* suffers, but there is no longer anyone to suffer, *our* suffering is taken away from us, as well as any ability to give up or to fight: *one* attends one's suffering without any longer being present oneself. All will, all strength abandon us.

Thus, in the great calm that sets in during true moments of despair, a sort of impersonal lucidity is revealed in which things begin to take on a life of their own, and the "world," stripped of all for-one's-own-sake, becomes a pure spectacle playing itself out before us with a relief all the more striking in that all selfhood has deserted it. Things deprived of world invade and block existence, begin to people the anonymous hyper-lucidity of despair, its impersonal vigilance; but they no longer reach us, or reach only the emptiness of our deserted "self." Whence the particular intimacy—that should not be interpreted too hastily—that sets in here with impersonal death, as an essentially inauthentic, a radically anonymous event, in which *they* die without the possibility of taking over their death and even being resolved to it. The anonymous hyper-lucidity attends the sinking of the world as if *one* were no longer there. One is dead, simply; that took place a long time ago already, it has always been that way, and that death, we didn't see it coming, and it didn't even happen; despair is, then, as Kierkegaard said admirably, that continual death, that death that cannot die and yet is already dead, that cannot take over or upon itself death, since the very decision of suicide always presupposes selfhood and a world-projection—which is precisely what sinks away in great despair—so well-described in a few dry sentences in *Sentimental Education*: "All that was necessary was a single movement. The weight of his forehead dragged him along—he beheld his own dead body floating in the water. Frederick stooped down. *The parapet was rather wide, and it was through pure weariness that he did not make the attempt to leap over it.*"[116]

Thus despair manifests the primary relation to death: in it we experience ourselves as if we were *already dead*,[117] as if fallen back on the hither side of all selfhood (a fall completely different from that of "the they") and of any world-projection, and therefore as incapable of *taking over* death, incapable of suicide. With despair there appears the *derived* character of authentic selfhood, reached in anxiety, qua thrownness into the not-to-be-outstripped possibility of death, and its subordination to impersonal events, to that dimension of essential anonymity that haunts all existence before any possible distinction between a "oneself" and a "they-self." The impersonality of despair, therefore, designates a phenomenon more originary than selfhood conquered in anxiety, and thus than any possible authenticity or inauthenticity, a phenomenon that affords the sole basis on which selfhood can be understood, not as ek-sistence in the project of a free potentiality-for-Being towards death, but as *insistence* on the face of the event: insistence that only appears *as such* when it collapses, when *I* can no longer "face" the event—in the originary and non-derivable phenomenon of despair.

5. The event, as a "gap (*faille*)" in existence (which can bring about its failure [*faillite*] in despair), by which the former world collapses, is not *experienceable* if all experience, all *empirie*, must be understood in the

sense of the experiencing of an innerworldly fact or state of affairs, of which the presential mode of being is that of *Vorhandenheit*. It may be noted in passing that the primacy given by Heidegger, as far as the event is concerned, to "experienceability" seems entirely problematic in a work that, like *Being and Time*, vigorously strives to distance phenomenology from the primacy of presence, hence from consciousness, and from what Husserl called "the principle of principles"—intuition. Why should "experienceability" be the measure of the event, if it is not the measure of existence? Or else should existence as such be defined by the exclusion of all events? By contrast, it must be maintained in an evential conception of existence that there is an experience of the event that has nothing "empirical" about it, because it is not the experience of a worldly fact: there is a *passibility* in front of events that remains irreducible to the traditional opposition (underlying the classical doctrines of "experience") of passivity and activity.[118] The event is not first possible, and then actual; its emergence is not subordinate to prior conditions of possibility in the subject,[119] to a "passivity" in which it would inscribe itself and that would belong to a transcendental apparatus. It is rather by springing forth that the event opens the space of play in which it can be "welcomed," that it unfolds the conditions of its own advent—at the same time as the conditions of the one to whom it happens. This is why, by contrast with the "worldly event"(*Weltereignis*) of which Heidegger speaks, the event in the sense I give this term does not simply take place as a *fait accompli* in a present that is completed and definitive. It *essentially overflows the present of its actualization* and only announces itself with the delay and deferment constitutive of what overflows all immediate consciousness, all contemporaneity, and all transparency of *Dasein* to itself. Having already irrupted into existence before any explicit consciousness of its coming, having already instilled or installed a meaning in existence that can only come to light according to an essentially delayed understanding, the event temporalizes temporality before any self-temporalization of *Dasein*. If "experience" always means coincidence and contemporaneity with oneself and with what is experienced, transparency of the given, readability, and immediacy of meaning for an intuition, then events are not, as such "experienceable": their present, constitutionally in-actual in its continuous coming to itself, overflows all contemporaneity of "self" with itself, precedes and grounds the "experience" I have of it, at the same time as it suspends it in the hiatus of surprise, at the same time as it destroys its bases and breaks its inner "continuity," announcing itself from a past "older" than any present, and opening the very dimension of its occurrence on the basis of which alone all "experience" can grasp it (and itself).

This "unexperienceability" of events by the standards of the empiricist concept of experience, that is, of experience as experience-of-facts, is revealed first in the impossibility in which we find ourselves to answer the question of "when." *When* did the event take place? This question is not about the event in its *factical* actualization, but about the event as that which always occurs in the margin of its actualization—the event in its eventialness as an impersonal reconfiguration of the world. An encounter, for example, is irreducible to the actual putting in presence of two persons before each other, as a fact occurring unproblematically within the world, because the dimension of surprise, of ek-stasis and forceful seizure that is introduced by the encounter "in the world," is indissociable from an upheaval of the world *as such*. Anxiety, self-consciousness, and timidity are surely essential phenomena in any encounter insofar as it interrupts our familiarity with the world, making us "lose our footing," exposing us to the risk of a radical alterity that eludes all mastery and all anticipation. Encounter is an upheaval of the world itself, because, as event, it does not take place in a previous world, in *my* world, in that "*Welt*" about which Heidegger says that it is an ontological constituent of *Dasein* whose Being is defined by *mineness*. On the contrary, encounter introduces into this world that is always "mine" the foreignness of an "other" world—incomparably so—the world of *another*, thus transforming mine through and through. In a true encounter, it is the event itself that enables my access to what I could not access on my own—the world of the other—allowing me to "see" my own world and to "see" myself from its foreign perspective. The encounter, shattering our solitary world and introducing into it possibilities not prefigured in it, thus signifies for the one to whom it occurs the unfolding of a new world. Speaking of his meeting with Milena, Kafka writes in one of his most beautiful letters, "You see, as far as I'm concerned what's happening [*was geschieht*] is incredible [*Ungeheurliches*: literally, immense, frightening]—my world is collapsing, my world is rebuilding itself [*meine Welt stürtz ein, meine Welt baut sich auf*] . . . . I'm not lamenting the falling apart, it was already in a state of collapse, what I'm lamenting is the rebuilding, I lament my waning strength, I lament being born, I lament the light of the sun."[120] Such an event only appears to the person to whom it happens when it has already taken place, so that the first moment, the beginning of a love, the beginning of a friendship, is always already "lost." When the event has taken place, it is already "too late"; we cannot truly experience it until after it has happened, and this is why the event in its eventialness happens only in accordance with the secret of its latency. The encounter is not the datable fact of the meeting of two beings, but what lies in reserve in that meeting itself, giving it its futural burden. It is this silent upheaval that comes in from the other into my own world, reconfiguring its possibilities from the outside.

As paradoxical as it may seem, what is true here of the extreme "passivity" of the encounter in which the other person comes to me on his or her own initiative—regardless of the attempts I might make to "promote" or "bring about" the meeting—is just as true of a behavior in which I show an initiative and a mastery. While in every encounter, according to the expression of Levinas, "the other strikes me with unpower [*impouvoir*]," in the decision, on the contrary, a power is manifested that it is entirely up to me to exercise; and yet, the great decisions, those that modify us in inscribing themselves in our lives as true *events*, are prepared within us in such a way that we are never truly contemporaneous with their origin. Not that, as Sartre thinks, we have always already decided, which would amount to hypostatizing human freedom, to conferring upon our faculty of choice an unconditional and properly demiurgic power (deliberation would be no more than a "comedy" we perform for ourselves, when, in reality, "the die is cast"), but because most true decisions, if they are truly *decisions*, are announced long before becoming fully pronounced. In a passage in *L'Herbe*, Claude Simon describes that impossibility of *dating* a decision, which belongs to its evential character: "But she didn't answer, and after a moment, he appeared: she could see him later the way he stood there, and she would wonder then if it wasn't at that moment that she made up her mind, although, she would think bitterly, it was about as futile to try to know the moment when a decision was reached and the reasons for that decision as to know the moment (and the reasons why) one catches a cold, the only possible certainty in the one case or the other (the decision or the cold) being when the one or the other reveals itself, and by then they have already been established for a long time."[121] Ironic though it may be, the comparison between a decision and a cold is not without a basis in "the things themselves." The event is what reconfigures by itself my possibilities (in this case, my love possibilities) in such a way that when it is carried out as an actual decision, when the decision intervenes or, more precisely, "reveals itself," it has already been established "for a long time"—in accordance with an "already" that is not to be understood in the sense of a factual chronology, but in accordance with that break that the event has produced between a past and a future that are irremediably sundered, out of which time itself emerges in its ecstatic disjunct [*discès*]—in the impersonal mode.[122] Basically, when the decision is made, the event had already taken place a long time earlier, and as much as the actualization of the event can be loud, gaudy, its coming is most often invisible, silent, so that Pasternak's exergue to Claude Simon's novel would epitomize by itself that unfathomable gap between the experienceable fact, on the one hand, and the event in its unexperienceable coming, its eventialness, on the other, insofar as I cannot experience it (a non-empirical experience, then) except *after the fact*, in the *essential a posteriori* of a necessary retrospection. "No one makes history, no one sees it happen, no one sees the grass grow." This is not only the case because we are reduced to a finite point of view on events, but because an event, essentially unexperienceable, as anonymous configuration of the world, always occurs *in the margin* of its actualization, silently and imperceptibly, "brought on the feet of doves"[123]: it does not make itself known till much later, when it has long since settled in; when the event becomes visible in its actualization, it has *already* occurred, and this is why, as Nietzsche writes, "the greatest events and the greatest thoughts . . . make themselves understood later; the generations contemporary with these events do not *live* them, but pass by them."[124] This delay is not accidental. It is consubstantial with the event. If I can never be contemporaneous with, live, or experience it, this is because its meaning itself only gives itself in an *essential a posteriori*—a "transcendental" *a posteriori*, so to speak, in accordance with which the *experience* of the event, as an impersonal reconfiguration of the world, eludes all *empirie* and all empiricism in the traditional sense.

F. Scott Fitzgerald, in his short story *The Crack-Up*, described this delay, this latency, this temporal reprieve peculiar to "great events," and indissociable from their suddenness. "Of course all life is a process of breaking down, but the blows that do the dramatic side of the work—the big sudden blows that come, or seem to come, from outside—the ones you remember and blame things on and, in moments of weakness, tell your friends about, don't show their effect all at once. There is another sort of blow that comes from within—that you don't feel until it's too late to do anything about it, until you realize with finality that in some regard you will never be as good a man again. The first sort of breakage seems to happen quick—the second kind happens almost without your knowing it but is realized suddenly indeed."[125] In this passage, Fitzgerald distinguishes two sorts of events: (1) those that come from outside and give the impression of happening very quickly. They do "the dramatic side of the work," he writes, but their suddenness does not preclude a delay, nor their dramatic side a certain latency (they "don't show their effect all at once"), a lag until it is "realized" always later, and by virtue of which this first sort of event ("that come, or *seem* to come, from outside") is close to the second; and (2) those that happen "almost" without one's being conscious of them, whose work, underground, seismic—the crack-up—has nothing remarkable or dramatic about it, but takes place slowly and imperceptibly;

thus, it is only once we have "realized" that they happened that they truly become events, for it is "suddenly indeed" that we realize their occurrence.

Whatever degree of relevance, from the phenomenological point of view, we may grant this distinction between two types of events (since *all events*, in engaging entirely our Being-in-the-world, are both more "internal" than all "subjective" interiority and more "external" than all within-the-world exteriority), the fact is that there remains in every event a constitutive tension between the sudden present of its emergence and the deferment with which it declares itself. As a result, we cannot experience it as such until it has *already* taken place, *already* transfigured our existence through and through, by opening it up to the excess of a meaning that it did not itself project. In the first sort of events, the explosive suddenness of the "first time" precedes the integration of the event into a world-projection, or on the contrary, the disintegration of the "fund" in which selfhood and existence are anchored. In the second sort, the latency and the delay "precede" the sudden occurring of the event as "realization" of this delay, this gap even, according to which the event has overturned, definitively "cracked," the person we were. In this second case, the delay, the period of latency, the incubation so to speak (the image of the cold in Claude Simon) belongs to the event in its *sudden* occurring. "Moreover, to go back to my thesis that life has a varying offensive, the realization of having cracked was not simultaneous with a blow, but with a reprieve."[126] But the opposition may not be absolute between the "crack" made from outside by the event (an event that never stops occurring and hitting existence with knockout blows until its progressive integration into existence, or else the disintegration of the latter), and the crack that comes "from within." For existence in its entirety must first be opened down to its depths, to the bottomlessness of a radical break, in order for the event, in its sudden explosion or silent latency, to invest the whole of existence and introduce this "crack" that reconfigures its possibilities in unforeseeable ways.

Only an analysis of birth will enable us to think through this bottomlessness (*Ungrund*), to borrow Schelling's expression, constituting an open break in existence that cannot be taken over by any project and alone makes the emergence of all ulterior events thinkable. This absolute break in which the event inscribes itself cannot be approached in terms of "facticity." If *Dasein*, in the anticipatory resoluteness toward death, *makes its facticity possible for itself*,[127] and masters, consequently, the unmasterable (in such a way that the ground-without-ground of existence still remains, in Heidegger's view, a *quasi-foundation*, which *Dasein*, as such, "possibilizes"), the event, by contrast, opens existence to the bottomlessness of a radical unpower, to the yawning gap of a break—passibility—that no project on the part of the self will ever be able to fill up, an originary dehiscence in which the event grows, in deferment of its own actualization, in the enhancement of a future transcending all possible projects. What can we say, then, of the inaugural and precursory event of birth, both a first event and an event par excellence? Is it possible, in conclusion, in light of the analyses developed above, to outline an *evential* conception of birth, which is lacking in *Sein und Zeit*? Birth is not an event that might or might not happen to the existent—that the existent might leave behind or on the contrary take over and resolutely repeat. *Dasein* is "native" at the bottom of its Being, because birth is the inaugural and anonymous event by which other events are in turn possible. Birth does not occur "in a history" but, like all true events, "makes history," opens the very possibility of a history and the dimension of its meaning. In answering the questions above, I shall attempt a deformalization of ecstatic temporality, in order to withdraw it from an ontological "point of view" and to understand it no longer on the basis of Being-towards-death but rather on that of the eventialness of birth.

The moment it emerges into being, no "self" can take it upon itself to be born. Birth is that gift of being that essentially exceeds all power of appropriation. Of course, in a sense, *I* am the one who is born, in the sense of a factical event that concerns *me*. However, I am involved in birth without ever being able to say that *I am being born*, but at most that "there has been birth." At the moment birth takes place, no "I" is there—understood existentially as the resolute project of a potentiality-for-Being—to take over this event. Selfhood in the sense Heidegger gives it can receive, in this respect, no more than a secondary status. It can only be something derivative, in the sense that only the event itself (*Er-eignis*) appropriates me to myself before all project-towards-death and all resoluteness, by configuring my possibilities for the first time and by opening my present to a past "older" than any past that can be taken over, than any "having been,"—to possibilities that I do not project and for which I cannot be answerable and to a prepersonal history that precedes and grounds my history. Existence as a whole, qua being-since-birth, is thus open to the yawning abyss of an absolute bottomlessness that cannot be caught up in any world-projection, an abyss prior to all foundation of *Dasein* in the sense of a "thrown foundation" and that gives every ulterior event to come. Birth as advent to the world is not, as such, experienceable. It designates an event *that has never taken place* in the sense of an innerworldly fact, and is consequently immemorial in a positive sense. Unexperienceable, nonempirical, birth is nonetheless constantly *felt* in what Heidegger calls

Befindlichkeit, the "finding-oneself-there" in the world, but this feeling never signifies a co-presence to the event, nor a consciousness or thematic grasp of it.

Birth thus opens up the possibility of a renewed analysis of temporality that describes its differentiated upsurge in the movement of temporalization as a dynamic structuration starting from events; because *Dasein* is first born, it does not temporalize itself originarily in light of the authentic future of its Being-towards-death, but rather in light of this immemorial past, impossible to take over for it, to which birth opens and that, in turn, opens *Dasein* to a future "ahead of" all project, conferring on *Dasein* what we could call a "task." If every task exceeds our own potentiality-for-Being, and calls us from a future that we do not project, this is because, since the origin, birth opens existence to more than that which it can take over or possibilize, giving that existence a meaning that it does not draw out of itself.

There are no events if not inaugural ones. An event, in order to occur in its incomparable novelty, must institute a true beginning, that is, be born out of itself, or, which amounts to the same thing, be born out of nothing, be prefigured by no possibility but reconfigure all possibilities unforeseeably in and by its very springing forth. An event is a radical beginning, a beginning that does not relay something else, a pure coming of itself into itself, free of all preliminary horizon. And at the same time, the present of the event appears constitutionally in-actual, "ecstatic" with respect to time as a whole by its continual coming to itself, already open to a past whose meaning it renews by shedding a new light on it, and a future that it unfolds before any project by its own dramatics. This is why my existence, insofar as it arises in an inaugural event, is open both to a "past" that is older than any present (a prepersonal past, older than any "having been" that confers a legacy and a history on me) and to a radical future that will never be present: my death.[128] The temporality of existence temporalizes itself originarily in the form of a past and a future that are radically heterogeneous, non-synchronizable and non-totalizable, since the never-happened arch-event (qua innerworldly, experienceable fact) of my birth is, by this very fact, still to come. I shall never cease being born, that is to say, coming to myself as something happens to me and, through this event that unforeseeably comes to me without coming from me, coming to myself as *other*. Suddenness of a beginning initially burst apart, star-spangled, not coinciding with itself and never an *origin*, and deferment of an event that never ceases occurring, and opens up for me, beyond any totalizing self-project, a task that does not end with my death: such is the most originary structure of temporality, as it is possible to apprehend it in light of events. According to such an analysis, temporality is *the non-happened event (birth) and the still-in-abeyance (task) event of its very upsurge qua beginning (present).* If temporality temporalizes itself in this way out of events, if it must no longer be considered solely within the horizon of the question of Being (the impersonal event precedes Being defined by mineness), it follows that human existence as a whole must be approached henceforth in its evential sense,[129] more originarily than in the existential analytic, in such a way that the ontological difference, which forms the starting point of *Sein und Zeit*, becomes itself an *event* springing forth with *Dasein*. As Heidegger puts it in a course of 1929–30: "It is not *we* who make it [the ontological difference], rather *it* happens *to us* as the fundamental occurrence of our *Dasein*."[130]

3

Bergson as Metaphysician and Critic of Metaphysics

Bergson's thought, like that of Nietzsche, Heidegger, and probably already Kant,[1] expressly brought to bear a critique of metaphysics in the sense of the unified conceptual apparatus, determinative of the history of Western philosophy as a whole. To my knowledge, this fact has rarely been emphasized, and even less analyzed for its own sake. By "metaphysics" Bergson meant not only, nor even primarily, the "science sought after" by Aristotle, but the coherent set of presuppositions governing philosophical inquiry as such from the pre-Socratics up to the time of his contemporaries. Furthermore, even before Heidegger, Bergson made the analysis of time the guiding thread of a characterization and critique of that same metaphysics. Of whatever speculative *hubris* one might suspect of this kind of undertaking (but is not *hubris* inseparable, since Plato, from the very definition of philosophy?), the twofold question of its historical *and* philosophical relevance is worth being raised. It is to this question that the following pages are devoted.

Metaphysics as a Lack of Understanding of the Radical Novelty and Unforeseeable Nature of Reality

Bergson himself sets out an affirmative metaphysics, and on the other hand, he conducts a critique of metaphysics. The term "metaphysics" has for him, as it did for Kant, two main meanings not only different, but opposed. For Kant metaphysics meant at the same time, in its positive sense, *the science of the limits of human reason* stemming from the irrepressible tendency of the latter to ask questions beyond the scope of possible experience, and, on the negative side—as subject to criticism—the dogmatic pretension of reaching a *knowledge* of things in themselves. For Bergson, metaphysics is at the same time—positively—the authentic method of philosophy, an intuitive science declining the use of symbols; and, as subject to criticism, what impedes the development of such a science, the whole of philosophy insofar as it has succumbed to the requirements of the intellect, has replaced duration as a qualitative and indivisible continuity, with homogeneous time, made up of juxtaposed instants, and the mobility inherent in reality with trajectory understood as a series of positions or stops. Understood in the latter sense, metaphysics, according to Bergson, has its historical source in Eleatism. "Metaphysics dates from the day when Zeno of Elea pointed out the inherent contradictions of movement and change, as our intellect represents them."[2] This intellectual representation of change and this spatializing conception of time, the paradigm of which is furnished by Eleatism, may be found throughout the history of philosophy and, in a sense, is identical with it. Since duration *is* mobility, and is even "mobility in its essence,"[3] the negation of the reality of movement is one with the misconception of the nature of duration. "It is thus that metaphysics was led to seek the reality of things above time, beyond what moves and what changes, and consequently outside what our senses and consciousness perceive."[4] Metaphysics replaces immediate experience with "a system of abstract general ideas," a theoretical scaffolding all the more fragile and shaky since it follows "the natural bent of the intellect,"[5] and distances itself from intuition. Metaphysics—understood now in its Bergsonian affirmative sense—must rather return to experience; it *is* that experience itself in its original form. Metaphysics must be experimental because experience is metaphysical: it is duration. But what does this mean? What does metaphysics—in its negative acceptation—overlook when it overlooks duration? What is obfuscated by intelligence when it replaces duration with a convenient, everyday representation, adapted to the needs of action?

The answer may be given in one word: the unforeseeable. The genealogy of metaphysics is the genealogy of the obfuscation of the absolutely new. "The truth," Bergson writes, "is that philosophy has never frankly admitted this continuous and unforeseeable novelty" that defines pure duration.[6] For the Greeks, Being is "given once and for all, complete and perfect, in the immutable system of Ideas." Time is the degradation of eternity, and therefore a privation. It delineates "the variations of a deficiency" and measures "the changing form of a void." As for the moderns, although they didn't conceive of time in light of eternity, they reduced it to a mere appearance: the temporal fades away into a system of relations. It is nothing but the sensible—hence confused—form of the rational. "The real becomes once more the eternal, with the single difference, that it is the eternity of the Laws in which the phenomena are resolved instead of being the eternity of the Ideas which serve them as models."[7] Experience is unrecognized in its unforeseeable nature; the "moving world of phenomena" is reduced to the differential equations of mathematics. Time lacks all positive determination, does nothing, is ineffective, since all the events to come can be legitimately represented on a line by points with different coordinates. "In short, time thus considered is no more than a space in idea where one imagines to be set out in line all past, present and future events, and in addition something which prevents them from appearing in a single perception: the unrolling of duration would be this very incompletion, the addition of a negative quality. Such, consciously or unconsciously, is the thought of most philosophers, in accordance with the demands of the understanding, the necessities of language and the symbolism of science. *Not one of them has sought positive attributes in time.* They treat succession as a co-existence which has failed to be achieved, and duration as a non-eternity. This is why, in spite of all their efforts, they cannot succeed in conceiving the radically new and unforeseeable."[8] Bergson's rhetorical modesty should not make us overlook his critical radicalness: his "most philosophers" refers to philosophy *as a whole*, all the more irremediably gone astray because their error is rooted in a *natural* illusion (along the same lines as Kant's transcendental appearance), an illusion resting at once on the requirements of the understanding, the laws of language, scientific necessity, and last but not least, the imperatives of action—which he does not mention here.

The radicalness of this critical gesture must be emphasized. What Bergson gives us is a characterization of "metaphysics" as a unified framework of thought determining the history of philosophy *as a whole*. His critique entails, therefore, the requirement of a recasting of the main concepts of metaphysics: possibility and reality, freedom and necessity, matter and life, religion and morality. The impossibility of thinking the fundamentally unforeseeable nature of duration means at the same time the impossibility of thinking freedom as entirely new action, life as creative élan, religion as creation and love, and so on. In order to understand this concept of "metaphysics" thoroughly we would have to expose of the entire panoply of Bergsonian concepts. But what about the relevance of Bergson's thesis for the delimitation of metaphysics in its essence? I will limit myself in these pages to the problem of time, since it has a priority over all others.

It is not difficult to find examples in the history of philosophy to illustrate Bergson's critique. The most obvious one is probably Aristotle. In Book 4 of the *Physics*, in approaching the problem of time, Aristotle gives an undisputable privilege, for the understanding of this phenomenon, to the dimension of achievement, hence of destruction, over that of generation, of novelty. "It is clear then that it [time] must be in itself, as we said before, a cause of destruction rather than of coming into being (for change, in itself, makes things depart from their former condition), and only accidentally of coming into being, and of being."[9] Through time, everything reaches its accomplishment and completion, but nothing comes about by essence, so that time is the very achievement of all that takes place within it: if something new appears in it, it is only by accident. This leveling down of novelty as such is obvious in other places of the Aristotelian corpus.[10] But this primacy of the phenomenon of passage, expressly emphasized by Heidegger, too,[11] is no less prominent, for example, in Hegel's characterization of time, in §258 [*Zusatz*] of the *Encyclopedia*, as "this abstraction of destruction," or in Husserlian phenomenology, which subordinates, despite the passivity of the arch-constitution of the temporal flux, the radical novelty of the *Urimpression* to the morphological acts and their respective horizons, whose fulfillment it ensures.

The Root of This Misconception: The Spatialization of Duration

But it is one thing to observe a lack, and quite another to determine the reasons behind it. What are these, in Bergson's view? What leads metaphysics to overlook novelty as a characteristic of duration, and to make unpredictibility into an adventitious, extrinsic character of phenomena? The answer, here again, may be expressed in one word: the *spatialization* of duration—that is, the adoption of what is at once "an idol of language" and "a scheme of our action on matter,"[12] namely the concept of a homogeneous time as it is presupposed from the pre-Socratics to modern physics. To question the legitimacy of Bergson's concept of metaphysics comes down to raising the following problem: is there a necessary connection between our misconception of the radical novelty of phenomena and the spatialization of duration? And consequently, does the Bergsonian determination of duration as a qualitative multiplicity of psychological states in constant mutation, interpenetrating each other and forming an indivisible unity, offer a real alternative to time as conceived by metaphysics?

But, first of all, is there in philosophy, or even in the sciences, such a thing as "spatialization of time"? Bergson has maintained that there is, on numerous occasions. For example, Kant's mistake was the following: "He did not notice that real duration is made up of moments inside one another, and that when it seems to assume the form of a homogeneous whole, it is because it gets expressed in space. Thus the very distinction which he makes between space and time amounts at bottom to confusing time with space."[13] Kant, in this respect, does not proceed otherwise than common sense, which figures symbolically heterogeneous inner states by juxtaposing them in a homogeneous milieu, "in such a way as to perceive them simultaneously, no longer in one another, but alongside one another"; in short, he "projects time into space, [he] expresses duration in terms of extensity."[14] This spatialization underlies any mathematical approach to duration that attempts to make it accessible to calculation, and thereby to prediction. This is a result of Bergson's conception of number, as set forth mainly in *Time and Free Will: An Essay on the Immediate Data of Consciousness*. Bergson adopts the Aristotelian definition of number as a "collection of units," the "synthesis of the one and the many,"[15] in order to show that such a synthesis presupposes the identity of the units that it unites, and that such an identity presupposes in turn the juxtaposition of the units in question in an "ideal space," so that "every clear idea of number implies a visual image in space."[16] Does Bergson not confuse, in that approach, "number" itself with its symbolic representation? The same question arises in the same terms for the concept of order that seems implied in all apprehension of time. For the astronomer who predicts an eclipse, time boils down to the calculable order of succession of a multiplicity of phenomena. Now, all order presupposes, in Bergson's view, a process of projection and figuration in space: "if we introduce an order in what is successive, the reason is that succession is converted into simultaneity and is projected into space."[17] Is this not again to confuse a relation of order that in itself is neither spatial nor temporal with its symbolic representation? Bergson would probably retort that for him, the ideas of order and number do not precede their symbolic representation, but are engendered by them.

In any case, it is first of all number, as *quantum* presupposing the homogeneity of the units it synthesizes, that is responsible, in the view of the philosopher, for the "mistaken idea" of a homogeneous duration analogous to space. From the Eleates to Kant and from Kant to modern physics, it is the same spatialization of time that is operative. For metaphysics, time is basically nothing other than space, and this is why time is so amenable to measurement. For modern physics, time boils down to an independent variable in the differential equations expressing the laws of matter. But does this claim have any relevance for understanding the traditional definitions of time? Should we not on the contrary concur with Heidegger when he says, "The time which is made public by our measuring it does not by any means turn into space because we date it in terms of spatial measurement-relations"?[18] Is this not equally true for Aristotle and for Kant, both of whom have recourse to the analogical representation of time by a straight line? For we are dealing with an *analogy* here, and nowise with a pure identification. Like all analogies, this analogy implies a heterogeneity between the items it puts in relation. In Aristotle's view, what legitimates the analogy is the *continuity* of time, a characteristic that time shares with both movement and spatial quantity. Just as the straight line is a continuous quantity, that is, a quantity that is infinitely divisible, of which the point is not a part, similarly time, qua numerical measure of movement according to the before and the after, is a continuous quantity of which the now is not a part, but merely a limit: in this sense, the now is indeed analogous the point. Moreover, the analogy here involves not four but six terms: the now is to time what the moving object is to movement and what the point is to the straight line: "the 'now' is no part of time nor the section any part of the movement, any more than the points are parts of the line."[19] It is precisely *because* we are dealing only with an analogy that time is not defined by Aristotle as movement itself, but as something that belongs to movement,[20] namely its numerical measure. Indeed, if time were, as some claim, a determinate movement (that of the sphere of the fixed stars, for example), we would have to agree that this movement itself takes place with more or less rapidity, for velocity is the distance divided by time. But this would amount to claiming that time accomplishes a certain movement within a certain time, and therefore that time presupposes time, which is absurd. This is why, between the now and the moving object, there is only a distant resemblance. Aristotle emphasizes this point by refusing to attribute to the now the mode of being of a *hypokeimenon*. By contrast with the moving object, which is the same qua substrate of movement and different as to its positions, the now is neither strictly speaking "the same," nor strictly "other," because identity and difference presuppose permanence and change, as the modes of existence of what is *in* time. The now is neither identical to itself nor other than itself, because it would have to be so *at a given time*, which is contradictory. As what measures all change within time, it cannot itself be given the determinations of what it measures. It neither remains the same nor changes, because it is not in time, or at least not in the sense in which things are, in being measured by time.[21] In order to establish the paradoxical identity of the now, Aristotle designates it not as *hypokeimenon*, but as *ho pote on*.[22] And what applies to the difference between the now and the moving object applies *a fortiori* to the difference between the now and the point. Whether in Aristotle or, later, in Kant or Hegel, the analogy between time and the straight line never constitutes anything more than a default representation of succession in simultaneity. Precisely "because this inner intuition yields no shape, we endeavor to make up for this want by analogies. We represent the time-sequence by a line progressing to infinity, in which the manifold constitutes a series of one dimension only; and we reason from the properties of this line to all the properties of time."[23] But Kant immediately points out the limitation of this analogy by stressing the fundamental "exception" that destroys this symmetry: "while the parts of the line are simultaneous the parts of time are always successive."

Under these conditions, nothing prevents our suspecting that Bergson made use of a formulation just as analogical to characterize metaphysics as the analogy he intends to denounce. Strictly speaking, giving the terms their proper sense, no philosopher has thought of time as being space; there is no "spatialized time."[24] Moreover, Bergson seems to waver between two claims. Sometimes he claims that the concept of time originated in its entirety from an illegitimate hybrid, an "endosmosis" between duration and space[25]; at others, more prudently, he seems to suggest, not that the time of metaphysics boils down to space, but that the *analogy* between time and space leads us to misconstrue the nature of duration: "All through the history of philosophy time and space have been placed on the same level and treated as things of a kind; the procedure has been to study space, to determine its nature and function, and then to apply to time the conclusions thus reached. The theories of space and time thus become counterparts of one another. To pass from one to the other one had only to change a single word: 'juxtaposition' was replaced by 'succession.'"[26] Hence it could be that no philosopher has ever proceeded, *properly speaking*, to anything like a "spatialization of time"; but it is the constraints of language, combined with those of the intellect, that force us into an inadequate symbolization of pure intuition and a series of erroneous analogies. For it is merely the admission of the possibility of an analogical relation between time and space that leads to misconceive the nature of duration. It is not that duration thereby becomes space; but, from the moment it becomes the *analogon* of space, it loses its essential property: its permanent creation of novelty. According to this alternative reading, Bergson is not saying, as Heidegger believes, that for metaphysics "time is space,"[27] but only that homogeneous time, as opposed to duration, is born of the interpolation of spatial concepts into temporal ones, the consequence of which is to engender an ambiguous admixture, which is *neither* duration *nor* space: time.

The Aporetic Consequences of the Idea of Spatialization of Time

However it may be with this nuance, to which I will have occasion to return, many questions remain. What does the intrusion of one concept into another mean? What is an admixture, a hybrid in the conceptual domain? This is not clear at all in Bergson's formulations. What does it mean to say that we are "impregnating the succession with simultaneity,"[28] if simultaneity and succession are distinct concepts, irreducible to one another, as is shown by the opposition of their characteristics (homogeneous/heterogeneous, inner/outer, physical/psychological, and so on)?

This obscurity has two consequences, both of them equally disastrous, and which are complementary.

If every concept that is common to time and space is the result of an illegitimate hybridization, what could the status of the phenomenon of movement be? Indeed, "Thus, within our ego, there is succession without mutual externality; outside the ego, in pure space, mutual externality without succession."[29] In space, there is only the oscillating position of the pendulum, since when this position exists, the preceding one no longer exists; as for succession, it only exists "for a conscious spectator who keeps the past in mind and sets the two oscillations or their symbols side by side in an auxiliary space."[30] But then, in pure duration, which is completely "interior," there could be no more movement than in pure spatial exteriority. In sum, *movement exists only in spatialized time*. The critique of the latter inevitably brings about the critique of the former. The radical dualism of duration and space leads to the conclusion that movement is impossible. Movement becomes a mere illusion, resulting from the illegitimate cross-contamination of two heterogeneous realities. "Immediate intuition," Bergson writes, "shows us motion within duration, and duration outside space."[31] But then motion is incompatible with exteriority, that is to say, with spatiality. In space, there is no movement, but in duration, which is mobility, there can be no *local* movement; the latter finds its place nowhere, neither in exteriority, nor in interiority; it becomes merely a fiction, the result of the projection of exteriority onto interiority. We come back, despite the criticism addressed to Zeno, to a new form of Eleatism.

Furthermore (this is the second consequence), because Bergson has radically split space and movement, true (and not only apparent) movement, which is no longer the successive positions of a body in space *partes extra partes*, must belong to interiority alone and be identical with pure duration. *Duration itself becomes a privileged movement.* Or more precisely, movement becomes double: on the one hand, movement understood as trajectory, that is, as a succession of immobilities, and on the other, a mobility belonging to inner duration and to it alone.[32] It is no accident that Bergson will go so far as to speak, in order to characterize motion in space, as opposed to the mobility of consciousness (that is, duration itself), of "two different worlds, incapable of communicating otherwise than by a miracle."[33] Even though, in his later work, he attempted to attenuate this dualism,[34] by thinking of it not, after the example of "ordinary dualism,"[35] as the opposition of the extended and the unextended, but as a difference of rhythms, the two extremes of which are formed by the relaxing of tension of matter and the tension or élan of life[36]—and therefore as a difference not of nature but of degree—the fact remains that this effort, however we may ultimately assess it, *does not solve the problem raised.* To assert that duration is mobility, whatever the "extension" one agrees to concede from duration to the material world, ends up in any case in insurmountable aporias. Indeed, if duration is "mobility in its essence,"[37] if it is therefore endowed with a "rhythm,"[38] an unchangeable rhythm that proceeds exactly as it proceeds, by contrast with the time of the mathematician that "could be enormously and even infinitely accelerated; nothing would be changed for the mathematician,"[39] the same paradox follows. Strictly speaking, duration cannot flow faster or slower, or even at the precise rhythm at which it flows, because that would amount to assuming that this flow has a duration, and hence that this flow of time is in turn flowing in time: we would inevitably end up in an infinite regression. Once we maintain that "the essence of duration is to flow,"[40] we have no choice but to identify time with a *change* that, as such, always takes place *in* time, that is to say, presupposes a series of states following one another *in a given time*, which is absurd. But is this not merely a matter of metaphors?

Indeed, as Bergson stresses, "it struck me that language was largely responsible for this confusion; duration is always expressed in terms of extension; the terms which designate time are borrowed from the language of space."[41] Are we to conclude from this that even "mobility," even "change" are terms that qualify duration only metaphorically? This is what Bergson seems to imply when he writes, "The inner experience [as opposed to the language of the understanding] will nowhere find a strictly appropriate language. It will be compelled to return to the concept, with at most the addition of the image."[42] But such assertions scarcely get us anywhere; of what is that metaphor a metaphor? What is the literal formulation, the strict one that would be the starting point of this transfer of meaning? The answer is that there is none and that there can be none: the intuition of duration is, in a literal, rigorous sense, ineffable, which means that it resists the terminological rigor that expresses it, or tries to express it. Here metaphorization is originary,[43] since the language of the intellect is the translation and transposition of an intuition, the very essence of which consists in transcending all symbolizations. Metaphorization is rather language itself. "Intuition gives us the thing whose spatial transposition, whose metaphorical translation alone, is seized by the intellect."[44] But if all is metaphor, there is no longer any metaphor: language is structurally inadequate, its indigence insurmountable, and intuition forever ineffable.

But can we not return to what is on the hither side of metaphor, despite Bergson's assertions to the contrary? I will leave this question in abeyance for the moment. Perhaps it is possible to make a case for the impossibility of metaphysics to give novelty an originary status in its determination of time, without thereby concurring with the diagnostic according to which that incapacity is in turn rooted in the confusion of duration and space.

What novelty are we talking about? If in some passages Bergson admits that there is novelty in the universe,[45] that claim appears to contradict his most constant assertions that it is life and consciousness alone that ceaselessly produce novelty. This ambivalence appears clearly when Bergson outlines an analysis of the event in *The Two Sources of Morality and Religion*. Are there events outside us? Bergson responds to that question in the negative. Take, for example, the San Francisco earthquake that William James describes in his memoirs. From the physical point of view, there is no such thing. All there is is an infinity of mechanical effects decreasing around an epicenter, as represented by science and our intelligence. We can only speak of an event, in Bergson's view, because we confer both its unity and individuality on it by a "myth-making function."[46] And Bergson proceeds to propose a psychological explanation for this operation resting on instinct and its protective and warding-off function against the misdeeds of intelligence: it is "a defensive reaction against fear" that, in order to "prevent a paralysis of the will brought about by an over-intelligent representation of a cataclysm entailing endless consequences,"[47] instigates the event, giving it a soul, so to speak, by a mechanism analogous to that of magic, in order to master it. But the only decisive question is not asked by Bergson: namely, how can the "intellectual instinct" "animate" *one* set of phenomena as opposed to some other one, if this set is not already invested, at the perceptual level, before any activity (even unconscious) on the part of the subject, with a certain relevant meaning determined by its relation to the total field within which it appears? In other words, how is such an operation possible if there is not before any sense-bestowal (and *a fortiori* any myth-making) an *order of meaning*, which gives the event its meaning within a context? Here Bergson commits the mistake typical of psychologists flagged by Koffka: "Never was a psychologist prouder than when he could say: A is not really A but something else."[48] What is given, in reality, is always the event itself as it springs up in the perceptual field and not some alleged mental mechanism of projection or myth-making exercising its powers over pure meaningless givens. In light of this example, it is clear that what prevents Bergson from granting the possibility of any event or any novelty whatsoever outside of an "interiority" approached according to a psychologistic model are still dualist presuppositions. In his view, there is no true novelty except the one created by the living (hence conscious) being in its continuous self-creation.[49] This obviously makes it very difficult to understand what it could mean, for a consciousness, that it "creates something new outside itself"[50] by tracing in space unforeseeable gestures or by creating works of art, paintings, for example[51]; for it is not the painting that is new, in Bergson's view, but the consciousness that creates it.

But then the duality of duration and spatialized time also results in emptying the very idea of "creation" of all meaning. In order for there to be creation, there must also be the *possibility* of not creating—that is, *contingency*. Now all possibility belongs to the well-known retrospective illusion, which boils down ultimately to a mere error; "for the possible is only the real with the addition of an act of the mind which throws its image back into the past, once it has been enacted."[52] If the possible has no reality outside the mind and is only the result of a projective, illusory mechanism, how could there ever be creation of anything, of the mind by itself, or of things outside it? How could the artist be defined as the one who "creates the possible"?[53] How could freedom be understood, in conformity with an artistic paradigm that permeates Bergson's entire work, as a creation of possibility?[54] In truth, possibility only appears as a "truism" for one who has set out by ascribing it to the mind, and in so doing, by excluding it from the universe: in short, for a dualism that coincides with a renewed form of Megarianism. By denying the reality of the possible, we commit ourselves to denying creation, and thus novelty, as well.

If we were to hold to these results we would have to conclude that Bergson's thesis on metaphysics is not only of little exegetic value for the rereading of the texts of the tradition, but of more than doubtful internal coherence. Should we stop at this conclusion? Is there not, in Bergson's analyses, a phenomenological kernel that resists these criticisms?

The Phenomenological Kernel

To ask such questions is to tread on slippery ground. We would have to interpret Bergson's critique of metaphysics in doing without the whole idea of "spatialization," as well as its corollaries (the event qua useful fiction, the possible as a retrospective illusion); we would have to recast it outside its metaphorical vocabulary and to abandon its central claim of an originary metaphoricity of language that forbids all rigorous rendering explicit of phenomena, all authentic "phenomenology." To understand Bergson with Bergson beyond Bergson and probably, to a large extent, against him: Does this endeavor make any sense? From the point of view of the history of ideas, certainly not. But from a philosophical point of view, possibly: on the condition, specifically, that Bergson saw aright, at least up to a certain point, in what he tries to say and show.

Leaving aside the problematic aspect of Bergson's conception of the spatialization of duration, is there, in what he says, a phenomenological kernel that can be salvaged from the criticisms formulated above? This question is but a reformulation of another: Does Bergson assert that metaphysics has apprehended time as being space, or does he only criticize the *symbolization* of duration by space—that is, a conception of time that, while not simply confusing the latter with its symbol, fails to recognize time's nature *by the very fact that* it allows that symbolization? According to this second reading, it is an inadequate conception of time *qua time* that opens the path to an illegitimate symbolization, without this in any way implying that metaphysics has expressly confused the thing itself (time, or rather duration) with its representation (space). In any case, this reading has the advantage of preventing our falling into the aporias raised by the idea of a hybridization of two heterogeneous concepts, along with the (historically untenable) assertion that there has never been, in metaphysics, an analysis of time *as such* that does not identify it surreptitiously with space.

Let us therefore try this other reading. If the time of metaphysics excludes all novelty *by principle*, the true target of Bergson's critique is perhaps not so much the interpolation of space in duration as the very concept of "succession" in its classic formulation: a given event is first future, then present, then past. Indeed, Bergson critiques a logic of retrospection by virtue of which the event is *realized* in advance in a future that is only the image of the present that it will be, in order soon to place it in a past that is but the trace of the present it once was. This retrospective logic is abstract, because it fails to recognize the positive phenomenological meaning of the experience of time as such. By contrast, we should grasp temporality not in accordance with the abstract schemes that make possible an analogical representation of it, but by returning to it, and without intermediaries. In other words, it is a question of "going to seek experience at its source," on the hither side of the "decisive turn" by which it "takes a bias in the direction of our utility"[55] and passes itself off for something else.

One of the ways of proceeding consists in taking as our guiding thread the phenomenon of novelty itself, the event inasmuch as it is precisely what is missed by the conceptualization of time by metaphysics. Consider, for example, the case of the emergence of a new artistic movement, such as romanticism: in itself, this event is strictly unforeseeable, even if, once it has appeared, it is not impossible to retrace its genesis *a posteriori*.[56] By virtue of its absolute novelty, the event preexists its own possibility, which cannot appear as such except retrospectively. It is not possible before being real; its possibility wells up from its realization itself.

We find here a *priority* of reality over possibility. This priority may be understood not as a refusal to confer any reality to possibilities, but as a positive elucidation of the status of the latter. True, Bergson concedes, if we take "possibility" in a purely logical sense, if we understand by that word the noncontradictory, all events are clearly "possible" before being actual: but in this sense what is understood by "possible" is nothing more than not impossible. On the other hand, if we take "possible" in a more rigorous sense—and probably *the only* rigorous sense—then every "possibility" refers to a *posse*, a power that determines it as such. The power in question is that of foreseeing the actualization of this possible. But do we have such a power? Clearly not. Most events are not possible before being actual, because they are not *foreseeable for us*; and, Bergson might add, even those events that are foreseeable for us—astronomical phenomena, and others—are only so approximately, with a certain margin of error. Thus interpreted, the primacy of reality over possibility does not lead to denying the reality of the latter, to making it into a mere "mirage"—despite some unfortunate formulations of Bergson[57]—which would lead him once more to a form of Megarianism, thereby agreeing with the determinism he challenges.[58] Quite to the contrary, it leads to restoring to possibility all its weight, to understanding it in its etymology, by making it rigorously proportional to a power of foresight. To say that possibility does not precede reality amounts to saying that reality is not foreseeable. It is not the discarding of all the possible into limbo; it is making it proportional to a *posse* by recognizing the radical finitude of the latter. "Possible," strictly speaking, is what I can foresee, anticipate, project, or bring about. Now, what happens is always other with respect to these possibilities: "The realization brings along with it an unforeseeable nothing which changes everything."[59] Unforeseeable, the event is thereby inexplicable—at least if what we mean by "explanation" is a nomological-causal explanation allowing us to deduce the particular effect from a universal law.[60] Arguably the event is only "explainable" in a completely different sense—in the sense of the interpretative reconstitution of a context.[61] When I come to events, I can only "explain" if I know *what* to explain, that is, *after the fact* (*après-coup*), by drawing from the context elements of causality, none of which was sufficient to allow me to foresee, according to a given law, the singularity of its effect.

Leaving aside Bergsonian terminology, it will suffice here to say that from the point of view of all the actual possibilities that depend on a prediction or a project, the event is always, and structurally, im-possible. All power of explanation, prediction, or anticipation is originarily late in relation to the event, so that the "possibility" of an event is always retrospective—which does not make it illusory, however. What is illusory is only the idea of a *preexistence* of the possible (in a nonlogical sense) in a well-informed understanding, that is, the idea that there are possibilities "in themselves," independently of the question of the modality in which a finite being is capable of relating to them.

What Bergson rejects, in other words, are four fundamental presuppositions that subtend the conception of time qua succession. (1) The future is something, somewhere: a "possible" in a divine understanding or a point on a universe line in Minkowski's four-dimensional space-time. (2) To the extent that the future is realized in advance and preexists in the form of possibilities, the occurrence of the event could be described as a change in temporal predicates ("future," "present," "past") that would affect a quasi-subject: it would be *the same* event that first would be future, and subsequently past, so that the change in question could be described as an extrinsic change. But, Bergson objects, it makes no sense to say that the same event is now future, now past, because "the same" can only be applied to an event once the event has taken place. The change in question, the "transition" from possibility to actuality, is not a modification affecting a substrate or a quasi-substrate; the event does not become present, it *occurs*, in the sense that what happens here is a change from nothing to everything, a drastic change, or, as Bergson eloquently says, a "change without anything changing."[62] (3) The occurrence of the event cannot, therefore, be described in inner-temporal terms, as we are invited to do by the metaphysical idea of "succession." An event is not *first* future, *then* present, *then* past; it is originarily present *as* past, that is, its presence is necessarily retrospective, and only to that extent, prospective: it opens up possibilities, obliges me to face them, reveals possibilities (and impossibilities) that did not exist before it. (4) Consequently, it is absurd to say, as metaphysics tends to do, that the past *follows* the future (and the present);

for the former could only "follow" the latter if the latter could precede the former, which, as we have seen, is absurd. It follows that the past is not the result of the *passage* of the present; it is given from the start as an originary, nonderivable dimension of time. The past is not a bit of abolished present, it is not first present, then destroyed: otherwise, it would be fair to ask *at what moment* that destruction takes place. This is probably what Bergson suggests, in an inadequately psychologistic language, when he says that memory is not formed after perception,[63] but accompanies it all along as its shadow. This is also why memory doesn't require any explanation: to explain memory would be to assume that the past is the present *minus* something, a present that, in a second moment, was abolished, and that must be rescued from nothingness. But such is not at all the case: "Memory therefore has no need of explanation. Or rather, there is no special faculty whose role is to retain quantities of past in order to pour it into the present. The past preserves itself automatically. Of course . . . it seems that the past is normally what is abolished and that there is something extraordinary about the preservation of the past: we think ourselves obliged to conjure up an apparatus whose function would be to record the parts of the past capable of reappearing in our consciousness."[64] But this is a mistake. Bergson could have shown it by rejecting the very idea of "preservation": if the past does not follow the present, if the "present" is rather the very mode of appearing of the past—in its increasing remoteness—for a consciousness that is necessarily retrospective, it makes no sense to speak of the "preservation" of the past (as a present that it *would have ceased to be*), nor to suppose a psychological mechanism fulfilling this function. As is frequently the case, Bergson's intuition is more rigorous and right than his final formulation—which conforms to his own theory! If the past and the present are co-originary, this is because the idea of "succession" does not account for their relation. The past is the in-itself of things, the present their mode of appearing for a consciousness that is always late in respect to them. The past is therefore not so much what "is preserved in itself" as what makes possible the appearance of every present as such. This is why there is a *continuity of appearance* between the past and the future. This is also why there is no possible symmetry between the past and the future.

Time, for Bergson, is therefore nothing but the enigma of the taking-place (*avoir-lieu*) of a radically new past (in its retrospective presence for a consciousness) from an unforeseeable future—*taking-place* that can no longer be conceived in any way in terms of *succession*. For succession presupposes a temporal change of status happening to a substrate *already given in presence*. Now, the taking-place of what is new as such cannot be described as the change of modal predicate (from "possible" to "real") of an event considered as *given*. By developing an (implicit) phenomenological analysis of the experience of time, Bergson accordingly sets forth a critique (it, too, implicit) of modal logic that considers the passage from the possible to the real as a mere change of status of certain events identified abstractly. The change from the future into the past, the taking-place of the new as such, is rather a drastic change that is synonymous with the *event* itself: the event is present only as past, its presence is solely retrospective; before being (present) it is nothing at all, it is absolutely not, and its occurrence is not thinkable as a simple *modification* of its temporal or modal predicates. In a sense, its temporality differs entirely from that of something that lasts, that is, from something the presence of which can be described first in one form, then in another, of something that, in lasting, remains subjacent to its determinations.

To reformulate Bergson's thesis in this way is, of course, to take considerable distance from literal Bergsonism. But perhaps it is also to remain as close as possible to it and to unfold its deep resources. It is true that Bergson most often formulates his own conception quite differently: he accepts succession as a determination of pure duration and critiques only a pseudo-succession projected onto space, the moments of which are juxtaposed: "That time implies succession I do not deny. But that succession is initially presented to our consciousness as the distinction of a 'before' and 'after' set side by side [*juxtaposés*] is what I cannot accept."[65] But if we are thinking with Bergson beyond his literal formulations and if we take seriously his critique of the conception of time according to which the novelty of the real would be no more than an accident, we are almost inevitably led to call into question the very idea of succession, and consequently, up to a point, the whole idea of "duration," since the latter is defined by the former.

What Bergson critiques, according to this reading, is therefore the understanding of the occurrence of the new, not as a drastic change, but as a mere modification of something—its transition from the status of "future" (possible) to that of "present" (real) and subsequently to that of "past" (unreal). The temporality of time as such, that is to say, the advent in presence of events and things, is then conceived on the model of the mere transition from one state of the world to another, of the mere succession of the states of something or the series of states enveloped in that succession. The advent in presence (novelty) becomes the mere modification of the already present. The distinction of the dimensionals of time (future, present, past) is understood on the basis of inner-temporal relations such as "precede" or "follow" (which at most only account for the relations taking place between things or events *already present* to a consciousness): the future thus *precedes* the past, which *follows* the present. In any case, time is no longer thought of as the condition for the appearance of the new but as the condition for the permanence or passage of the already-there; it is even often mistakenly identified with that passage.

But this being the case, Bergson's critique has yet another consequence, less obvious but just as radical. Indeed, what induces us to consider the future as already given (or already present) in its own way, and hence to misconstrue the taking-place of events as the transition from one state of the world to another, as a change of temporal and modal status? The following answer might be advanced: the subordination of time, as the condition for all novelty, to subjectivity in the metaphysical sense of the term. Indeed, by understanding time as succession, we interpret the *taking-place* of something as a change in its status. We envisage the future as already present (and how, if not in expectation?) and the past as still present (in memory). We posit therefore *a presence underlying everything that can present itself to it* [that is, to that presence] *qua "present"*: a *subjectivity*, precisely. Thus, we make the future not into absence pure and simple, but into the "present of the future," as it fulfills our awaiting, and we make the past into what is preserved in the presence of the mind to itself, a "present of the past" given to memory.[66] We make subjectivity, as originary presence to self, the origin of time and the condition of possibility for the succession of phenomena. This operation is, of course, only possible as long as we understand time on the basis of inner-temporal determinations, essentially as succession.

I have attempted elsewhere to show how, in Augustine, this spiritualization of time operates on the basis of his inner-temporal understanding as "passage" and "transition."[67] Let me just reiterate that time only exists, in Augustine's view, because awaiting anticipates and memory retains instants that do not cease passing away (*transire*) and flowing by: "But if the present were always present, and did not pass into past time (*nec in praeteritum transiret*), it obviously would not be time but eternity."[68] Indeed, it is necessary that time itself be understood as a certain passage or a certain change occurring from the future toward the past (the future *becoming* present and the present *becoming* past), in order for the question to arise about the condition of possibility of this passage; about that which, by pouring the future into the past through the present, ensures time's cohesion and confers upon it its immutable structure; and this "something" can be nothing but the mind itself [*ipse animus*].

Thus the impossibility to apprehend time on the basis of inner-temporal relations, as the *succession* of the future, the present, and the past, not only leads to missing the novelty of the real itself as its essential, positive determination. It also leads (even if Bergson never analyzed this consequence), by thinking time itself as an arch-change, a passage or a *transit*, to assigning to the mind, by the intermediary of its three acts (awaiting, attention, and memory) the task of *making possible* such a change—in short, to grounding time itself in the spirit and to establishing a relation of subordination between an originary spiritual time and the time of the world, which is merely derived from it. Thus, if there is a phenomenological kernel in Bergson's critique of metaphysics following to the guiding thread of the question of time, it could be formulated by means of three closely correlated claims: (1) Time is not something (inner)-temporal; (2) It is not originarily subjective, in the sense that subjectivity would itself be understood as a presence underlying the three dimensions of time; (3) It is the condition of possibility of novelty qua positive determination of phenomenal reality. These claims, only the last of which was expressly thematized by Bergson, lead *a contrario* to circumscribing the site of an understanding of time having ignored this triple requisite.

Despite the largely fictive nature of this reconstruction of Bergson's thought, it will perhaps be possible to draw instruction from it both for a positive phenomenology of time and for a critical reading of the history of philosophy, and, eventually, for the delimitation of the set of common structural presuppositions that delineates, within that history, the boundaries of a "metaphysics."

PART II

Beyond Subject and Object?

4

Sartrean Freedom, or Adam's Dream

In *The World as Will and Representation*, Schopenhauer writes, "The will is subject to necessity in all of its appearances, while in itself it can nonetheless be considered free and even omnipotent."[1] The "even" [*ja*], in this formulation, is key to all that precedes it. Indeed, given that freedom is defined as a characteristic of the will, and the will, since Peter John Olivi, John Duns Scotus, Bernard of Clairvaux, and Descartes, is conceived of as the very site of the *imago dei*, that is to say is as infinite, considered "formally and in itself," as the divine will, it follows that freedom of the will is a power that cannot be subjected to any other power (at least from the natural point of view), hence cannot admit of degrees: it must be complete or not be at all. To be sure, the doctrine of indifference still finds its complement, in Descartes, in a doctrine of natural (and gracious) light, which makes indifference no more than "the lowest degree of freedom." But the internal logic of the modern concept of freedom would have it that, once indifference is admitted, it becomes inexpugnable, as it were. Freedom no longer deserves the qualification of "omnipotent" in a merely contingent way; it *is* omnipotence itself as befalling man by virtue of his status as image—an omnipotence not exercising its power *ad extra*, as in the divine creation, but *ad intra*, in the inner self, and consisting in the fact of affirming or denying, of following or fleeing any state of affairs that might present itself to the subject in the form of a representation or an idea. Limited to the inner sphere, man's omnipotence remains analogous to God's, despite the iconic distance that separates them, despite the unbridgeable gap between the increate and the created.

But what happens when a philosophy subscribing to an atheism of principle adopts the Cartesian concept of "freedom"? What does this concept, borrowed from the problematic of the *imago dei*, become in a radically atheistic thought? Can atheistic thought free itself from this initial problematic, and is it not content with repeating or transposing it (in which it would show itself to be less *free* than it thinks in respect to its historical rootedness)? This is indeed, or so it seems, the situation of Sartre's philosophy. On the one hand, it draws the most extreme consequences from the modern concept of indifference as received by Descartes from Molina; on the other, precisely by virtue of a militant atheism, it reverses the order of priority that made human indifference the reflection and image of the divine omnipotence: it is no longer human freedom that is in the image of that of God, but it is God's freedom that becomes the illusory projection of human freedom. But does not the inversion or subversion of a theological position remain a theological position through and through?[2] Far from breaking with the tradition, does not Sartre give us, at the very most, a parody-like inversion of it in which freedom ends up canceling itself out? In drawing the most extreme consequences from the concept of indifference, in pushing on to the end—that is, to the point of paradox—the logic of the modern concept of freedom, does he not reveal, despite it all, and reluctantly, something of that logic?

In Descartes's Footsteps

A well-conceived and well-constructed atheism must put the human at the center of everything, of the whole of being. "The sole point of departure is the interiority of the *cogito*."[3] Before human reality, there is nothing, but human reality has this particularity that it brings the Nothing with it: man is he through whom nothingness comes into the world (59). To be a consciousness, a for-itself, is to "nihilate" from the outset any given situation, to introduce into the heart of being, into the raw and massive in-itself, a nothingness that separates from it. This "nihilating withdrawal" from any given that defines human reality finds its faithful and first expression in Descartes's methodological doubt: "Descartes, following the Stoics, has given a name to this possibility, which human reality has, of secreting a nothingness which isolates it—it is *freedom*" (60).

Freedom as nihilation—this is Descartes's brilliant discovery. "No one before Descartes had stressed the connection between free will and negativity."[4] How should we approach such a connection? It is realized essentially in hyperbolic doubt: "Doubt strikes at all propositions which affirm something that is outside our thought; that is, I can place all existence between parentheses: I am exercising my freedom when I, who am a nothingness and a void, *nihilate* all that exists."[5] Freedom "is" nothing other than this nihilating stepping back by which I say no to what presents itself to me as true at first sight in order to put it out of play and hold it literally to be *nothing*. However, Sartre no sooner acknowledges his indebtedness than he blames Descartes for lack of radicality: "He did not push his theory of negativity to the limit."[6] Indeed, the negation of the *ego cogito* only bears upon non-being (the false, the merely apparent) and not upon being itself. Descartes only conceived of free will as a mere "negation of negation." "In short, he failed to conceive negativity as productive."[7] According to Sartre's declarations here, the primary inspiration of *Being and Nothingness* is indeed Cartesian, but of a revised and corrected Cartesianism, stripped of its theological implications. Indeed, his religious background kept Descartes from developing his doctrine of freedom as negativity to its ultimate and radical consequences. Cartesian freedom is freedom before evil and error, and not before the Good: it only denies the negative, and bows before Being. God supplies the sole measure of being and the good, and, as a consequence, man has freedom only to turn away from Him, to plunge into the nothingness of evil, error, and sin. Conversely, to push the conception of a productive negation to the end, as Sartre invites us to do, is to conceive of the for-itself, after the example of Descartes's God, as above truth and goodness, as positing them by its free fiat. This is why, Sartre adds, Descartes only really grasped human freedom in its full metaphysical essence when he thought of divine freedom: the freedom of God, "is . . . his [Descartes's] own freedom, such as he would have conceived it without the fetters of Catholicism and dogmatism."[8]

This avowal has far-reaching consequences: God's freedom is human freedom thought through to the end. Atheism is indistinguishable from this reversal of precedence by which man finds himself in God's place, invested with his attributes. Indeed, the freedom of for-itself is limitless. It coincides with the choice by which man decides as to himself and the world in deciding on his own values. This freedom is "infinite," not only in the sense in which for Descartes man's will considered "formally" — that is, considered essentially—is infinite, regardless of the "matter" of the ideas to which it is applied, but infinite with *that same infinity* that makes God the creator of his ideas, by virtue of which, consequently, will and understanding are indiscernible in him. Freedom of the for-itself is indeed beyond all reasons and motives [*motifs et mobiles*], recreating them behind itself by its very upsurge: "I am condemned to exist forever beyond my essence, beyond the reasons and motives of my act. I am condemned to be free. This means that no limits to my freedom can be found except freedom itself or, if you prefer, that we are not free to cease being free" (567 [translation modified—Tr.]). In the image of the freedom of the Cartesian God, such a freedom is not subordinated to any preliminary idea, any essence, any value, any good; it creates essences as well as existences, and it is not because something is good that it chooses it, but because it has chosen it that this thing is good. The claim that the for-itself has no other values than those it has itself created, that is to say, that it is totally "unjustifiable," does nothing more, consequently, than repeat and transpose in a different register Descartes's view on the divine omnipotence: "To one who pays attention to God's immensity, it is clear that nothing at all can exist which does not depend on Him. This is true not only of everything that subsists, but of all order, of every law, and of every reason of truth and goodness."[9] In other words, God does not create the world by conforming to a model of goodness; he does not create the world thus because he judges it to be good, but the world is good because he creates it so: "Because He determined Himself towards those things which ought to be accomplished, for that reason, as it stands in Genesis, *they are very good*; that is to say, the reason for their goodness is the fact that He wished to create them so."[10] Now human freedom, according to Sartre, presents more than an analogy with this divine freedom: being on principle beyond all reason or motive, it confers on reasons and motives their *meaning*; it *constitutes* them precisely as such. It is because human freedom chooses them that they are good, and not the other way around. "We ought to ask," Sartre writes, "how a reason (or a motive) can be constituted as such" by the act of freedom (564 [translation modified—Tr.]). The for-itself retroactively *confers* on its motives the value they have in light of an autonomous project of its unmotivated—and hence unjustifiable—freedom. "It is only because I escape the in-itself by nihilating myself toward my possibilities that this in-itself can take on value as reason or motive" (564 [translation modified—Tr.]). Hence, all voluntary deliberation is always "a deception" (581). Indeed, since by deciding on my acts according to an absolutely unmotivated decree, my freedom projects back, like its shadow, its own reasons and motives, "constituting" them as such, the result is that I never deliberate to choose, but having chosen, I try to confer a specious motivation on my freedom by simulating a purely fictive deliberation. I have decided to join the resistance, or to stay home and take care of my mother, as in a well-known example, and now I am looking for good reasons for doing so. The deliberation is a comedy I perform for myself. "When I deliberate, the die is cast" (581, [translation modified—Tr.]). After the example of the God of Descartes, human reality is therefore pure productive spontaneity. Nothing preexists its own free decrees; all motivation that would confer meaning on them comes necessarily too late. Such a freedom, determined *theologically* through and through, is "an absolutely new production, the germ of which could not be contained in an earlier state of the world" so that "freedom and creation [are] one and the same."[11] If God's freedom is creation outside, human freedom is initially exercised "within": it is a continuous creation of self. The for-itself does not cease choosing itself and thereby creating itself. The inaugural act of this creation is defined by Sartre as an "originary choice."

But how is this freedom attested phenomenologically? Based on what privileged phenomenon can its emergence be described concretely? The primordial experience of freedom is anxiety. But where can a pure description of it be found? Sartre's phenomenology, on this point, has less in common with the existential concept of *Grundstimmung* forged by Heidegger in *Sein und Zeit* than with Kierkegaard's analyses in the *Concept of Anxiety*. This amounts to saying that human freedom cannot grasp itself, once again, without measuring itself against an Adamic freedom, the possibility of which has been meditated by Christian thought. What is at stake in this confrontation? How does Sartre read Kierkegaard's text? And in the discrepancy brought about by his interpretation, in the reorientation introduced into Kierkegaard's thought, is it not theology that still provides the fundamental orientation, even in the formulation of an atheistic philosophy?

Anxiety, or Freedom Dreaming Itself

In Kierkegaard's thought, Sartre does not hesitate to see—as he did in Descartes—a prefiguration of his own conceptions. "Anxiety, Kierkegaard asserted, is the possibility of freedom." *Being and Nothingness* repeats and develops this assertion in many ways. But it does so by modifying its meaning entirely. Anxiety was understood by Kierkegaard in light of a properly theological questioning: through it, it was a matter of seizing the concrete possibility of the first sin. How was Adam's first sin possible, given that before this sin the difference between guilt and innocence did not exist? This is the question formulated by Kierkegaard: anxiety answers it, while all explanation in terms of "concupiscence" fails to do so. Indeed, to hold that there is a concupiscence of sin in Adam is to presuppose sin in him, and consequently to fail to understand how, with him, sin "entered into the world."[12] For Adam does not choose evil, but it is by him alone that evil appears. "The first sin constitutes the nature of the quality: the first sin is the sin."[13] Here there is an inexplicable leap from innocence to evil, which is the very leap of freedom: "The new quality appears with the first, with the leap, with the suddenness of the enigmatic."[14] To explain sin by temptation would be to commit a *hysteron proteron*: the latter is rather the result of the former. But how, then, are we to account for this qualitative "leap" by which sin appears in the world?

To understand this mystery, we must analyze man in the state of innocence, that is, in the state of ignorance in which, the distinction between good and evil not having yet been posited, freedom exists as if in a dream state. "This," asserts Kierkegaard, "is the profound secret of innocence, that it is at the same time anxiety."[15] How so? What is ignorance (or innocence) anxious about? Literally *nothing*, since it is unaware of sin. But this nothing is the absolutely indeterminate possibility, possibility in the pure state. The concept of anxiety, Kierkegaard specifies, "is altogether different from fear and similar concepts that refer to something definite, whereas anxiety is freedom's actuality as the possibility of possibility."[16] What freedom is anxious about is not an ontic correlate, but the nothingness of its own possibility, that is, itself, insofar as it is capable of everything, the pure possibility of being able. Thus, all anxiety is anxiety about the absolute novelty of the possible inasmuch as possibility is itself directly dependent on freedom. "Anxiety is at this point always present as the possibility of the new state."[17]

The whole issue here, in an analysis that Kierkegaard qualifies as "psychological," is to preserve the "qualitative leap" from innocence to guilt, to avoid already presupposing guilt in the state of innocence. Only anxiety as openness to the *nothingness* of possibility guarantees this qualitative leap "psychologically," which is precisely what the explanations by means of concupiscence fail to do. Anxiety is indeed temptation, if you like, but it is temptation before itself, that is, before nothing—temptation before the pure possibility of the possible. It is through anxiety that Adam becomes guilty, and he does so without departing from innocence. He is guilty to the extent that he succumbs to anxiety. The prohibition raised against Adam—"Only of the tree of the knowledge of good and evil thou shalt not eat"—cannot arouse temptation in him since, being unaware of the difference between good and evil, Adam cannot even understand the meaning of this injunction. Therefore, the prohibition does not arouse desire, concupiscence, in Adam, but solely anxiety. "The prohibition induces in him anxiety, for the prohibition awakens in him freedom's possibility. What passed by innocence as the nothing of anxiety has not entered into Adam, and here again it is a nothing—the anxious possibility of *being able*. He has no conception of what he is able to do; otherwise—and this is what usually happens—that which comes later, the difference between good and evil, would have been presupposed."[18] Anxiety is therefore the self-experiencing of this freedom preceding the distinction between good and evil, of that freedom *in the dream state* that lets itself be dragged along by its own possibility, and that, completely fascinated, holds itself beneath its own sway. Thus it succumbs to "the anxious possibility of being able" brought on by the prohibition. Anxiety is this vertigo of a freedom allowing itself to be snapped up by its own abyss, a freedom closed in by the circle of its self-reflection, which is not yet the real freedom for good and evil, but a specular freedom, prior to their division. No one, moreover, can say what that freedom can do: "Of what it can do, [Adam] has no idea." This is why this freedom in the state of innocence is not yet a real freedom. While actual freedom is operative in the *choice* between good and evil, Adam's does not yet have before it clearly distinct objects upon which it could bring its choice to bear. It remains an oneiric freedom, a freedom *sub specie possibilitatis*: "Freedom's possibility is not the ability to choose the good or the evil. . . . The possibility is to *be able*."[19] Behind this apparent tautology, the whole enigma of anxiety lies hidden.

Kierkegaard, moreover, distinguishes *two* anxieties, which Sartre will tend to conflate for reasons soon to become obvious: (1) the anxiety felt by Adam in the state of pure innocence, before any distinction between good and evil, any self-reflection and any positing of an ego—that is, "objective" anxiety; and (2) the anxiety that can strike every human being after original sin, provided he discovers himself to be sinner before God, and in so doing takes up a guilt older than his own, becomes a full-fledged member of humanity, and acquires a place within his species: reflective, "subjective" anxiety, as Kierkegaard calls it. Now, objective anxiety is the experience of a freedom that has only itself as counterpart and is only "actualized" in self-reflection: it is "anxiety belonging to innocence, the anxiety that is freedom's reflection within itself in its possibility"[20] This self-reflection of freedom arouses the ambivalence of a fear that is at the same time desire, desire for what we fear, fear of what we desire, in which we are alternately attracted and repelled by possibility in its pure state, like a man tottering at the edge of a cliff. "Anxiety," Kierkegaard writes, "is a desire for what one fears, a sympathetic antipathy."[21] Whence the comparison with dizziness, which Sartre adopted, though not without changing its meaning. "Anxiety may be compared with dizziness. He whose eye happens to look down into the yawning abyss becomes dizzy. But what is the reason for this? It is just as much in his own eye as in the abyss, for suppose he had not looked down. Hence anxiety is the dizziness of freedom, which emerges when spirit wants to posit the synthesis and freedom looks down into its own possibility, laying hold of finitude to support itself. Freedom succumbs in this dizziness. Further than this, psychology cannot and will not go."[22] This dizziness of freedom has nothing of the sublime about it in Kierkegaard's view. Adam's freedom is only a *negative* freedom, a freedom to sin: for it turns away from the freedom of God and sinks down egotistically into itself. The anxiety in which "freedom faints" before its own possibility, though prior to the positing of an ego, is "of all things the most selfish,"[23] since freedom wants itself, wants nothing other than its own possibility, and lets itself be taken captive and snapped up by its own nothingness: "In that very moment everything is changed, and freedom [which has fainted], when it again rises, sees that it is guilty. Between these two moments lies the leap, which no science has explained and which no science can explain." This is why anxiety is always anxiety before possibility in its most "terrible" form. Possibility is, according to Kierkegaard, "the weightiest of all categories. . . . Whoever has truly been brought up by the possibility has grasped the terrible as well as the joyful."[24]

Interpreting these passages in his 1964 lecture "The Singular Universal," Sartre presents a series of variations on the theme of Kierkegaardian anxiety. First, he conceives of all anxiety in the mode of Adam's anxiety, that is, he makes no mention of the distinction between Adamic anxiety and anxiety stemming from sin—objective and subjective anxiety. Adam's freedom becomes the model for *all* human freedom: "For we are all Adam," he declares.[25] Then, since God does not exist, Adamic freedom, which is purely negative in Kierkegaard's view, is transformed into positive freedom. It is freedom by which the for-itself chooses itself, that is to say, "creates" itself.

Sartre freely interprets Kierkegaard's claim that Adam "has no interiority prior to anxiety."[26] But he makes a very different use of it than does the Danish thinker. "The real 'self,'" we read in *The Concept of Anguish*, "is posited only by the qualitative leap. In the prior state there can be no question about it"; "the concepts of sin and guilt posit precisely the single individual as the single individual."[27] But what does Kierkegaard mean here? It is by discovering himself to be a sinner before God that man accedes to a consciousness of himself as unique and acquires a true "self." Sartre understands this quite otherwise: "Anxiety," he says, "is the abandonment of being to the forbidden possibility of choosing itself finite by a sudden retreat of the infinite."[28] Sartre therefore interprets Adam's freedom as if it meant *choice of oneself* and *self-finitization* of the ego. "The Self is chosen finitude, nothingness affirmed and delimited by an act . . . the finite is now constituted as loss of the infinite, freedom as the necessary and irremediable foundation of the formation of the Ego."[29]

But if freedom means henceforth this choice by which Adam (that is, *any* for-itself) constitutes himself egoically and determines his own finitude, are we still talking about Adam, even as an allegorical figure? Are we still talking about man? Or has not a new figure already begun to replace the former one? Indeed, only a *positively infinite* being is capable of something like a "self-finitization"; only he is capable of lowering himself infinitely to the point of taking upon himself a *chosen* finitude, and thus making it his own. It is no longer of Adam that Sartre is speaking to us; it is of the New Testament God and of the movement of his kenosis. This is only possible, incidentally, by virtue of another, more subtle shift, that by which "sin" is emptied of its theological meaning and identified with choice *in general*: "Sin . . . is choice."[30] Not this particular option by which Adam disobeyed God, but the repeated act of the for-itself of choosing itself and thereby "finitizing" itself. If we are all Adam, it is in the sense in which "each of us commits on his own behalf and on behalf of all a singular sin: in other words finitude, for each person, is necessary and incomparable."[31] In short, through this strange "sin," the for-itself does not become guilty but discovers himself finite; man, that is, appropriates his essence. "The essence of the human being is suspended in his freedom" (60). In order for the for-itself to be able to become man, after the example of the God of the New Testament, in a choice that is itself unconditioned, it is necessary for it to be *never born* and to create literally himself. We will soon have confirmation of this.

Returning for a moment to the Kierkegaardian point of view, it is as if Sartre's freedom were the Adamic freedom as it *dreams* itself in the state of pure innocence. From this nothingness, of which Kierkegaard says that it fascinates the "dreaming spirit," Sartre makes the very origin of human freedom, the supreme activity of a for-itself. But then, doesn't the for-itself dream itself free as Adam did by projecting his freedom in an imaginary exteriority, before succumbing to its specular image? Kierkegaard probably would not have seen anything in that infinite freedom but an illusion of our narcissism (that is, a consequence of original sin).[32] This is why, between him and Sartre, the experience of dizziness takes on an entirely new meaning. While anxiety as dizziness, far from signifying the victory of freedom as self-positing, manifested for Kierkegaard its defeat and literally its fall, Sartre interprets the dizziness of anxiety as the purest revelation of our human freedom. For vertigo, as Sartre explains, is not the fear of the void but the fear felt before myself as capable of everything: as not determined by any raison [*motif*] that would assure me that I am not going, the next moment, to hurl myself into the void, as having to decide at every moment about my reasons on the basis of a sovereign and unjustifiable freedom. What anxiety is anxious about, what dizziness reveals, is the nothingness of a freedom that, in its absoluteness, gratuity and lack of justification is always beyond its reasons and motives: "This freedom which reveals itself to us in anguish can be characterized by the existence of that *nothing* which insinuates itself between motives and act" (71). In conformity with this absolute and autarkic freedom, man—or rather the for-itself—becomes the creator of man, so much so that God is superfluous. "Everything happens as though God needed sin in order that man might produce himself in front of him, as if he had solicited it in order to bring Adam out of his state of ignorance and give meaning to man."[33] If God, according to this odd parable, has become superfluous, it is because man has filled his vacancy. This subversion of theology is no more than its parodic reversal.

Freedom in the Making

In light of the preceding considerations, we can now approach Sartre's doctrine as set forth in *Being and Nothingness.* Not only will we find confirmation in it of the theological origin of the Sartrean concept of "freedom," but we will see the paradoxes that ensue from the attribution of this limitless power to man.

Sartre's whole philosophy is contained in the assertion of this discretionary freedom by which human reality chooses itself and fashions its own *I.* "The freedom that manifests itself through anguish is characterized by a constantly renewed obligation to remake the *Self* that designates the free being" (72 [translation modified—Tr.]). Now the possibility of "remaking the *Self*" by choosing it assumes quite obviously that I am not initially myself. As early as in *The Transcendence of the Ego* Sartre broke with an egological phenomenology, to assert that all egoity is a transcendence constituted out of a neutral transcendental field, that every self is an object in the world posited by a nonpositing consciousness of self. This pre-egoic consciousness given to itself in a prereflective *cogito* is called by Sartre "for-itself" in *Being and Nothingness.* The for-itself, structured by intentionality, is entirely on the outside, alongside the world. It is nothing but its own exteriorization, the bursting forth toward . . . the world by which it opens itself to it. Hence it differs *toto caelo* from the in-itself or objective being, which is purely what it is in its ontic massivity. The for-itself, on the other hand, whose very being consists in transcending itself, is only graspable for itself as *not* being *in-itself,* as introducing by this very fact into the massive in-itself a first negation that will prove decisive. It is by the for-itself that nothingness surges forth at the heart of plain being, and if the for-itself possesses the signal privilege of producing nothingness (of nihilating it), this is because it is for itself a nothingness: it is *never* graspable as an in-itself, it is never what it is, but always at a distance from itself. It is what it is not and is not what it is. Indeed, the characteristic proper to the for-itself is to never coincide with itself, by contrast with plain being, but to make itself be what it is, and hence to not yet be it, to not be what it is, since it has to make it be—in other words, to be pure freedom, pure, self-producing spontaneity, existence preceding all essence. Anxiety "as the manifestation of freedom in the face of self means that man is always separated by a nothingness from his essence" (72). He can never define himself by what he is, by an essence, since he must recreate himself at every moment by a free decree of his freedom, so that his essence to him only refers to what he was, and not what it has yet to be. His essence is always past, outstripped in the very movement in which he chooses himself. In Hegel's phrase, which Sartre takes up, essence, for human reality, is what it was: "*Wesen ist was gewesen ist.*"

Thus, since the for-itself by which nothingness wells up in being as the origin of all negation is irreducible to any essence, the result is that human reality, unless it steals away and flees from itself in bad faith, can never define itself in the mode of the in-itself. It can never take shelter, to escape the infinite power that characterizes it, behind any given nature, behind timeless values, behind unchanging causes that would furnish a justification for its acts. It is *absolutely* free, inexcusable, unjustifiable. All essence is essence only for a freedom that chooses it; all value is value only for a freedom that posits it. Nothing can solicit freedom that freedom has not first itself activated; nothing can erode or obstruct it in its exercise: "In anguish freedom is anguished before itself inasmuch as it is instigated and bound by nothing" (73).

Sartre supplies a very concrete example in order to show this freedom in action. I am sitting at my desk with the intention of starting to write a book when suddenly I am gripped with anxiety. It is the famed "anxiety before the blank page," but how can it be accounted for? In this case as in the others, Sartre points out, what makes me anxious can be nothing other than my own freedom. Contrary to appearances, my writing is not inhibited by objective reasons: the issue is not that I am not certain that the book will be a good one, that its subject matter is interesting, or that it is not redundant with another. Indeed, all these objective reasons have no bearing on this book as *my* possible; that is to say, on this book insofar as its realization is dependent on my freedom. For me to be able to feel anxiety about the book I am writing, I must experience the radically unmotivated nature of my project. I was "wanting-to-write-this-book," but what I was, my essence, doesn't define me, since I must constantly choose it afresh. I am separated from it by a nothingness; I am *not* he who was "wanting-to-write-it." There is *nothing*, in my past reasons, that can force me to carry out my project. I am free, at every moment, to reject it entirely. Moreover, I am separated by a nothingness of he who I will be, since nothing can guarantee to me that the reasons I presently have for writing will still be my reasons in the future. I will always be free to give up my undertaking. It is precisely this double nothingness of freedom, both with respect to what I was (my "essence") and to what I will make myself into (my project), that arouses the anxiety of the blank page. The for-itself is therefore its own nothingness in two senses: with respect to the past, in that it is never done, never in-itself, always to be done; with respect to the future, in that it is separated from itself by the possibilities of itself that it projects, by the nothingness that it isn't but that it has yet to be.

Nothing, no in-itself, can relieve me of the infinite responsibility of my freedom. When my alarm clock rings in the morning and I automatically respond to its call, it is not the alarm that prescribes my possibilities for me, but I who prescribe the possibilities for the alarm: I am the one who freely constitutes it as "signal to get up." It is I, and no one else, who confers the imperious requirement on the alarm. In other words, it is freedom, and freedom alone, that is the "original source of my possibility" (79–80). The possibilities that offer themselves to me are not quasi objects, as is believed by common sense: they only acquire their being from my potentiality-for-being. Consider this boulder that stands blocking my path, to take another well-known example. It only presents itself as "steep" in light of a project preceding it. In itself, it harbors no possibility. It is neither easy nor hard to climb. It is what it is, period. So it is I who "constitute the possibilities that surround me as "*having the possibility of becoming my possibilities*" (80). This expression may seem redundant, but it is strictly accurate. What, then, is the possible, asks Sartre, if not that on which, by my own power, I *confer* its possibility, literally what I am capable of (*ce qui est pu par moi*), or, according to "a paradoxical doubling up" insisted upon by Jankélévitch, "what I am capable of being capable of (*ce que je peux pouvoir*)"?[34] In sum, it is my freedom, and it alone, that raises possibilities as a hunter flushes partridges, and it is only at the cost of a misconstruction of its essence that the possible can be thought of as "a transcendent and purely logical being," according to Leibniz—in short, as a kind of thing.

A freedom that can be neither limited nor curtailed by anything, that is the only source of all the possibilities and standards according to which it decides, a freedom that does not well up out of an already reified *I* that would have the mode of being of the In-itself, but that has as its task to "remake the *I*" at every moment by its free decrees—such an infinite freedom is arguably a source of anxiety. Now anxiety inevitably arouses behaviors of concealment and flight, the main one being "bad faith." To escape the burden of a freedom that is at once unlimited and absolutely unjustifiable (since all justification rests on reasons, and I am the only one who chooses these reasons), the for-itself disposes of a parry, consisting in passing oneself off for someone else, or rather for some*thing* else: it thus mimics a mode of being that is not its own—that of the in-itself. Sartre's example is the following: "Let us consider this waiter in the café. His movement is quick and forward, a little too precise, a little too rapid. He comes toward the patrons with a step a little too quick. He bends forward a little too eagerly . . . he is playing at *being* a waiter in a café . . . the waiter in the café plays with his condition in order to *realize* it" (101). But how can the waiter play at being what he is? For we are not talking about a professional actor: this "human reality" coming toward me in his typical black and white attire *is* in fact a café waiter. But, as we have just seen, the for-itself can never be what he is without qualification. Between his non-positing self-consciousness [*conscience non-thétique (de) soi*] and his *I*, a slight discrepancy, an *écart*, insinuates itself, so that he never adheres to his being, he is always "at a distance," he is himself in the mode of not being it—that is, he makes himself freely be this way or that. The café waiter's bad faith therefore consists in sneaking away from his ontological condition (to be what he is not and not to be what he is) by pretending to be in-itself, that is, by assuming a mode of being that is incompatible with that of human reality.

Now, for Sartre, all feelings belong to a fundamental bad faith. "Should we not say that being sad means first to make oneself sad?" (104). To be sad, therefore, is to identify oneself with what is only a transcendent correlate of consciousness, my sadness, and act as if I *were* nothing but sadness in the mode of the in-itself. All feeling is a comedy that we play for ourselves, a condition we mimic in order to realize it. To be sad is to play being sad the same way the waiter in the café incarnates his own role. It is to give to the feeling that haunts the nonpositing consciousness the consistency of plain being: "If I make myself sad, it is because I *am* not sad—the being of the sadness escapes me by and in the very act by which I affect myself with it" (104). The inevitable consequence of this thesis is that it becomes impossible to distinguish between the feeling we play and the one we feel, between sincere and affected love, true anger and histrionic anger, and so on. Indeed, how could we distinguish between them, if the nature of all feeling is such that I cannot feel it without playing it, or rather, if to feel it is *nothing other* than to play it? But if pretending to be sad and being sad are phenomenologically identical, there are no more feelings. Furthermore, how could there be feelings, for Sartre, if all is dependent on my freedom, which is pure activity, absolute spontaneity exempt from all passivity, all *pathos*? To be sad, for Sartre, is nothing, basically, but to choose oneself sad—*that is, not to* be *sad!* "Moreover, as Gide has very well said, a sentiment that is play-acting and one that is vital are two things that are hardly distinguishable one from another. To decide that I love my mother by staying beside her, and to put on an act the upshot of which is that I do so—these are nearly the same thing."[35] But between Gide and Sartre, there is the difference of the "nearly"!

Every felt feeling is a feigned one: this is only the first paradox generated by the Sartrean thesis of an absolute freedom in which the for-itself makes itself be what it is: "My own consciousness . . . is because it makes itself, since its being is consciousness of being. But this means that doing sustains being; consciousness has yet to be its own being, it is never sustained by being . . . *consciousness is not what it is*" (105 [translation modified—Tr.]). Freedom is pure spontaneity without any prior passivity. "For human reality, to be is to *choose oneself*; nothing comes to it either from the outside or from within which it can *receive* or *accept*" (568–69). Freedom cannot be supported, as we have seen, by any reasons whatsoever that precede it; its choice can be nothing other than totally unmotivated, irrational, absurd, in a word. "Such a choice made without base of support and dictating its own cause to itself, can very well appear *absurd*, and in fact it is absurd" (616). Such a "freedom"—the source of all meaning, all values, and at the same time absurd—is it still worthy of the name? Does it not hang over human reality as the most implacable, the most incomprehensible of fates? Indeed, as Luigi Pareyson insists, "freedom is not as such without being. A freedom that is activity and nothing but activity, activity that stands balanced on itself, activity abandoned to itself, is not properly speaking freedom. There is nothing surprising about the fact that whoever conceives of freedom in this way ends up sooner or later considering it as a condemnation and a prison, as was the case with Sartre."[36] This is precisely the turning point in which Sartrean freedom, by dint of being infinite, absolute, turns into its opposite and becomes a blind fatality. Let us try to better understand it.

The Original Choice and Existential Psychoanalysis

The problem for Sartre is the following: If freedom, as power of nihilation, is beyond all reason and all motive, if it creates its reasons and motives by its unmotivated upsurge, what distinguishes such a freedom, by which the for-itself creates and recreates itself ceaselessly, from a pure and simple *whim*? A whim, Sartre says in *Notebooks for an Ethics*, is a way for man to relate to his being "as if he were a chance [*un hasard*] for himself." Now, if freedom is absolute or else it doesn't exist at all, if it has no "other" that would limit its exercise, since being does not determine it, since it is itself nihilation of all being, since it rests entirely on itself, that is, on its own nothingness—how can it still escape arbitrariness? How can it avoid reducing itself to "a series of capricious jerks, comparable to the Epicurean clinamen" (583)?

Here Sartre must back off, so to speak, before the consequences of his own doctrine, which would make human reality into a succession of arbitrarily chosen *I*'s and something like a series of continuous creations. He must, as it were, reinject some being into that originary nothingness by which the being of consciousness always eludes itself, by which I can never adhere to what I am but am perpetually "at a distance." To reinject the nothingness that I am with being would be to imagine an originary choice in which the for-itself decides about its being, conferring on the latter a *constancy* that its subsequent choices will express. Indeed, how is it possible that I observe in my choices a certain continuity, and that the "values" I hold to do not change at every moment—in short, that in the daily life and routine of my existence it seems to me that I do not have to keep choosing myself? Sartre's answer is the following: "All these trivial passive expectations of the real, all these commonplace, everyday values, derive their meaning from an original projection of myself which stands as my choice of myself in the world" (77).

But does Sartre not back off here before the anxiety of freedom that he himself has described? If what makes my freedom is the fact that for me, at every moment, everything is possible, what prevents me from doing anything and everything? The only possible answer is: nothing. It is from this nothing that anxiety is born. Now, Sartre must not only account for the anxiety-producing character of my freedom, he must also account for the circumstance that, in the facts, it is rare that I explore the infinity of this "all is possible." What is more, in most cases my choices seem to make themselves automatically, as a matter of course, so to speak. Where, then, does this relative constancy of what psychology would call "my character," and sociology "my conditioning," come from? *Neither from my character, nor from my conditioning*, since there are no such things, according to Sartre. The for-itself is a being such that its being is choice; it has neither essence nor any given nature. Consequently, the constancy of my choices itself can come only from a previous choice, but a foundational one. The nothingness of my freedom ultimately rests on the grounding of a being that I myself have chosen by an originary decree: for "whatever our being may be, it is a choice" (607). Thus, concrete freedom, the freedom that decides in each case in a given situation, is a freedom always already determined by a first general decree. "I emerge alone and in anguish confronting the unique and original project which constitutes my being" (77). Therefore, anxiety changes its "object," so to speak. Since in my daily actions in reality I do no more than ring the changes on this first, originary choice, develop the consequences of my being as I originally chose it, true freedom appears to be led back in its entirety to that original choice, the ultimate free foundation of all the others. But does not this thesis of a founding decision contribute to obscuring anxiety rather than to arousing it? Does it not reintroduce a manner of determinism from which Sartre was trying to free himself? The characteristic of determinism is "to provide us with a *nature* productive of our acts" (78). But is this not also the consequence of this theory? There are at least two differences, Sartre would probably reply. For one thing, I can *modify* this originary choice at any moment; for another, it is no longer an external, stubborn, inert nature that is the cause of our acts, but an entirely free choice. But does this not boil down to saying that *it is our freedom itself that is nature*, that is, at once absolutely free and absolutely fatal? To put the freedom of God in the place of that of man—is this not precisely to expose oneself to the paradox of a freedom that cannot exercise itself without self-destructing?

How, moreover, is it possible to think an absolute *first choice*? How could possibilities give themselves to an originary, free decree, if the possible only emerges in being by freedom and freedom alone? For I am, qua free, "the original source of my possibility" (79–80). Hence, this fundamental first choice does not get its possibilities from a prior situation and a deliberation on that situation. "It is the foundation of all deliberation . . . because as we have seen, a deliberation requires an interpretation in terms of an original choice" (594). A choice of an originary freedom that secretes its own possibilities, since no possibility precedes it, no deliberation; a choice without selection, since the latter supposes prior possibilities. Such a choice, writes Sartre, is the "ontological foundation" of selection (595), but can it then itself be a *selection*, can it be itself a *choice*?

Sartre, however, attempts to describe its possibility. Freedom does not reside in the deliberation and choice between possibilities. It is the very foundation of the possible. "It is in lighting this cigarette I learn my concrete possibility, or if you prefer, my desire to smoke" (73 [translation modified—Tr.]). Here we have not only, as in Aristotle, primacy of actuality over potentiality, but actuality that *precedes* potentiality and produces it as such. It is *by* freedom that there are possibilities, reasons, a situation. But then freedom can no longer be defined as a choice *between possibilities*, and it is hard to see what authorizes Sartre to continue speaking about "choice." Must we not make the same objection to this original decree that Sartre makes to Kant's doctrine of choice of the intelligible character: "A choice which would be a choice *in terms of nothing*, a choice *against nothing*, would be a choice of nothing and would be annihilated as choice" (617)?

What differentiates, then, this first decree of my freedom—irrational, unmotivated, and unbeknownst to myself—from the worst of destinies? This alleged originary "choice" does not get its possibilities from the world: it is "beyond the world" (77) in the sense that what is at stake in such a choice is not this or that possible; it is my being-in-the-world as such, that is, as a whole. What I choose, in the original choice of my being, is my very way of being in the world. "I choose myself as a whole in the world which is a whole," so that this choice designates precisely "the first phenomenon of being in the world." For I choose all the possibilities that articulate the world for me by choosing "my ultimate and total possibility" (594); "we choose the world—not in its contexture as in-itself but in its meaning—by choosing ourselves" (596).

This will be shown by the example of fatigue. What happens when, during a hike in the mountains, I fall exhausted by the side of the trail while my hiking companions happily continue up the trail? Is it my strength that is giving out, my determination that is lacking, my morale that is sagging? No, says Sartre, none of the above. Or rather, if they have some relevance, these physical or psychological explanations do not get to the root of the problem. My fatigue involves and reveals "a free and global project of myself" by which I have decided on how I relate to my body, physical exercise in general, walking, and hence also to the mountain, its level of difficulty, to everything that gives me the occasion to exercise my own strength, and to which I relate either in the mode of cheerful challenge, or of a reticence and distaste for continuing as soon as I feel the first signs of tiredness. Thus, he who falls by the side of the trail is only tired because he has chosen himself "fatigueable," whereas his traveling companions have chosen themselves "sportsmen," "spunky," "in good shape," "courageous." There is nothing, therefore, in what constitutes my contingency that does not ultimately go back to that first choice of myself. Am I ugly? Am I little? Am I poor, sick, oppressed, the victim of an inferiority complex? If so, it is because I have *chosen* myself thus, says Sartre. "In one sense it is I who choose my body as weak" (628). And it is not different with my inferiority complex, "this inferiority which I struggle against and which nevertheless I recognize, this I *have chosen* from the start" (591). This is a consequence of the "general assessment of my being" that is the founding act of my being. Even my ugliness is included in it. My ugliness is nothing other than what announces itself to me from my original project, for example, the project of being successful with women; it is "the apprehension of the coefficient of adversity which is presented by women or by society to my enterprises" (592). We must say, therefore, that strictly speaking I choose myself ugly just as I choose myself inferior. There is no one, not even the exploited factory worker, who does not choose his way of being exploited, by deciding to accept it. It is true that Sartre does not deny that there is such a thing as contingency; but he thinks of that contingency as dependent in its entirety on the decree of a freedom. For the *meaning* of my contingency comes from that decree. Thus, nothing prevents me from "deciding to be handsome," in the sense that I will cease living my ugliness as a handicap: I will do everything I can to improve my physique and, in spite of my inherited defects, I will in fact become handsome. Here there is something right in Sartre's description: my ugliness is *also* what I make of it. But it is not *only* that. What is striking in these descriptions is their constantly hyperbolic character. Sartre does not say how "to decide to be handsome" would be something different from "to spruce up (*faire le beau*)," which is very different from actually being handsome! For if it is true that my ugliness is also what I make of it, it is not true that I am the one who makes my ugliness; if it is true that all facticity can be recast and taken up in a free project, it is not true that it *comes from* a free project. Now, it is indeed in the direction of that conclusion that Sartre would like to draw us. At first, the for-itself *is* nothing but the free decree of its freedom by which it chooses itself as a whole at the same moment it decides on its world. It *is* nothing but that—freedom; that is, it is its own nothingness, the nothingness of all being. Its being itself, its facticity, is "in suspense in its freedom." This comes down to saying that none of its determinations determine it; they determine it only to the extent that it chooses them. I choose myself French, bourgeois, sick, a man of the twenty-first century, and so on. Actually, strictly speaking, it must be said rather that *I* do not choose myself thus, since the freedom that chooses me and makes me into myself is not yet *myself*; it is not I who choose my freedom, it is my freedom that chooses me, and me who am chosen by it. Am I not therefore a plaything of its power?

This is what emerges in another example Sartre gives of this "contingent and unjustifiable" "initial choice" (611–12), which an "existential psychoanalysis" will attempt to bring to light: stuttering. Here stuttering is supposed to illustrate the thesis that "whatever our being may be, it is a choice; and it depends on us to choose ourselves as 'great' or 'noble, or 'base' and 'humiliated' " (607). Stuttering expresses the originary decision by which I have chosen myself inferior in the mode of a complex. Hence correcting my stuttering does not suffice to change my project itself at its root. As in Freudian psychoanalysis, there can be symptom shifts. Naturally, Sartre adds, even revolt, indignation, and despair, which can be the result of the humiliation that I have chosen, are co-chosen, so to speak, in my originary choice. I cannot choose myself inferior without at the same time choosing myself bitter, rancorous, and so on. Thus, "to choose to be an inferior artist is of *necessity* to *wish* to be a great artist" (608; my emphasis on *necessity*). One must insist on this *necessity*: not only does the choice itself appear entirely arbitrary and incomprehensible for the person who makes it, as irrational to him as the blindest of destinies, but also, in this choice itself, all the concomitant bad faith behaviors are "necessarily" implicated. Does this leave room for any freedom whatsoever?

Sartre the Megarian

None, Sartre would reply, if we continue to define freedom as the power of contradictories. Or more precisely, Sartre will maintain an extremely paradoxical claim that could be summed up, in scholastic terminology, as follows: While for Thomas Aquinas the freedom of specification (to choose this rather than that—the power of contraries) is grounded on freedom of exercise (to be able to choose or not to choose—the power of contradictories), Sartre accepts freedom of specification, but rejects all freedom of exercise: for the for-itself *cannot not choose (itself)*. Freedom is always *in medias res*, always in the process of making itself; it is never a pure undetermined potentiality preceding its actualization. It does not exist before its effectuation in a given choice, since not to choose is to have already chosen. It exists only in actuality, and never in potentiality; therefore, it cannot define itself as the undetermined potentiality to choose or not to choose. "The freedom of the for-itself is always *engaged*; there is no question here of a freedom which could be undetermined and which would preexist its choice. We shall never apprehend ourselves except as a choice in the making. But freedom is simply the fact that this choice is always unconditioned" (616). The choice is unconditioned in the sense of being pure spontaneity. "In addition it is necessary to point out to 'common sense' that the formula 'to be free' does not mean 'to obtain what one has wished' but rather 'by oneself to determine oneself to wish' (in the broad sense of choosing)" (621). Freedom means self-determination (spontaneity) or yet again "autonomy of choice" (622). This freedom—and this is the essential point—cannot go back in time to a moment when it has not yet chosen, when it would be pure undetermined potentiality preceding all determination. "Not to choose is, in fact, to choose not to choose" (619). This is precisely what, in Sartre's view, constitutes the absurdity of freedom. "This choice is absurd, not because it is without reason but because there has never been any possibility of not choosing" (616). What Sartre wants to reject, in substance, is the distinction between a pure power of contradictories, an undetermined potentiality for choosing or not choosing, and its actualization in a concrete choice. "Freedom is not a simple undetermined power. If it were, it would be either nothingness or in-itself; and it is only by an absurd synthesis of in-itself and nothingness that it could have been conceived as a bare power preexisting its choices" (624 [translation modified—Tr.]). Freedom exists only in actuality: choice and act, Sartre comments, are inseparable; choice exists only in the act of choosing (622), "we are wholly choice and act" (618). Freedom is wholly actual or else it is not at all.

In other words, there is never, in Sartre's view, a blank moment when freedom is not already engaged in choices. This is what he expresses in the formula that freedom is not its own foundation (623); it cannot decide *freely* on its being free, it cannot itself choose itself as freedom: "In fact we are a freedom which chooses, but we do not choose to be free. We are condemned to freedom" (623). The facticity of freedom consists for it in not being able to separate itself from its actualization. When I choose not to choose, I am still performing an act of freedom: thus "we are not free to cease being free" (567).

I am condemned to freedom: How are we to understand this odd expression? If it is true that all determination is choice of that determination, that freedom is the alpha and omega of all existence; if it is true that my very being in its entirety comes from a completely irrational originary decree, to the point that it can play the role of the Freudian unconscious in a "psychoanalysis" of a new kind; then, it becomes obvious that freedom, by its very absoluteness, by its infinity, escapes my power. It locks up the for-itself like a chain.

The paradox of this freedom is that its power escapes it by its very immensity. On the one hand, Sartre maintains the idea of an absolutely first choice that is entirely within the power of human reality, and by which the latter decides about itself in totality: the idea of a demiurgic power, of a first and founding *fiat* thanks to which nothing of what I am is left to chance, but all that I am, including my most singular contingency, is submitted to my decision. In other words, according to this view, the for-itself is endowed with a total, flawless presence to itself, such that nothing of itself can escape it, because it is up to it, from the beginning, to decide about it. Against Freud and his idea of the unconscious, Sartre maintains that the original choice is "a conscious choice" (594), that the prereflective consciousness is "totally translucent" to itself (688), and therefore that the for-itself is present to itself and its own master from one end of its existence to the other. "Thus we are always wholly present to ourselves" (596). But here is the paradox: precisely because the for-itself *is* only the being that it chooses to be, because it is all transparency, inalienable presence to itself, it is also *by that very fact* opaque, otherwise no "existential psychoanalysis" would be required. Let us read the rest of the sentence I have just quoted, in which this about-face appears: "Thus we are totally present to ourselves, but precisely because we are wholly present, we cannot hope to have an analytical and detailed consciousness of what we are" (596). It is our omnipotence itself that turns on us: it is precisely because we dispose, according to Sartre, of this exorbitant power to choose ourselves in totality by choosing our being-in-the-world, that this titanic and total choice, precisely *because it is total*, escapes us entirely. The for-itself, then, is no longer Adam but Atlas, condemned to "carry eternally on his back / the vault of heaven and the crushing weight of the world" (Hesiod). Because it is infinite, this freedom that haunts the for-itself has something of the inexorable.

Such a fatalism must be understood, moreover, in a strict and rigorous sense. It might not be unwarranted to compare it to the only coherent fatalist doctrine that philosophy has ever known, that of the Megarians. Their teaching consisted in accepting the two first premises of the Master Argument, (1) "all true propositions concerning the past are necessary" and (2) "the impossible does not logically follow from the possible," while rejecting the third, (3) "something is possible which neither is nor will be true."[37] Thus from the irrevocability of the past (1), the necessary realization of all possibilities (3) is deduced, by means of a fundamental rule of modal logic (2). Now, this is what Sartre does when he accepts, first, that "in order for the future to be realizable, it is necessary that the past be irremediable" (638), and when he maintains, second, that there is no possible that will not be realized: "Why should we attribute to Racine the capacity to write yet another tragedy, since he did not in fact do so?"[38]

Therefore, accepting the above-mentioned fundamental rule of modal logic (2), we must conclude—as Aristotle refused to do in *De Interpretate*—in favor of a backward movement [*retrogradation*] of truth such that, from the future to the present, the consequence holds: for a painter, writes Sartre, "the picture that ought to be painted is precisely the one he will have painted."[39] Then, it is true already now that what will be true tomorrow ("*x* painted such and such a painting") will have been true now, while its opposite will have been false now. For possibility is nowhere present except in the act of choice. It only exists as realized, and for human reality there is no possibility of not choosing. All possibility, qua dependent on an act of freedom, is therefore already necessarily in actuality, realized through and through, since all refusal to choose remains once again a way of having chosen.

Faced with these criticisms, Sartre would probably not be completely unprepared. It is true that freedom is not its own foundation, that I am condemned to be free, that my freedom announces itself to me in the guise of destiny; but this "condemnation" is not a deprival of freedom; it can only be conflated with a destiny at the cost of a simplification. The absolute choice that founds all the others, the initial "assessment" of my being, would only weigh on me like a destiny if I were forbidden ever to modify it. Now, Sartre, on the contrary, supports the "perpetual modifiability of our initial project" (598) by a complete metamorphosis of our existence. He describes this "radical conversion of my being-in-the-world," this "abrupt metamorphosis of my initial project" (598) in pages as beautiful as strange. For we must admit that the idea of a transformation of my entire being at the moment of an absolute decision seems problematic, to say the least. This idea is psychologically implausible, but Sartre is not concerned about that, because freedom is situated on an entirely different plane than that of psychological determinism. Where the psychologist sees only continuities, the philosopher should see discontinuities: freedom is a leap, or else it is not at all. But it is at this point that the problem arises. Sartre specifically rejects a philosophy of time as made up of instants, fashioned after Descartes's continuous creation (599). It is not true that time is in itself, at every instant, a beginning *ex novo*; it is, on the contrary, freedom, he asserts, that in bringing about a metamorphosis of its initial choice, introduces into time a "nihilating rupture" (602), thus "causing the instant to spring forth." Here again, everything rests in the final analysis on freedom, as the source of the temporalization of time[40]—everything, including that freedom itself! Indeed, must the instant not be there already in order for there to be a free decision such that it liberates me from all my prior choices and brings about a totally new project of my being? No, Sartre answers. It is freedom, on the contrary, that causes the instant to spring forth in the *continuum* of temporalization—in other words, it is choice itself that is the condition for the emergence of the instant, which, in introducing a rupture with the past, is the condition for the emergence of choice. Thus, it is choice that is the condition for choice. There is, doubtless, a vicious circle here. This circle is the very one of a freedom that rests on itself alone. It confers on freedom something properly magical. Freedom causes the instant to emerge as the condition of the metamorphosis of existence, that is, of freedom. What was psychologically mysterious appears, therefore, ontologically dubious. To account for the possibility of this metamorphosis in the instant, that is, of freedom in the absolute sense he gives this term, Sartre resorts to freedom as the only thing that is able to account for itself.

Infinite Responsibility

A freedom that rests on itself alone cannot have any other limits than itself. Sartre, however, has reminded us that freedom is not its own foundation. In this lies its facticity. I am not free not to be free. But "facticity" thus understood, far from restricting freedom, far from setting a factual limit that would be the mark of its finitude, is but the other side of its infinity. I am not free not to be free: for Sartre this means that my freedom alone limits my freedom. To assert that the for-itself cannot return to the hither side of the fact of its own freedom, from the point of view of this ontology, is not to limit the range of this power that belongs to its transcendence, but rather to emphasize the unlimited nature it possesses on principle: whatever it may do, the for-itself is free—free even from its contingency, since the latter boils down to what the for-itself does with it. Even the adversity of the world and the situation in which the for-itself is plunged are products of its freedom: for there would be no adversity without the project of an end to be realized. Along these same lines, the situation does not constitute an obstacle to its freedom, since there are only situations *for* a freedom. "There is freedom only in a *situation*, and there is a situation only through freedom. Human-reality everywhere encounters resistance and obstacles have meaning only in and through the free choice which human-reality *is*" (629).

There occurs an approach to the limit. From the fact of their being situations only for a freedom, Sartre draws the conclusion that I am entirely responsible for my situation, since I chose it by choosing myself. Indeed, the counterpart of this "facticity"—that is, of the fact that I cannot choose to be free or not free—is an infinite responsibility. This world that I have not wished for, into which I was born, I have nonetheless chosen it to the extent that I have chosen myself, I am completely responsible for it. Since I cannot escape my freedom, it follows that I am responsible for everything, for the whole world, and that my responsibility is consequently limitless. "I am responsible for everything, in fact, except for my very responsibility, for I am not the foundation of my being" (710). Like Atlas, man "carries the weight of the whole world on his shoulders" (707); "I carry the weight of the world by myself alone" (710). But let's leave aside mythological comparisons. Actually, the for-itself plays less the role of a Titan than of God, the creator *ex nihilo*; he "is the one by whom it happens that *there is* a world" (707); he is responsible for it to the precise extent that he is its "author" (707).

Here the Sartrean hyperbole reaches its apex. We must read and give all their weight to the expressions in which Sartre says, for example, that in a war, everyone (here we are to understand women, children, babies, old people) is responsible for that war. "Is it not I who decide the coefficient of adversity in things and even their unpredictability [*sic*] by deciding myself? Thus there are no *accidents* in a life. . . . If I am mobilized in a war, this war is *my* war; it is in my image and I deserve it" (708). This is not only true of the soldier who can indeed desert, evade mobilization, but of every man, every woman, every child. "We must, therefore, endorse Jules Romains's phrase: 'In war there are no innocent victims'" (708). If we wish to give their full meaning to these expressions, we cannot overlook the fact that *Being and Nothingness*, published in 1943, was reprinted several times after the liberation. If Jules Romains wrote the quoted sentence after the First World War, Sartre is repeating it on his own behalf after the Second. We must carefully ponder the following *unpardonable* sentence that could be addressed to the victims of genocide, to deported innocents, to children: "One has the war that one deserves."

With this example, which is not just an example, we touch upon what this assumption by man of a divine freedom—this inverted theology—may have of absurdity and monstrosity about it. To assert that *human* freedom has no limits, that is, has only the limits it chooses for itself ("my freedom, in choosing freely, chooses its limits for itself," 678), is, strictly speaking, to abolish all freedom at the same time as all responsibility. All freedom, as we have seen, since this hyperbolic freedom by which I am God's equal, in claiming to master all, itself escapes all mastery and turns into its opposite. All responsibility, since if I carry the entire world on my shoulders, if I am responsible for everything, I no longer have any personal, inalienable responsibility toward what I alone could do in a given situation; my task, in becoming titanic (or "Christlike"), becomes by that very fact unassumable and vanishes qua *task*.

Whence a certain number of formulations that betray the absurdity of such a freedom. How, for example, are we to think that the for-itself, which *creates itself* in the very act of choosing itself, can *be born*, if to be born is not to be the origin of one's being? "To be born," Sartre replies, "is *to take one's place*, or rather . . . to *receive* it" (630). But how could the for-itself, a pure spontaneity, *receive* anything at all? "As we have seen, for human reality, to be is to *choose oneself*; nothing comes to it either from the outside or from within which it can *receive or accept*" (568–69). No *event* can befall the for-itself, and especially not the event of being born. Indeed, on the one hand, the for-itself is never surprised by anything—not even its birth. "There is nothing which astonishes in the world, nothing which surprises us without our determining ourselves to be surprised" (651); but on the other hand, and above all, no *event* can befall it, since, as Sartre writes, "what happens to me happens to me through me" (707 [translation modified—Tr.]). There is consequently nothing astonishing about my being the only one responsible for the event of being born. "To be sure, in being born *I take a place*, but I am responsible for the place I take" (636). If I am responsible, it is because the place I take, or in other words my situation, is always understood in light of my fundamental project. It is by choosing myself and by choosing the world that I am responsible for my own birth. From there, it is but a short step to conclude, "Thus in a certain sense I *choose* to be born" (710 [translation modified—Tr.]).

But what does "choosing to be born" mean here? In order to understand this, we must push Sartre's logic to its conclusion: To choose to be born is nothing other than *to choose to be a man*. Does the for-itself enjoy a privilege like the one that, in Christian theology, is that of Christ alone in the event of the Incarnation? The response is clearly affirmative. This is what Sartre emphasizes when it comes to the analysis of death as a contingent and absurd fact. By contrast with Heidegger, who sees in mortality, and therefore in finitude, the very being of man, death for Sartre represents no more than a "limit of fact" to my freedom, so that even if the for-itself did not die, it would be no less a man, since in choosing itself, it would decide itself in favor of finitude. "In other words human reality would remain finite even if it were immortal, because it *makes itself finite by choosing itself as human*" (698). By choosing itself, by delimiting its possibles, the for-itself "finites" itself [*se finitise*], that is, creates itself finite: "The very act of freedom is therefore the assumption and creation of finitude" (698). But *only an infinite being can create itself finite.* To make oneself finite is *not to be it*—and there is nothing surprising in that, if we reflect that Sartre's starting point for thinking human freedom was none other than the Cartesian God.

Hence the for-itself can no more die than it could be born. Death "is never *encountered* by the for-itself since it [death] is not *of it* [the for-itself]" (699 [translation modified—Tr.]). And indeed, the for-itself must be immortal in order to be able to choose itself or create itself finite (mortal). To "experience" death is therefore for the im-mortal for-itself to *assume* it freely as a limit of fact to its absolute and limitless freedom, and thus to choose oneself mortal freely, in an unconditioned choice. "There is basically no difference between the choice by which freedom assumes its death as the inapprehensible and inconceivable limit of its subjectivity and that by which it chooses to be a freedom limited by the fact of the Other's freedom" (700). For it is only for the other that I am dead: "*death* represents the future meaning of my present for-itself for the other" (699 [translation modified—Tr.]). Consequently, my death never limits my freedom, since "freedom never encounters this limit" (700). Whence this expression of Sartre that, in its very equivocation, sounds like a confession of powerlessness for thinking any human finitude: "Freedom is total and infinite, which does not mean that it has no limits [it has those of my fundamental project: limits that are *de facto* but not *de* jure] but that it never *encounters them*" (680).

This forgetting of finitude—Sartre's philosophy, even in his ethics, will never be done paying the price for it. Once the for-itself occupies the place left vacant by God, once it sets itself up as the ultimate basis for all Good and all values—since it must be considered as "the being through which the Good comes into the world"[41]—the other person cannot appear, given that he or she is "a *real* limit" (672) to my own freedom, except as the incarnation of Evil. The look of the other is the look of the Medusa, petrifying my freedom; it is already *in itself* a malediction, the *evil eye*: "The eye is always evil because it fixes things."[42] The contingent fact of the existence of the other person is already *by itself* a principle of oppression, of intolerable violence. "Originally, each person is an oppressor inasmuch as he is Other, oppressed insofar as he is himself," so that it is necessary to conclude that "*every* individual relation has to be alienating."[43] Alienation, oppression—these do not represent *one* of the possible modes of the human relation, but the *essence* of all relations in which each is for the other and for him- or herself alternately oppressor and oppressed in an infernal circle of violence that can never have beginning or end. "Every form of behavior of one toward another is alienated behavior, even generosity, even disinterest. . . . I am alienated insofar as I am the Other for the Other, I am alienating insofar as the Other is Other for me."[44] Therefore the simple fact of the existence of others can be designated, in *Notebooks for an Ethics*, in a comparison that is rigorous even in its exaggeration, as "an initial fact analogous to the original sin," which is a sin toward the Absolute—in the present case, myself. This theological vocabulary of sin does not occur here fortuitously; it is required by the entire economy of a thought whose blind spot is alterity. Pushing that logic beyond the positions taken in *Being and Nothingness*, Sartre affirms that this "original sin" is not any particular act of violence that would as such be imputable to the other, "but rather the fact that man is first of all present to himself as other. The springing up of man in the world is a sin against freedom, through alienation."[45] My freedom, powerless because total, takes itself captive by choosing itself, but it only experiences that captivity beneath the look of the other, and only conceives of it as being taken captive by the other. A reflection on absolute freedom can be brought to completion only in a reflection on absolute alienation, in which the fate of freedom, which is to turn into a fate, is a fate that the other inflicts on me.[46] The absolute of freedom is the summit of alienation and the empire of violence: rigorously, a Hell.

5

The Mirror of Narcissus

On the Phenomenology of the Flesh

Contemporary philosophy, particularly in France, has a tendency to consider the phenomenological relevance of the concept "flesh" (*Leib*) to go without saying, with a few rare exceptions.[1] According to this widely held opinion, the distinction between *Leib* and *Körper* offers the only sure starting point for an analysis of our corporeal condition,[2] not only because it gives a satisfactory account of the phenomena themselves, but also because it is the only distinction capable of setting a limit to the scientific objectivism (and its technological prolongations) that claim to demote the human body to the rank of a being among others in nature. The defense and illustration of subjectivity (raising the question of whether it does not turn into a rehabilitation of metaphysics) and the anti-naturalist claim thus constitute the main arguments, in authors whose philosophical orientations are as diverse, incidentally, as Merleau-Ponty, Sartre, Michel Henry, and Jean-Luc Marion, in favor of a return to the theme of flesh, despite many nuances added to this concept. However, in all the cases cited, this permanence of the flesh is accompanied by a more or less explicit critique of Husserlian idealism. Thus, on the one hand, the Husserlian distinction [between *Leib* and *Körper*] is maintained, and on the other, it is transplanted outside its original domain. But is such a transplantation possible? Does the flesh-body distinction make sense outside the context of constitution and intentional analysis? More generally: Is the flesh the best starting point, is it a starting point at all, in analyzing our corporeal condition? In order to attempt to do justice to these questions, I will dwell on the example of Merleau-Ponty, which is not only that of a precursor for all subsequent phenomenology of the flesh, but that of a thought that has placed the latter at the center of his investigation and has attempted to furnish us with one of the most complete and coherent doctrines concerning it. Through this example, we will be able to examine the modalities of the shift introduced in this concept, which aspires and conspires to move toward new ground—the whole problem being whether this shift remains or not fundamentally tributary to the presuppositions inherent in what it has shifted or recast.

The Husserlian Conception of the Flesh: Sensualism, Idealism, Theoreticism

In order to do this, it will be useful to set out from the analyses of Husserl himself and to assess the innovations of subsequent phenomenology with respect to them. From these celebrated analyses of the flesh or of the lived body (*Leib, Leibköper*), I will retain only the elements necessary to carry out my task. In the most important text for this question, *Ideen II*, the thematization of the flesh is situated in the more general framework of an analysis of the constitution of the animal nature (*animalischen Natur*) insofar as it contains—in man at least—two layers of being (*Seinschichten*): that of the flesh, and that of "soul" or the "empirical ego." These two layers, Husserl insists, are not just superimposed, they are closely connected: they "interpenetrate each other," they are "interwoven" (*verflochtene*) with one another in a characteristic manner,[3] in such a way that by their unity they constitute the complete and concrete man in the fullness of his phenomenal determinations, "the ego-man (*Ich-Mensch*)." The goal of intentional analysis is to uncover, on the basis of their respective modes of givenness, these different statra of meaning, which are strata of constitution for and by a transcendental ego. Therefore it is under phenomenological reduction that this analysis unfolds in its entirety.

The intentional elucidation of the constitution of the body of flesh (*Leib*) in its difference from the body-object (*Körper*) has its starting point in the analysis of self-contact. Indeed, what happens when one of my hands touches the other? Husserl distinguishes, in a famous passage, a "double sensation . . . and [a] double apprehension."[4] When I touch my left hand "I perceive and have appearances of a soft, smooth hand, with such and such a form."[5] Therefore, I perceive objective properties of my hand as a body among bodies. But at the same instant in which I thus perceive the physical thing, left hand, "I also find in it a series of touch-sensations, which are '*localized*' in it, though these are not constitutive of properties."

These sensations are not merely added to my perception of the hand as a physical thing. They are different in kind, since they alone make of this perception a perception of *my* hand. "It is not that the physical thing is now richer, but instead *it becomes flesh* (*es wird Leib*), *it senses*."[6] In this experience of double contact, I not only feel my left hand, but in feeling it as *my* hand, I localize the tactile sensations stemming from the contact with my right hand in it; and the same process is repeated in my right hand. Each of my hands is therefore at once touching and touched, so that this double modality of feeling is doubled in each of my members. In sum, "the sensation is *doubled* in the two parts of the flesh (*dergleichen* [*empfindungen*] doppelt *in beiden Leibesteilen*), since each is then precisely for the other an external thing that is touching and acting upon it, and each is at the same time flesh (*Leib*)."[7]

What does Husserl mean here by this enigmatic phrase: a "similar sensation duplicated"? Wouldn't I also have a similar sensation duplicated in each of my hands in the case in which I explored tactilely a symmetrical object, for example that "ball of lead" that Husserl himself mentions in the course of his description? In this last case, each of my hands would be at once touching (they would perceive, or rather the ego would perceive through them, the objective properties of the physical thing—its smooth surface, its roundness, its coldness) and touched (they would feel "inside itself" or "on itself" corresponding sensations). Furthermore, these two series of sensations would respond to each other, so to speak, from one hand to the other, would follow each other and espouse each other in a characteristic way, by virtue of the symmetry of the object. So what is the difference? It lies in the fact that the ball of lead is touched, but not touching. No sensation is localized in it. It feels nothing. It is not touched by me at the moment I touch it. Things go differently with my left hand, which awakens when touched by my right hand and vibrates in unison with it. Consequently, in the case of the ball of lead, I have analogous sensations "in" both hands, the regular correspondence of which, term by term, so to speak, ensures at once the coherence of the object and its empirical reality based on the continuous concordance of the two perceptual flows. But in Husserl's view, the phenomenon of self-contact is very different: in it, we have a most remarkable and astonishing situation. Indeed, by virtue of the fact that each hand can be felt alternately as touching and touched, not only is there a regular correspondence between these two series of phenomena, but a correspondence *of a new kind*, in which each of these series of phenomena is in turn duplicated, in that it is open to a double apprehension: "The same touch-sensation is apprehended as a feature of the 'external' Object and is apprehended as a sensation of the flesh-object (*Leib-Objects*)."[8]

Let me emphasize the paradoxical nature of this last expression. In a sense, the flesh is precisely what cannot become an *object*. And yet on the occasion of this redoubling of the two tactile flows of adumbrations, each of which can be apprehended both as exposing the object and as sensations in the lived body, it does seem that *I experience my flesh* as an "object" of a new kind. But in order for me to be able, so to speak, to feel my flesh, or as Husserl says, to "touch myself," a transitivity and an immediacy of my relation to myself must be established that raises new problems. Indeed, as opposed to what happens in the case of vision, in which the eye is not itself seen, and in which the color sensations are not localized in the eye, the touch possesses that particularity that it allows me to apprehend myself directly. In the experience of self-contact, "my flesh as touched flesh is a touching-touched."[9] Here we have a phenomenon that is of the order of a *pure self-affection*: on the occasion of the phenomenon of doubled touch, I apprehend myself in the process of feeling, I witness, as it were, the birth of touching as brought about in my twin hands. I *touch myself touching*, while I do not see myself seeing. And this is true even if I observe my eye in a mirror, for it is still in that case an *Einfühlung* that is occurring: I perceive my eye only as that of another. It is not surprising that in the first version of *Cartesian Meditations* Husserl dared to speak, apropos of that experience, of "a kind of reflection (*eine Art von Reflexion*)."[10] To the reflection in the mirror that only gives me an external double, we must contrast a reflection of touching—not specular, but immanent—by which the latter relates to itself immediately and without intermediary. If Husserl eliminated this phrase from the definitive version of the text, it is probably because it introduced a source of confusion with the strict phenomenological concept of "reflection," the concept that characterizes the reflexivity of transcendental consciousness. The reflexivity that is born of the palpation in which my flesh relates to itself is not reflection in the sense in which this term is applied to the pure ego: indeed it is in turn something *constituted*, while originary reflection is an ultimate determination of the *constituting* ego in the originary temporalization of its living present. To conflate these two sorts of reflection would probably be tantamount, in Husserl's view, to placing the order of the constituting and that of the constituted on the same level, that is, it would imperil transcendental idealism itself.

Flesh (*Leib*) is therefore nothing but the manner in which every sensation is doubled when my body (*Körper*) relates to itself in the experience of self-contact. Running my hand over my skin and thus awakening in its depths a dormant or potential touch responding to my fingers' call and following them in their trajectory, I can say, "from here to here is me!"

This is an unquestionable fact, a fact the meaning of which no phenomenology can abstain from calling into question. This body only seems mine because it answers to the solicitation of touch by stirring at its contact and echoing it in response. But it is here, precisely, that the difficulties begin. The first one is the following: How do we move from the idea of doubled sensations to that of pure self-affection? Isn't this transition more like a leap? Indeed, the idea of a reduplication of sensations in each member implies the *duality* of tactile sensations: each hand is felt *successively*—never at the same time—as touching and as touched. But if we were to stick with that duality of tactile flows, the experience of self-contact could enjoy no primacy for the constitution of the flesh-body. Whenever I touch *any object*, I can experience the "double apprehension" Husserl speaks of: I can alternatively feel objective tactile properties and tactile sensations localized in the flesh itself. We must therefore go a step further to reach the idea of an immediate experience of self, a self-affection prior to the constitution of the world, of spatiality, of others, of language. We must accept, in a way, no longer merely a reciprocity or a reversibility of the touching and the touched, but a quasi identity between them. We must presuppose, by a kind of approach to a limit, that there is, actually, only *one single* flow in which the touching and the touched do not cease exchanging their roles, to the point of becoming indiscernible from one another for each other. This possibility is perhaps never thematized by Husserl, but it magnetizes all his analyses like a kind of tropism, that of a coincidence of touching with itself by which flesh would be constituted precisely as such in its unity.[11] Indeed, without this *telos* of one sole undivided experience of the touching-touched, that is, of a coincidence of flesh with itself by means of a true self-affection, how could the experience of self-contact have a paradigmatic character? But then we slip surreptitiously from the idea of double sensations to that of a single flow of sensations that can be apprehended in two ways. This is the whole equivocation of the expression used by Husserl: *so haben wir dergleichen [Empfindungen]* doppelt *in beiden Leibesteilen*. The mistranslation of the French translator when she renders *dergleichen* by "the same" ("the same sensation duplicated in the two parts of the body") is in a sense required by the context.[12] Indeed, it is *as if* there were but one and the same sensation duplicated in both hands and alternately active and passive, a simple self-affection of self by self, a quasi-coincidence between those phantom-hands of which Husserl immediately specifies that they are "much more" than material things.[13] Indeed, my hands are no longer experienced as parts of the physical body, as *membra disjecta* external to each other of a body that is itself extended over space; they seem to become neutral and undifferentiated incarnations of one and the same undivided palpation that comes back over itself and harmonizes with itself. If there is something like *a* flesh, it is therefore because sensibility turns back onto itself and agrees with itself immediately, before all constitution of a spatial body; whereas if there is *a* body, it is only by the intermediary of the flesh, that is, in a mediate way, by unification and synthesis of heterogeneous parts. But there is nothing obvious in this, and from a self-evident phenomenon we have slid imperceptibly into a speculative theory. Where is the border? Precisely at that point where the reduplication of the touch is imperceptibly transformed into a coincidence of the flesh with itself, into the constitution of a preobjective, prespatial nature, entirely penetrated by soul. And how is this transition carried out? Thanks to the concept of "sensation" (*Empfindung*). It is the presupposition of the existence of a *hulē*, preobjective and yet localized in the flesh, in a prespatial and yet structured locality, that indeed dominates all Husserl's descriptions. "Obviously, the flesh . . . becomes a *flesh* only by incorporating tactile sensations, pain sensations, etc.,—in short, by the localization of the sensations as sensations."[14] The fundamental function of the flesh, for Husserl, is that of furnishing a localization for the sensations *qua* sensations, that is, before all objectifying apprehension (and, as a matter of fact, mainly for the tactile sensations). But do such "sensations as sensations" exist? Do they have the slightest phenomenological meaning? This is highly doubtful. The whole enigma of perception is precisely that I never perceive *sensations*, but always properties of the world and of my body-in-the-world. If we were to suppose, in any case, that the answer to these questions is negative, the problem of primary localization of the sensations of touch would vanish, along with the very necessity for a phenomenology of the flesh.

So there would be no flesh, as Husserl understands it, without a form of sensualism. The flesh is the originary, preworld and preobjective place in which all tactile sensation is located before its intentional apprehension and objectification—for instance, the pure hyletic data of heat, cold, or pain.[15] Husserl clarifies that it is a question of an "immediate localization,"[16] as opposed to the localization of objects by the intermediary of the flesh in objective space, which is only a mediate one. Therefore flesh can be defined as the "hyletic substrate (*hyletische Unterlage*)" of consciousness.[17] To the question of where a pain is, for example, I cannot answer by localizing my pain in the objective space of the already objectified physical body, because my pain is not there the way damaged tissue is; but neither is it just in my consciousness. This question must rather be answered by referring to this "substrate," by localizing my sensation *qua sensation* in the locality or prespatial dimensionality of the flesh. This entails that the flesh does not only presuppose the distinction between *hulē* and *morphē* (and the sensualism underlying it) but that to a great extent it founds it. If it makes sense, from the point of view of intentional analysis, to distinguish between really immanent (hyletic) contents and objective properties of the noema, this is mainly because certain hyletic givens, the givens of touch, are localized in a spatial volume that does not find its place in objective space, in that exteriority that belongs to me originarily and that remains the locus of my intimacy, in this carnal fold that is neither a pure worldly exteriority, nor a simple egoic interiority, but an interface between the world and me.[18] To say that flesh *founds* the distinction between *hulē* and *morphē* amounts to saying that it is no longer a constituted instance, but a constituting one. From the point of view of transcendental phenomenology, that amounts to saying that it has a highly paradoxical status.

It is true that Husserl does not go that far. He never makes flesh the origin of the fundamental phenomenological distinction between *hulē* and *morphē*. Flesh is always *constituted* and cannot be an origin, properly speaking. But the analysis of flesh opens a breach in transcendental idealism, a breach that, however slight, will not close up again. Thus Husserl must acknowledge that "The flesh has from the first an exceptional constitutive place,"[19] given that "*what, as world*, stands over and against the subject depends on the flesh (*Leib*)."[20] This is why the latter appears fundamentally ambiguous from the point of view of the distinctions made in intentional analysis. Flesh is neither a "component of the I" (*Bestandstück des Ich*) nor an "over-and-against the *I*" (*Gegenüber des Ich*)[21]: it is neither transcendent in the sense of a worldly objectivity, given in an inadequate manner through a flow of adumbrations, nor identical to the pure *ego*. As the "hyletic substrate" of consciousness, it has the same structural ambivalence as the hyletic contents, at once really immanent to consciousness qua pure unapparent sensations, and immediately overstepped, interpreted by morphological acts in order to be able to appear as exponents of the object, residue of the centrifugal movement by which consciousness transcends itself toward the world. This is why flesh stands precisely in the equivocal "in-between" of world and consciousness and appears thematically only in the singular experience of the doubled touching. All constitution presupposes the flesh qua kinesthetic system inseparable from all givenness in the flesh (*leibhaft*) of an object in space; and at the same time, the flesh is itself constituted, even if that constitution is "imperfect."[22] On the one hand, the flesh body is presupposed by all constitution, as appears in the case, for example, of the taking of narcotics—Husserl says, more bashfully, of stimulants—substantially alters the way things appear. Here we have the manifestation of how "the *appearing external world shows itself as relative . . . to the flesh,*"[23] a relativity on which the difference between the thing (*quid*) and its mode of givenness (*quomodo*) is based, that is, nothing less than the prime phenomenological distinction for all intentional analysis; from another point of view, the flesh remains foreign to the pure ego (*Ichfremdes*); there is a "foreignness-to-me of the flesh (*Ichfremden des Leibes*)" that forbids making it the site of constitution itself.[24]

It is obviously this structural ambivalence and the aporias it elicits for Husserl's transcendental apparatus that give Merleau-Ponty's analyses their starting point. How could the flesh be constituted by the pure *ego*, if all constitution rests on the distinction between the thing and its modes of appearing, and if the flesh, in its preobjective locality, qua "hyletic substrate" of every consciousness and all constitution, gives no purchase for such a distinction? How could constitutive analysis admit of a *tertium quid* neither really constituted nor really constituting, between the ego and the object? It might be countered that the flesh is "constituted" in a very peculiar sense of the term, since, given as is the *hulē* itself in the real immanence of consciousness, in no case can it pertain to the constitution of *objects*. What we are dealing with here is the exceptional case of a "purely hyletic constitution" lacking "both the hyletic multiplicity of profiles and animating apprehension."[25] However, even if we were to accept the possibility, as problematic as it can be, of a constitutive analysis stripped of any true "transcendental guide," that is, without any possibility of a distinction between a given and its modes of givenness, we would further have to accept a "constitution" that presupposes necessarily itself, since the flesh can be apprehended as such only on the basis of tactile hyletic *data* that, in order to appear phenomenally, themselves presuppose the flesh. In any case, either the flesh is given in its entirety in real immanence, but then it is hard to distinguish it from consciousness: it is no longer the latter's "substrate" (*Unterlage*) but becomes identical to it; or else it must be an appearing moment after all, it must pertain to an objectifying apprehension, be perceived, present itself as a quasi-object, all things required in order for an analogizing apprehension to take place based on it: but then it is no longer "immanent" in the same sense as are impressional *data*.

There paradoxes, incidentally, arise to a great extent from the fact that Husserl's break with Cartesianism is not total: it is not without a deeper complicity. The flesh is an object invested with spirit, "filled with the soul through and through,"[26] but at the same time, it is a "substrate" for consciousness, necessarily distinct from it. Between the soul and the flesh there is a "fusion" so intimate that "the apprehension of soul must necessarily take into itself the sensation states of the flesh,"[27] and at the same time—since the pure ego is, of course, not identical to its soul, nor *a fortiori* to its flesh—"Certainly a consciousness without flesh (*leibloses*) and, paradoxical as it sounds, also without a soul . . . is imaginable."[28] On the one hand, Husserl's philosophy takes a step beyond Cartesian dualism by initiating what Levinas has called an "idealism of the sensible," which restores to the lived body its rights and proscribes its being thought of as a pure, disincarnate subject; but on the other hand, it takes a step backward, since, as opposed to Descartes's substantial distinction that ended up with a substantial union, this flesh, in Husserl's view, is never truly me. "Soul and psychic ego 'have' a flesh,"[29] but they are not their flesh. The lived body is only something I "possess," an adjoining [*dépendance*] of my *pure ego*; it "does not belong to the realm of what properly pertains to the Ego (*Ichliche*),"[30] or more precisely, it only belongs to the "*Ego-like* (*Ichlichkeiten*) *by the grace of what is originally Ego-like*."[31] My body is only *my* body, in other words, an ownness or an adjoining of the pure ego pertaining to its sphere of ownness, because the ego preexists its body, that is to say, is distinct from it, and bestows on it its *egoicity* only in a derivative way: "This flesh (*Leib*) is *my* flesh, and indeed mine in the palpable special sense, because I already am and in a certain sense bestow on it its special virtues."[32] The flesh is never more than "the ego's first 'subjective possession' "[33]—the ego remaining alone subjectivity in the only authentic and originary sense.[34] The concept of flesh does not break with idealism, even if it may at times threaten its internal equilibrium, or with the Cartesian sources of idealism: basically, it derives rather from the presuppositions governing them.

It is hard to see, under these conditions, how the lived body could bridge the gap between the ego and other subjectivities or furnish the necessary tool for a thinking of intersubjectivity. Here again, Husserl's description is ambiguous—and structurally so. Indeed, on the one hand, the flesh must be the very locus of the presentation of others, in the sense that the flesh of the other is directly perceived, as originarily as mine is; "indeed, the other's lived body is perceived in my spatial environment, and entirely originarily just as my own; not, however, the psychic that is embodied in the former [the other's lived body]. It is not really and actually self-given, only appresentatively co-meant."[35] If this were not the case, indeed, if the flesh of the other were not accessible to me directly in a perceptive manner, all passageway between my own subjectivity and foreign subjectivity would be cut, and there would be no means of reestablishing it by any "analogizing transfer" from the *eidos ego* to that flesh facing me. It is only on the basis of a carnal similarity, an originary resemblance between the sensible aspect of the other (his expressions and conducts) and my own, that I can bring about the coupling (*Paarung*) by resemblance that Husserl describes at length in *Cartesian Meditations* and thus confer on him or her the meaning "other." In short, if the other did not *present* himself to me (by means of a *Gegenwärtigung*) as flesh, I would not be able to realize the least analogizing transfer of the meaning "ego" to him, or consequently apprehend him through an act of *appresentation* (*Vergegenwärtigung*) as *alter ego*. This analysis, however, remains unilateral; for, on the one hand, we must maintain that if a body is only one's *own* body to the extent that it is proper to, or the ownness of, an ego, an originary giving of the flesh of the other is impossible without the apperceptive transfer itself. The correlate of this is that the sphere of ownness (*Eigenheitssphäre*), as Husserl determines it on the basis of a new reduction, an "*epochē* of a specific type" in which I exclude "*all constitutional effects of intentionality relating immediately or mediately to other subjectivity*,"[36] in §44 of *Cartesian Meditations*, is a radically and inexorably solipsistic sphere in which the other can never *present* itself to me as one's own body (*Leib*), because everything that is "one's own" there draws its ownness from me alone, and no (foreign) flesh can evince the least title to ownness of which I am not myself, initially, the owner. If, in this sphere of ownness, all that is "one's own" is *my* ownness, belonging to my transcendental ego, then naturally there cannot be, within it, presentation of any *foreign* "one's own body" (that expression itself being absurd), and therefore no analogizing transfer, either. No additional transcendental operation will make me exit my initial solitude.

Sensualism, idealism, solipsism—and, of course, theoreticism of the flesh: this last trait is so manifest that it scarcely needs commentary. The flesh is my body as I apprehend it, that is, as I experience it in a theoretical act of knowledge. If it exists, the phenomenological legitimacy of the concept of flesh rests therefore entirely on the possibility of a certain *cognitive* grasp that comes to light in a privileged (but not exclusive) way in the experience of self-contact. Of course, one's own body is also, for Husserl, the organ of an "I can," but as for one's own body in movement little mention is made, and for good reason: one's own body as such is not in the world the way a physical object is, and it is very difficult to understand what "to move" means for it, since it must be defined as an "ultimate central here," that is, "a here which has no other here outside itself, in relation to which it would be a 'there.'"[37] Such an absolute here cannot move, if all movement in space presupposes the relativity of a "here" and a "there" at the same time as a transition from one to the other. "For it [my flesh body], change of place . . . has no meaning."[38] Only the body (*Körper*) seems to be able to move through space and not the arch-immobile flesh—by which this flesh receives, once again, one of the most traditional attributes of the soul.

A First Reorientation: The *Phenomenology of Perception*

This fourfold horizon in which the concept of "flesh" is caught up in Husserl—sensualism, idealism, solipsism, and theoreticism—must it lead phenomenology to abandon the concept altogether, assuming, of course, that phenomenology is able to free itself from the philosophical options of its founder? Unless the concept of flesh is recast, and thereby withdrawn from this fourfold presupposition. But is that really possible? Does such an operation even make sense? This is, in a way, the whole problem of Merleau-Ponty's thought, in which the reworking and deepening of the notion of flesh are accompanied by an increasingly deep rift with respect to transcendental idealism.

Rather oddly, the first thematization we find of this phenomenon, in *Phenomenology of Perception*,[39] marks a retreat rather than an advance vis-à-vis Husserl's analyses. The fundamental distinction at that time, in Merleau-Ponty's view, is not between *Leib* and *Körper*, but between "phenomenal body" and "objective body." Now, the two distinctions are not homogeneous. For Husserl, the body-object is as "phenomenal" as is my own body: they simply belong to two distinct layers of phenomenality. Merleau-Ponty's translation-treason, in this respect, is already significant: it tends to present the body-object not so much as a stratum of constitution, having its own right and validity, but rather as the result of a *misconception*—or even of a falsification—of the only truly *phenomenal* body, that is, the one that is the subject matter of an authentic phenomenology. This theme will, moreover, lead Merleau-Ponty, several years later, to elaborate an autonomous ontology of the flesh that is irreducible to the objectivistic ontology of the sciences. In reality, if the opposition (rather than the distinction) between the phenomenal body and the body-object takes precedence, in *Phenomenology of Perception*, over the distinction between *Leib* and *Körper*, this is because Merleau-Ponty's main interlocutor during these years is not so much Husserl as Sartre. Merleau-Ponty is mainly preoccupied with establishing, against Sartre's ontology of the in-itself and the for-itself, that the phenomenal body possesses neither of those two modes of being; in short, that the distinction between the phenomenal body and the body-object at no point intersects that of the body for me versus the body for the other (*PP*, 106 n1). It is in order to dissolve the antimonies to which the opposition between the for-itself and the in-itself leads us that Merleau-Ponty takes the phenomenal body as his subject matter and that he maintains that others do not appear initially as body-things amid the in-itself, but manifest themselves from the start "at the top of [their] phenomenal body" (*PP* 351). He thus reformulates, in a different vocabulary, Husserl's claim according to which the flesh-body of the other subjectivity must be able to be given as originarily as mine is, in order for a transcendental intersubjectivity to be possible. As he will reiterate a bit later, "The whole riddle of *Einfühlung* lies in its initial, 'esthesiological' phase; and it is solved there because it is a perception" (*S* 170).

But Merleau-Ponty actually does not aim at repeating Husserl. His purpose is rather to make the flesh itself the key to a critique of transcendentalism. The decisive sentence in this perspective, which may be considered as encapsulating the whole project of *Phenomenology of Perception*, is the following: "The body is a natural self and, as it were, the subject of perception" (*PP* 206). The reserve introduced by "as it were" is, moreover, provisional—and entirely rhetorical. The purpose of Merleau-Ponty is without restrictions to make "the body [into] the subject of perception" (*PP* 225). But how is this transposition of the Husserlian problematic onto the terrain of a "natural" *I* possible? It would, in any case, be impossible without an in-depth recasting of the phenomenological conceptuality. But did Merleau-Ponty give himself the resources necessary to carry out this task? The whole difficulty with his enterprise, which, on the one hand, borrows its terminology and concepts from Husserl, and on the other rejects to a considerable extent the transcendental apparatus, appears in this type of assertion: "But I am not in front of my body, I am in it, or rather I am it" (*PP* 150). Are we talking about the *Leib* or the *Körper*? Husserl would say that I am in front of my *Körper* and not in front of my *Leib*, because the latter is not, properly speaking, an ob-ject. But he would not say that I *am* my body of flesh either, because as a transcendental subject I am only an ego who *has* a flesh, to the precise extent that it *constitutes* it as such.

But let us look more closely at what (voluntary) distortions Merleau-Ponty introduces into the conceptualization of his predecessor. The first one consists in a reinterpretation of Husserl's claim that the flesh is "incompletely constituted." It was very difficult for Husserl to account for this from the standpoint of his presuppositions. Indeed, this *necessary* incompleteness is such that it is not the product of a law proper to the transcendental ego but of a situation that could appear merely contingent with respect to pure eidetic distinctions, namely the fact that the body becomes an obstacle to itself in its exploratory function, that it constitutes an impediment for its own perception: thus, my eye-sockets and my head limit the field of my vision, the flexibility and length of my arms limit the domain offered to tactile apprehension, and so on.[40] But since the body is understood by Merleau-Ponty as "that by which there are objects" (*PP* 92), that is, as the true and sole subject of perception, what appears as a *de facto* necessity from the point of view of transcendental analysis, here becomes a *de jure*, or a "metaphysical" necessity (*PP* 91). Since the body-subject is never, properly speaking, constituted, the incompleteness of its constitution becomes a *constitutive* (Merleau-Ponty will later say "ontological") feature of this body, and can be described as latency, as a "marginal presentation" (*PP* 95), or as an oblique presence. "To say that it is near me is to say that it is never really in front of me, that I cannot array it before my eyes, that it remains marginal to all my perceptions, that it is *with* me" (*PP* 90 [translation modified—Tr.]). The oblique presence of my body is the indication of my inherence in it. It can lead only to an indirect ontology that will take form in *The Visible and the Invisible*. This latency, moreover, because it is fundamental, oversteps the distinction between the senses; it is not valid for touch alone. It is not just my tactile constitution that is incomplete, as Husserl thought,[41] but "it is no different, in spite of what may appear to be the case" (*PP* 92) for my visual body, as it appears to me in a mirror; for just as my tactile body is doubled with a touching body that is itself intangible, so my visual body refers back to a latent one that is invisible on principle.[42]

Finally, the double-touching phenomenon itself should be analyzed differently. "My body," Merleau-Ponty reminds us, "is recognized by its power to give me 'double sensations'" (*PP* 93). But how should this phenomenon be interpreted? Here Merleau-Ponty completes *in fine* Husserl's analysis of the touch with a more personal "touch." "In passing from one role to the other, I can identify the hand touched as the same one which will in a moment be touching. In this bundle of bones and muscles which my right hand is for my left, I guess for an instant . . . that other right hand, agile and alive, which I thrust towards things to explore them" (*PP* 93 [translation modified—Tr.]). But how can I "guess" that other right hand? Is it by this sensation of movement that is the indication of agility and life? Not at all: it is by the application of a function of knowledge that goes out from my body and returns to it, that is, by the outline of a *reflection* in which my body grasps itself no less immediately than a transcendental consciousness. "The body catches itself from the outside engaged in a cognitive process; it . . . initiates 'a kind of reflection' which is sufficient to distinguish it from objects" (*PP* 93). This last distinction, in reality, is the first, because it is the only one that is entirely *sufficient*, as Merleau-Ponty specifies. Only one's own body is able to grasp itself "in its exploratory function," that is, on the occasion of touching, to apprehend its own tactile capacity. What is new here is not the theme of reflection, already largely outlined in Husserl, but rather the status conferred on it: this reflection of the body is the primary reflection, which presides over any other, since the body is the ultimate origin, the true "subject."

Many aspects of this body-subject are partially left in shadow—particularly that of its movement. On the one hand, the phenomenal body is the body in movement—although Merleau-Ponty hardly details how it can be, qua distinct from the body-object that is moved through space—but on the other hand, it is primarily, not to say primordially, approached starting out from a theoretical attitude (the "function of knowledge" referred to above: *PP* 93), as an object of experience.[43] Actually, there is no "my own body" except in my own experience of the body or in the body as proper object of my experience. This is why, as Jacques Colette has insisted, reflection, even transposed to the body itself, anchors the analysis in an entirely gnoseological context from which Merleau-Ponty detaches himself only ostensibly. "Thus breaking with the phenomenology of consciousness, he cannot leave the pathways of a phenomenology of perception and of a gnoseology governed by the reflective model. This is why he must discover, even in the sensible, an elementary form of mediate consciousness, and this form is, inevitably, specular."[44]

The Reflexivity of the Sensible: The Developments in Signs

The article in *Signs*, "The Philosopher and His Shadow," represents a decisive step along the path leading Merleau-Ponty toward the progressive abandonment of transcendental phenomenology and to the elaboration of an ontology of the flesh. Once more, the phenomenologist reproduces and comments on Husserl's characterization of the lived body, but this time it is the changes he introduces—both in relation to the text of *Ideen II* and to his earlier descriptions—that are meaningful. Husserl's assertion that a real mind "essentially can be only . . . a real mind of an animate organism" already indicates clearly that phenomenology is not a philosophy of mind that contrasts mind with a nature in itself.[45] On the contrary, the description of the flesh leads toward a "third dimension" that corresponds neither to mind nor to nature—is situated on the hither side of objectivity and subjectivity, rendering these distinctions problematic (*S* 162). Unfortunately, Husserl scarcely tried to elucidate how the entry into this third domain modified his own instruments of analysis. "Does it make no changes at all in our conception of noesis, noema, and intentionality—in our ontology? . . . We know that Husserl never made himself too clear about these questions" (*S* 165). This lack of an *ontology* of the flesh must be filled by trying to deepen this domain situated between transcendent nature and the immanence of mind. "It is into this interval that we must try to advance" (*S* 166). But how does this ontological approach to the flesh break with the transcendental approach? While Husserl's whole intention was to *distinguish* the subject from the object, the flesh as the ego's primordial possession, and the body as an object for the positive sciences, and by this very fact, to hierarchize the given, to bring out layers of constitution (material nature, animal nature, the spiritual world), Merleau-Ponty's goal consists in seeking in the body as lived body a *tertium quid*, neither subjective nor objective, that is, a locus for the *overcoming* of these oppositions. In this sense, his purpose is "ontological": it is to elucidate the mode of being of this third dimension, and thus to carry out a recasting of the whole conceptual apparatus that presides over the analysis of the other two. Nothing shows this apparently very slight and yet radical shift better than a new point of "translation." Indeed, in a footnote Merleau-Ponty slips in a correspondence between two of his expressions relating to flesh: a "feeling thing" and a "subject-object," and two "equivalent" expressions in Husserl: *empfindendes Ding, das subjective Objekt*. Of course the equivalency of these phrases is anything but obvious: to say that the flesh is a "subjective object" for Husserl is to maintain that it is both the closest and the most one's own object in that it is the transcendental possession of a pure ego; it is perhaps to attribute to it an intermediary mode of being, between constituted objects and the constituting ego, but certainly not to attempt to *overcome* this alternative. It is unlikely, in this respect, that Husserl, with his concept of flesh, "overturned the relationships between the constituted and the constituting" (*S* 172 [translation modified—Tr.])—or rather, if he did, it was despite himself.[46]

It is in light of this change of attitude that we must understand the renewed description of the experience of the double-touching. "There is a relation of my body to itself which makes it the *vinculum* of the self and things. When my right hand touches my left, I am aware of it as a 'physical thing.' But at the same moment, if I wish, an extraordinary event takes place; here is my left hand as well starting to perceive my right, *es wird Leib, es empfindet*" (166). How does Merleau-Ponty interpret this phenomenon henceforth? From the point of view of an ontology of the flesh, the decisive question is no longer that of its mode of givenness to a consciousness, but that of its mode of being in and for itself. What determines this mode of being is *reflexivity*—and no longer merely the *reversibility* of touching and touched. In *Phenomenology of Perception*, Merleau-Ponty cautiously affirmed that the body "tries to touch itself touching" (*PP* 93 [translation modified—Tr.]), but without success; and if he alluded to a "reflection," it was only metaphorically. Here, on the contrary, he does not hesitate to take the decisive step and conclude from the preceding description, "Thus I touch myself touching; my body accomplishes 'a sort of reflection'" (*S* 166). How could I *touch* myself *touching*, palpate my own palpation, have contact with my own "tact"? What I touch is still my hand, a given part of my body, and not my own touching! And yet Merleau-Ponty goes further: "My right hand was present at the advent of my left hand's active sense of touch" (*S* 168). What does "to be present at" mean here? And furthermore, *who* is present at? Can "my right hand" "be present at" anything at all? Without overlooking all these difficulties, we must understand the reasons that suggest these formulations. They were teleologically inscribed in the assertion that the body perceives. If the body perceives, if it is a subject, it must be an immediate and continuous relation to itself, and hence it must receive the traditional attributes of consciousness, reflection for a starter. There is no embodiment of the mind without a corresponding mentalization of the body. But we must go even further. Since the flesh is ontologically a third dimension, irreducible to the distinction between subject and object, it is universalized until it becomes the name of the being itself. This universalization of the flesh can avail itself of a basis in Husserl. "When we say [Husserl says!] that the perceived thing is grasped 'in person' or 'in the flesh' (*leibhaft*), this is to be taken literally: the flesh of what is perceived, this compact particle which stops exploration, and this optimum which terminates it all reflect my own incarnation and are its counterpart" (*S* 169). There is therefore a flesh that 'reflects' my own flesh, and this is why reflection here is no longer only an immanent reflection (in the sense of the immanence to itself of a consciousness), but rather transgresses the division between nature and mind. The relation between flesh and the world itslef takes on a specular cast, for "from now on we may literally say that space itself knows itself through my body" (*S* 167 [translation modified—Tr.]). *Literally?* This sensible that knows itself is the very body qua sensible and sensing; it is the sensible-sensing qua body. But is this body identical with space *in general*? Or is Merleau-Ponty just talking about the spatiality of one's *own* body? Probably so, but not exclusively. "If the distinction between subject and object is blurred in my body . . . it is also blurred in the thing, which is the pole of my body's operations . . . thus woven into the same intentional fabric as my body" (*S* 167). One sole intentional fabric interlaces the thing to my body: the latter "is caught up in the context of my body, which itself pertains to the order of things only through its fringes or periphery" (*S* 168). But where, then, are the boundaries between the world and me? Are we not in full hylozoism? Or rather, have we not entered into a new form of idealism, an idealism of the flesh?

How is it possible to move from an ontology of the flesh governed by the reflective model, and freed from any subordination to another constituting level, to an ontology of the sensible in general that extends the paradigm of reflection to the world itself as a whole, in which my body plays no more than the role of a thread in a fabric, to borrow Merleau-Ponty's image? The author of *Signs*, in any case, oversteps the difficulty and unhesitatingly takes the plunge: we must show that the flesh and the thing—but not the object—belong to one selfsame sensible weave. This is what objectivism naturally was incapable of: not only the objectivism of the sciences, for which an *I* as "pure 'knower'" is able to "grasp all things without remainder—to spread all things out before itself—and to 'objectify' and gain intellectual possession of them" (*S* 162), but also what remained of objectivism in Husserlian idealism. This double insertion or this double inscription that later Merleau-Ponty will call "chiasm" and "intertwining"—does it not destroy intentionality? "Certainly there is a problem here. What will intentionality be then if it is no longer the mind's grasping of an aspect of sensible matter as the exemplification of an essence, no longer the recognition in things of what we have put there?" (*S* 167). We must, in order to address this issue, give up the very concept of *hulē* that conditioned through and through Husserl's characterization of the flesh. Flesh is no longer the substrate of sensations, but the locus of an undivided "sensing," cutting across the distinction of the senses and understood as a relation of totality between the subject and its world.[47] But above all, the extension of reflexivity to the sensible as a whole and the insertion of the thing and of flesh into one sole reticulation leads to extreme difficulties when it comes to elucidating the status of others in perception. Does not carnal idealism lead to a carnal solipsism? The question may be raised with good reason in view of the formulations—often extreme—of Merleau-Ponty. "My body annexes the body of another person in that 'sort of reflection' it is paradoxically the seat of" (*S* 168). Indeed there does not seem to be any fundamental difference here, in Merleau-Ponty's view, between the act in which my right hand witnesses the birth of touching in my left hand, and the one in which it touches the flesh of others. It suffices, for example, that I shake the hand of someone else to immediately and without remainder perceive it as a prolongation, as it were, of my flesh. "The other person appears through an extension of that compresence [of my two hands]; he and I are like organs of one single intercorporeality" (*S* 168). These analyses, however, suffer no lack of coherence; they flow logically from prior decisions. Since the true subject is corporeal, the other cannot give himself to me as a spiritual source constituted on the basis of a first esthesiological stratum; in short, it is no longer a question of constituting another mind for a mind, but another man for a man (*S* 169). The dynamics of *Einfühlung*, with its moment of perception, and its moments of coupling by resemblance and of analogizing transfer by appresentation, is powerless to account for it, for all "'*Einfühlung*' goes from body to mind" (*S* 169), and consequently remains abstract. "If the other person is to exist for me, he must do so to begin with in an order beneath the order of thought" (170). The intercorporeality must already take place at the level of sensibility. And it is precisely because flesh transcends the partitions between the objective and the subjective that it also transcends those between mine and yours. The "annexation of the other" to my flesh is inseparable from a depersonalization of the latter. It is because my own body already harbors within it an anonymous dimension, which will be stressed even more strongly in *The Visible and the Invisible*, that "the barrier between us and others is impalpable" (*S* 174). My flesh is not constituted before that of the others as the condition for a higher constitution; and conversely "the constitution of the others does not come after that of the body, others and my body are born together from the original ecstasy" (*S* 174). Husserl did not manage to account for the fact that the other is presented to me *perceptually* at the level of the flesh; Merleau-Ponty attempts to unpack all the consequences of this fact. And since the flesh no longer refers to private sensations and their immediate localization, but to an originary intersensoriality, the sharp division between the senses also disappears. "I see that this man over there sees, as I touch my left hand while it is touching my right" (*S* 170). But is it possible to abandon so easily both the sensualism that dominated Husserl's definition of flesh and the idealism that irremediably left the other subjectivity outside the sphere of ownness? If flesh is entirely defined by its reflexivity and if the latter remains the privilege of subjectivity, it is hard to see how we can escape a solipsism of a new variety. Unless we can slip from description into imagery. The transposition of Husserl's concepts here has as its limit the generalized transfer of the metaphor. The increasingly marked metaphorical style of Merleau-Ponty is not the result of a contingent idiosyncrasy: it has a significance primarily *philosophical*, indissociable from a thought and method of which it forms the rigorous correlate.

The Ontology of Flesh in *The Visible and the Invisible*

Is it possible to have a concept elaborated in a transcendental context bear the full weight of a critique of its original context? Does the adoption of flesh as a master concept allow us truly to exit the idealism and the objectivism that are as the Janus Bifrons of Husserlian phenomenology? In order to delve into these problems, it is worth examining the most rigorous and radical attempt Merleau-Ponty made in this direction—his posthumous and unfinished work, *The Visible and the Invisible.* On the subject of the concept that is the most central to that entire undertaking, Merleau-Ponty wrote, "What we are calling flesh, this interiorly worked-over mass, has no name in any philosophy" (*VI* 147 and 139). This assertion also obviously applies—first and foremost—to Husserl's phenomenology. In order to grasp the meaning of this caveat, we must try to perceive, behind the recurrence of the descriptions (sometimes even to the point of being word-for-word), the new change of perspective that is taking place. It is a question this time, beyond doubt, of positively elaborating the ontology of flesh of which "the philosopher and his shadow" afforded us scarcely more than a hint of the possibility. What is at issue, to this end, is to take a position resolutely beyond the distinctions of consciousness/object, phenomenal body/objective body, subject/object, mind/nature, external/internal, and constituted/constituting. The physicist and the psychologist, in Merleau-Ponty's view, make the same error, when they both adopt, as a "pre-scientific prejudice," "the ontology of the Κοσμοθεωρός and of the Great Object correlative to it" (*VI* 32). Against such an ontology, it must be shown "that the being-object and the being-subject conceived by opposition to it and relative to it do not form the alternative, and that the perceived world is beneath or beyond this antinomy, that the failure of 'objective' psychology is—conjointly with the failure of the 'objectivist' physics—to be understood not as a victory of the 'interior' and of the 'mental' over the 'material,' but as a call for the revision of our ontology, for the re-examination of the notions of 'subject' and 'object'" (*VI* 22–23). How can this renewed ontology be formulated?

In any case, it doesn't leave behind the descriptions of the flesh of the earlier works from which Merleau-Ponty takes up and re-orchestrates the main elements: "veritable touching of the touch" (*VI* 133–34), "carnal adherence of the sentient to the sensed and of the sensed to the sentient" (*VI* 142), "texture that returns to itself and conforms to itself" (*VI* 146). If there is an added nuance here, it is in the expression of a reservation—albeit a slight one—concerning the literalness of these formulations. Indeed, "if my left hand is touching my right hand, and if I should suddenly wish to apprehend with my right hand the work of my left and as it touches, this reflection of the body upon itself always miscarries at the last moment" (*VI* 9). A reservation about their literalness, probably, but not about their well-foundedness, because that inability, as is immediately pointed out, "is not a failure" (*VI* 148), or at least if there is a failure, "this last-minute failure does not drain all truth from that presentiment I had of being able to touch myself touching" (*VI* 9). Elsewhere it will no longer be a question of a "presentiment," but of an "imminent" experience, yet never realized in fact: "In fact I do not entirely succeed in touching myself touching, in seeing myself seeing, the experience I have of myself perceiving does not go beyond a sort of *imminence*" (*VI* 249). I am always *at the point of* feeling myself feel without ever succeeding, but that impossibility does not contradict the truth of that experience *that I cannot actualize*! This "justification," however difficult it may be to accept, is capital, because it gives us the key, in a sense, to the phenomenological concept of flesh: "My body does not perceive, but it is as if it were built around the perception that dawns through it; through its whole internal arrangement, its sensory-motor circuits, the return paths that control and release movements, *it readies itself, as it were, for a self-perception*, even though it is never itself that it perceives or itself that perceives it"(*VI* 9 [CR's emphasis; translation modified—Tr.]). There is a coincidence of self with self, a pure self-affection, an immanent reflexivity that is, in all feeling, what makes it possible, and flesh thus makes a circle with itself, it is built entirely on a mirroring of itself, there is a "fundamental narcissism" (*VI* 139) of all feeling, of which the experience of self-contact is the revealer par excellence. To what extent are we still on phenomenological ground, here, if "imminent" experience takes precedence over actual experience, if it is not the fact that has value of law, as in all actual description, but law that prevails over the fact by virtue of a *sui generis* necessity?

Whatever the response to that question may be, the experience of self-contact no longer appears here as one experience among others, essential for the apprehension of my body as flesh; it becomes *the paradigm for all experience*. There is not a sensing turned toward the world by which external things are given to me, and a sensing of what is "my own" by which my flesh is apprehended, but the essence of sensing is the sensing of what is my own.[48] All sensing is constitutionally turned toward the self and devoted to self. "To touch is to touch oneself" (*VI* 255), to see is essentially to see *oneself*, and so on. "To touch *oneself*, to see *oneself*, accordingly, is not to apprehend oneself as an ob-ject, it is to be open to oneself, destined to oneself (narcissism)" (*VI* 249). In short, to feel that one feels, to see that one sees, to touch oneself touching, is to feel *period*, to see *period*, to touch *period*. This reflection, naturally, is no longer a property of consciousness, but of the body as such. "Reflexivity must be understood by the body, by the relation of the body to itself" (*VI*, 246 [translation modified—Tr.].) Here, the *de facto* impossibility of a perfect coincidence of touch with itself, this experience on the point of being completed that always fails at the last moment, far from contradicting carnal reflexivity, brings it a paradoxical confirmation: for in order for there to be fundamental adhesion of flesh to itself, there must first be dehiscence or hiatus; "fission that already takes place in the touch (duality of the touching and the touched) and that, with the mirror (Narcissus) *is only a more profound adhesion to itself*" (*VI* 256 [CR's emphasis; translation modified—Tr.]). It is because flesh never coincides entirely with itself, but is always basically turned toward itself, that flesh can be defined as "*a mirror phenomenon*," and that the mirror, as implement, can be considered a simple "prolongation," in the world, of my own flesh (*VI* 255).

Under these conditions, it is not only the implement-mirror that is the prolongation of my flesh in the world, but *the world itself.* An assertion to be taken rigorously and literally: "To touch is to touch oneself. To be understood as: the things are the prolongation of my body and my body is the prolongation of the world, through it the world surrounds me" (*VI* 255). Since things are but the prolongation of my body, because of that coiling over itself of the sensible that makes all feeling a feeling *of oneself,* since in going toward things flesh, at bottom, does no more than adhere more profoundly to itself, it is the whole world that becomes flesh at the very moment the flesh becomes world. Merleau-Ponty never stops scrutinizing the possibility of this double movement. "The thickness of the body, far from rivaling that of the world, is on the contrary the sole means I have to go to the heart of things, *by making myself world and by making them flesh*" (*VI* 135 [CR's emphasis; translation modified—Tr.]). This crisscross movement of the flesh and the world, this "intertwining" in which the hold of my flesh on the world is a hold of the world on my flesh, is what is also designated as "chiasm" in *The Visible and the Invisible* (*VI* 261). There is a twofold captation of the world by my flesh and of the flesh by the world: the world is modification (or mundification) of my flesh; my flesh is reflexivity, turning of the world back over on itself, mirror phenomenon. The fundamental "narcissism" of my flesh is extended here to the entire *cosmos*, which feels itself, touches itself, sees itself through the flesh. Merleau-Ponty goes very far in the affirmation of this cosmic narcissism of the flesh, taking up once again the phrase from *Signs*: "We are the world that thinks itself" (*VI* 136, note). It is only if we bear in mind that the reflexive model governs all these analyses that we can also understand what appears, at first glance, to be a *non sequitur*: the transition from the twofold captation (or chiasm) to the model of the mirror. "The seer being caught in what he sees, it is again himself he sees" (*VI* 139 [translation modified—Tr.]). It is one thing, it seems, to assert that flesh, a precipitate of invisible in the visible, is accessible to itself only in the body—*its* body; it is another to assert that bodies *in general* are nothing but the specular reflection of myself and that in surveying them it is still myself that I am examining. To stop at this incoherence, however, would be to remain on the surface of the text, to miss the necessities that command its economy and that derive from both the pregnancy of the reflexive model, the only one able to make the flesh into the locus of a concrete *subjectivity*, and from the internal logic of the *Leib* concept since its Husserlian institution. Flesh, because it is without limits, does not, at bottom, admit of any outside-the-flesh. Its a-cosmism almost inevitably calls for its extension to the entire cosmos. Merleau-Ponty's approach, if it advances further in this direction, is at least consequent with that of his predecessor.

It is because the "reflexivity" of touch extends to the totality of the sensible, and first of all to vision, which is its synecdoche, that Merleau-Ponty can assert that what I look at looks back at me, to the point where I cannot say which of us is seen and which is seeing. "The vision he exercises, he also undergoes from the things"; "as many painters have said, I feel myself looked at by the things" (*VI* 139) and, consequently, "it is by the world first that I am seen or thought" (*VI* 274 [translation modified—Tr.]). It is very difficult to say, at this stage, whether this generalized narcissism means the pure and simple dissolution of others in a world that has become wholly an extension of my flesh, or whether, on the contrary, my flesh has been so changed that everything that appears to me shows me, henceforth, a rudimentary face, and *looks at me* in a kind of silent companionship. "There is an *Einfühlung* and a lateral relation with the things no less than with the other. . . . Like madmen or animals they are *quasi-companions*" (*VI* 180). And indeed we can detect two movements here, which, though opposite, are nevertheless of a piece: one by which the flesh is mirrored in the world, transforming it into a quasi-mirage, and another by which the flesh is depersonalized to the point of including in it an essential alterity, that of the other no less than that of things. "What we call flesh," Merleau-Ponty writes, is "this innate anonymity of myself" (*VI* 147 [translation modified—Tr.], 139). Here it is as if one paradox called for another, as if it were possible to palliate the aporia of a thoroughgoing egological cosmology with a depersonalization of the ego itself. But in any case, the other loses all privileged status; he is no more than a fold in that fabric by which flesh and world appear as variants of one single sensible texture. In this narcissism without Narcissus, the world itself appears constructed according to a specular model, to the point that I can no longer say "who sees and who is seen" (*VI* 139). All the differences are abolished in the immediacy of a Nature that calls to mind that of Schelling, in which the same and the other, touch and vision, my flesh and that of things, seem indiscernible.

The Flesh as Openness to Vertical Being

But even more than Schelling, it is Heidegger that is of decisive relevance here. The "middle path" of the new ontology, beyond the opposition between subjectivism and objectivism, opens a new domain of research in which the flesh is no longer thought of as one ontic region among others, and not even, after the example of the transcendental ego, as *the* region par excellence, the arch-region (*Urregion*) of all regions, but—such is the fundamental innovation of *The Visible and the Invisible*—as the openness *to* the world and *of* the world according to the diversity-unity of the sensorial registers, or as the openness of Being itself. "Carnal being" designates "a prototype of Being" (*VI* 136), in the sense that "it is the perceptual life of my body . . . that accomplishes the primary openness to the world" (*VI* 37). "This perceptual world," Merleau-Ponty adds, "is at bottom Being in Heidegger's sense" (*VI* 170), the Heideggerian *Seyn* thought as *Offenheit*. Thus, we must think "the *Umwelt* of a carnal subject as *Offenheit*, as *Verborgenheit* of Being" (*VI* 185) and consequently apprehend flesh as the site of a difference that we must perforce qualify as "ontological." This difference is not thought as the unconcealing overwhelming (*entbergende Überkommnis*) as it tends to hide itself in the arrival that keeps itself concealed (*sich bergender Ankunft*) of the entity,[49] but—since the "visible" here has a tendency to designate the sensible in general, by virtue of a primary and basic intersensoriality[50]—as the disjunction between the invisible and the visible that remains a modality of their junction and of their co-belonging. The invisible in its primordial acceptation, as it is inseparable from the phenomenon of the flesh, designates neither a contingent privation of visibility, a *de facto* invisible as in the case in which one object blocks our view from another, nor an absolute invisible, inaccessible *de jure* to the senses, in the manner of a Platonic ideality; it is rather "the invisible *of* this world," as Being is always the Being *of* an entity, or yet again "pure transcendence, without an ontic mask" (*VI* 299). In this respect, it is rather what accompanies all visible and makes it possible as such, "its own and interior possibility, the Being of this being" (*VI* 151). The withdrawal of the invisible is the condition for the coming of the visible to visibility, so that, between them, there is not opposition, but rather mutual belonging: what Heidegger sometimes calls *Zwiefalt*, fold. And indeed Merleau-Ponty also speaks of a "fold" that he compares to a "central cavity of the visible" articulating, at the heart of vision, "these two mirror arrangements of the seeing and the visible, the touching and the touched" (*VI* 146), or yet again, in a similar sense, of a "folding back," of an "upholstering," of an "invagination" (*VI* 152 [translation modified—Tr.]). The flesh, as at once seeing and seen, invisible and visible, is precisely the point where this difference is knotted and articulated, where the invisible is manifested as what makes the visible visible, and the visible as that which recovers the invisible by masking it. "The flesh is, we said, the dehiscence of the seeing into the visible and of the visible into the seeing" (*VI* 153). This fold of the visible and the invisible as it is formed at the level of the flesh is precisely what has a tendency to be obscured by objectifying thought, by the idea that the visible is arranged and displayed completely to a high-altitude overview, and, correlatively, our bodies entirely accessible for a Κοσμοθεωρός. By contrast with this ontology (or ontics) of the ob-ject, the flesh can be given only marginally, in an irreducible latency, as primordial invisible, the matrix of all visible: it is accessible exclusively to an *indirect* ontology (*VI* 179).

It is precisely because the flesh cannot be thought of as a particular ontic region, but only as the openness to/of a "vertical" and "wild" Being—that is of a Being prior to all "representation" and all "objectification" (*VI* 253)—that it makes sense to designate the world itself as "flesh," without annexing it, however, to one's own body. What Merleau-Ponty calls "flesh of the world" cannot be thought, in this respect, as a mere extension of my body. Indeed, the openness of the lived body is not in the first instance a characteristic of man or of his soul; it must be understood independently from all anthropology, because "it is indeed a paradox of Being, not a paradox of man, that we are dealing with here" (*VI* 136). And conversely, "When we speak of the flesh of the visible, we do not mean to do anthropology, to describe a world covered over with all our own projections, leaving aside what it can be under the human mask" (*VI* 136). The openness of Being no more involves anthropology than the extension of the flesh to the sensible in general involves anthropomorphism. The Heideggerian concept of "openness" comes to the rescue of what might appear to be a subjective hyperbole. The "one's own body" / flesh of the world distinction must be understood prior to all distinction between subject and object; it is more originary than that distinction. Not only is the flesh of the world not identical with the flesh of the body (*VI* 261: "flesh of the world—distinct from my flesh"), and in particular, it is "sensible and not sentient" (*VI* 250), but additionally, it cannot be approached in the same way. How, then, may we interpret their difference? Precisely as *the* difference, the one that unites and articulates the visible and the invisible, the one that distinguishes them in relating them to each other. Every flesh is at the same time body, every seer is at the same time visible—the flesh is the invisible *of* the visible, the intangible *of* the tangible, etc. To assert that the flesh is also body is henceforth no longer to think of it as an *object* in the world. The ontology of flesh presupposes the rejection of all objectivistic ontology, since it is born of the latter's insufficiencies. The determination of the body (*Körper*) as an *object* is no longer, as Husserl thought, a legitimate determination, but a *falsification* of its mode of being. Under these conditions, what Merleau-Ponty henceforth calls "flesh of the world" is nothing other than the body itself thought outside all horizon of objectivity, removed from all high-altitude thinking and from all falsifying ontology (or ontics). The flesh of the world is the body—both my own and that of things—qua seen, touched, *as long as it is no longer belongs to any objectifying approach* (*VI* 250–51). The flesh is therefore the place where this difference is carved out, that "spread" [*écart*] or that "shift" (*VI* 148) between the seeing-invisible, the touching-intangible, on the one hand, that is, that effulgence, that marginal presence-absence, and the visible, the tangible, on the other hand, that is, its own presence to itself as body, its incorporation in the world, amidst things. Between my flesh and the flesh of the world, there is henceforth a difference analogous to the one that is established between the openness of Being and the coming into presence of beings.

As a result, the problem as it is formulated in Merleau-Ponty is not so much, as in Husserl, that of the distinction between flesh and body, as two superimposed layers of being, each one with its irreducible status, but rather that of their fusion, or their paradoxical unity. In opposition to the ontic model of superposition by layers, we must set the ontological model of a lateral relation: "there is no *hierarchy* of orders or layers or planes. . . . This in virtue of the 'ontological difference'" (*VI* 270). The unity of flesh and the body, that texture that joins and disjoins them in one and the same movement, must be able to be exhibited, of course, without recourse to a transcendental ego. The foundation of this unity must be discovered at the level of the flesh: "The body is one sole body in its two phases, it incorporates into itself the whole of the sensible and with the same movement incorporates itself into a 'Sensible in itself'" (*VI* 138). This is why any relation of mere subordination between flesh and body, any relation of derivation, must also be rejected, along with any relation of inclusion of the latter in the former. "We have to reject the age-old assumptions that put the body in the world and the seer in the body, or, conversely, the world and the body in the seer as in a box" (*VI* 138). Neither flesh nor body are parts of the world, layered realities coming from a constitution by strata[51]; rather it is a matter of two poles at the heart of one single dynamics; a dynamics in which the flesh becomes world, and the world flesh. Thus the intentional correlation, which is the nonreal inclusion of the noema in the noesis, the immanence of the object in consciousness qua transcendental correlate of the latter, becomes, on the occasion of this metamorphosis of the concept of flesh, the inextricable intertwining of the sensible and the sentient. From a correlational structure we must move to a "circular" one (*VI* 138), since the flesh refers back to the body and the body to the flesh in an endless whirlpool: I can only feel myself feeling on the occasion of a sensible in actuality, and there is no sensible but by the intermediary of a sentient. But as for this spiral, Merleau-Ponty must admit that it is distorted or vitiated from the start, deflected in any case in the direction of the *percipi*, which enjoys a true primacy over the *percipere*. "It is by the flesh of the world that in the last analysis one can understand the lived body [*corps propre*]—The flesh of the world is of the Being-seen, that is, is a Being that is *eminently percipi*, and it is by it that we can understand the *percipere*" (*VI* 250). But then does not this primacy of the *percipi* have ruinous consequences? Does it not indicate that there is no circularity or narcissism of the flesh, that the flesh is not of a mirror-like construction, that what I experience on every occasion is always already a *body*—be it mine or that of things—and *solely a body*? That therefore I cannot return on the hither side of this evidence, the evidence of the world on which my perception is built, that there isn't anything like a precosmic flesh prior to its apprehension as body, that there is no possible return to the origin, no coinciding of flesh with itself, no proto-spatiality prior to that of things, and that the temptation of this return to the origin that constituted the basis of Husserl's approach of constitution must be repudiated in its very principle?

How can the relation between flesh and world be circular and at the same time decentered? How can it be maintained, by virtue of the reflexive paradigm, both that "my body is made of the same flesh as the world" (*VI* 248) and that these two fleshes are "distinct" (*VI* 261), by virtue of the ontological paradigm? How can we envisage both the touching of touching as the ultimate model of all perception, and the discrepancy [*écart*] and noncoincidence with itself as the primary phenomenon? For the flesh, on the one hand, is defined by its immanent reflexivity, by its immediate givenness to itself, and on the other hand, qua site of *Unverborgenheit*, it is inseparable from its own concealment; "to touch *oneself*" is not "to reach *oneself*, it is on the contrary to escape *oneself*, to be ignorant of *oneself*, the self in question is by divergence *(d'ecart)*, is *Unverborgenheit of the Verborgen* as such" (*VI* 249). Is it unconcealment that must be understood here on the basis of the reflexivity of flesh (Merleau-Ponty italicizes the reflexive pronouns) or the other way around? Is there not something basically incompatible in these two models? How are we to reconcile the mirror of Narcissus with the openness of vertical Being? How can we accommodate the one to the other, if sensible reflexivity must always, after all, refer to a subject ("reflection" is what "qualifies [us] as subjects of vision" [*VI* 202]), and if, on the other hand, the conceptuality of Being as *Offenheit* is elaborated precisely in order to break away from a metaphysics of subjectivity (and its attributes: egoity, reflexivity, immediate presence to self)? How can we make a philosophy of carnal *generality*, in which the latter is understood as primordial unity of different fleshes, cohabit with a thinking of the oneness (*Einzigkeit*) of Being that is neither general nor particular,[52] is nowise an ontic generality subsuming a manifold of beings, and cannot be captured by these distinctions? Is there not, here, a kind of "grand écart" in the realm of thought, in preparation for a *saltus mortale*?

Must we not rather conclude from these difficulties that *The Visible and the Invisible*, despite its terminology of Heideggerian inspiration, remains faithful, fundamentally, to a perspective of transcendental inspiration, which it limits itself to inflecting slightly? True enough, Merleau-Ponty seems to criticize sensualism, and, to a degree, Husserl's theoreticism. But does he really break with his idealism? To think of the flesh as the origin of the world is still to think of it as not being of the world, to confer a status of origin on it, and thus retain the main features of the transcendental attitude. This attitude resides in a "well-known" paradox, which Merleau-Ponty already stressed in *The Structure of Behavior*. "Every theory of perception tries to surmount a well-known contradiction: on the one hand, consciousness is a function of the body—this is an 'internal' event dependent upon certain external events; on the other hand, these external events themselves are known only by consciousness. In another language, consciousness appears on the one hand to be part of the world and on the other to be co-extensive with the world."[53] It suffices to substitute "flesh" here to "consciousness" to enter into the problematic of *The Visible and the Invisible*. In transcendental idealism, the ego for which the world appears is at once the origin of the world, since it constitutes it, and a part of the world, since it constitutes itself qua empirical ego, by means of a worlding apperception. And the same is true of flesh, which remains, in this respect, a quasi-transcendental. It is at once a "part of the world," as it perceives itself as a body alongside others, is visible and touched, and "coextensive with the world," since the world as such—including the flesh itself as a body—appears only by its intermediary. Thus, to the a-cosmism of the pure ego there corresponds a no less radical a-cosmism of flesh. "Where are we to put the limit between the body and the world, since the world is flesh?" (*VI* 138). The flesh, as origin of the world, can have no contours in the world; its limits are those of the world itself that, being made up of its stuff, appears included in it. Being without limits, it has no skin, either[54]; its ubiquitous presence is a radiance whose center is everywhere and circumference nowhere. Nor does it have matter. It is without beginning or end. It is that "glorified body" (*VI* 148) that stands opposed to the "momentary body" and of which we should probably say, as of the pure Husserlian ego, that it has neither birth nor death. There is an eternity of flesh extending even to its temporalization ("Posit the existential eternity—the eternal body" [*VI* 265]) that is the rigorous analogon of the eternity of the transcendental ego.[55] To be sure, this flesh is caught up in the nets of the world, is enveloped in it, this intertwining defines it. But there are distinctions that do not admit of a middle term: transcendentalism cannot be amended by a position that denies it. And when Merleau-Ponty asserts, "in part I retained the philosophy of consciousness" (*VI* 183), the reader can arguably ask what this "in part" means. Is it not precisely this "in part" that continues to be audible in assertions such as "my consciousness . . . is sustained, subtended, by the prereflective and preobjective unity of my body" (*VI* 141–42)? "Sustained" and "subtended" here refer back to Husserl's *Unterlage* [substrate]. How can one at the same time affirm and deny such a relation of subordination? How can one abandon the sensualism of the *hulē* and yet retain the *Unterlage*, which forms, literally, its infrastructure?

And if it really became necessary to decide between understanding flesh as reflexivity and understanding it as the openness of vertical Being (*Verborgen* of an *Unverborgenheit*) it is always to reflection that primacy would be granted. Just as all reflection, for Husserl, harbored an unthought and was consequently inseparable from an *Ichspaltung*, a splitting of the *I* into thematic (reflected) ego on the one hand, and "anonymous" (reflecting) ego on the other, similarly, the latency of flesh for itself is always of the order of a truncated reflection, or of the impossibility of an integral reflection (impossibility itself, attested to by a "hyper reflection" [*VI* 38, 39ff]). Merleau-Ponty himself decides the issue in stressing that the dehiscence or "fission" that takes place in the touch confirms the preeminence of reflexivity and "is only a more profound adhesion to Self" (*VI* 256). It is reflexivity that makes flesh thinkable as the very site of *Offenheit* and not vice versa. But probably what most radically prohibits all reconciliation between the conceptuality of the ontological difference and that of sensible reflexivity is the fact that for Heidegger the thinking of Being always means a thinking of its intrinsic *finitude*. Nothing similar in the case of flesh: its innerworldly unlimitedness, its ubiquitous radiating, its glorious eternity by virtue of which it is, like nature "at the first day" (*VI* 267) makes it at least difficult to imagine what its finitude could be.

It is therefore because flesh remains, despite all Merleau-Ponty's denials, a quasi-transcendental, that the attempt to acclimatize the ontological difference to a post-Husserlian framework seems destined to fail. That failure is not initially or mainly bound to the unfinished state of *The Visible and the Invisible.* But then, the question arises as to what the abandonment of transcendentalism, from the point of view of a philosophy of the body, may mean. Does it not necessarily amount to the abandonment of "flesh"? To abandon flesh—without renouncing philosophy: is this project consistent? To answer these questions, we must return to our starting point.

Touching and the World

Must we confer primacy to the experience of proprioception for the apprehension of the body qua one's own? This is not at all certain. What I touch, in self-contact, is always only a skin, having a specific warmth, flexibility, and texture; it is my hand qua thing in the world. To be sure, since that hand is mine, I also feel the contact of my other hand at the very moment when my hand feels it. That is all there is. To speak of "flesh," of "reflexivity," of "coincidence of touching with itself" is to have already ventured too far. What is going on here *is basically no different* than what goes on in any other contact with things. To touch a thing, to engage into tactile relationships with it, is always necessarily to be touched by it as well, to initiate a reciprocal contact with it. Tactile perception appears, in this respect, as an event structured by two poles, that of the world and that of me, in continuous interaction with one another. In grasping properties of things, I also apprehend myself as being affected by them, and conversely, I only experience myself tactilely—which also means corporally—on the occasion of my contact with things. Therefore touch is simultaneously and *inseparably* proprioceptive and exteroceptive: on the occasion of an exteroception, I also perceive myself, for without that proprioception, there would not be any possible exteroception, either. This implies that even before all experience of a self-contact, touch offers me the perception of my own body and of my body as *my own*, of my body as *mine*, in an original and originary way in the experience of my contact with what is foreign to me. Indeed, as Eugène Minkowski stresses, "touch contains an element of reciprocity, and that is what, along with the affirmation of being, distinguishes it from all other fundamental qualities. All that touches is touched, or at least can be touched. That is essentially what we translate with the word contact."[56] Touching things is always to be touched back by them. This is why all contact should be understood literally and etymologically as con-tact, that is, touch-with . . . in which I am inseparably touching and touched, in which I experience myself by exposing myself to things. By virtue of this element of reciprocity, perception is always a being-*with*-the-world rather than being-in-the world in Heidegger's sense; it establishes a communication with the world that is not, however, communion or fusion with it, and in which, by touching other bodies, I do not find myself—like Narcissus at his fountain.

This is why touch is immediately "cosmological," according to another expression of Minkowski's: it exposes us to the world in its primary alterity. It is the sense of exteriority par excellence—that is, of foreignness to me, and it is only by its intermediary that the world appears solid, palpable, to us. As Condillac already remarked in his *Treatise on Sensations*, "The sensation of solidity is unlike the sensations of sound or color or smell," in which "the soul naturally perceives its modifications in which it finds itself and itself only"; it is, on the contrary, the first sensation "by means of which the soul passes beyond itself,"[57] jolting against an exteriority that it cannot assimilate. What Condillac asserts here of the soul is valid first of all—and probably *only*—for the body: since what I touch is always outside me, including when I turn my touching toward myself, and since I only apprehend myself, in touch, as a skin, with its depth of bones and muscles, the touch is always "eccentric" to itself, as Maurice Pradines writes,[58] it attests to the essential eccentricity of my own body to itself. The skin is, in a certain sense, the being-outside-itself that defines the body as such, and it does so because it is not only, with respect to my body, the first tangible and the tangible par excellence, but also the medium of touch, that which opens it onto things. It is because the body appears always fundamentally outside itself in the experience of touching (that eccentricity to itself being what we call "skin") that it also has an "inside" that is as the outside of its outside, "darkness stuffed with organs" that is the intangible of this body, not the intangible as a modality of active touching, but the inaccessible, the out-of-reach, the other side of a skin.

Consequently, what applies to the touching of things applies no less to the touching of my body: the tangible of my body is always my body as "other," my body as skin. This is why touch is always an initiation to the world, and therefore to spatial exteriority. Indeed, if there is no spatiality without exteriority, and if all exteriority necessarily presupposes an alterity vis-à-vis me—then touch, the sense of alterity, is the sense of exteriority itself, and consequently of space. What an analysis of touch leads to putting in doubt is precisely the idea that, just as we have a body that is our own, we also have a space that is our own, an originary, preobjective space, that of our flesh as the substrate of localized sensations, preceding the objective space of things and making possible its constitution. Maurice Pradines has formulated this critique with particular insight in his *Philosophie de la Sensation*: "No more than simple contact," he writes, "does the double contact reveal to us a space that is *ours*. We only know 'our' corporeal space by the organs that allow us to touch other bodies and at the moment and to the degree that we touch them. This amounts to saying that this space has nothing 'ours' about it, that it is foreign, or that it only belongs to us to the extent that we feel foreign to ourselves. In short, there is but one space that is external to us, because it is exteriority itself, and our body enters it without any privilege."[59] This amounts to saying that if my body has a space, that space, given the natural eccentricity of touch, is always necessarily further outside than any alleged "inner space." It is this depth carved out in the world itself that I explore with my fingertips through the elasticity of a skin, through this permeable yet closed membrane, and I can feel its closure precisely to the extent that I feel it *from the outside*. What I feel in this way can no longer be a private flesh, a primary and primordial locality prior to worldly determinations; henceforth it can no longer be anything but a *body* that is itself, in its own way, in the midst of things, but without being any of them, nor comparable to any of them, since it alone possesses the notable property of being in turn touched by what it touches, and in initiating with the world a true con-tact.

If the touch, then, like all the other senses and perhaps even more so, is a cosmological sense—if what I touch is never a private, a-cosmic flesh, but a body-in-the-world qua organ of con-tact—it follows that the experience of self-contact, from which Husserl and Merleau-Ponty set out, can no longer have any privilege. Since all exteroception already possesses in itself a proprioceptive dimension, since I can never touch anything without being touched myself by it, the experience of self-contact is not required for my apprehension of the body as *mine*. It is derived and subordinate to a more originary experience, namely the one by which, by exposing myself to the world, I apprehend myself in my relation to things. *It is not the pure self-affection of a monadic "I" that grounds the possibility of my contact with things, but only the reciprocity of an originary con-tact that makes the proprioceptive experience thinkable.* "The 'me and the other' in their 'reciprocity' is a much more primitive phenomenon than the 'I' all by itself, which, at bottom, means nothing at all. . . . This reciprocity included in the touch also determines the particular way of being of everything that is; beyond this, it projects a reflection in the universe and makes it solid and palpable."[60] It is in its relation to palpable bodies that my body becomes palpable qua body, that it acquires a sensible relief; and this is no less true of the meeting of my two hands, in which each send back to the other, alternately, its own tactile consistency. It is always toward the other that my touch is oriented, and I always touch it as other; but in so doing, I also experience myself. The "self" given to itself in the touch is none other than the pole of a relation that, by relating to itself, is reduplicated. Husserl, incidentally, was very close to recognizing this, but he interpreted the flesh immediately as an autonomous stratum of phenomenality, and thus he forged the artificial problem of the constitution of the flesh by the intermediary of the ego, and of the world by the intermediary of the flesh.

But it is not enough to abandon the primacy of self-contact for the constitution of the body as mine; or rather, that abandonment inevitably entails another, that of its incompletely constituted character. Indeed, if all tactile perception is structured in relation to two poles in such a way that it is always the experience of oneself as embodied and experience of the world in its fundamental exteriority and solidity, then we must make the claim that my body appears to me necessarily *in its entirety* by the intermediary of my contact with what is foreign to me—air, water, solid matter. When my body is immersed, for example, I feel more vividly what the French rightly call my "carnal (or corporeal) envelope," I feel this membrane that binds me to the world by separating me from it. And, similarly, athletes today often use suits made of synthetic materials that allow them to better perceive, to keep a closer "contact" with, their own movements. In all these cases and in many others, we have no need for self-contact to feel our body *as being "ours"*: its "ownness" is given to us originarily in and by the eccentricity of feeling. If I needed to touch myself—let alone touch myself touching—to be aware of the unity of my body, not only would that awareness always have to be begun afresh, like Penelope's task, but, always remaining incomplete, it would be strictly impossible: I would never have more than a phantom-body. I would haunt the world with a spectral presence incommensurable with that of things.

And furthermore, the consequences of these criticisms must be even more radically drawn. It is not only necessary, as we have just seen, to reject the primacy of self-contact and the incompleteness of the carnal constitution, but first and foremost *the primacy of touch as such* for the apprehension of what it is no longer possible to call my "flesh." Indeed, according to Husserl, flesh "can be constituted originarily only in tactuality,"[61] and this is the case because touch is considered the only one among the senses capable of relation to itself, of initiating this sensible reflexivity of touching-touched by which the body is defined as my own. Now, not only does the possibility of that so-called "reflection" appear doubtful, to say the least, but it must be maintained that it is not just touch but *all* the senses, or better yet, all the perceptual systems,[62] that possess a double dimension, proprio-and exteroceptive, that is to say, that constitute the differentiated yet undivided modalities of the permanent encounter of a living organism with its environment. Incidentally, it may be a particularity of our languages that led Husserl and his heirs to miss this phenomenon. In French, but also in German, the dimension of con-tact, hence of reciprocity, is much more marked in the case of touch than in that of the other senses. We say that to touch is always to be touched by what one touches, while we do not say that to see is to be seen, nor to taste, to be tasted. But this remark is purely linguistic. It means that "to touch," as opposed to "to see" or to "to taste," can have as its grammatical subject the names of persons as well as the names of things. I touch things, but things touch me as well—with varying degrees of violence. That does not imply, however, that things touch me *in the same sense* in which I touch them. The rules of usage of the verb "to touch" do not tell us anything about the phenomenological state of affairs. We must rather maintain that there is just one touch, the one of which I am the active or passive subject. Through it, a relation is established from me to things. Now, if we look closely, the same is true of the other senses. To see is not just to see something, to take a bird's-eye view on the world. It is also to see the relation that things have to my body, to see myself, at the occasion of things, as situated in the world in which they appear to me, to explore a portion of the world according to that unique perspective that is born of the singular position of my body amidst other bodies and by virtue of which it appears itself to be inscribed in the spectacle of their array.[63] Similarly, to hear is not just to register a noise, but also to localize a sound source, which can only be performed in reference to my body. I apprehend myself at the occasion of a noise by perceiving the relation of the sound to my organs. To hear is always to hear something *somewhere*, to situate a sound source in relation to myself. In all cases my body is co-perceived, co-given. It is an integral part of perception that has a necessarily relational structure. The dimension of reciprocity and contact, far from constituting a particularity of touch, applies basically to all the senses. There is no reason, in this respect, to want to draw from a particularity of the grammatical use of the verb "to touch" more than it can give us, and especially not a whole implicit phenomenology.

What happens, under these conditions, to the *unity* of what we must call—distinguishing it both from the Husserlian "flesh" and its "objective" counterpart, the *Körper*—my "body"? We can answer this question in omitting the so-called carnal "reflexivity." In truth, there is no problem here, as long as proprioception and exteroception are thought of as being co-originary. I recognize this foreign and exterior-to-the-other hand as being *my* hand, not because my other hand "coincides," so to speak, with it in feeling (according to the reflexivity of the touching-touched), but because this *reciprocity* of the con-tact through which I apprehend myself by apprehending things *is doubled in each hand*, consequently making possible their grasp as "mine." *It is therefore the doubling up of a reciprocity (that of contact) that allows me to apprehend my body as mine in the experience of auto-con-tact, which actually is always the experience of a hetero-contact.* The doubling in question is therefore always the doubling of a *relation*, the relation in which my body and the world constitute complementary poles. It is in the world and nowhere else that my body relates to itself according to the reciprocity of the double con-tact and that it experiences itself as exterior to itself, commensurable with things and exposed to them.

This reciprocal exteriority of my members is what brings about the singular *vulnerability* of my body, which is thoroughly open to the world in an originary dehiscence, and incapable of coinciding with itself in pure immanence. For where immanence reigns, there is not yet space, since space, as Pradines remarked, is nothing but exteriority itself. That wound from which my body cannot recover and that founds all the others, this bath of exteriority, this primitive exposure, is spatiality itself. This is why touch is already, in itself, initiation to space. The empiricists, especially Condillac, did not explain the experience of proprioception otherwise. Indeed, let the hand place itself on any part of the body, on the chest, for example; "Then its hand and its chest will be distinguishable by the sensation of solidity that they send mutually and *that places them necessarily outside of each other*. But in distinguishing its chest from its hand the statue will find itself in each, because it will feel itself equally in both."[64] How will the soul recognize what is "its own" in members that are yet different and external? To answer this question, Condillac forms the concept of "response": as soon as it (the statue) places its hand on parts of its body, "the same sentient being replies in some way from one to the other: *this is myself.*"[65] In order for my body to be able to respond to itself in this way, it must already differ from itself—it is necessary that it not coincide with itself in a pure immanence. For there can be no response unless it is between two, where there is already difference. The body is already the other of itself, that exteriority to itself is what defines it: it is originary exteriority to itself insofar as it responds to itself, that is, insofar as the "self" of exteriority constitutes itself in and by such a response. Therefore, between the double touching of my hands and the simple touching of an external thing, there is only one difference, "that the 'I' which responded in the one case ceases to respond in the other," that therefore there is no longer a double, but a simple reciprocity, a simple con-tact. In this way, Condillac concludes, the statue can experience "that it is not all that it touches" and assign limits to its body, limits that are not drawn in the prior unboundedness of a flesh, but are born immediately from con-tact, at the surface of the skin.

But if the body is originarily eccentric to itself, if it is constituted in itself by an originary being-outside-itself, if its unity, such as it is attested at the level of touch in the reciprocity of the double con-tact, is always inseparably of concordance and foreignness, if it can only apprehend itself through a skin that places it from the outset outside itself, if my hands can only grasp themselves as twins because they are also experienced, *at the same time*, as *membra disjecta*—then we must definitively give up the Husserlian concept of "flesh" and replace it with a corporeity as experience of the world, the self-intimacy of which can no longer mean anything other than a modality of this primary eccentricity, the eccentricity by which takes place from one member to another a reciprocity of response. Completely exposed to the world, my body is the sensible (and sentient) modality of this primitive being-outside-oneself; if it is experienced in a self-contact, it is precisely because the latter is self-con-tact, that is, self-experience of itself always already traversed by the rays of the world, self-estrangement by which I exist alongside things and with them. What the phenomenon of self-contact thus reveals is that there is no proprioception without a corresponding exteroception, that reciprocity of contact is never without the exteriority of touching and touched, and that in them or with them—reciprocity and exteriority—my body appears open to the world in an originary dehiscence without ever being able to retrieve or constitute that openness. An openness of an originary being-outside-oneself and for itself, the body can only appear to itself in the midst of things; it is always of the world and in the world, and it is in this, precisely, that it escapes itself: constituted by the openness, the fault of its exteriority, it cannot play the role of constituting instance. What must be called "body" is precisely this disjunction, at the level of touch, of the touching and the tangible, this impossibility of all coincidence, and thus, this primary eccentricity to oneself, or yet again this openness that precedes and prohibits all distinction between constituting and constituted, between transcendental and empirical.

6

The Ecological Phenomenology of J. J. Gibson

> And do you think that you can know the nature of the soul intelligently without knowing the nature of the whole?
>
> **—Plato, *Phaedrus*, 270 c.**

Merleau-Ponty, in an article in which he reflects on the philosophical contributions of *Gestaltpsychologie*, points out that although "classical psychology made perception a real deciphering of sense data by the intelligence, a beginning of science, as it were,"[1] the superiority of the "new psychology," that of the Berlin School, consists precisely in the fact that, for it, "perception is not a sort of beginning science—an elementary exercise of the intelligence." And he adds, "We must rediscover a commerce with the world and a presence to the world which is older than intelligence."[2] The work of the American psychologist James J. Gibson, himself a friend of Koffka and an adept of the Gestalt approach during its early stage, illustrates that fundamental thesis perfectly—even better, probably, than does *Gestaltpsychologie*. Perception, in his work, is conceived as a permanent encounter, as primordial communication of a living organism with its life environment. It is never considered as a science in its infancy.

In the mid-1940s, Viktor von Weizsäcker had preceded Gibson on this path. "Authentic perception," he writes in *Der Gestaltkreis*, "constitutes in a way a joint meeting between me and the world."[3] To understand perception in this way, as encounter, is to no longer understand it as knowledge, that is, to oppose a tradition that in the West stretches back to Plato's

Theaetetus; it is, more precisely, to replace the paradigm of *objective* knowledge, which is but one with the advent of modern science and philosophy, with a very different paradigm, stated by Weizsäcker as follows: "In opposition to the old formulation, 'knowledge reaches something objective,' stands the new, 'an *I* encounters its milieu.'"[4] What kind of consequences follows from so radical a reformulation of the problem of perception, on the condition we take it seriously?

But to begin with, what does it mean to say that perception is of the order of an encounter, and of one that takes place between a living being—a human being, eventually—and its surrounding world (*Umwelt*)? Every "encounter," in the most general sense of the term, is an event. But every event is also, in its own way, an encounter. At least this is the case as long as it happens to someone, as long as it lends itself to being experienced. The "experience" in question is not only the reception of sense *data*. It differs from the concept of "experience" inherited from empiricism. It is not an experience in the sense of lived experiences belonging to a subject, but of a life experience we cope with according to who we are. What is at stake in such an experience is the world in its moment of appearing, as it arises *for me*. Very different from this are the concepts of "event" and "experience" underlying the psychology of empiricist and associationist origin—which still today furnishes many contemporary endeavors in the field of the "cognitive sciences" with their conceptual framework in order to understand and explain perception. These accounts rest on atomic events of a physical nature, called *stimuli*, neurological processes of conduction thanks to which these stimuli are conveyed to the brain, cognitive processes enabling us to decode this information and to transform it into sensation, and, finally, annexed systems thanks to which the sensations are combined or associated by the brain in such a way as to bring about perception itself. This analysis, constantly repeated since Descartes and Locke, rests at least as much on assumptions about the body and the mind, the status of causality, and the relations among the different sciences (physics, physiology, psychology), as on a specific analysis of events. According to this analysis, every event boils down to an atomic, meaningless and structureless occurrence. By interrelating "events" of this sort by means of a concept of "cause" borrowed from classical physics (the univocity and universality of which is presupposed, by the way), these undertakings aim at accounting for perception as a psychological or mental phenomenon. As Whitehead noted at the beginning of the last century, "Every special science has to assume results from other sciences. For example, biology presupposes physics. It will usually be the case that these loans really belong to the state of science thirty or forty years earlier. The presuppositions of the physics of my boyhood are to-day powerful influences in the mentality of physiologists."[5]

These two concepts of "event" are not only different—they are incompatible. The perceptual event in the first acceptation is global, undivided, harboring a certain vital meaning for the one experiencing it, structured temporally and spatially, but also structured according to two complementary poles, that of the living being and that of its environment, in close connection with each other. The event in the second acceptation is an elementary, measurable, physical fact, causing the appearance of a corresponding mental fact, understood in the same way. The first option sets out from the relation of the living being with its world as from an originary given, impossible to reconstruct out of more primitive elements. The second is installed, with a clear conscience, within the "subject/object" distinction, and depends inevitably on a theory of mental representation. The first holds that the finality of perception lies in the vital function it has for an organized life form; the second assigns to perception a mere function of knowledge. The first approach may be qualified as "ecological," the second as "cognitive." Let us inquire further into their respective presuppositions.

The Cognitive Approach to Perception and Its Aporias

In order to understand the problems raised by the cognitive approach, we must return to the origin of its formulation, that is, to the beginning of the modern era. Its elaboration is inseparable from the scientific and epistemological revolution associated with the names Kepler, Galileo, and later Newton, and from the philosophical revolution contemporaneous with them, inaugurated by Descartes and further pursued by Locke. It is no accident, in this respect, that the birth of modern optics in Kepler's *Ad Vitellionem paralipomena* was approximately contemporaneous with the formulation of the law of falling bodies and the principle of inertia in Galileo's *Dialogues Concerning Two New Sciences.* Here and there, geometry is applied to problems traditionally belonging to psychology and physics in Aristotle's sense. In assimilating the eye to the optical apparatus of the camera obscura, Kepler thinks he has established that man sees according to geometrical laws—those laws that enable us to calculate the convergence of light rays inside the eye, thanks to a series of refractions. Nature, according to Galileo, is made up of solids endowed with gravity, in relative movement with respect to each other in the infinite, homogeneous, and isotropic space of Euclidean geometry. In both cases, according to Galileo's famous phrase, nature is written in mathematical language.

To the unification of the field of knowledge under the impetus of a mathematized physics there corresponds the elaboration of a monist ontology of nature as a manifold of objects amenable to calculation and measurement. The only reality is that which yields to the criterion of objectivity inaugurated by the new physics. This elaboration of a neutral ontology of the object in general is the true conquest of the modern era. The revolution it inaugurated, in this respect, was not the advent of a new theory of subjectivity or of innerness, as has sometimes been claimed, since we find already in the Middle Ages, in Duns Scotus in particular, an extremely precise and developed theory of mental representation, based on the distinction between *esse objective* and *esse reale*. The originality of the modern age lies rather in the subordination of the old theory of mental representation to a unified doctrine of "objective" knowledge (in a sense entirely unrelated to the scholastic doctrine of the *objectum*). There is only one nature, and it can be understood—or decoded—in its entirety by means of a universal science, a *mathesis universalis*. The only field eluding such an objective knowledge, because no longer considered a part of objectified nature, was that of the interiority of the mind. The Cartesian distinction between *res cogitans* and *res extensa* and the Lockean distinction between primary and secondary qualities did no more, in a sense, than draw the ultimate consequences from that new "representation of nature," as Heisenberg calls it.[6] These distinctions ended up in the radical separation of ego and world, subject and object, and, at the heart of the "subject," in the opposition between body and mind. Thereby a new alternative appears, which today seems insuperable: that between a conception that envisages the mind as a part of nature, knowable by means of the same principles as it (materialism, naturalism), and conception supporting the opposite claim (idealism).

The philosophy of perception, from Kepler to our day, rests entirely, in its very formulation, on the emergence of the new concept of objectivity and the monist ontology of nature underlying it. Indeed, the theory of perception sets out from physical processes to understand the causality they exercise over the senses, and through them, over the brain. It thereby establishes a strict correspondence among objective physical phenomena, sensors, and psychological contents. To the chemical phenomena there correspond the senses of taste and smell; to the mechanical, optical, and acoustic phenomena there correspond the senses of touch, vision, and hearing. At the same time, the idea comes to light that the physical cause of the stimulation is never known in itself, since what is known is only its *effect*, that is, the corresponding neurological influx. If the senses can teach us something about the outer world, this can only be thanks to what

Johannes Müller called "the specific energy of the nerves."[7] What we know through the sensations are never objective stimuli, but only the state of our own nervous systems. The sensation, as Müller says, is nothing more than "the consciousness of the state of a nerve." It follows that the causes of our sensations can never be known directly, but only *deduced* thanks to "unconscious inferences" (Helmholtz), whence the origin of the distinction between purely inner *sensations* and the *perception* of the outer world, with all the discrepancies and distortions separating the two. According to this conception, these discrepancies attest to the cognitive processes through which the brain "interprets" and "decodes" the sensations.

The first difficulty raised by this doctrine is purely internal to it. Neither the stimulus nor the sensation—that is, none of the so-called "causes" of perception—can be defined without already involving perception, that is, without a mention of their so-called "effect." Here we find ourselves in the presence of a paradoxical situation, without analogy in classical physics, in which a cause cannot be defined independently of its effect, which contradicts the *physical* concept of "causality" as nomological interdependence among *several* phenomena. Now, it is precisely on this concept of "cause" that the proponents of the cognitive approach want to base their reasoning, by virtue of their monist ontology of nature and their unconditional allegiance to the modern concept of "objectivity."

This paradoxical situation is well illustrated by Newton's theory of optics. On the basis of the property of white light's being decomposable into a polychromatic spectrum by means of a transparent prism, Newton wants to advance a purely physical definition of color that makes a different index of refraction correspond to each hue of the spectrum (he distinguishes six of them, probably by analogy with the seven tones of the musical scale).[8] Thus, "to the same degree of refrangibility ever belongs the same color, and to the same color ever belongs the same degree of refrangibility."[9] This definition is ambiguous, and Newton is not unaware of it. It leaves out perceived color. This is why its author feels the need to correct it immediately: "For the Rays to speak properly are not coloured. In them there is nothing else than a certain Power and Disposition to stir up a Sensation of this or that Colour. . . . So Colours in the Object are nothing but a Disposition to reflect this or that sort of Rays more copiously than the rest; in the Rays they are nothing but their Dispositions to propagate this or that Motion into the Sensorium, and in the Sensorium they are Sensations of those Motions under the Forms of Colours."[10] But then are we not going from one extreme to the other? To the purely physical definition of color by the index of refraction of light—or as we would say today, by the wavelength of the electromagnetic spectrum—Newton simply *juxtaposes* a definition of color as sensation. Sometimes it seems that color can be equated to a property of the physical stimulus, light, or to the object insofar as it can reflect light selectively by virtue of its own physical properties, and sometimes color is defined as a sensation aroused by light stimuli. Newton's efforts to overcome this tension between the objectivist and the subjectivist aspect of his definition of color have something desperate about them. Recourse to the idea of "disposition," here, introduces more confusion than clarity. Indeed, color is purported to be not so much an objective property of the rays themselves as their ability (or disposition) to provoke, in the subject or in the sense, such and such a sensation. But what is a disposition? Something can only have a disposition in reference to something else (or to itself in another respect) that is able to actualize this disposition. For example, salt is soluble in water; it possesses this dispositional property—letting itself be dissolved—only in relation to this other element: water. Physics tries to explain this phenomenon by reducing this dispositional property ("water-soluble") to simple (nondispositional) physical properties pertaining to the molecular structure of salt and to the chemical interactions taking place when it comes into contact with other substances. But this is precisely what is excluded in the case under consideration. Colors can only be dispositional properties of light (or of objects insofar as they reflect light), *in reference to the subject* that perceives them and that alone can actualize such a disposition. This link cannot be further explained by means of purely *physical* analyses. To say that color is a dispositional property is therefore to include in the definition of the stimulus itself the perception this stimulus is intended to explain. Now, if color in its physical definition already includes a reference to color as perceived, the former cannot *causally explain* the latter. What is lacking here is the distinction among *several* phenomena that is the requirement for any nomological connection between them. Furthermore, color cannot really be at once objective and dispositional. If it is dispositional, it includes a reference to the perceiving subject—it is not purely "objective." It is the very idea of an optical physics, and the distinctions supporting it—between cause and effect, subject and object—that are problematic from the start.

This tension between objectivism and subjectivism is the true legacy of Newton's optics. It can be found nearly everywhere in the most contemporary philosophy of perception. It is present in every theory that attempts to explain perception on the basis of physical stimuli by virtue of a linear relation of causality. It was already in Kepler, when, in order to discuss retinal stimulation, he resorted to the notion of "image" and expressed the alleged "cause" of vision in terms of vision itself.

However, to this first difficulty threatening the internal coherence of his doctrine, others are added of an experimental nature. In order for the distinction between stimulus, sensation, and perception to make sense, it must be assumed that each sensorial receptor is able to transmit specific information. The specificity of the sensation (which must be distinguished from perception) is strictly a function of the specificity of the stimulus. Now in spite of in-depth research, nobody has ever been able to discover specific tactile receptors, for example, for the "sensations" of hot and cold, smooth and rough, or even for pain. In the case of the senses of smell and taste, this absence of a simple correlation between the elementary chemical properties and the sensed odors or tastes is even more striking. As Gibson writes, "For more than a century, physiologists have been trying to discover the chemical causes of sweet, sour, salt, and bitter tastes, and of the bewildering array of smell qualities. . . . Sugars are sweet, more or less, but so is saccharine. Acids (hydrogen ions) are sour, but so are other chemicals. Salts are often but not always salty. . . . The chemist cannot predict what the smell or taste of a chemical will be until he tries it, for no theory is available. Conversely the psychologist cannot explain a smell or taste in chemical terms for he does not know what the stimulus is."[11]

The situation might seem different in the case of vision. We know that the retina has only two kinds of photoreceptive cells, called cones and rods; as a consequence, it does not have specific receptors for each different color. Yet the hypothesis has long been made that it is possible to establish a strict correlation between a wavelength of light and its perceived color. This hypothesis is doubly contradicted—on the conceptual and the empirical levels. On the conceptual level, because the wavelengths form a *continuum*, while perceived colors form a *scale* structured around primary hues (red, yellow, blue, and green) and exclusive hues (red/green, yellow/blue). Nothing in the electromagnetic spectrum corresponds to these structures—on the empirical level, because all attempts to establish in the visual field a univocal relation between wavelengths and colors have failed. This is what has been shown by the experiments of Edwin Land,[12] among others. Different-colored paper squares are placed on a board in random order; then one of these squares (called "Mondrians") is chosen—a yellow square, for example. The experimenter measures separately the percentage of short, middle, and long wavelengths reflected by this piece of paper; then he regulates different light sources in order to project the same wavelengths in the same proportions on another "Mondrian," a white square, for example. Henceforth this square reflects the same percentage of short, middle, and long wavelengths as the yellow square originally chosen. Will this square be perceived as yellow by the observer? The response is an unequivocal no: it will continue to appear white. Color possesses a relative constancy under very variable lighting conditions. The composition of light in a location within a visual field does not determine the color perceived at that location. The reason for this phenomenon is probably that we never perceive isolated colors, but only relations between colors in changing conditions of lighting and in a given visual context. As Gouras and Zrenner observe, "Color vision is not concerned with analyzing the wavelength composition of light reflected from an object's surface but with exposing an object in its background. . . . The colors we see in objects are those that best set them off from their backgrounds under the prevailing light conditions."[13] This implies that different optical stimuli can give rise to the perception of the same color and identical stimuli to the perception of different colors. Under these conditions, the notion of "stimulus" is more puzzling than helpful in order to explain these phenomena. It postulates a series of atomic processes, whereas perception seems rather characterized by a form of syncretism or fundamental holism.

But then it is not only the notion of "stimulus" that must be critiqued, but that of "sensation" itself. Indeed, sensation is nothing but the "subjective" counterpart of stimulation. The cognitive approach of perception postulates the possession, by the subject or the animal, of elementary sensations, the combination, association, or computation of which would give rise to perception itself. But is it possible to describe the situation in that way? First of all, what are these sensations themselves? Are they of a neurophysiological kind or of a psychological kind? Are they atomic *perceptions* or are they situated under the threshold of perception? The objection has often been raised that these alleged "sensations" could only be postulated after the fact, through a process of abstraction setting out from perception itself. They describe no more than an impoverished perception, in very specific conditions of experimentation, or particular phenomena such as visual *afterimages*. What is a pure, visual sensation that is not already a perception of something? On the snow, in conditions of heavy fog, an immobile onlooker, compelled to a monocular vision, might well be unable to grasp anything, in all directions, but homogeneous white light, without any form or recognizable object. This would almost be a null degree of perception, a perception of *nothing*. Would he have a *sensation* of light? This conclusion rests on a sophism. An almost null perception is not at all a nothing of perception: it is still a perception, but an extremely impoverished one. Not to be able to see anything is not the same thing as not seeing; it is still a modality of vision. At no moment is this observer in the presence of a *pure sensation*. Hence the idea that perception is based on sensation has nothing necessary about it in itself. James J. Gibson's strength is to have drawn this consequence with the greatest clarity: "Sensation," he writes, "is not a prerequisite of perception."[14] Perception is not a matter of organs undergoing a certain external stimulation and transmitting sensations to the brain, but rather of "perceptive systems," most often comprising several hierarchically interconnected organs and integrated with the organism as a functioning totality. While receptors are stimulated, an organ is activated and a perceptive system *goes into activity*: the analysis of perception can only take place at this last level.[15] In sum, stimulation by physical energies is only a necessary, and not a sufficient, condition for perception. The latter is always performed by an animal endowed with perceptual systems in a given environment.

Shouldn't this critique of the sensation of the empiricists lead, then, to a calling into question of the cognitive model? If there are no atomic sensations, there is no cognition either, strictly speaking—that is, no calculation or unconscious computation through which information is processed—first coded, and then decoded. This is Gibson's basic idea. Sometimes he explains it in a questionable form—that of a naïve or, as he says, "direct" realism. To him, the information present in an environment is already structured in such a way that the role that can be attributed to the nervous system of the animal is not to confer an order on atomic sensations, nor to reconstruct an array putatively lost at the moment of stimulation, but only to control the perceptive systems in such a way that they can function *optimally* and thus gather the information already contained in the environment as a permanent source of stimulation. Two main types of argument are furnished to support this thesis. The first is comparative: the bee has a remarkable perception of certain characteristic properties of its environment, while possessing no organ of sight that would make possible the formation of a retinal image (the study of which becomes incidental for the study of vision). The second consists in showing that in most of the cases in which something like an "unconscious inference" at the basis of perception is assumed to exist, the reasons inviting us to do so reside in an insufficient description of what is in fact *given* as *already available* information in the phenomenal field. In other words, the study of perception has as a prerequisite a *phenomenology* (though Gibson doesn't use the term), and it alone is capable of showing that everything necessary for perception is already available within perception itself.

One of the most striking examples Gibson gives us on this subject is that of the phenomenon of distance in visual perception. Since Descartes and Berkeley, it has been admitted that it is impossible to *see* distance directly, because the distance of objects to the eye of the observer cannot be indicated in the retinal image. If we take that so-called "image" as our starting point to understand the phenomenon of vision, the problem becomes that of how a three-dimensional perception can be obtained from the two-dimensional "image" formed on the back of the eye. Descartes's solution, in his *Dioptrics*, consists in making distance perception dependent on an angular relation between the two visual axes, that is, on a judgment of the mind grounded on a "natural geometry."[16] This description envelops at least three debatable presuppositions: (1) that perceived space is three-dimensional Euclidean space; (2) that the eye is in fact comparable in its functioning to a camera obscura and that the retinal image is the starting point for any adequate explanation of vision; and (3) that the problem of distance perception must introduce something more than what is given in the image, namely "an action of thought," "a reasoning quite similar to that used by surveyors."[17] Against these presuppositions, Gibson shows very convincingly that the perception of an object's distance has nothing to do with the reconstruction of an abstract three-dimensional space on the basis of pure *data* of sensation. Distance is rather a structural property of the visual field itself; it is seen directly. How does Gibson establish this point? An experiment he carries out at the end of World War II consists in posting an observer in the middle of a field that is ploughed, without furrows and extending almost out of sight, and in asking him to assess the height of a stake fixed in the ground at distances ranging over a distance of one kilometer. It is generally assumed that the phenomenon of the size constancy has a tendency to "break down" beyond a certain distance: the size of an object would then be regularly underestimated. Gibson's experiment invalidates this hypothesis. At a great distance, the estimation of the height of the stake becomes *variable*. The size of the object looks less definite, *but not inferior*. In any case, the estimation continues to be relatively accurate. This accuracy rests on the grasp, by the observer, of certain structural invariants. Like all objects, the stake hides a part of the ground in which it is standing. In the example chosen, the texture of the ground is more or less uniform. It increases in density in the same visual angle with increasing distance. But the proportion of ground of analogous texture that is hidden behind the stake remains constant. The observer posted at one end of the field does not have to make any particular calculation; he grasps this invariant directly. "No matter how far away the object was, it intercepted or occulted the same number of texture elements of the ground."[18] There is no visual space without a ground, that is, without a continuous surface whose texture density or texture "compression" varies as a function of distance, that is, as a function of the optical angle, and against which all the other surfaces stand out. Gibson noticed this principle of ecological optics very early, and called it *texture-perspective*.[19] Another structural invariant, in the cited example, is the point of intersection of the stake with the horizon. This point corresponds exactly to the point of observation. The height of the eyes of the observer is in a sense "carried over" or indicated on the stake at the precise point of its intersection with the horizon, and this is true *whatever the distance may be*. In sum, "For any distance the proportion of the stake extending above the horizon and that extending below the horizon was invariant."[20] This invariant does not have to be inferred or deduced. It is given at the perceptual level. This does not mean at the level of the retinal image. The size of the object in that so-called "image" is not relevant to the understanding of the phenomenon of visual constancy. The latter is based on relations that, even though they may pass unnoticed in ordinary perception, structure it and are given in it alone. Things happen quite differently, for example, in the evaluation of the size of objects up in the sky, where these invariants are missing. In this case, the assessment rests on a true *judgment* based on acquired knowledge. Certain soldiers must undergo specific training to be able to estimate the distance of enemy planes: they must learn to recognize the silhouette of a plane, identify the model, and, thanks to a knowledge of its size or wingspan, evaluate its altitude. The errors are sometimes considerable. But this form of inferential knowledge—and this is the point—cannot be taken as a paradigm for ordinary perception.

If the information concerning distance was not given by perception itself, it is hard to see how it would be possible to acquire it. Indeed, on what basis, on what knowledge, would the first inference be based? Unless we assume the existence of an innate knowledge, which most theoreticians of consciousness reject, it must be obtained from prior inferences. Thus we are drawn into an infinite regression: cognition presupposes cognition to account for cognition.[21] This in no way excludes that the *perception*—not the cognition—of these structural invariants may be more or less fine and be capable of progress in the course of the development of the individual: we can learn to see better what is before our eyes. Learning, here, is a process of differentiation.[22] But this precludes that *seeing* already in itself puts into play a different type of knowledge, a knowledge of a different order, unless we take "knowledge" [*co-naissance*] here in Claudel's sense of a reciprocal birth,[23] by the interplay of a continuous encounter. If perception is such an encounter, this presupposes a complete change of paradigm from the point of view of an approach to perception, and in particular the abandonment of the concept of "knowledge" [*connaissance*] and of the cognitive model in general.

The Ecological Approach to Perception: Beyond Psychology?

To conceive of perception as an encounter is to start out from the "mutuality" or reciprocity of the animal with its environment as from an ultimate given,[24] impossible to analyze further into its "elements," prior to the distinction between subject and object. It is to start out from a "fundamental relation," as von Weizsäcker called it, the basis of which is unobjectifiable[25]—that is, removed from objectivity and objectification on which, since Galileo and Descartes, the modern ontology of nature rests. That relation, he adds, "is the ultimate authority." By it, we are "attached and glued, so to speak, to our environment" in such a way that our bodies and their perceptual systems remain constantly in contact with certain parts of the world, unless an overpowering disturbance comes along to disassociate them. Weizsäcker designates this phenomenon as "coherence."[26] All perception manifests not only an intrication of movement and perception, but also a coalescence of the *I* and the environment in which either the perceived movement is sacrificed to the benefit of one's own movement, or one's own movement and the perturbation it engenders in the perceived phenomenon are sacrificed in favor of the perceived phenomenon: thus, for example, "as long as the butterfly interests me, I neglect, I sacrifice the other movements engendered by my own movements."[27] Here it is not at all a question, of course, of a subjective choice, but of a reciprocal and complementary obfuscation that is a structural given of the relation itself, and that von Weizsäcker compares, for good reason, to Heisenberg's uncertainty principle.[28] In the perception of movement, "it is either the identity of place that is sacrificed [that is, of my own movements] or that of the thing perceived."[29] There is a basic intrication of the subject and the object. "Intrication contains within itself this necessary condition that the activity by which something appears to me does not itself appear, and that while something appears to me, I am also active."[30] I can let the abovementioned butterfly fly away, but as soon as I try to fix my look on its fragile, vibrant silhouette, I must sacrifice both the movement of my own eyeballs and the background movement to its relative stability. This is what makes the amateur photographer surprised at seeing that the background of his wildlife snapshot, as frozen by the camera—unless artificially corrected—is blurred, although he saw it sharp. Why do we not see the retinal image tremble while our eyes spell out the world? Because this so-called image is not in fact what we *see*. The coherence here is the primary phenomenon on the basis of which the breaks in this coherence may subsequently be understood.

These analyses foreshadow in a striking way certain traits of Gibson's ecological approach, beginning with his critique of the objectivist ideal of classical physics and its uncritical application to the problem of perception. *To speak of perception only makes* sense*, in Gibson's view, at the level of the dynamic relations that unite the animal with its environment.* This is a question of *definition*, that is, a fundamental issue. A mind does not perceive, nor does a body, but only a living being immerged in its milieu. It is necessary, under these conditions, to dismiss as a starting point a physics of stimuli, and, while not ignoring the givens of physics, to pose the problem of the refraction of light or of the diffusion of sound at the relevant level: in short, to elaborate an ecological optics, chemistry, and acoustics. These latter rest on the abandonment of the notion of "stimulus" in its classic acceptation, as a punctual, meaningless, momentary phenomenon. Such stimuli make sense only for a physiology of sense receptors; they are identifiable only in the very artificial conditions of the laboratory—but become irrelevant at the level of the perceptual systems themselves. Perception is not involved with a mosaic of such stimuli, the organizational principles of which would have to be explained in a second stage, but with a flow of stimulation structured from the start. Perceived light, for example, is not a mere electromagnetic radiation such as it is conceived through abstraction by physics, but a diffuse illumination structured by multiple and complex phenomena of reverberation, filling the transparent medium of air and water. It already possesses an order of its own, made up of contrasts, transitions, and configurations displaying information about their source. This is what Gibson calls an optical array. It is because classical psychology and physiology conceived of stimuli along the lines of too simple a physical model that they were led to understand perception as a construction of the mind. Their error lies in a lack, and not in an excess, of physics. The physics of perception is not that of the manuals; it is far more complex.

For Gibson also, as for von Weizsäcker before him, reciprocity is the fundamental phenomenon. This implies first of all the proscription from analysis of all linear causal schemes between more or less elaborated stimuli and responses. Neither perception nor behavior, as Goldstein has forcefully established, can be characterized in terms of "responses." Perception and behavior in their mutual intrication are both finalized activities that can only be described at the level of the cohesion of an organism with an *Umwelt*: they presuppose a circular causality, or, in von Weizsäcker's vocabulary, a "cycle of structure [*Gestaltkreis*]." It is unlikely that this causality could be described in terms of *input* and *output*—the terminology of cybernetic theory. As Gibson remarks, this distinction between nervous influx coming from the periphery, called "sensory," and influx coming from the center, designated as "motor," "is based on the old doctrine of mental sensations and physical movements."[31] It is fundamentally dualist. We must on the contrary maintain that behavior is constantly guided by perception and perception continually based on a behavior. Behavior, as opposed to a montage of reflexes, is neither stimulated nor commanded; it is neither purely voluntary nor involuntary. Indeed, "to say that some control is voluntary is to say nothing."[32] If behavior is, from the start, *controlled* perceptually and not *commanded* by the center, the theory of behavior based on the comparison between *feedback* motor commands and afferent *inputs* leads us astray. It overlooks a fundamental fact: all perceptual modalities are at once exteroceptive and proprioceptive. They inform us inseparably about ourselves and the world; or rather, about ourselves-in-the-world. Even vision, considered in general by psychology as one of the senses of exteriority par excellence, contains irreducibly proprioceptive and kinesthetic givens. These givens concern three privileged types of movement: that of the observer in relation to his environment, which Gibson studies under the rubric of "motion perspective"[33]; that of the limbs in their relations to the torso and head; and that of the head and the eyeballs. In each of these cases, Gibson shows that the deformations of the optic field occasioned by movements are of an *exclusively* proprioceptive nature and that they cannot be provoked by any other circumstance in the world.[34] Proprioceptive kinesthesis does not therefore correspond to any particular "sense," whose alleged sensory *data* would come exclusively from articular innervation and the sensibility of the internal organs. *All* perception is inseparably proprioceptive and exteroceptive, since it bears on *the relation* between an organism and its milieu. The definition of proprioception itself is formulated in relational terms: proprioception is "the consciousness of self that *accompanies* the perception of the environment."[35] This is why coherence is the fundamental phenomenon: it cannot be reconstructed after the fact by the comparison between efferent and afferent information. It is given from the start. Therefore it is presupposed by any other partial process.

Now, to insist on the presence of proprioceptive information in each of the different sensory systems is the same as showing the fundamental intrication of perception and behavior. Indeed, the distinction between "sensory" and "motor" may make sense at the level of the physiognomy of the sense organs: it becomes meaningless at the level of the animal. Movement has a constitutive role for perception itself, for the latter is essentially a grasp of invariants across a flow of variations. Here a double critique of

Gestaltpsycholgie takes place. The first criticism addressed by Gibson to the Gestalt school is the primacy it gives in the clarification of the principles of organization and segregation of the perceptual field, to experiences in which the observer is passive and immobile, more easily reproduced in the laboratory. Of course, the Berlin School did not fail to recognize the presence of dynamic forms of organization, as in the perception of a melody or in the stroboscopic phenomena analyzed by Wertheimer; furthermore, it thought of dynamism as providing the ground for the organization of any perceptual field; but it overlooked to a considerable degree the role played by bodily movement at the level of perception itself.[36] Koffka, Gibson notes, "made no reference to head turning,"[37] which allows structural modifications (modifications of the visual angles and mutual occlusion of surfaces) to arise in normal perception, that is, in perception taking place under natural conditions, in order for significant invariants to emerge. In the woods, for example, it is very difficult to distinguish, in the intertwining of branches, those belonging to a given tree. But as soon as the observer begins to walk, this intertwining automatically undoes itself, each leafy branch recovering its unity thanks to the angular hiding of certain surfaces.[38] Perception as an ecological phenomenon has to do with precisely this sort of phenomena, and not with the convoluted Gestalt illusions. These illusions for the most part have the essential flaw of being two-dimensional images, probably due to the tacit assumption that the two-dimensional retinal image is an adequate starting point for a study of vision.[39]

But *Gestaltpsychologie* has not only failed to recognize the constitutive role of bodily movement, replacing it by an abstract "dynamism" stemming from artificial conditions; it has misinterpreted the very idea of "structure" by virtue both of its physicalism and its intellectualism. In postulating an isomorphism, that is, a community of structure between physical, physiological, and psychic forms, it has merely endorsed the Cartesian dichotomy. Now, there are only perceptions, as Gibson reminds us, for a living being considered in its environment. As a result of its dualistic assumptions, *Gestaltpsychologie* has embraced the classical idea that two-dimensional vision is immediate and three-dimensional vision only mediate or derived, because it is obtained by the application of laws of field organization to a mosaic of excitations in themselves amorphous. Now, according to Gibson, vision is rather concerned from the outset with surfaces, angles, and solids and their temporal and spatial transformations. As for the "impression of a visual *field*, [it] involves a way of seeing of the most sophisticated sort,"[40] and cannot, as such, furnish any explanation of *normal* perception. What needs to be explained is not the vision of relief and depth on the basis of that of images, but, on the contrary, the perception of pictures—and their artificial depth—on the basis of the normal vision of an arrayed environment according to structural laws. *Gestaltpsychologie* is misguided, in this respect, by the equivocity of the notion of "form" (*Gestalt*), which can mean many different things: a form drawn on paper, a sketch, an outline, an abstract geometrical form, and the shape of objects the visual angle of which may vary, which can hide other objects and be hidden in turn by them, and so on. Gestalt psychology conceives of shape itself as a form among others.[41] It thus misses the specificity of vision *in its natural conditions*. This critique of Gibson's does not always do justice to the discoveries of the Berlin School, for which it must at least be said that it does not confuse the notion of *Gestalt* with those of "form" in the ordinary sense, of diagram, of contour, etc. *Gestalt*, as a dynamic structure, is rather *presupposed* by these latter. But the corollary of Gibson's critique is the following: *perception is not first perception of invariable forms, but of informal invariants.*

The vision of an environment consists indeed in the grasp or the "pick-up" of structures that only manifest themselves in or through a change, that is, rest on the living and dynamic relationship of the animal to its environment, or rather on the system whose two complementary poles are the body and the environment. These stable configurations can be evinced through a description of the optical field in terms of movement perspective, mutual occlusion of surfaces by modification of the visual angle, etc. They constitute the very object of vision. They do not correspond, Gibson maintains, to the *Gestalten* of the psychologists of form: they are formless.[42] What vision as apprehended in its ecological context attempts to grasp through the modifications of the ambient light from sunrise to sunset is not momentary forms, but invariants that are meaningful for the animal. For instance, a rodent will identify a potential predator by a certain number of structural features. To maintain that these structures are formless is to give a new solution to a traditional problem of the relation between the percept and the concept. The identity of a perception must not be sought in its relation to a concept, but strictly on the plane of perception itself, in the *perceptual* invariants structuring it; thus, what is seen is not the frontal or the lateral view of a cat, but the cat as such through its various presentations. Here the reader may have recognized the Husserlian problem of *Abschattungen*: in Gibson's view, their unity does not depend on an objectifying apprehensional act coming to inform a formerly given sensible material, but on laws immanent to the perceptual transformations themselves.[43] What is seen originally is not sensations, or forms, or "objects" in the Husserlian sense, but ordered transformations and their qualitative invariants.[44] When I read, for example, what counts is not the form of the letters or their disposition on the page; generally I do not even notice them, and I would be quite incapable of saying, for the page I just read, what typographic typefaces it was composed of or what the spacing was between the lines. What matters are solely "the distinctive features of letters and their combinations."[45] In this example—which is after all a reworking, in other terms, of very similar analyses by Köhler or Koffka—it becomes clear that the critique of *Gestaltpsychologie* does not simply mean its abandonment (the "forms" of the Gestalt psychologists are also, in many ways, "informal") but rather its reformulation in a new theoretical framework. The same is true of another key concept of ecological psychology: that of "affordance."

This notion is probably the transposition of Köhler's requiredness or Lewin's *Aufforderungscharakter* in a new conceptual framework. Indeed, if, on the one hand, the animal's movement, as *finalized*, takes on a constitutive character for perception itself, and if, on the other, what is perceived is always formless invariants for an animal in a given environment, these invariants cannot be without vital significance. Their "significance"—in a preconceptual, precategorical sense of the term—lies in the possible behaviors they afford: whence the neologism *affordance*. These implicit meanings are embedded into the perceived world from the start, before any theoretic act of knowledge. For example, the branch affords the monkey the possibility of hanging from it; it is a thing-from-which-to-hang in order to catch fruit or play. This theory of affordances contains many implications and epitomizes all by itself the main aspects of the ecological approach. First, it manifests the priority of action over knowledge and situates the problem of perception on this plane of action. Second, it tacitly implies that any definition of perception that does not take into account the ecological level of the interaction between a living being and its milieu is meaningless. Perception is not a neurological function of the brain, nor is it the passive reception of sensations, nor the active elaboration of perceptions by a "mind" considered in the abstract and indifferent to its life conditions. It is a *faculty* of the animal as such, considered not in isolation, but in its relation to a given milieu. Perception is an aptitude, a disposition of the animal—that of grasping significant invariants of its environment—and as such it can be the object of a learning process. As a faculty of the animal-in-its-environment, its meaning is relational. An affordance, Gibson insists, is neither subjective nor objective: by this word "I mean something that refers both to the environment and the animal in a way that no existing term does."[46] *Gestaltpsychologie*, because of its dualism, has failed to understand the true status of affordances:

these suggestions for action "are properties of things *taken with reference to an observer* but not properties of the *experiences of the observer*. They are not subjective values; they are not feelings of pleasure or pain added to neutral perceptions."[47] Finally, the idea of "affordance" confirms the coalescence or indivision of movement and perception, inscribing the ends of behavior in perception itself. "The perception of a goal, its affordance, controls locomotion in one way whereas the visual proprioception of the optical outflow controls locomotion in an entirely different way. The bee who lands on a flower needs to both perceive the flower and control his flight. He has to see an invariant environment in order to identify the flower, and to see himself moving through the environment in order to guide his locomotion. The perceiving and the behaving go together but they are not the same process."[48]

The richness of these analyses must not hide the theoretical difficulties they harbor. In rejecting stimuli, but in continuing to speak of an influx of stimulation, Gibson limits himself to shifting the problem rather than solving it; furthermore, the notion of "information" he uncritically makes use of holds him prisoner to a form of objectivism that his analyses were meant to challenge. Furthermore, Gibson is probably wrong in defining his own position as a variant of "realism," a "direct realism."[49] While believing thereby to emphasize the novelty of his theory, he is in fact reinscribing it entirely within the traditional alternative of realism versus idealism and overlooks to a certain extent its originality. This originality lies for the most part in the claim that perception is a process structured by two complementary poles, that of the self and that of the world, that is to say, a necessarily two-faced phenomenon, at once and inseparably proprioceptive and exteroceptive and, as a result, impossible to analyze according to the subject-object dichotomy. The perceptual process takes on a third status, neither objective nor objective, but relational. Such a "relation" does not derive from its relata: it precedes them and makes them possible. The relation is such, here, that its relata themselves are *relative* to each other. There is no animal except in relation to an *Umwelt* and no *Umwelt* except in relation to an animal. The ecological approach does indeed constitute, in this respect, a *conjoint* critique of idealism and realism. This is what Gibson's hesitations show when he comes to state the principles of his doctrine. On the one hand, he seems to retain the basic distinction of modern philosophy, when he asserts that perception belongs to the "objective pole" of experience, while the sensations, as purely occasional phenomena, "consciousness of the state of our nerves" (Johannes Müller), such as a ringing in the ears or an afterimage, belong to its subjective pole.[50] On the other hand, he insists on the fact that what is perceived, namely the environment and its affordances, "is neither 'subjective' nor 'objective.'"[51] Indeed, *the pick-up of information as such always depends on the animal*, both as species and as individual. "In short, whether or not a potential stimulus becomes effective depends on the individual. It depends on the species to which he belongs, on the anatomy of the sense organs, the stage of maturation, the capacities for sense organ adjustment, the habits of attention, the activity in progress, and the possibilities of educating the attention of the individual."[52] This quotation alone suffices to show how little Gibson's "realism" has to do with what has been labeled with this term by the philosophical tradition. More faithful to his thought is probably the distinction he makes, more rarely, between sensation as the "private" pole and perception as the "public" one[53]; for the private makes sense only *in relation* to the "public" and *vice versa*. "Private" and public are notions relative to each other. We cannot truly understand what Gibson means unless we completely abandon the idea of a subjective contribution and an objective one to perception. "For me," Gibson writes, "perception is an awareness of the world. An awareness of the self *accompanies* it but does not *contribute* to it. Proprioception, as I put it, goes along with perception but is not the same thing. There is a subjective aspect and an objective aspect to every phenomenal experience but this does not mean that there is some degree of subjective *determination* of objective perception. The old idea that a perception is determined partly from the outside and partly from the inside is nothing but a muddle of thought."[54] The pole of the *self* cannot "contribute" to anything at all, since it only appears as such in and by perception itself! If it were absolutely necessary to fashion a word to describe Gibson's thesis, it could only be a word foreign to the lexicon of modern philosophy—"mutualism," for example. This is why the ecological understanding of perception, just as it leads beyond the modern metaphysics of the subject and the objectivist ontology of nature, surely leads beyond "psychology," despite Gibson's repeated denials.

The Critical Potential of the Ecological Approach

In any case, if there is a generic name that is suitable for Gibson's approach, it is "phenomenology." His is even a phenomenology of the first order. But its importance should be measured equally in terms of its empirical and conceptual contribution, on the one hand, and of critical potential with respect to traditional phenomenological idealism, on the other. It is the latter aspect that deserves a closer look and presupposes our extending Gibson's claims beyond psychology to the philosophical realm.

The reader familiar with Husserl or Merleau-Ponty who takes up the study of Gibson will of course be struck by the affinity of some of their analyses, but even more by a strong sense of estrangement. It is as if phenomenology were suddenly stripped of its entire idealist infrastructure, of its whole Cartesian and Kantian background, while losing nothing of its descriptive rigor. Gibson is a "phenomenologist" almost unknowingly. He never quotes Husserl or Heidegger. If their legacy infiltrates his work, it is probably via Köhler or Koffka. But which legacy? Phenomenology, from Husserl on, is based on a critique of objectivism and naturalism in the sciences, psychology in particular. The history of the phenomenological movement is marked throughout its history by this same leitmotif: Erwin Straus, Viktor von Weizsäcker, Kurt Goldstein, F. J. J. Buytendjik, and a bit later Maurice Merleau-Ponty take up this anti-naturalism on their own behalf, opposing the behaviorism of their times and the associationist empiricism underlying it. This same position is assumed by Gibson. For him, perception is exactly what it was for his predecessors: a *sui generis* phenomenon that must be described on its own basis. This description is not a mere prelude to experimentation: it has a constitutive role for science, which it furnishes with a conceptual framework and the formulation of its leading problems. Of course, within the framework of an experimental phenomenology like Gibson's, there is a continuity between experimentation and description, which complete and correct one another. But in sharp contrast with his predecessors, Gibson abandons—or simply is ignorant of—the very principle of Husserl's opposition to naturalism, that is to say, his choice in favor of transcendentalism. This choice remains determining for most of the phenomenologists who have brought their analyses to bear on perception, including Merleau-Ponty.

Husserl's critique of the objective sciences did not consist in denying their validity, but only in restricting the scope of this validity; as a consequence, the transcendental reduction made it possible to accede to a "field" beyond the reach of their objectifying methods, that of "pure phenomena in the phenomenological sense." But in thus withdrawing into the realm of the pure lived experiences of a transcendental ego, and in detaching itself, by means of an *epochē*, from all the objective problems stemming from neurophysiology, biology, or physics, phenomenology sanctioned the Cartesian dichotomy between subject and object, lending it an even greater legitimacy. In doing so, it incurred the risk of facing the objection that, far from being a neutral method of "bracketing" or "parenthetizing," it, too, was based on the implicit and unexamined assumption of a particular ontology—the one that, since Descartes, sets up a diametrical opposition between nature and mind. There is one author whom Gibson certainly read, who formulated this argument against the Husserlian *epochē*: Wolfgang Köhler. "I do not believe that we are justified in putting certain phases of experience in brackets. . . . It is otherwise to be expected that even if the brackets are introduced as mere methodological tools, they will sooner or later turn out to be weapons of an ontological prejudice. In fact, I am not sure whether Husserl himself has not used them as such weapons."[55] It matters little what the Gestaltists themselves did about this warning. Gibson, for his part, drew the most radical consequences from it, though they have remained largely implicit in a work not primarily meant to be philosophical. He replaced the modern dualist ontology of mind versus nature with a *relational* "ontology" (but does the latter term apply?) quite able to do without those notions.

Husserl believed he could free himself from empiricism by asserting that the hyletic contents were not to be defined, as were traditional *sense data*, by the extrinsic and causal criterion of their origin in the senses, but rather pertained to lived experiences as intrinsic, purely descriptive characteristics. He thought he could free himself from Kantianism by maintaining that the constitution of perception had no need for additional categorial acts. Yet he did think of perception as a relation of *knowledge* between a *subject* and an *object*. He consequently characterized perception itself as a *subjective* phenomenon, in the sense of belonging to a transcendental subjectivity purified by the *epochē* of all worldly inscription. He analyzed the perceptual noema as the result of the *objectifying* apprehension, by means of morphological acts, of previously given hyletic contents. He accepted, by this very fact, the dissolution of perception into a multiplicity of apparently discrete acts (to which the temporal proto-constitution alone could confer a deeper continuity) and into a multiplicity of material contents of consciousness, apprehended by means of those acts: he thus embraced a certain psychological atomism.[56] Last, he understood intentionality itself, not of course as an extrinsic relation establishing itself after the fact between independent relata, but as a relation whose ultimate *fundamentum* was located *in subjecto*, in the ultimately constituting subjectivity, that is, as a relation *inaugurated* or instituted by the pure ego insofar as it enjoys, as transcendental ego, an unconditioned preeminence and prerogative over all that can present itself to it as an object. The intentional relation is a relation such that it is established by the subject, since the latter is an absolute (in the sense that *nulla re indiget ad existendum*),[57] in relation to which the world itself possesses a meaning (and an existence), but that does not draw its meaning (and its existence) from the world. From this perspective, no meaning can come into the world except by the transcendental ego and its sense-bestowing (*Sinngebung*). It is strictly excluded to subscribe to the idea of meanings or values immanent in perception itself, to an "order of meaning" prior to all sense-bestowing, because stemming from the interdependence both vital and "historical" of a living being and its life environment.

Gibson's ecological approach, if we are to take its most radical philosophical implications seriously, leads to a very different understanding of the perceptual phenomenon. The phenomenological reduction puts out of play and consequently abandons to classical physics the problems concerning the nature of light or sound, that is, concerning the natural energies as sources of perceptual information. Gibson believes, on the contrary, that we have first of all to analyze these physical phenomena *at the only level at which they are relevant for the understanding of the nature of the information available for the animal's perceptual systems*, namely at the ecological level. We have to analyze, for example, not radiant light (considered according to its two physical models, wave or particle), but ambient light, structured according to multiple phenomena of reflection, and thus to elaborate a phenomenological optics.

Husserl characterizes perception as one among the possible *modes of givenness* of objects to consciousness, specifically the one in which they are given *in the flesh (leibhaft)* through a flow of sensible *Abschattungen* or silhouettes. For him, the originary phenomenon is the noetic-noematic correlation. For Gibson, it is primordial reciprocity, that is, codetermination or codependency between the body and its surroundings. Perception is no longer the objectifying apprehension of a *hulē* by a constituting subject, because *hulē* is a hybrid concept that bespeaks, at the very heart of phenomenological idealism, a residue of empiricism. Perception cannot be understood on the basis of a series of isolated intentional acts and the multiplicity of their objective correlates, that is to say, on the basis of a manifold of empty intentions and the corresponding intuition filling them or failing to do so. Perception is not primarily an *act* (or a multiplicity of acts) but an *ability*, which in its exercise admits of degrees, that is to say, can be refined and developed, and belongs not to a pure ego, but to an embodied, living being, endowed with perceptual systems and situated in a world imbued with vital meanings.

As a consequence, the "horizon" can no longer mean the in-principle unlimited network of intending acts by which a subject, by his own initiative, is assumed to exceed all given and anticipate all possible manifestation, but rather the embeddedness in the perceptual field (and to begin with, in the visual field) of the very conditions of perception (and vision); and thus of the *conditioning* of perception itself. Thanks to the mutual determination of the perceiver and the perceived, there is no perception unless it is conditioned by the very conditions of its actualization. To perceive, one must be situated, that is, inscribed within a specific environment. All environment imposes on perception its own conditioning; for example, in the case of terrestrial vision, this particular line of horizon in which the visible collapses and fades away in the distance. The *finitude* of vision is not understandable as a characteristic of the subject considered in itself, but belongs to the living being as located in the world, that is, as conditioned in turn by its own life conditions. These life conditions can only be *corporeal*. At this point, Gibson's analyses have to be completed. To the remote horizon, to this indistinct fringe where earth and sky meet—or vanish—there corresponds a proximal horizon, this aura of invisibility surrounding my own visual field and corresponding to the way my body itself obstructs my vision. The latter deserves no less to be called "horizon" than the former: their complementarity derives from the necessarily dual—both extero-and proprioceptive—nature of all perception.

A philosophy of perception that does not set out from subjective lived experiences cannot subscribe to the Husserlian notion of *reality* defined as a "concordance" of the lived experiences of a subject, according to the teleological unity of an intuitive fulfillment endless by principle. For this philosophy, reality designates rather the univocal and orderly nature in time and space of both perceptual variations and their structural invariants. Thus the opposite of reality, illusion, cannot mean a failed or truncated knowledge, a discordance in the unity of fulfillment, an *error*, since perception does not belong primarily to the theoretic realm. Illusion is rather a characteristic of the ambiguity or ambivalence of certain perceptions: it is less the result of an interpretation on the part of the subject than of impoverished information, or information ill-adapted to our perceptual systems. This applies, for example, to the illusions of the Gestalt psychologists: they do not take place under *normal* conditions, but only in those—abstract and highly sophisticated—concocted in the laboratory. For example, when a figure drawn in perspective changes into its opposite, or when a full solid becomes hollow, "that 'inversion,'" as von Weizsäcker suggests, "does not, however, demonstrate the addition of subjective factors to the event produced by the stimulus; it only shows the polyvalence of the stimulus."[58] The perceptual antilogies do not entail that perception is a construction of the mind, a quasi-fiction. On the contrary, two paths remain open: either—and this represents at least a certain tendency of Gestalt psychology—to maintain that illusions are a privileged example of the laws of organization of the perceptual field, which comes down to making them into the model of all perception (at least there is a tendency in this direction); or inversely, according to the path chosen by Gibson, to understand illusion as a lacunar side effect of normal perception, an ambiguous, indeterminate, or underdetermined by-product. In this case, the illusion can no longer function as the paradigm for understanding perception. It is nevertheless a boundary case of perception, which implies that illusion and reality are not opposite concepts, but complementary ones. Alas, Gibson scarcely thematizes these concepts of reality and illusion—which would have enabled him to inflect his position in the direction of a less naïve adhesion to "realism."

Nor did Gibson furnish an analysis of the body as relational pole in the I-world system. But we may suspect that his interpretation of this phenomenon would have been very different than the idealist phenomenological concept of flesh (*Leib*). Of course it is possible to interpret this concept, in Husserl himself, as an attempt to overcome Cartesian dualism and as the thematization of a reality of a third type, neither subjective—in the sense of the pure ego—nor objective. As the medium of reduplicated tactile sensations, flesh, Husserl claims, is neither a "component piece of the *I*" (*Beständstück des Ich*) nor an "over and against me" (*Gegenüber des Ich*)[59]; it is neither transcendent in the sense of a worldly objectivity, given inadequately through of flow of adumbrations, nor identical to the constituting ego. And at the same time, as a phenomenon that is constituted—although imperfectly[60]—in the experience of self-contact, the flesh is merely the "hyletic substrate (*hyletische Unterlage*)" of consciousness.[61] It is never really me: "Soul and psychic Ego 'have' a flesh,"[62] but they are not their flesh. The latter is never anything but a dependency of the pure ego, which remains subjectivity in the only originary sense. Even in the late philosophy of Merleau-Ponty, who endeavors to make flesh the true subject of perception, this attempted transplantation of a transcendental concept turns out to be ambivalent, because it retains the essential part of the transcendental apparatus. This essential part is what Merleau-Ponty formulated as a "well-known" paradox as early as in *The Structure of Behavior*. "Consciousness appears on one hand to be part of the world and on the other to be co-extensive with the world."[63] The same may be said of flesh: "The thickness of the body, far from rivaling that of the world, is on the contrary the sole means I have to go unto the heart of things, by making myself a world and by making them flesh."[64] But in order for flesh to be able thus to "become world," it must *not belong to* the world from the beginning—or it must be the origin of it. Flesh remains, in this regard, a quasi-transcendental. But is it possible to accede to such an origin? Is it possible to grasp the flesh before its being made worldly?

Gibson's response would probably be no. First, because the primary phenomenon is not flesh as origin of the world, source of all constitution, but the originary *relation* between a body and a world. The body is uniquely one of the poles of a *system*, and it makes no sense to try to understand it outside this system. Second, because the privilege conferred on touch for the constitution of flesh makes of this "sense" a sense apart from all others, the very sense of proprioception. Now, *all* perception, as Gibson insists, is *both proprioceptive and exteroceptive*. In this respect touch has nothing specific about it. In hearing, for example, I hear not only sounds, but their localization in relation to my body; through the sounds I hear, I apprehend myself in space. And when I hear myself speaking, I "hear" not only the sounds emitted, but also the vibrations of my larynx and cranium. In vision, I grasp my own movements at the same time as those of things by means of the "visual kinesthesis" described by Gibson. As for touch, just like the other "senses," it is a co-perception of myself and the world; and this is precisely the reason it is so different from a pure self-affection. I seize this hand as being my own, because I feel in it the contact with my other hand, in what Husserl called "double sensations"; but I also apprehend—and *simultaneously*—my hands as being *other* from one another, that is, as "things in the world." Inseparably other and my own, things of the world and my own body, and not inseparably flesh and body; for if flesh and body are *co-originary*, like the front and back of one and the same phenomenon, the principle of their distinction (hence also of their *subordination*) disappears entirely. Never would I experience my body as mine if I did not experience it at the same time as other, and *necessarily* so. In this exteriority of my body to itself, my body receives its unity, in its continuous commerce with other bodies or other things, from different sensorial systems and not from a privileged sense, elevated to the rank of sense of self-affection or "reflexivity," that is, sense of self par excellence.

Conclusions

Has Gibson succeeded where others have failed? Has he been able to draw philosophical consequences from his own discoveries? This was not, assuredly, his purpose, which was initially that of a man of science and an experimenter. It is permissible, however, to attempt to formulate, after him, the stakes involved in his approach. His realism, as I have said, has something "naïve" about it in a different sense than the one he would like to give this term. The ecological approach, precisely because it sets out from an indissoluble relation—that of the living being with its life milieu—is necessarily beyond the distinction between realism and idealism. This is precisely what makes its strength—and its difficulty. But does the ecological paradigm *suffice* to account for the perceptual phenomenon, and does it not also remain "abstract," in certain respects, at least? Is perception just the way a living organism adapts continually to its life conditions and grasps the *vital* meanings contained in its *Umwelt*? Is there not a profound difference, in this regard, between animal perception and human perception? When, for example, Gibson analyzes the *affordance* of a letterbox,[65] can he account for the fact that a letterbox is only what it is for a living being capable of using it by getting his or her mail from it, and not for the rodent seeking shelter or the bird building its nest in it? Wouldn't he, in order to do so, have to complete the ecological paradigm with a hermeneutic approach according to which all perceiving is always a *perceiving as* . . . , is always, consequently (as long, at least, as it is a question of human beings) a way of interpreting what appears to us by means of symbolic and linguistic referents, in which the phenomenon and its interpretation appear inseparably linked? The figural sense, prior to all sense-bestowing (*Sinngebung*) by a subject, which belongs to perception itself, would thus arise from an "order of meaning" prior to a great extent to any subjective performances, and yet would not arise from nature alone and its ties with the living being. It would also arise from a *history*. Not a natural history, to be sure, but a history of meaning, and thereby a *history of perception* to which art, among other things, attests. But this would imply leading perception back not only to the closed economy of a "circle of structure," but to the open economy—or the "an-economy"—of an unforeseeable becoming in which the meaning of what is perceived cannot be entirely determined in advance. Then perhaps, and *only* then, perception could well appear—to return to our point of departure—as that "*historical* encounter" of which von Weizsäcker speaks.

PART III

The Nothing and the "There Is"

7

Is a Phenomenology of Nothingness Possible?

The Carnap-Heidegger Controversy

> It is the mark of a cultivated man to require exactness in each class of subjects only so far as the nature of the subject admits.
>
> —**Aristotle, *Nicomachean Ethics***

"Western thought abhors a vacuum. The Open for it is but dizziness. Banished by Parmenides, the Nothing triumphs in sophistry, and later in the mystics and the theologies of Kenosis. But this relation to the Nothing arouses suspicion; and being qualified as sophistic is most often dismissive. It stigmatizes a thinking that is accused of having no other relation to Nothing than the relation to itself of its own inanity."[1] This statement of Maldiney's—absolutely accurate—immediately raises a question. Can thought have a different relation to what is designated here by three synonymous names—the Nothing, vacuum, and the Open? Can it avoid perpetuating, be it by omission, Parmenides's interdiction regarding non-being—disallowing it as null and void? Indeed, what justifies this interdiction is mainly logical requirements linked to the principle of noncontradiction. Of "non-being" it is impossible to say anything without presupposing that the words designating it name something, that is to say, without asserting about it that it is—which is to contradict oneself. The question is therefore decided even before being posed: All that we can say about nothingness is that it isn't, which amounts to excluding it from the universe of the logos. One can say nothing about the nothing, except that it is nothing and that there is nothing to be said about it. But then, by the same move by which nothingness is crossed out, so to speak, from the thinkable, by thought, it is paradoxically reaffirmed. For to maintain that nothingness is nothing amounts to nothing but to define it in its essence. Heidegger has drawn our attention to this point. "We know it, the nothing, in that we wish to know nothing about it."[2] Through this paradox, naturally, nothing has yet been said about the nothing, about its status, or about the necessity of thinking it. But a domain is at least marked off, as the domain in which the question itself is posed, and this domain is that of the relationships between thought and logic. The problem is, as Heidegger emphasizes, whether " 'logic' is of supreme importance" to assess thought or whether, on the contrary, "the idea of 'logic' itself disintegrates in the turbulence of a more original questioning."[3]

But where does such a turbulence come from? Heidegger would reply: from the question of Being itself. Being and nothingness, in his view, are "the same" (*dasselbe*), and their shared foreclusion seals the unity of Western thought as onto-theology. But doesn't the sole fact of submitting logic to a higher authority already plunge us into full-fledged irrationalism? That is indeed how the lecture "What Is Metaphysics" has often been understood and judged. Such was the case in the first instance by a whole philosophical tradition that, in the twentieth century, sees in the analysis of propositions the only rigorous method, and in logic itself "the essence of philosophy."[4] But must not logic rather play, in philosophy, the modest role of an organon, an instrument in the search for truth, the very role that Aristotle attributed to it? Nothing, then, would stand in the way of our questioning logic in turn, with respect to its presuppositions, its possibilities, and its limits. Such is, if we examine it closely, Heidegger's claim. But is that claim worthy of being defended? In order to attempt to answer this question, we must go back to the historic debate setting at odds, at the beginning of the 1930s, Carnap and Heidegger. Subsequently, I will try to broaden the problem, and to formulate on the subject of nothingness the question of whether (and on what conditions) phenomenology can say something meaningful about it without relinquishing what grounds it as such—as phenomeno-logy: the very requirements of logos.

The Starting Point of the Controversy: Two Figures of "Metaphysis"

Before entering into the Carnap-Heidegger disputation, it will not be superfluous to recall the main content of the 1929 lecture "What Is Metaphysics?" to which Carnap's article, published in *Erkenntnis* 2, "The

Elimination of Metaphysics through Logical Analysis of Language,"[5] is a response.

The whole originality of the Heidegger lecture lies in its phenomenological style. Indeed, what it involves is a manner, without equivalent in the philosophical tradition, of presenting metaphysics in its own light, as it were, or rather of letting it present itself on the basis of the way it penetrates and permeates existence, of letting it appear, as it were, at the level of human existence, since the latter, in its essence, is "metaphysical." "Metaphysics," writes Heidegger, "is inquiry beyond or over beings, which aims to recover them as such and as a whole for our grasp."[6] But such a question could not even cross *Dasein*'s mind if the latter were not, in its being, "metaphysical," that is, if its existence were not constitutively transcendence, the outstripping of beings as a whole toward Being, to the extent that this passing beyond (meta) is the condition for the comprehensibility and the appearing of any being. Not only does not metaphysics designate here an academic discipline that we would be encouraged to approach in a historical perspective, but it is not a science rooted exclusively in a theoretical interest on the part of the subject, either. The understanding of Being is itself a modality of existence conditioned by the behavior (*Verhaltungen*) of *Dasein* and by the thoroughly practical—or "praxical"—manner with which it relates to its Being to dodge it or resolutely assume it. The same goes for metaphysics, to the extent that it is precisely a modality of existing. "Metaphysics" is existence itself insofar as its going beyond, its transcendence, by exposing it to Being, relates it and opens it originarily to itself. "Going beyond beings occurs in the essence of *Dasein*. But this going beyond is metaphysics itself. This implies that metaphysics belongs to the 'nature of man.' . . . Metaphysics is the basic occurrence of *Dasein*. It is *Dasein* itself."[7]

It is not surprising that we find, the same year, in *Kant and the Problem of Metaphysics*, an assertion that is identical almost word for word.[8] Like Kant making metaphysics an ineradicable need of human reason, Heidegger makes it the innermost constitution of existence. But, by contrast with Kant, Heidegger does not want to limit his claims by having it enter "the sure path of a science." On the contrary, setting in opposition from the outset the "rigor" of thought and "exactness" of science, Heidegger must finally conclude that their paths diverge radically. "For this reason no amount of scientific rigor attains to the seriousness of metaphysics. Philosophy can never be measured by the standard of the idea of science."[9] Discreet, but persistent, this anti-Kantian claim is first of all an anti-neo-Kantian claim. It is the "epistemological" interpretation of the *Critique of*

Pure Reason by the Marburg School that is his primary target. The question of metaphysics is the question of Being as such in its historicality for a thought that is historical through and through, that is, intrinsically finite, and stands as far as possible from the modern requirements of "science." Moreover, borrowing Kant's phrase, Heidegger asserts in his epistolary preface addressing the 1969 translator that there is no "metaphysics of metaphysics," that is, no "critique" in the Kantian sense.[10] To interrogate the essence of metaphysics is not to delimit its legitimate powers by the measure of the modern idea of science, but to seek its root in human existence as transcendence.

The analysis of boredom, and even more that of anxiety, will serve as guiding threads to show this. Through these moods (*Stimmungen*), *Dasein* feels itself as situated at the heart of beings as a whole. This expression, "as a whole," already implicitly leads us back to the phenomenon of the world. In every *Stimmung*, the world itself manifests itself to *Dasein* in keeping with a specific tonality or "color"—for example as joyful, frightening, or disturbing. But as *Sein und Zeit* emphasizes, there is an essential difference between anxiety and most of the other moods. In the case of anxiety, what *Dasein* is anxious about (*Wovor*) is not an entity in the world, it is "the world qua world" (*Welt als Welt*)[11] to the extent that this world "exists" beyond all entities, that is, pertains to existence as transcendence. The "object" of anxiety is not, therefore, different from the "subject" of anxiety: its *Wovor* and its *Worum*, its "in the face of which" and its "for which," in Heideggerian terms, coincide. Anxiety is felt in the face of the world as such in its uncanniness (*Unheimlichkeit*) by an entity that is ontologically Being-in-the-World. Or rather, anxiety is felt by *Dasein* in the face of itself to the extent that it is thrown into the world and that this thrownness (*Geworfenheit*) is a feature of its Being. This is why, in this fundamental mood—"fundamental" since it leads *Dasein* before itself and removes it from its own concealment in the They—the object of anxiety is nowhere (*nirgends*) and is, properly speaking, "nothing" (*nichts*); or rather, the object of anxiety is the "nothing and nowhere" (*das Nichts and nirgends*) that means, phenomenally, the same thing as "the world as such" (*die Welt als solche*).[12] Here we have the first occurrence of the expression "the nothing" to designate the world itself. Heidegger passes from the assertion that the vis-à-vis of anxiety is completely undetermined and, in truth, is nothing (*nichts*) to the assertion that this vis-à-vis is the nothing, the nothingness (*das Nichts*), that is, the world in its ontological sense. He replaces an indefinite pronoun with a noun, which will become the nodal point of Carnap's critique. He even expressly equates the nothing with the world—*das Nichts, das heißt die Welt as solche*—and hence, even if this last point is not formulated, the nothing with Being, since the phenomenon of the world is originarily rooted in the Being of *Dasein* as *In-der-Welt-sein*.

Reiterating the main points of this analysis, "What Is Metaphysics?" makes an additional step. This time what is at stake is the further determination of the meaning of the expression "the nothing," an expression that Heidegger seemed in *Sein und Zeit* to use in a still rather indeterminate way. Indeed, why speak of the nothing and not "quite simply" of Being? To understand this, we must return to the phenomenon of anxiety. In anxiety, Heidegger specifies, beings as a whole withdraw, recede into the distance, and sink away, as it were, into insignificance. But in this reflux and this drift, they are not annihilated. They only appear more forcefully in their radical injustification. The nothing that manifests itself here, on the occasion of the withdrawal of beings, must not be thought of as the consequence of an annihilation (*Vernichtung*), but as being of a piece with the "nihilation" (*Nichtung*) that structures the ontological difference. Being in the face of which anxiety places us is the pure and simple other of all beings, that which is not itself a being. This "not" belongs to it by essence. The nothing "is" therefore nothing other than Being itself, or the "*als*" [as] in the expression *Welt als Welt*. Consequently the nothing—in that it designates the worldliness of the world, the same (*dasselbe*) as Being—can no longer be thought of as the application of the logical operator of negation to beings considered "as a whole" and in their entirety. It refers to a positive phenomenon, that of the ontological difference. It signifies "the original opening (*Offenheit*) of entities as such."[13] Or, as Heidegger writes, "For human existence, the nothing makes possible the openedness of beings as such. The nothing does not merely serve as the counterconcept of beings; rather, it originally belongs to their essential unfolding in presence [*Wesen*] itself. In the Being of entities the nihilation of the nothing occurs."[14]

Heidegger's analyses are well-known, and my summary was not intended to provide a commentary on them. It was only meant to introduce a further question. This question is of the possibility of a thinking of nothingness with respect and in opposition to the criticism raised against it. The whole problem is to determine to what extent what Heidegger says is meaningful, or whether it is just a vain play on words. Carnap, whose target is more generally metaphysics as a meaningless set of pseudo-propositions that pretend to the status of knowledge, saw the 1929 lecture as a perfect sample of that "metaphysics." In so doing, he obviously started with a concept of "metaphysics" quite different from Heidegger's.

To use an analogy, it could be maintained that while Heidegger is influenced in part by a Kantian definition of metaphysics borrowed from the "transcendental dialectic," Carnap limits the meaning of that term to what Kant calls "dogmatic metaphysics," that is, to "a completely isolated speculative science of reason, which soars far above the teachings of experience, and . . . rests on concepts alone."[15] This is what emerges from a definition like the one given in a brief, final "supplement" to the *Überwindung* . . . : "This term is used in this paper, as usually in Europe, for the field of alleged knowledge of the essence of things which transcends the realm of empirically founded, inductive science."[16] According to this definition, metaphysics is this discipline that pretends to the status of science, and therefore that believes it can compete with the empirical sciences, because it produces a "new knowledge,"[17] which remains nevertheless inaccessible to all experimental verification. Two years earlier, in the *Aufbau*, Carnap already characterized this alleged "science" as "the extra-scientific domain of theoretical form" (§176). And he found in Bergson and his metaphysics of intuition the best representative of this tendency. But he objected that the alleged "non-rational," "ineffable" knowledge could not pretend to the status of knowledge, since it could be neither confirmed nor invalidated experimentally. "There is no road from the continent of rational knowledge to the island of intuition, while there is a road from the country of empirical knowledge to the country of formal knowledge, which thus shows that they belong to the same continent" (§181).

But this characterization of "metaphysics" is not yet sufficient. Indeed, precisely because Carnap defends not only an empiricism in the traditional sense, but a logical empiricism, his claim is not only that metaphysics is a pseudo-knowledge because it remains outside all verification; his claim is that metaphysics is meaningless, that is to say, that its statements cannot even be properly constructed in a logical language. Therefore, metaphysics does not rest, as Kant believed, on a mere epistemological illusion, but on a logical "illusion." Its statements are not only false, empty of all knowledge content, because without any relation to experience, nonfactual. They are *sinnlos*, meaningless. They "say nothing but merely express a certain mood and spirit."[18] This is why it is no longer possible, as Kant believed, to continue to promote a critical metaphysics after having eradicated its dogmatic forerunner. All that remains is a purely immanent dissolution of the problems left behind by metaphysics, by means of a logical analysis that exposes them as pseudo-problems: such is the first task, if not the only task, of philosophy.

But is Heidegger's goal to promote a "metaphysics" in the sense in which Carnap understands it here, that is, a knowledge capable of competing with scientific knowledge? In other words, is not Carnap's critique of metaphysics only the critique of a specific metaphysics—the one that claims for itself the title of "science"? Is it not to that extent dependent on the metaphysics it critiques, and from which it borrows its main concepts? Is it not a metaphysically conditioned critique of metaphysics? And conversely, if "metaphysics" in the sense in which Heidegger attempts to expose it belongs to the precinct of thought and no longer to that of science, if it declines the title of "knowledge," if it designates the very structuration of human existence and the interpretation it gives of itself in a relation to itself that is "practical" from the outset, if the problems it raises do not even constitute the sort of problems that can receive scientific solutions, if they relate to the way each *Dasein* appropriates its own existence and tries to make its meaning transparent by maintaining to that existence a first-personal relation—can Heidegger's undertaking fall beneath Carnap's critique at all? Does it not pertain, on the contrary, to a kind of question that belongs to a completely different domain than that of science, without being able to enter into competition with the latter, and yet without being absurd?[19]

At about the same time, Wittgenstein christened this kind of question "ethical." For him, ethics does not consist in a science of good and evil, but in an "enquiry into the meaning of life." Thus understood, it rests on an experience that Wittgenstein qualifies as "experience par excellence," and about which he asserts, "I believe the best way of describing it is to say that when I have it I wonder at the existence of the world."[20] That experience, Wittgenstein goes on to say, leads us beyond the domain of what can be the object of science, at the same time that it brings us to the limits of meaningful language. The experience of "seeing the world as a miracle" cannot be said, he continues, in a logically correct language. It confronts us with the limits of the sayable, it leads us to a "running against the walls of our cage." And yet, he concludes, "it is a document of a tendency in the human mind which I personally cannot help respecting deeply and I would not for my life ridicule it."[21] What Wittgenstein refers to here with the word "ethics" is very close to Heidegger's existential philosophy—close to the point of merging with it. This is testified to by a conversation between Wittgenstein and Waismann, reported by the latter and constituting at the same time an extremely clear repudiation of Carnap's enterprise:

> A propos of Heidegger. I can certainly see what Heidegger means by Being and anxiety. Man has the urge to thrust against the limits of language. Think for instance about one's astonishment that anything exists. This astonishment cannot be expressed in the form of a question and there is no answer to it. Anything we can say must, a

priori, be only nonsense. Nevertheless we thrust against the limits of language. Kierkegaard, too, recognized this thrust and even described it in much the same way (as a thrust against paradox). This thrust against the limits of language is ethics. I regard it as very important to put an end to all the chatter about whether there is knowledge in ethics, whether there are values, whether the Good can be defined, etc.

> In ethics, one constantly tries to say something that does not concern and can never concern the essence of the matter. . . . But the tendency, that twinge, means something. Augustine knew this when he said: "What, scoundrel, you don't want to speak nonsense? Come on, say one, at least one, who cares?"[22]

Not only does Wittgenstein show himself to be remarkably perceptive in his reading of Heidegger; not only does he squarely oppose any enterprise of pure and simple elimination of what he calls "ethics"—his free translation of *Confessions* I.4: *et vae tacentibus de te, quoniam loquaces muti sunt*, sounding in this respect like a veritable affront to Carnap, who thought at the time he could avail himself of his backing—but especially, Wittgenstein emphasizes in this passage the difference of level between Heidegger's interrogation and the positivist project, a difference making any parallel and any dialogue between their respective positions almost impossible. However, Heidegger is at least in agreement with the Vienna Circle on a decisive point: ethics, although it corresponds to a tendency deeply ingrained in man, impossible to "eliminate" and deeply respectable, cannot be formulated without giving rise to "nonsense." Under these conditions, Heidegger's affirmations remain foreign to philosophy. There is no possible phenomenology of existence in its "ethical," which is to say existential, dimension.

Therefore we must fully engage this question of the meaningfulness or lack of it in Heidegger's statements, and more specifically in those involving "nothingness"; and in order to do so, we must revisit Carnap's text.

Carnap's *Überwindung*

The Vienna Circle project announces itself as "science free of metaphysics."[23] Philosophy has no other goal than to elucidate and systematize scientific statements by bringing out their implicit logical architecture. It is nothing but a contentless method that, on its negative side, makes possible the elimination of logical errors and meaningless words in the language of science and philosophy, and, on its positive side, "serves to clarify meaningful concepts and propositions, to lay logical foundations for factual science and for mathematics."[24] The *Überwindung*, the "overcoming" or rather the pure and simple elimination of metaphysics, has, from this point of view, merely a preliminary function: it paves the way for a situation in which, philosophy having itself become a "scientific" activity, "there will, I hope, come a time when one no longer needs to present lectures against metaphysics."[25]

To understand to what extent "metaphysics in its entirety" presents meaningless statements[26]—which are therefore no more than pseudo-statements—we must understand positively what condition a proposition must satisfy in order to be meaningful. That condition, in reality, is twofold: (1) It must be syntactically well-formed (in the sense of logical, not grammatical syntax); (2) It must contain a vocabulary that is itself meaningful. This second criterion only applies, as we will see, to synthetic statements, that is, to statements that are true not just by virtue of their form alone, but also by virtue of their relation to experience.

From this typology, two categories of pseudo-statements ensue: first, those in which one or more of the words of the vocabulary (variables and predicates, as distinct from logical connectors and quantifiers) are meaningless; second, those that are incoherent from the point of view of their syntax, and for which any logical paraphrase is impossible. The former are examined by Carnap in sections II and III of his article, the latter in sections IV and V.

Before tackling Carnap's analysis of these two kinds of nonsense, it is necessary to expose the doctrine of meaning of logical positivism in its main lines. According to the Vienna Circle, all propositions are either analytic or synthetic. An analytic proposition is a tautology, that is to say, a statement that is necessarily true by virtue of its form. For example, the statement "It is raining or it is not raining" tells us nothing about the current weather conditions. It has no empirical content, refers to no fact about the world, but limits itself to illustrating the syntactic rules that preside over the use of the connector "or": the proposition containing this connector is true when at least one of the two expressions it connects is true. For Carnap, as for Wittgenstein, the propositions of logic and mathematics are all analytic in this sense. They are tautologies or tautological transformations of tautologies. In the case of these propositions, to understand their meaning and to understand that they are true by virtue of their form alone, that is, to understand that they are tautological, are identical. With the second kind of propositions, things are otherwise; their truth depends on a nonlinguistic criterion: the experience to which they refer. They are true if the state of affairs to which they refer exists, and false if that state of affairs does not exist. But in order to be able to be true or false, they must first be meaningful. Here, the problem of truth and that of meaning are distinct, as opposed to the case of analytic statements.[27] If the statement is true, it is thereby meaningful, but its being meaningful does not imply its being true; it can also be false by virtue of its content. On what conditions, then, is a synthetic statement meaningful? This is a fundamental problem in the view of the Vienna Circle, since it leads to distinguishing scientific statements (or those that can become so) from nonscientific ones (and that cannot become so): metaphysical statements.

The answer to this problem—for every problem, in the view of logical empiricism, has only one solution—is the following: A synthetic statement is meaningful if it has a determinate relation to experience, that is, if that statement can be made to correspond to facts capable of either confirming or invalidating it. This empirical criterion is duplicated, in the framework of logical positivism, by a strictly formal criterion making it possible to establish inferentially which statements are meaningful and which are not: a synthetic statement has a meaning if and only if it can be deduced from a finite class of observational statements. This criterion assumes, first, that a synthetic statement must be well-formed from the point of view of its syntax, because failing this it would not be deducible from any other statement. Second, it implies that it must be possible to deduce a class of simpler statements from it until we reach immediately verifiable statements, also called "protocol statements" (*Protokollsätze*) because they furnish experience or observation protocols, the verification of which allows the verification of the statement in question. For example, the proposition "*x* is an arthropod" is meaningful if it can be derived from observational statements of the type: "*x* is an animal," "*x* has jointed legs," "*x* has a segmented body," "*x* has a chitinous skin."[28] Then we can construct the following inference: "If *x* is an animal and if *x* has jointed legs and if *x* has a segmented body and if *x* has a chitinous skin, then *x* is an arthropod," which supplies the criteria of the meaning of the word "arthropod." Here we have a purely formal and consequently objective criterion for the meaning of a word, quite independently of the psychological question of what we "mean" through that word—what mental representation, what emotions we associate with its use. In short, we can, then, furnish the following general definition of the meaning of a synthetic statement: "The meaning of a statement is its method of verification" (Schlick).

This logical procedure of "reduction" (*Zurückführung*),[29] as Carnap also calls it, makes it possible henceforth to eliminate metaphysical statements by exposing them as nonsense of the first type—nonsense relative to vocabulary, not to logical syntax. It is hardly necessary to insist on this first aspect of Carnap's argumentation, for several reasons. First, this part of his exposition is entirely tributary to the verificational theory of meaning, which, targeted by criticism coming from various sides,[30] would later be abandoned by Carnap in §34 of *Logische Syntax der Sprache*. For us today, it is of no more than doxographical interest. Second, even if we consider only its application to the critique of metaphysical statements, this doctrine turns out to be astonishingly confused, arbitrary, and marred by presuppositions. The most naïve among them is probably the assertion that each word having originally been introduced into the language "for no other purpose than to express something or other," it must have had a definite meaning "from the very beginning of its use."[31] On this view, it is only later, "in the course of historical development," that that meaning would begin to fluctuate. Metaphysics does nothing more than play, as it were, on this semantic indetermination: in metaphysics "the word has been deprived of its earlier meaning without being given a new meaning," and the former mental images associated with it are now replaced by "new mental images and feelings"[32]; metaphysics thus invents "pseudo-concepts." According to this Adamic doctrine of language, language at the beginning is made of perfectly univocal meanings, and it is only subsequently that it is perverted by a kind of philosophical Babel. Not only does Carnap never justify this assertion (and how could he on the basis of his own principles?), but this assertion leads to obvious mistakes. The example chosen to illustrate it, the word "ἀρχή" is a case in point. This word, Carnap contends, had an "original meaning," namely "beginning," and then was turned away from its usage and used metaphorically by philosophy. It suffices to open a dictionary, however, to see that the word "ἀρχή" has had several main meanings since the time of Homer.[33] Furthermore, Carnap's claim is not only false; it proves to be, on analysis, utterly unclear. This is shown by the second example, the word "God." According to Carnap, this word has three, and only three, distinct uses: (1) mythological—in this first case, it concerns "physical beings . . . enthroned on Mount Olympus" and who, on occasion, can manifest themselves to man, and thus be "empirically observable"[34]; (2) metaphysical—the word "God" in this case refers to nothing observable; it thus gives rise to a "pseudo-concept"; (3) theological—this third use, Carnap maintains, ceaselessly "oscillates" between the two former ones. What are we to make of this typology? First, it is simply false to assert that, from the point of view of the metaphysician (and accessorily the theologian), there is no possible experience of God; without even mentioning the mystic experience, theology accepts the possibility of a beatific vision, and metaphysics distinguishes many modalities of experience of the divine: for example, the contemplation of the Prime Mover according to Aristotle, or the idea of infinity according to Descartes. It may be that these "experiences" are not experiences; but this must be first established. Now, Carnap takes it for granted. What he denies, therefore, is not that the word "God" has a meaning, but first and more fundamentally that there is in general a possible experience of God, that is to say, that any such thing as "God" exists. This assertion is called "atheism." But what it involves is a philosophical (or metaphysical) thesis, not just a logical clarification. If there is no possible experience of God, there is no doubt that many areas of metaphysics are entirely meaningless, but that is for an entirely different reason than the one given by Carnap.

But this is probably not the main point. Indeed, whatever may be the relevance of this first part of his critique, it remains for us to examine the second type of metaphysical nonsense that Carnap believes he is able to expose, and that, in his view, is by far the most serious: the one concerning logical syntax. The passages from Heidegger devoted to nothingness belong to this category. But before dwelling on that, we must again consent to a brief digression.

Before getting to the "Heidegger case," Carnap gives us a sample of this category of nonsense that he says he owes to Russell's theory of types: "Caesar is a prime number." This proposition, he says, is akin to metaphysical propositions, because although it respects the grammatical syntax of English, it is incoherent from the point of view of its logical syntax. To a number predicate that can only be satisfied by the name of a number, it applies a person predicate: in short, it mixes up names and predicates that belong to different logical spheres. Can we resort to the theory of types to justify this assertion?[35] No, since the theory of types is a strictly syntactic theory,[36] and it is impossible to specify what Carnap means by "different logical spheres" without resorting to semantic considerations. But there is more: Carnap's assertion according to which the proposition "Caesar is a prime number" is syntactically incoherent necessarily leads to a paradox. Indeed, if such is the case, the negation of that proposition must also be incoherent. Now, if we consider "Caesar" as a definite description in Russell's sense, its negation is the following: "Either there is an *x* such that that *x* is Caesar, and *x* is not a prime number, or it is false that there is an *x* that is Caesar and that it is a prime number." Not only does that negation make sense, but it is true. As a result, it appears at least legitimate to ask whether the proposition "Caesar is a prime number" is not simply false, and not "meaningless," as Carnap would have it.

Syntactic Nonsense and the Problem of Nothingness

These remarks, however, do not entirely remove the edge from Carnap's analysis of metaphysical nonsense and therefore from his critique of Heidegger. What are we to understand, first of all, by this "metaphysical nonsense"? As I have insisted, it is no longer a matter of "statements devoid of meaning because unverifiable and without content,"[37] but of statements that constitute a violation of logical syntax as such. Although grammatically correct, they cannot be expressed in "a logically correct language."[38] In sum, the metaphysician is deluded here by the surface grammar of the natural languages, and he is mistaken about their deep grammar. Carnap's strategy in order to establish this point is to draw a table allowing the reader to put in relation and compare expressions borrowed from ordinary language (column I), expressions from Heidegger's text, most often mutilated and decontextualized—(column II), and last, "logically correct" expressions written in the formalized language of first-order predicates logic (column III). What is the purpose of this operation? To show that Heidegger's statements, by contrast with those of ordinary language, are not amenable to any appropriate logical paraphrase. But that is not all. If the problem were only to know how to paraphrase Heidegger's expressions—and in particular those pertaining to nothingness—it would be superfluous to mention expressions from ordinary usage such as "rain is outside," "we know the rain," and so on. If Carnap mentions them, it is because his goal is to show not only the logical incoherence of Heidegger's expressions but also and chiefly their metaphysical character. Now, to establish the latter point, it is necessary to show both that Heidegger's expressions are drawn from ordinary use and that they are diverted from their ordinary use.

Thus, from the start, a tension is revealed in Carnap's argumentation. At first sight, his thesis is the following: Heidegger believes he is using language according to its everyday usage but, in doing so, he lets himself be deluded by its grammatical syntax and is mistaken about its deep syntax. Yet if it were truly a matter of "mistakes," they should be corrigible. Nothing, then, would bar our objecting to Carnap that these mistakes are contingent, that there is nothing particularly significant about them, and that in any case they have nothing to do with what he calls "metaphysics." Carnap is therefore forced by the logic of his argument to go a step further. He must establish not only that Heidegger is mistaken in his use of the word "nothing" (*Nichts*), but that he deliberately uses this word in a way that deviates from ordinary usage, and that, since that ordinary usage is logically correct, he also, in so doing, deliberately violates the logical syntax of the word: the "author of the treatise" he writes, "is clearly aware of the conflict between his questions and statements, and logic."[39] But here Carnap exposes himself to the objection that Heidegger deliberately violates ordinary usage because he does not take the words in their ordinary usage. But if that were the case, it would no longer make sense to pretend to correct him, as Carnap is forced to acknowledge: If "the word 'nothing' has in Heidegger's treatise a meaning entirely different from the customary one . . . then the mentioned logical errors in sentences IIB would not be committed."[40]

Carnap has therefore no way out: he addresses two critiques to Heidegger about which there is strong evidence to suggest that they are not compatible with each other. On the one hand, he maintains that Heidegger is using words in their customary and prephilosophical sense. Thus, when he uses the word "nothing," he means nothing other than what is said in a sentence such as "outside there is nothing," which can be paraphrased in first-order predicates calculus by a negative existential quantification. In this case, Heidegger is simply committing a logical error, since he does not have the right to replace "nothing" (*nichts*) with "the nothing" (*das Nichts*). In making this substitution, he lets himself be deluded by grammar, since he is "employing the word 'nothing' as a noun."[41] On the other hand, this error cannot be simply a thoughtless blunder; it must reveal something about the metaphysical enterprise qua enterprise of systematic violation of logic. And Heidegger is then accused of consciously violating the deep syntax of language. Carnap can quote, in support of this interpretation, the passages from the lecture in which Heidegger attacks the sovereignty of logic within philosophy. Heidegger's questions and answers, Carnap concludes, "are irreconcilable with logic and the scientific way of thinking."[42]

But doesn't Carnap have to choose? Either Heidegger deliberately violates syntax or he lets himself be deluded by grammar; either he uses words in their habitual sense or he gives them new meanings that rule out the possibility for logical paraphrase to take as its model sentences grammatically analogous in ordinary language. Either logical paraphrase reveals errors or Heidegger uses language in such a way that he knowingly rejects any logical paraphrase of what he is saying. And actually Carnap must choose between these two possibilities, because this last scenario would make his critique pointless. If it turned out that Heidegger did not in the least take as model for his statements analogous statements from ordinary language, if he used words in a sense different and without relation to their ordinary meaning, if he therefore refused the very principle of a logical paraphrase that would bring his propositions in line with those of everyday language, Carnap's critique would lose all bearing; it would be without object, superfluous, and even ridiculous.

Thus, in order to be meaningful, Carnap's critique must constantly waver between two incompatible assertions: Heidegger must speak in ordinary language and not speak in ordinary language; he must speak a nonmetaphysical language and transgress it constantly and deliberately; he must be both corrigible and incorrigible, etc. But actually, since the second hypothesis leads to the collapse of Carnap's critique—since, if it were true, "the mentioned logical errors in [Heidegger's] sentences IIB would not be committed,"[43]—the only option is to revert to the first. This is what Carnap does a little bit further on. "But the first sentence of the quotation at the beginning of this section proves that this interpretation is not possible. The combination of 'only' and 'nothing else' shows unmistakably that the word 'nothing' here has the usual meaning of a logical particle that serves for the formulation of a negative existential statement. This introduction of the word 'nothing' is then immediately followed by the leading question of the treatise: 'What about this Nothing?' "[44]

This argument is extremely weak for at least three reasons: first, it assumes it is possible to conclude from the fact that a word is used once in its "habitual" sense that it will always and necessarily be used in the same sense in all its subsequent occurrences. This assertion, as observed by James Conant,[45] violates Frege's contextual principle as formulated at the beginning of *Foundations of Arithmetic*. A word has meaning only within the context of a proposition, but the examination of this occurrence does not suffice to fix the rules of its usage for the entirety of the proposition in which it appears.

Next, and above all, the assertion that Heidegger uses his words in their habitual sense and that therefore the word "nothing" (*nichts*) for him "has the usual meaning of a logical particle that serves for the formulation of a negative existential statement" contradicts the evidence of the texts themselves. Indeed, Heidegger always distinguishes between the pronominal and adverbial use of the word "*nichts*" and its nominalized use. Moreover, he is not the only one who makes this distinction: first and foremost, German grammar itself does so. How could it be that Heidegger lets himself be deluded by the grammar of his language if the latter marks the difference between an indefinite pronoun and a noun by capitalizing the latter? How could Heidegger confuse the logical syntax of the word "*nichts*" with its grammatical syntax, given that the difference between "*nichts*" and "*das Nichts*" is already marked in German at the grammatical level by the very way these words are written?

Last, Carnap's argument encounters the objection that the noun "*das Nichts*," the nothing, nothingness, has no usage in ordinary language, but only a strictly philosophical (or theological) one. It is hard to see, in these circumstances, how its use could be the result of any "mistake" whatsoever. To sum up, the "error" Carnap imputes to Heidegger, which consists in taking the word "nothing" (*Nichts*) for the name of an object, because "the word 'nothing' [*Nichts*] here has the usual meaning of a logical particle that serves for the formulation of a negative existential relation,"[46] is nowise an error, nor can it be, because this expression is not used at all in everyday language in the noun form (*das Nichts*) attributed to it by the metaphysician. As to whether Heidegger in fact uses this expression as the name of an object, this is a question we must, for the time being, leave aside.

The fact is that far from furnishing a faithful paraphrase of Heidegger's "statements," Carnap deliberately introduces an "error" into the text of "What Is Metaphysics?" to suit his purposes. He decides, a priori, as it were, regardless of the context, that Heidegger can only mean by "the nothing" (*das Nichts*) what everyday usage means by "nothing" in a sentence of the type "Outside, there is nothing," that is, "there is no thing that is outside." He thus decides that Heidegger's statements can be legitimately paraphrased by negative existential quantifications. Thus, not only does Carnap abolish the distinction that Heidegger repeatedly makes between *das Nichts* and *nichts*, but, by proposing this paraphrase, he contradicts himself. In order to be coherent, Carnap should say, "I don't understand anything about Heidegger's use of the word '*Nichts*' because this word cannot be paraphrased in first-order predicates logic." But this is precisely not what he says. He rather says, "I understand perfectly well what Heidegger means by *Nichts*, and what he means is exactly the same thing as what everyday language means by the indefinite pronoun *nichts*, but what I understand perfectly well, and what can be so paraphrased, I don't understand it, and am incapable of supplying a paraphrase of it."

Furthermore, contrary to the translation he himself has just given of Heidegger's phrases (transformed for the occasion into assertions, since only an assertion can be true or false, and it alone can have a meaning satisfying Carnap's criterion), phases such as "We seek the Nothing," "We find the Nothing," Carnap is forced to recognize that the word "*das Nichts*" in its actual usage by Heidegger is not at all used in the same sense as "nothing" (the negation of an existential quantifier), but quite clearly as a noun. Carnap thinks he is entitled to conclude from this that this noun is the name of an object: "For even if it were admissible to introduce 'nothing' as a name or description of an entity, still the existence of this entity would be denied in its very definition, whereas sentence (3) ['The Nothing exists only because . . .'] goes on to affirm its existence."[47] Here Carnap addresses to Heidegger the only coherent argument in his whole critique, but one that is also the most traditional, the most worn-out one in metaphysics against the possibility of speaking of nothingness, since its first formulation dates back, in a sense, to Parmenides himself. If every noun must have a referent, and if to have a referent means to refer to an object, then the word "nothing," used as a noun, must refer to something, to an object: nothingness. Now, nothingness is the negation of all objects. Therefore the word "nothing" can nowise be used as a noun. We will have occasion to revisit this problem. For the moment, it will suffice to formulate two questions: Is every noun necessarily the name of an object? And is nothingness necessarily the negation of any object?

Heidegger saw that there was a problem here, and he expressed it directly. He also outlined a response—not without a touch of irony—in the second volume of his *Nietzsche*. "As the 'negation' of everything 'objective,' nothingness 'is' for its part, not a possible object. To talk about the nothing and to pursue it in thought are shown to be projects 'without Object,' vacuous word games that furthermore do not seem to notice that they are always flatly contradicting themselves, because no matter what they stipulate about the nothing they always have to say that the nothing is such and such."[48] It is still too soon to assess the value of this response, which puts into question the relevance and importance of the logical—as well as metaphysical—notion of "object": we shall have to return to it.

As for the last "nonsense" that Carnap draws our attention to, it needs no additional commentary. In his view, "*das Nichts nichtet*" [nothingness nothings] is, of course, of all nonsense, the most serious, since it adds to a syntactic nonsense a lexical one. It forges a new verb, "to nothing," about which it is easy to see that it does not satisfy Carnap's criterion. "A new word is introduced which never had a meaning to begin with."[49] But what does "to begin with" mean here? Is Carnap suggesting that all new words, precisely because they are new, are meaningless? Of course not. He means that the only new meaningful words are those about which it is possible to indicate a method of verification and that therefore increase the vocabulary of science. But does ordinary language create new words in order that they may someday be included in the scientific lexicon? It is useless to insist on this issue. Things are otherwise if Heidegger uses his words "with an entirely different meaning than elsewhere," which for Carnap means two things at once: in a use different from their ordinary use (which is a triviality) and in a use that excludes in advance any possible paraphrase.

But in that case, Carnap's demonstration, by his own admission, would collapse; for Heidegger's phrases would no longer contain the errors he points out.

But is this not in fact the case? Must we not even go so far as to maintain that Heidegger's use of the word "nothingness" would have led him—assuming that the question could have had for him a genuine interest—to reject any paraphrase at all of it in the language of modern symbolic logic? The lecture "What Is Metaphysics?" is entirely devoted to attacking "the reign of 'logic' in philosophy" at the same time as all forms of positivism.[50] In this regard, it is not so much Carnap who, in 1931, initiated hostilities against "that metaphysical school which at present exerts the strongest influence in Germany"[51]; rather, it was Heidegger himself who, two years earlier, had attacked logical positivism in covert words[52]—Carnap's article being interpretable in turn as a response. Incidentally, Heidegger points out in a marginal note to his lecture, alongside the passage dealing with the way science excludes the question of nothingness by claiming it has to do with entities "and nothing else" [*und sonst nichts*], that he is borrowing this phrase from Taine, that is, from a positivist.[53] Heidegger subsequently reaffirmed with the greatest clarity his rejection of all logico-mathematical formalization of what he calls "nothingness": in what concerns Being (and therefore the nothing), "we do not wish to capture what opens up here in a formal schema of formal thinking."[54]

But what is the value of such a line of defense? Does it not rather weaken the one adopting it? Indeed, what is the value of a thought that rejects all logical paraphrase of its own assertions? Have we not, after all, reached something that can hardly be understood otherwise than as an "irrationalism"? Nothing is less certain. This defense may, on the contrary, turn out to be a very strong one, provided we understand its meaning—especially provided the critique of logic is not itself arbitrary, not the result of a personal preference or opinion of any kind, but rather grounded in an analysis of the possibilities and impossibilities of that discipline, whose meaning it probes philosophically. Before running into the breach opened up by a supposed "irrationalism" on the part of Heidegger, we must ask a preliminary question—if we are not ourselves to participate in the very irrationalism we oppose. What does Heidegger's rejection of mathematical logic and its primacy in philosophy mean? What is the meaning of his rejection of any and all enterprise that would claim to assess the sense and nonsense of his assertions by the standards of the logical formalism of Frege and Russell?

Logical Formalism and Its Philosophical Meaning

Let us note, first of all, that Heidegger never said anything—neither in the 1929 lecture nor elsewhere—against logical formalism per se that would tend to cast doubt on its validity or fruitfulness. The target of his attacks is the application of logic to philosophical problems—an application that is blind and lacking all critical investigation on its own conditions of possibility. Furthermore, Heidegger rejected throughout his work the idea that philosophical reflection on the essence of the "logical," whose source lies in a reflection on logos in its original Greek sense, could be reduced to the formalism of mathematical logic, or of what he calls—using a term borrowed, incidentally, from the Vienna Circle—"logistics." His claim is the following: Logistics, far from exhausting the field of logic (or of the logical), is but a deterioration and late by-product of it. Without entering into the details of this difficult topic, I will limit myself here to two texts; separated by an interval of fifty years, they testify to a rare constancy, regarding this question, in Heidegger's thought.

The first is the conclusion of a text of his youth: *Neuere Forschungen über Logik*, from 1912. It follows analyses devoted to the logical doctrines of Meinong, Russell, and Whitehead. "It is in my view especially necessary," he writes, "to point out that logistics does not come out of mathematics at all [*überhaupt nicht aus der Mathematik herauskommt*] and that it is incapable of proceeding to genuinely logical problems. I see the limits in the applications of mathematical symbols and concepts (in particular, the concept of function), which conceal the meanings of concepts and their shifts in meaning (*Bedeutungsverschiebungen*). The deeper sense of principles is left in the dark. The calculus of judgments (*Urteilskalkül*) is, for example, a calculating with judgments (*Rechnen mit Urteilen*). Logistics is simply not familiar with the problems of the theory of judgment (*Urteilstheorie*). Mathematics and mathematical treatment of logical problems reach limits at which their concepts and methods fail, more precisely, there where the conditions of their possibility lie."[55] This passage asserts—albeit allusively, and without furnishing any argumentation and rather peremptorily—that mathematical logic is nothing but an extension of mathematics into the domain of judgment, and that that extension, not questioned as such as to its conditions of possibility, leaves the main philosophical problems in suspense.

The second text is excerpted from *Die Frage nach dem Ding* (1962), and bears upon "a view and treatment of logic which today and for a number of decades has been much talked about." It characterizes this view as follows: "With the help of mathematical methods people attempt to calculate the system of the connectives between assertions. For this reason, we also call this logic 'mathematical logic.' It proposes to take on a possible and justified task. However, what symbolic logic achieves is anything but a logic, that is, a reflection upon λόγος. Mathematical logic is not even logic of mathematics in the sense of defining mathematical truth, nor could it do so at all. Symbolic logic is itself only a mathematics applied to propositions and propositional forms."[56]

There is certainly reason to question this characterization of mathematical logic, particularly when it is seen as a calculus of "the system of the connectives between assertions" (which, strictly speaking, can only apply to the calculus of propositions, and not to the calculus of predicates, nor to Russell's logic of relations) and a fortiori when this calculus is conceived of, a little further on in the text, as "a mere combination of representations" despite Frege's anti-psychologism. In giving special emphasis to the concepts of "connectives" and "combination," Heidegger understands contemporary logic in terms of the *synthesis* and *diaresis* of Aristotle's syllogistic; he misses their true novelty. But that is not the essential point, which lies rather in the assertion that not only mathematical logic is not a logic of mathematics (Heidegger is probably referring to the failure of the project of logicism to provide a foundation of mathematics), but it consists only in a "mathematics applied to propositions and propositional forms." Again, Heidegger gives no arguments to support his claim, and if we wish to assess its importance, we must try to fill in this gap. In what sense is mathematical logic no more than an "applied mathematics," a mathematics applied to the traditional problems of logic? And especially: What does follow from the application of this logical formalization to the elucidation of philosophical notions?

The task seems very vast. Where should we begin? In Part 6 of the "The Elimination of Metaphysics," Carnap said that all the logical problems raised by Heidegger's concept of "nothingness" eventually came down to "the logical faults infecting the use of the word 'to be' in our language,"[57] and more particularly to the "confusion" consisting in taking existence for a predicate of objects, whereas its true logical form is that of a quantifier applying to the whole proposition. If we want to elucidate the potential presuppositions of the application of a logico-mathematical formalism to philosophical notions, we may therefore start with this concept of "existence," since it is presupposed by that of "nothingness."

The Logical Problem of Existence

By making manifest the logical relations that remain insufficiently expressed in the natural languages, the goal of symbolic logic, as developed by Frege, is not only to avoid the ambiguities and errors associated with our spontaneous use of language, but also to bring out the deductive structure of mathematics by means of an adequate *formalismus*, at the same time distinct from that of arithmetic (by contrast with Boole's algebra of logic) and liable to be combined with the latter in order to complete it. This ideography, "at first just for arithmetic,"[58] would subsequently make possible the logicist foundation of arithmetic, that is, the project aimed at establishing that "arithmetic is a further development of logic; that a more rigorous establishment of arithmetical laws reduces them to purely logical laws and to such laws alone."[59] Now, in order to thus enlarge the symbolism of mathematics by means of signs originally conceived for logical relations, Frege borrows from mathematics the notions of "function" and "argument." Thus, even if it is not logic that is derived from mathematics but quite the opposite, the invention of symbolic logic is linked to the extension of certain mathematical concepts outside their original domain.

A function is a formula having one or several empty places (for example: "$y = 2x + 4$") that can be saturated by one or several arguments (here symbolized by the variables "x" and "y"). Frege proposes to extend the concept of "function" beyond mathematical functions with one or several unknowns and the concept of "argument" beyond the sphere of numbers. But how is this extension possible? In the first place, what does the equality in the function "$y = 2x + 4$" denote? Not a numerical value, but a truth-value. If I make "5" correspond to "y" and "7" to "x," this equation is false; in the case where y = 8 and $x = 2$, this equation is true. This consideration makes it possible to apply the function versus argument distinction to propositions in general. Consider the sentence "Caesar conquered Gaul." It contains an unsaturated part, a function: "conquered Gaul," and a part that saturates this function, an argument: "Caesar." "Not merely numbers," Frege writes, "but objects in general, are now admissible; and here persons must assuredly be counted as objects."[60] According to the element that saturates it, this function, has as its value truth or falsity. "Caesar conquered Gaul" is true, but "Hannibal conquered Gaul" is false.

Frege calls "concept" a function that receives as arguments objects, and as values, not numbers, but truth-values. "A concept is a function whose value is always a truth-value." And he calls "object" "anything that is not a function," that is, anything the expression of which "does not contain any empty place."[61] The two truth-values are therefore objects. They constitute what is denoted by a proposition.

What becomes of the traditional problem of existence in this new logical framework? The problem addressed by Frege is that of the translation, within a logic based on the notion of function, of the Aristotelian distinction between the universality and the particularity of propositions having a subject-predicate form ("All *S* are *P*" and "Some *S* is *P*"). Frege proposes to translate these formulas by creating two logical operators, the existential quantifier and the universal quantifier, which generate the propositional forms (*x*) (F*x*) and (∃*x*) (F*x*) ("for every *x*, F*x*" and "there exists at least one x such that F*x*").[62] These quantifiers do not bear upon objects but upon the propositional function itself. This amounts to saying that in a sentence of the type "Whales exist," that is, "There are whales," I am not asserting anything about an object, this whale, I am not attributing any new property to it, but I am limiting myself to asserting something about a concept, that of "whale." I am asserting about this concept that something comes under it. The statement "there are whales" says something about the concept *whale*, but it says nothing about the whale I am looking at. That particular statement is no more about this observable whale than is the universal statement "All whales are mammals."[63] Actually, what I say in both cases is something "general." The proof of this is that universal propositions and particular propositions can be expressed by one another. "All men are mortal" is equivalent to "there is no man who is not mortal." This amounts to saying that they are both true even in a world in which no man exists: they express nothing other than a relation of the inclusion of properties.

What the existential quantifier says is consequently equivalent to the form of Aristotle's particular judgment, expressed in a more powerful formalism. "But if the content of what is predicated in the judgement 'Men exist' does not lie in the 'exist,'" Frege writes, "where then does it lie? I answer: in the form of the particular judgement. Every particular judgement is an existential judgement that can be converted into the 'there is' form. E.g., 'Some bodies are light' is the same as 'There are light bodies.' . . . It is more difficult to do the opposite and convert a judgement with 'there is' into a particular judgement."[64] The superiority of the formalism invented by Frege over that of Aristotle is twofold: (1) it makes possible the translation of Aristotle's particular judgments, while the reverse is more difficult: to translate "there are men," Aristotle would have to say, "Some animals are rational"; (2) above all, it permits one to avoid Aristotle's error consisting in believing that general propositions are necessarily instantiated, that is, that they imply existence. For example, the syllogism in Darapti, "All Greeks are men, all Greeks are white, some men are white," is only true if there are Greeks, and if not, it is false. Aristotle proceeds as if the major of his syllogism in fact included two propositions: a proposition of existence, "There are Greeks," and a general proposition, "If something is a Greek, it is a man."[65]

But then, if "existence" means nothing other, or nothing more, than the form of the particular judgment, if "Some men are Germans" is just as much a judgment of existence as "Some men exist,"[66] why call this judgment a "judgment of existence"? Why call the logical operator invented by Frege an "existential quantifier," and not, for example, a "particular quantifier" and propose to read it not "there is at least one x" but "for some *x* . . ."[67]? This would at least have the merit of drawing attention to the fact that in the existential quantifier it is emphatically not a question of the existence of individuals in the ordinary sense. But Frege not only invents a formalism, he accompanies it with a philosophical interpretation. His purpose is not only to furnish a logical paraphrase of Aristotle's particular judgments, but to show that the philosophers were entirely mistaken about the concept of existence when they made it into a property of individuals. When they speak of "being" and even of "absolute being," philosophers end up, says Frege, in an "apotheosis of the copula."[68]

In short, what is existence from a logical point of view? It is a property of a function (or a concept) and not of an object, or it is a second-level concept, a concept of concept, expressing a "classification": "When you say 'There are men' and 'There are no centaurs' you are also making a classification. But you are not classifying things, which in one case are not there at all, and in the other case are not being assigned to one of two classes, but you are classifying the concepts 'man' and 'centaur' by assigning one to the class of concepts under which something belongs, and excluding the other from this class. This is why I hold that in these sentences the concepts are the real subjects."[69] To take another example, this time borrowed from the domain of mathematics, if I assert that "there is at least one even number between 2 and 8," I am not asserting the existence of this number (what does the "existence" of a number mean?) but only that the concept "even number between 2 and 8" is not empty, and that it includes at least one x that comes under it. We can see to what point this concept of "existence" is adapted when it is a matter of the existence of numbers, that is, of purely ideal entities having no reality in space and time. But does it suffice to account for our ordinary concept of existence such as we use it in our natural languages?

Its being tailored, so to speak, to the measure of mathematics is further attested to by the fact that "existence" taken in this sense (as a concept bearing upon concepts) has exactly the same logical status as number. Indeed number is not a predicate or a property of things (like color is, for example). "This is perhaps clearest," writes Frege, "with the number 0. If I say 'Venus has 0 moons,' there simply does not exist any moon or agglomeration of moons for anything to be asserted of; but what happens is that a property is assigned to the concept 'moon of Venus,' namely that of including nothing under it. If I say 'the King's carriage is drawn by four horses,' then I assign the number four to the concept 'horse that draws the King's carriage.' "[70]

Here we have an analogy with the concept of existence that doesn't assert any property of thing, either, but only a property of concept—that of not being empty. To quantify existentially, consequently, is nothing other than to number. "In this respect," Frege specifies, "existence is analogous to number. Affirmation of existence is in fact nothing but denial of the number nought."[71] Like number, existence is a property of concepts, a concept of concept. Just as to number is to attribute a property to a concept and not to the individuals subsumable under this concept, so to assert existence is to assert of a concept that it subsumes at least one individual—and this can be true even in a world in which no individual corresponds to this concept. But the question that cannot fail to arise here is the following: Does this concept of existence allow us to account for the way we use existence when we attribute it to objects that can be or not be, that begin to exist and cease existing, that is, that are subject to time? In other words, isn't this formalization inextricably bound to philosophical presuppositions—bound, for example, to Frege's Platonism?

In any case, the consideration that ultimately justifies the assertion that it makes no sense to speak of objective (or individual) existence is the following: As soon as I speak of an individual, I presuppose its existence by the simple fact of referring to it, and the assertion of its existence adds nothing further. When I say "*A*," or "*A* exists," strictly speaking I am saying the same thing. If existence were a predicate, as "wise" is, I should be able to assert it about something, but also to deny it. For example, I can say "Socrates is wise" and "Socrates is not wise." But it makes no sense to say "Socrates is not existing," for then I attribute an existence to Socrates, but, at the same time, I take it back. "If you want to assign a content to the verb 'to be,' so that the sentence '*A* is' is not pleonastic and self-evident, you will have to allow circumstances under which the negation of '*A* is' is possible; that is to say, that there are subjects of which being must be denied. But in that case the concept 'being' will no longer be suitable for providing a general explanation of 'there are' under which 'there are *B*'s' means the same as 'something that has being comes under the concept *B*'; for if we apply this explanation to 'There are subjects of which being must be denied,' then we get 'Something that has being comes under the concept of not-being' or 'Something that has being is not.'"[72] We have here the same argument that Carnap will take up, and that leads both authors to the same conclusion: the concept of "being" is a pseudo-concept, since either it says something superfluous or it asserts a predicate that is not a predicate, since its negation is impossible. "In this way we form a quasi-concept—'being'—without content, since its extension is unlimited."[73] We must emphasize how much this assertion itself is overdetermined from a metaphysical point of view. The assertion that there is a "common concept of being" and that, since being is a concept, it must be the most universal in extension, therefore the most empty in understanding, so empty that it is superfluous and in reality says nothing, is connected to a metaphysical tradition—that of the univocity of being—dating back to Duns Scotus and extending its influence to Kant and even Nietzsche, and the main thesis of which Heidegger includes in the number of "prejudices" that he enumerates in §1 of *Sein und Zeit*: "'Being' is the 'most universal' concept." But if it is the most universal concept, it should be added, it is still a concept, that is, it still has a certain right to be considered a predicate. And does it suffice to say, in order to dispose of the problem, that this predicate cannot be denied? On the contrary, there are contexts in which the sentence "The table does not exist" has meaning; it is when I mean that it does not exist here and now (it existed, or it will exist). But Frege's logico-mathematical concept of "existence" precludes this sort of consideration, precisely because this existence thus understood is a property of concept, that is, a property of something that is not subject to time.

Russell, in his *Philosophy of Logical Atomism*, makes an important clarification on this subject. In general, and with the exception of a few terminological modifications (he replaces "concept" with "class," because he no longer adheres to Frege's Platonism—but is it sufficient, in order to escape Platonism, to make that replacement?—and he replaces "object" with "individual"), his analysis of existence coincides with Frege's. What we mean when we assert that "there are men" is simply that "that propositional function is true in at least one instance."[74] This amounts to saying that this propositional function is at least sometimes true. But what does "sometimes" mean here? To say that this function is sometimes true amounts to saying that it is possible that this function is true. But then "existence" in the logical sense says strictly nothing other than possibility. In Fregean terms, it is the possibility that a concept is not empty. This possibility actually tells us nothing about the eventual existence of individuals or objects subsumed under this concept.

Russell draws this consequence, which remained implicit in Frege, with the utmost clarity. From the point of view of existential quantification, "existence" means nothing other than "possibility." "It will be out of this notion of sometimes, which is the same as the notion of possible, that we get the notion of existence. To say that unicorns exist is simply to say that '(*x* is a unicorn) is possible.'"[75] But then why call this quantifier "existential"? Is it not the logician—and not the philosopher—who lets himself be misled by the use he makes of the word "existence" here, thinking that he is paraphrasing the sentences of ordinary language that speak of it? To what extent does the existential quantifier really allow the formalization of the notion of existence as it is used in our natural languages?

For the reasons we have seen, Frege and Russell reason on the existence of things exactly as they might reason on that of numbers; for them, there is a perfect univocity of existence. But then we have to do with a metaphysical thesis and not with a logical one. When we say, for example, "This table exists," do we mean the same thing as when we assert, "There exists a real number between 2 and 4"? In the first case, "existence" refers essentially to time and space. "This table exists" means, "There exists a table here and now." Before having been produced it did not exist, after having been destroyed it will no longer exist; if it is moved by someone, it will exist continually during its successive locations. Such a concept of "existence" obviously cannot apply to a number. Now Frege and Russell give no importance to this distinction. And it is by virtue of this univocist conception of existence that Russell can conclude at the end of his analysis, "The actual things that there are in the world do not exist, or, at least, that is putting it too strongly, because that is utter nonsense."[76] But the fact that Russell accepts to formulate—and a fortiori to write—such "nonsense" at least reveals something: that he believes he can draw general philosophical lessons from what is actually only a logical formalization. He thereby proceeds as if a logical formalization had in and for itself a philosophical significance, without having to be interpreted. He thus changes into a metaphysical thesis what is and remains a formalism.

Now it is not at all obvious that existence, in the statement "this table exists," or "this table does not exist," can be formalized in the language of Fregean mathematical logic. In the event that it can't, we would begin to understand what Heidegger means when he says that mathematical logic is merely mathematics applied to logic—namely, mathematical logic implicitly attributes the way of being of mathematical objects to the whole of what is. Now as Heidegger reminded us in *Sein und Zeit*, and as he repeats in his 1929 lecture, "mathematics is not more rigorous than historiology"[77]; it only rests on a different regional ontology. And this is why there is actually no sense in extending the mode of being of mathematical objects outside their own domain. Moreover, if that extension takes place, it can only lead to serious difficulties.

This kind of difficulty appears precisely when we try to reduce the spatiotemporal concept of existence to "existence" in the Fregean sense—notions that, as we shall see, are not equivalent.[78] Can we, by means of the concept of "existence" underlying existential quantification, paraphrase a statement from our natural languages as banal and intuitively obvious as "*x* is dead," that is, "*x* has ceased existing"? The answer, as C. J. F. Williams has shown, must be no. One might, at first view, try to paraphrase this statement in the following way (the author takes as his example the death of a horse named "Black Beauty"): "For some time before time *t* there was a horse which was *F, G, H*, etc., and was called 'Black Beauty' but after time *t* there was no such horse." Is this translation satisfactory? No, because it remains ambiguous on an essential point, that of whether it is the same horse that is called "Black Beauty," possesses such and such properties, etc., and of which something is asserted before and after time *t*. In order to dispel this ambiguity, it is therefore necessary to add a specification on the identity of this horse over time. By specifying this last point, we are led to a second paraphrase: "For some time before time *t* there was a horse which was *F, G, H*, etc., and was called 'Black Beauty' but after time *t* there was no horse which was *F, G, H*, etc., and was called 'Black Beauty' and was identical with the horse which was *F, G, H*, etc., and was called 'Black Beauty' and existed before time *t*." Are we now in possession of a logical translation making it possible to account for temporal existence and its cessation in terms of existential quantification? Nowise. Indeed, as Williams shows, the preceding statement is absurd for at least two reasons: (1) it reintroduces, at the end, a sense of existence ("and existed before time *t*") different from that of existential quantification, namely the existence of an individual over time that the paraphrase was intended to eliminate; and (2) it has a logical defect stemming from the use of the expression "identical with." Indeed, to return to the terminology and expressions of Frege, when we say that "the Evening Star is bright" we are saying something about the reference (*Bedeutung*) of the expression "the evening star," but when we say that "the Evening Star is the same as the Morning Star," we are expressing something about its meaning (*Sinn*). Thus, every proposition of the type "which *is F, G, H*, etc., and is identical with" constitutes a solecism. All in all, the attempted translation thus turns out to be a "failure," by Williams's own admission.[79]

What applies here to the cessation of existence also applies, and rigorously in the same terms, to the appearing, the coming into being, of something.

This failure—if indeed it is such—is obviously crucial for the problem at hand. It undermines the very foundation of Carnap's project of "elimination" of metaphysics. It manifests in an irrefutable manner the philosophical presuppositions inherent in the Fregean conception of existence and, by this very fact, the structural limits of all attempts to reformulate traditional ontological problems in the logico-mathematical formalism. Can this difficulty be solved? Tugendhat, for example, has tried to do so by proposing to restrict the scope of the existential quantifier by a spatiotemporal clause.[80] With Frege and Russell, Tugendhat maintains that existence is not a predicate of individuals, but against them he defends the claim that there is a concept of existence that is irreducible to the Fregean concept and that means the presence of something somewhere for a certain time. "The traditional notion of being, absolutely speaking," Tugendhat writes, "reappears within the modern context" of the logic of predicates,[81] far from being purely and simply eliminated by it. Only if we adopt this "classical" concept of existence does it make sense to speak of the being of an individual through time, and therefore also of its coming into existence and of the cessation of its existence. But what are we to make of Tugendhat's logical solution? First, we must note that this author does not propose a new formalism capable of giving rise to a logical calculus. Nor does he solve the paradox raised by Williams. His thesis appears stronger in its critical scope than in its positive contribution. In *Self-Consciousness and Self-Determination*, Tugendhat seems more cautious about the importance of the innovation he proposed in his article and about the possibility of continuing to formulate the problem of existence in the classical sense, as existence of individuals in space and time, within the Fregean formalism. "I can leave the question open here as to whether it is still possible to reduce existence in this sense to the existential quantifier (as I once maintained), or whether a genuine—though unique—two-place predicate is involved in this sense of existence." The fact remains—and this is the essential point—that the concept expressed through the "there are" of existential quantification and the "singular (predicative) concept of existence" have "two different grammars."[82]

Thus, the logical paraphrase provides no philosophical solution to the traditional problem of existence, unless we presuppose a univocity of existence that nothing can legitimate from the strictly logical point of view. Conversely, it leads logically to difficulties as soon as we have to account for the use of the notion of "existence" simultaneously in its ordinary and philosophical senses, since here they are not at odds one with another. In this respect, as Heidegger insisted, Frege's logico-mathematical formalism goes hand in hand with largely unexamined philosophical presuppositions. It is precisely these presuppositions—Platonism and the thesis of a univocity of existence from mathematics to metaphysics—that Heidegger rejects. The impossibility of translating statements about the coming into existence and the cessation thereof into the Fregean formalism shows obviously the latter's limitations, and it does so by purely logical means. It follows that Heidegger probably had good reasons for dismissing the paraphrases that logical positivism claimed to make of his assertions regarding the problem of existence. Since existence, in the sense in which he understands it, is certainly not a property of classes or concepts, it has a fundamentally temporal meaning.

What are we to make, then, of his "statements" about nothingness? This is, obviously, the pivotal question, if it is true that in "What Is Metaphysics," the Nothing "is the sole topic of the lecture."[83]

Once Again: The Logical Problem of Nothingness

But first, what can bring philosophy to confront the nothing, nothingness? How, in connection with what problem, can the nothing make its appearance in philosophy? Is this problem, as Carnap would have it, only a pseudo-problem?

The answer to these questions has already been sketched out in connection with the logical paraphrase of an expression such as "x died." The first context in which we are induced to bring up the nothing is when we say of something—a thing in our surroundings, for example—that its destruction has reduced it to nothing, when we speak of its annihilation, or, on the other hand, when we say of something that it springs forth, appears, is born, when we refer to its coming into existence. To appear, to disappear is to spring forth out of nothing and return to nothing, as is already attested in ordinary language. In the phrase "A is reduced to nothing," nothing, nonexistence, refer to the absence of something in time and not to a property of its concept. It is in this sense, for example, that Thomas Aquinas can say that *omnis creatura est vertibilis in nihil.*[84] It is so to the extent that it is subject to becoming, and therefore to change, to destruction, to disappearance. It is therefore in the first place to the experience of temporality that the consideration of nothingness belongs. Time presupposes that one can attribute to something (thing, person, event) now being, now nonbeing. There are phenomena such as "to spring forth" and "to disappear" of which we could give no account unless we accepted at least a certain concept of "nothing." As Heidegger remarks, "if the nothing is nothing, if it is not, then neither can beings ever founder in the nothing nor can all things dissolve in it. Hence there can be no process of becoming-nothing (*Nichtswerden*)."[85] Now, is not the process of "becoming-nothing" a phenomenon—which immediately entails the corollary that the nothing must be, at least in some sense, given? "The nothing itself . . . must be given beforehand."[86] Nonexistence, that is to say, nonpresence, absence (*Absenz*),[87] which constantly gnaws away at presence, here has a phenomenological right equal to that of presence, the actually given. If the nothing is "given" in this sense, it is not as a zero-point of givenness, but precisely as the givenness of an absence, of a nonpresence, as what is at play in all givenness and without which the givenness of a given would not even be possible. Therefore, only if the nothing and Being are understood in light of time is it possible to accede to their phenomenological meaning. Furthermore, the nothing does not have an exclusively temporal meaning, but to some extent also a spatial one. In the distance, at the point where the horizon trembles, the world collapses into itself and loses itself in the nothing. This nothing is precisely not nothing; it is the condition of the appearing of the world, or, more precisely, it is the appearing of the world itself as conditioned, as dependent on our finitude. It belongs to the world itself in its moment of appearing, suspended between past and future, insofar as its openness (*Offenheit*) determines the very existence of *Dasein*, that is to say, "the Being of those beings who stand open for the openness of Being in which they stand, by standing it."[88] The nothing is therefore nothing other than Being; it is Being itself.

Is all this only metaphors, inconsistent statements, nonsense even? Does not this phenomenological description—insofar as it is phenomenological—have its own right? But if so, what supports this right? Heidegger continually asserts it: the nothing in the sense in which he understands it, as openness of the appearing, withdrawal, latency articulating all presence, *Un-entborgenheit* belonging to all *Unverborgenheit*, is not nothing—which comes down to saying that it cannot be paraphrased by a negative existential quantification. Or, to express it differently, the phenomenological concept of nothing, the nothing as "given,"—albeit obliquely—in all givenness, is not a nothingness of givenness: it is not a *nichtiges Nichts*,[89] an absolute nothingness, a "null nothing"; it is not what we refer to when we say "it's nothing," because it is indeed, as such, something—the "condition" of the appearing for all appearing. Of course, this nothing is of no concern to science, since the latter, by virtue of its objectivism, completely and definitely overlooks the appearing of the world.

This comes down to saying that nothingness is not the negation of all things, that it is not thinkable as the application of the logical operator of negation to all that can be thought (to all that falls under a concept). This is Bergson's main mistake, to which Heidegger dedicates a few lines without naming him, in his 1929 lecture. The nothing is neither the application of the logical negation to the entirety of imagined beings nor its application to the totality of conceived beings, as apprehended by the understanding.[90] There are two reasons to reject this formulation of the problem. The first is purely phenomenological. This formulation misses the very problem it was supposed to solve, namely the problem of the absence conditioning all presence, of the finitude of all manifestation, in other words, of the intrinsic temporality of the phenomenal world. Indeed, if the nothing were "the entire negation of the totality of beings," that totality itself would have first to be given. But to whom could it be given? "The totality of beings must be given in advance so as to be able to fall prey straightway (*schlecthin*) to negation—in which the nothing itself would then be manifest."[91] But this is precisely what is impossible. Such a straightway givenness of beings as a whole to which negation as logical operator could be applied misconstrues the phenomenological conditions of all givenness; it presupposes, so to speak, a divine, infinite understanding, which is precisely excluded by our finitude. The second argument, which runs through the entire lecture, concerns not only Bergson, but more generally every conception that makes nothingness the result of a negation. If nothingness were nothing other than the application of negation to all that falls under a concept, it would assuredly follow that nothingness, like negation itself, would have nothing real about it. This is what Kant had already said: "Reality is something, negation is nothing; that is, it is the concept of the absence of an object, as shadow or cold (*nihil privativum*)."[92] But what does it mean, here, that negation is nothing? Can this "nothing" in turn be thought on the basis of the logical operator of negation? Is it not necessary to maintain exactly the opposite? Is not nothingness prior to negation, rather than being made possible by it? At about the same time, Husserl also posed, in a different context, the phenomenological problem of "the origin of negation."[93] This question seems all the more absurd in that logic gives us no definition of negation, or rather, in that the very definition it gives of this "functor" (for example, by its truth table) necessarily presupposes negation through the opposition between true and false.

But does what I am saying here still have meaning? A first response to that question follows from the considerations above. Indeed, if the problem of nothingness is first of all that of temporality itself—and as a result, of the world, insofar as its appearing presupposes temporality—then the critique of the concept of existence underlying existential quantification applies here first and foremost. If existence cannot mean everywhere and uniformly the "denial of the number nought," but signifies in most cases the presence of something over time (and eventually space), it follows that nonexistence, non-being, signifies its absence, its nonpresence. To the question I raised, there is, therefore, a response both simple and univocal: the concept of nothingness is legitimate as long as we maintain the irreducibility of the spatiotemporal meaning of existence to the formalism of existential quantification. Nothing then prevents us from positing, more generally, the question not of the absence of this or that being (ontic concept of "nothing") but of the withdrawal or absence constitutive of all coming into presence as such, and therefore of the nonappearing as it articulates all appearing, of the Openness of phenomenality or yet again of the world in its originary phenomenological meaning—and such indeed is the ontological question of the nothing for Heidegger.

But at this point a supplementary difficulty appears, which resides in the application of the principle of noncontradiction to statements about nothingness. When we speak of nothingness, do we not transform it surreptitiously into an object, do we not make of the expression "nothingness," inevitably, a "name of object," as Carnap said, so that we affirm of nothingness that it is as long as and to the same extent as we assert that it is nothingness? We thus witness the reformulation of the argument of Parmenides in the setting of contemporary logic.

Let us recall that Frege's fundamental argument against the conception of existence as a predicate of objects was the following: If existence were a predicate, it should be able to be denied like any other predicate. If, in the expression "*A* exists," existence had a predicative meaning, it would make sense to assert "*A* does not exist." But, in the assertion "*A* does not exist," if that statement is true, *A* must have a reference. I therefore posit the existence of *A* by assuming that this word has a reference, and, at the same time, I deny its existence through its predicate. I therefore fall into a logical contradiction. It follows both that existence is not a predicate and that it does not make sense to speak of the nonexistence of something, of its non-being. And we can even less speak of non-being in itself, that is, transform it into an object, since in so doing we would assert the existence of that object.

The first part of this argument rests on a concept of existence whose philosophical limits we have attempted to show: there is no reason to go over it again. As for the assertion that nothingness cannot be the name of an object, it rests on the following prior assumption: All we can speak of meaningfully are either objects or concepts. Indeed, besides the logical constants and the operators of quantification, that is to say, the elements of its syntax, the language of the logic of predicates only admits of functions (concepts) and objects (arguments, truth-values). Now, nothingness cannot be a concept, because a concept always has an extension, it always bears upon objects, even if this extension is null. Nor can it be an object, the argument of a function. This is why, as Frege would conclude, "nothingness" has no other meaning than that of a previously denied existential quantification, and is logically the equivalent of the empty set. "Nothing" therefore cannot be used as a substantive: we cannot pass, as Carnap claimed, from "nothing" (*nichts*) to "the nothing" (*Nichts*).

But perhaps there is, after all, a way to grant nothingness a place within logic, and that is precisely to make it into a "concept." This project is as old as philosophy itself: When Plato, in the dialectic of the "great kinds" in the *Sophist*, decides to transgress Parmenides's interdiction by speaking of a being of non-being, he can only do so because he has previously reduced non-being to an Idea, a genus, that is, discarded absolute non-being as the opposite (ἐναντίον) of being and accepted only a relative non-being, alterity.[94] An analogous strategy presides over contemporary logical undertakings. If nothingness has a logical status, it can only be a conceptual status. In this way it is possible to dissipate the paradox linked to the pseudo-referential status of the propositions about the nothing. In the proposition $(\exists x)$ (. . . (x)), existence as expressed by the existential quantifier is to be understood, as we have seen, as a predicate of predicate of individuals, that is, a second-order predicate. The same is true of "nonexistence" in the sense of the negative existential quantifier. If I assert, for example, that "there is no largest prime number," I am asserting that nothing instantiates the property "largest prime," that is, that the extension of this concept is null or that every statement of the form "___ is greatest prime" is false. Now in the third-order predicate calculus, nothing would preclude the assertion that "there was a second-level property of first-level properties of individuals (namely, noninstantiation) such that it qualified some first-level property (for instance, largest prime number)."[95] It follows that the paraphrase of the concept of nothingness is the following: "concept of a first-level concept with no extension." "Its extensional counterpart," as Wiggins remarks, "would be the extension of the concept 'concept with no extension' or {{ ^ }}, the unit-set of the null set." Thus, if I assert the existence of such a concept, namely the concept of an empty concept, I do not contradict myself. The only question remaining is whether it is indeed to that that a thinking of nothingness refers. Indeed, not only do we have to do once more with the existence of a concept (and therefore of something and not of nothing), but with the existence of the concept "concept with no extension," and consequently of the existence of a concept having a certain extension (since many concepts have a null extension); not only is this concept something, but a number of objects fall under it.[96] By his refusal to make nothingness the name of an object, the logician has solved the problem of the pseudo-referential status of this term, but he has done so by making of nothingness a property of concepts, by assigning it a reference, and, finally, by idealizing it. The principle of noncontradiction has been preserved, but the problem of nothingness, which is certainly not that of the extension of certain concepts—and, more precisely, of their null extension—has been missed. For nothingness is not the number nought.

Here we can see to what extent the two problems—that of "existence" in the logical sense and that of quantification—in reality are one and the same: to reject the definition of the former ("affirmation of existence is nothing but denial of the number nought"), or more precisely to restrict its scope, is thus also and at the same time to question the latter and to inquire into its limits. The question that arises, indeed, is the following: if everything that pertains to mathematical logic must be an object (falling under a concept), if all concepts must be quantifiable, isn't there anything that is neither an object nor quantifiable and that thus eludes in principle all formalization in that logic? Let us give a few examples.

What of perception? Is it quantifiable? Are perceptions different objects (in the Fregean sense) capable of falling under a concept? But where does one perception end; where does it begin? What determines its numerical identity? How can perceptions be added up? What is the unit here that is to be considered relevant? We might answer that this unit can be conceived of as a temporal one: for example, one-tenth of a second. Thus we could measure the perceptual continuum by means of temporal units of measurement. However, this answer is somewhat irrelevant, for the experiences of other people are also perceptions, and yet, they belong to two different categories. My perception and theirs are not placed on the same level; they cannot be added up together. The same goes for other phenomena—therefore also for other words, which are not strictly singular or plural: "consciousness," "the world," "the body," "others," "the phenomenal field," "the visible," "the appearing." There is, and there can only be, one sole world, and at the same time, it is inevitable to assert that there must be several, that there must exist between them an implicit "geometry," a congruence and articulation that do not enter into the unity-multiplicity distinction. For unity and plurality are not on the same plane here—are not addable and form no sequence in the arithmetic sense.

It goes without saying that "nothingness," in the sense Heidegger understands it, belongs to the same category—and that is how he escapes mathematical logic. If the only thing that can be considered an object is what falls under a concept, if the only thing that is quantifiable is a concept, it follows that the nothing is neither an object nor a concept in the sense Frege and logistics attach to these terms. Thus, when Heidegger asserts that nothingness is older than negation, and that it does not mean the negation of all things (in the sense of a negative existential quantification), this is not only because he refuses to conform, in order to conceive of it, to the formal concept of existence underlying existential quantification, but also and chiefly because he rejects, in order to give an account of the world as a phenomenon, the principle of quantification. The world is neither an object, nor a multiplicity of objects, nor the concept subsuming that multiplicity: it possesses its own phenomenal structures, irreducible to any account in the language of mathematics. This is why the nothing, just like Being, cannot come under the jurisdiction of conceptual thought, not only in the classical sense of the term, in which the concept is primarily related to the representation of a subject, but also in the sense in which logistics understands it. "Being thus denies itself every concept (*Begriff*)"[97]—which is also true of nothingness. If what I have said above is true, there can be no question of taxing such an assertion with irrationalism.

Not only does mathematical logic not exhaust the field of the sayable and the thinkable, but by presupposing the universality of the realm of the quantifiable, it begs the question: it is indeed this "applied mathematics," of which Heidegger speaks, which does not question the limits of its legitimate application and remains, in this respect, infra-philosophical. This *petitio principi* is of no consequence if it is a question of seeking, like Frege, the logical foundation of arithmetic, since one does not see, in that case, how the nonquantifiable could be of any concern to philosophy. But it becomes a serious lapse when it is a question of applying mathematical logic indiscriminately to philosophical problems as a whole, or of claiming to translate the totality of the sayable into a formal language. To those who would proceed along these lines it should be reminded of what Plato said of mathematicians—he who held mathematics in such high esteem: ὀνειρώττουσι [μὲν] περὶ τὸ ὄν, "they dream about being."[93] It is impossible for them to have a waking vision as long as they proceed as mathematicians, that is, as long as they do not question their own presuppositions and give no rational justification for them (μὴ δυνάμεναι λόγου διδόναι αὐτῶν). Their dream is rigorously the same as that of an unrestricted application of mathematical tools to ontological problems. For, as Plato says in Letter VII, the tools of philosophy are not philosophy itself. And to Carnap, who claimed that "metaphysicians are musicians without musical ability,"[99] one is tempted to reply that logicians who think they can solve philosophical problems through the positivity of a formalism alone are, on careful consideration, hardly more than mathematicians without mathematical genius.

8

“Between Emptiness and the Pure Event”: Phenomenology

“The sun is new every day.” Aristotle comments on this famous fragment of Heraclitus in the following terms: “we should obviously not only have a new sun every day, as Heraclitus says, but a new sun every moment.”[1] What does “new,” νέος, mean here?

At every moment, before our astonished eyes—and “new,” as it were—the sun is born. Its flaming insularity stands vertically erect upon itself in that place of precarious and jeopardized equilibrium of its own upsurge; “it forms and dissolves, and it approaches and departs,”[2] that is to say, it renews itself at the very site of appearing. Ceaselessly it perpetuates the appearing in its rising. Its presence is that of an event, but a continuous one. What is true here of the sun is true more generally of the world. Subjected to the dominance of fire, itself being fire, it flames up and devours itself rhythmically, “an ever-living Fire, with measures of it kindling, and measures going out.”[3] Of that vanishing appearing, the thunderbolt (κεραυνός) “that steers all things” is like a cryptogram.[4] Bursting forth, it hides all the more within itself in that it flames without. The appearing, here, is this contradictory tension, this polemical irresolution between the pure outpouring of an endless source and its deeper disappearance into itself: for “eclosion remains hidden (φύσις κρύπτεσθαι φιλεῖ).”[5] But then how can we describe it? How to try to approach it (ἀγχιβατεῖν)?[6] How to say what is not, and is never given? How to speak of this world in the process of becoming of which Roger Munier rightly says, "It appears . . . does nothing but continually appear. Pure and constantly reconducted event, in a fulminant forward movement that can only be approached by freezing it."[7]

One can only try to approach it, says Heraclitus, through a contradictory discourse, a constantly polemical logos, discordant and unreconciled. Thus, in the famous fragment 49a handed down by Plutarch: "We step and do not step into the same rivers; we are and are not." The same rivers? This is indeed what Heraclitus writes: ποταμοῖς τοῖς αὐτοῖς. At every moment, the rivers remain identical to themselves through the continual change of their waters; but this current that carries them away, and carries itself away with them, also constantly renews them: "On those who enter the same rivers, other and other waters flow."[8] What Heraclitus is asserting here is not the universality of movement—which Plato was to label with the name "mobilism"—but the mobile perenniality of appearing, its incessant renewal in itself. To try to approach it, it is necessary to reunify by the logos these opposites that common mortals hold to be disconnected: the same and the other, to enter and not to enter. The river is only an image by which we should not be obsessed, like sleepers by the vapors of their dreams. Through it, Heraclitus "scrutinizes appearing" at its origin.[9] His intent is not to deny the stability of things and to reduce their constancy to a continual flux; he only tries to recapture, in his antinomic logos, the rise to the phenomenon, its lacerating, fleeting radiance—this unapparent event in which the world is in suspense: unfinished and finished, transitory and immutable. For what he says here about the river—it should first be said about the world—and the instant: μεταβάλλον ἀναπαεύεται—"It rests by changing."[10]

Here, it is not a particular understanding of the logos that determines, in the view of Heraclitus, a particular understanding of the *phainesthai* but rather the other way around. It is because he attempts to bring the enigma of the appearing to light, and with it that of time, that he must think the logos as what relates the opposites the one to the other, and maintains them—in accord and discord—in a harmonic union, in a tension comparable to that of the bow or the lyre.[11] Parmenides is deaf to this antinomic logos: "Uncritical tribes, by whom being and not-being have been thought both the same and not the same."[12] Parmenides, and after him Plato, and after him philosophy as a whole, are deaf to it as well. "We must prove to them and convince them, writes Aristotle, that there is a kind of nature that is not moved."[13] But to whom is this warning addressed? Not to Heraclitus, in any case. It is Cratylus and he alone who sustains mobilism's thesis according to which "one cannot enter the same river even once."[14] The union of opposites that constituted the logos itself is thus entirely dissolved, at the same time as any possibility of speaking of a selfsame river, of being able to name it and to say anything at all about it. But by interpreting Heraclitus in that way, Aristotle, like Plato,[15] fails to even understand his question. Heraclitus, as opposed to Cratylus, asserts nothing—and certainly not that all things move: πάντα ῥεῖ. He simply asks, How can changing and remaining be fundamentally the same thing? Or, how can appearing and disappearing be one in all phenomena? Thus, while conforming themselves to one of the most profound characteristics of the Greek language—the equivalency of *gignesthai* and *einai*[16]—he contents himself with investigating the *phainesthai* as such. He is, in this regard, the very first phenomenologist. Indeed, how could phenomenology ever do without a meditation on appearing in its innermost mobility, as a gushing forth, a wellspring, an event? How could it avoid this question without cutting itself off from what lies at its basis, the attention to what shows itself when it shows itself, and to the modality in which it shows itself? But on the other hand, can phenomenology investigate the very event of appearing without adopting—be it only momentarily—the antinomic logos of Heraclitus? Can it escape, by faithfulness to the "things (*Sachen*) themselves," which are never just things (*Dingen*), a paradoxology?

We have every indication to the contrary. When Husserl speaks of time, that is, of "the definitive and true absolute" of the self-constitution of the immanent flow of consciousness, he must indeed try to account for this springing forth of appearance itself—in the form of the *Urimpression*, and, later, of the "living present"—and he rediscovers, without realizing it, the antilogies of Heraclitus. The originary impression is pure springing forth, *genesis spontanea*,[17] and at the same time, this originary change (*Urwandlung*) cannot even be described as a change, for "it is in no time."[18] This is why "the originary flowing (*das urtümliche Strömen*), as pre-being (*Vorsein*), is inexperienceable and ineffable" unless it is "ontified."[19] One can only try to describe it in rigorously antinomic terms, as flowing and staying, as the unity of these opposites: it is an "original staying . . . present (*urtümliche stehende . . . Gegenwart*)—[a] staying present that, in a certain sense, is the *nunc stans*, for which the word 'present,' insofar as it already refers to a temporal modality, is not truly appropriate."[20] At such a level of radicality, in which we are dealing, ultimately, with the very appearing of all that appears even before anything appears, there are no longer any more "phenomena," but only a sudden springing forth that is ever missed, essentially "anonymous," since it can only become conscious in a second, retentional consciousness that, illuminating the former one, has already modified it.

Husserl's question here is no longer what a phenomenon is or how it is to be described in its essential features. Rather it is how phenomena phenomenalize themselves. How does that which comes to appear enter into appearing? Through what drama? Through what event?

As for Heidegger, when he thinks of Being itself as a phenomenon, and as the phenomenon par excellence, he essentially thinks of the "is" in a verbal, "transitive" sense, as the event of the revealing of beings, of their coming to appear in disclosure (*Unverborgenheit*), and at the same time he also thinks of it as that which, in this revealing, escapes and withdraws—precisely as what does not appear. What is first and foremost a phenomenon, the appear of all that appears, the Being of all beings, is also, by the same token and for that very reason, the unapparent par excellence. The unconcealing overwhelming (*entbergende Überkommnis*)[21] of Being is thus what hides itself in the disclosure of beings, the unapparent of all appearing, its invisible Openness. Through distinct conceptualities, it is as if phenomenology had done nothing but rehearse from one end to the other the same enigma, giving it different turns: in the event of appearing itself something withdraws in favor of what appears, and this "something" is the event itself—its nonappearing advance, its unapparent occurrence. The nonappearing occurrence of appearing thus reigns over that which appears like an invisible sun whose zenith is perpetual: "How can one hide from that which never sets?"[22]

If we were unable to describe the "movement" of the appearing itself—which is just as much a "rest"—its auroral rise, its "there is," its novelty—if we were unable to take up the challenge of Heraclitus, the notion of "phenomenon" itself would become a dead letter and lose all meaning. In this regard, appearing is not only a possible object for phenomenology, but its object par excellence. But to describe the "movement" of appearing itself is strictly speaking to describe its eventialness [*événementialité*]. The event is the primary "object" of all phenomenology, even when it is only implicitly so.

The Paradoxes of the Event

Now in wanting to describe the eventialness of the event, its occurrence, it is quite difficult to escape paradox. Phenomenology—as long as it strives to remain at this level of a description of appearing in and for itself—almost inevitably reinforces the retrospective triumph of Heraclitus over Parmenides and the entire tradition stemming from the latter.

There is no event without change. But does it suffice that there be a change for there to be an event? Among changes, some take place in such a way as to presuppose a permanent substratum: a barge floats on the river, a bird sits on a branch. Others, on the contrary, "blaze," so to speak, without it being possible to designate in them, or "under" them, anything that remains: lightning flashes, a sound reverberates. From a linguistic point of view, the use of nouns refers in the first case to beings ("the barge," "the bird"), and in the second to the event itself. But of these two types of change, the first is no less an event than the second. For both can appear. On the other hand, there are transformations that are practically imperceptible at the human level, such as, for example, gradual chemical modifications taking place deep down in the earth's subsurface. These transformations are not events. In order for there to be an event, a change has to appear, or rather, the event is the appearing of the change itself. The answer to the question we were asking—whether it suffices that there be a change for there to be an event—can now be given. In order for a change to "rate as an event" ["*fasse événement*"], it has to appear to someone as change, that is, it has to modify something from the point of view of one's experience. In order for there to be an event, it does not suffice that something changes; it is necessary for this change to make a change *for* someone. The event is not the transformation itself, it is the appearing of that transformation in the world, or yet again: it is the taking place of that transformation, its occurrence. But how is the latter to be described? Do not the words "happen," or "occur" refer to changes? If the event is not a change, but the occurrence of such a change in the world for the person who experiences it, does it not logically follow that the event must be described as a change of a change? But is this consequence not paradoxical? Doesn't it lead to an infinite regression? Is it not necessary to speak in this case of this second-level change—this occurrence—as having itself to occur, and to postulate a third-level change by which this change of change happens, and so on? Perhaps this consequence is not inevitable. Indeed, there is no indication that by "occurrence" we must understand a "modification" of the same structure as the transformation that occurs. To most of the changes of the world Aristotle's description applies: "Everything that comes to be comes to be by the agency of something and from something and comes to be something."[23] All change is an alternation of predicates or properties within a substrate. But the occurrence of such a change, the taking place by which it rates as an event for the person witnessing it, is not a change of this type. Here we return to the antinomies of Heraclitus. This occurrence can be nothing other than "a change without anything that changes," according to Bergson's phrase, or a change from nothing to something, a radical change [*changement du tout au tout*]. This is the intrinsic character of appearing: It is an immobile transformation into itself. What applied only to some changes—like lightning—which are exactly their appearing and nothing more or less, applies here to the very appearing of all change. All appearing is a transformation from itself into itself in which nothing subtends the transformation itself, pure "mobility" in which nothing moves and that is also, and by this very fact, pure immobility. A blossoming in which nothing changes and in which everything changes in relation to this "nothing": in which mobility and immobility are but one, and rigorously designate the same. If we couldn't describe this phenomenon, we would be equally unable to say anything about the event according to its mode of appearing—and especially not that it takes place, happens, or occurs. But how can we express this last phenomenon?

Perhaps we could formulate that same difficulty otherwise, this time taking our lead from the idea of "novelty." No event without "novelty." But how can we think the latter? "Novelty" in general is taken in a relative sense. When I purchase a new pair of gloves, this pair of gloves is new compared to other, older ones. It is its brand "novelty" that will tarnish—this novelty itself is perishable. Nothing indeed ages quicker than the new. Novelty is perishable because relative: it only exists in comparison. But does this hold for what is ever new in all appearing? To say of an event that it is new—is this saying anything about the date it appeared? Is it to relate it in any way to another event? Is it not rather to assert nothing about it but itself, to say nothing else about it but what characterizes it as itself—that it is, precisely, an event? "Novelty" as used here does not describe one aspect among others of the phenomenon (as it constitutes a property among others of the pair of gloves) but the very phenomenality of the phenomenon as a pure appearing in its own light, that is to say, a pure appearing out of nothing, an advent of itself to itself in the opening of the instant. This is why we have to do here with a novelty that must not be understood in a relative sense—with a novelty that neither comes about nor passes away and that, by the same token, cannot "get old" either, with a novelty that in its own way—like the present—is "always there." Like the present, of which Georges Braque has grasped the living source, "We will never have rest. The present is perpetual."[24]

Thus, whether it is a question of the concepts of "change" or of "novelty," as long as we try to recapture the event placing ourselves at the very site of its appearing, the determinations that applied to things or states of affairs that have already appeared are no longer suited to its description, or only on the condition of being modified in their meaning. Change must be understood as "absolute" change, novelty as imperishable and irrelative novelty. These "absolutes" may be the despair of the painter or poet when he attempts to recapture the world in an initial moment that Claudel calls *co-naissance*.[25] Thus, Hölderlin thinks, the word can only reach all things by going back, as it were, before all institution of a language[26]—and, in reconnecting itself to a universe as new as it is unknown, in being attuned to its tone, to say what has never been said before, to harken to the never-heard-before of its own poetic virtualities. Similarly, Cézanne appeals to this "echo" that the painter must be vis-à-vis the world grasped in its "virginity." To return to this instant of the world's virginity is to recover the world *in fieri*, not as a fact or as already made, but in the renewed surprise of its arising—and in order to do that, to place oneself at the beginning, in the nothing: in "this dawn of ourselves above nothingness."[27] Only at the edge of nothingness can beauty thus declare itself at the highest degree of what Oskar Becker calls its "fragility": "The simply 'wrought to perfection' of truly great works of art consists precisely in that any conceivable further elaboration, which would necessarily involve changing them in any way, would inevitably destroy them."[28] Beauty, too, "springing forth" from the apex of the work itself, is also and by this very fact, that which is the most fragile and exposed. This is why "the phenomenon of 'success' only appears if the power [of the artist] is uncertain. Luck, which success bestows by 'gratuitous favor,' does more than all ability." The existence of the artist is essentially adventuresome; "Tyche plays an essential rôle" in it.[29] But is it right to oppose, as does Oscar Becker, artistic to historical existence?

Among events, some have a bearing on the very meaning of the existence—or better, of the adventure—of the one they affect or overwhelm. These events, in which our destiny is at stake and that bring us to encounter ourselves as ourselves in an adventure in each case unique, presuppose, in order to be thought, a different concept of "man" than Heidegger's *Dasein*. They are determinations of the advenant.[30] By "advenant" I designate the very humanity of the human being, qua "capacity" to undergo the unsubstitutable experience of what happens to him or her. Thus understood, the "advenant" does not designate a neuter essence of man, somehow prior to his factual existence, but the evential constitution of the adventure itself, indissociable from its historical act of birth and the initial possibilities that condition that birth. Events befall the advenant insofar as, open to the world, he is affectively situated within it and projects himself into it in order to understand it. More precisely, these events are the upheavals of the world itself as the advenant understands it—and himself in it—and as he experiences himself affectively in this world. A mourning, an encounter, an illness, but also a decision or a promise can be upheavals of this sort. What is at issue here is a crisis in which the advenant is challenged to abandon what hitherto ensured his coherence and to change himself at the risk of his self: to "annihilate oneself for the purpose of existing."[31] Every event, from this perspective, addresses Goethe's imperative to us: *Stirb und werde*—"die and become." Now, not only must events of this kind be able to be described as (drastic) transformations of the world as such, not only is the novelty of meaning they introduce into their context unprecedented for those whom they befall, but on the occasion of their description new paradoxes, concerning the determinations peculiar to these events, such as "possibility," "world," and "temporality," arise.

First of all, an event is what transcends all foresight, all expectations, and all projects, that is, what breaks with all the possibilities that articulate, for the advenant, his or her world. With respect to these preliminary possibilities, it appears strictly im-possible: its possibility as event resides precisely in that impossibility. This is attested by the expression of surprise: "But that's impossible!" The event is the openness—to the impossible—of its own possibility for us: it is the configurator of possibilities according to its own forestalling initiative exceeding any possibility of ours, according to an initiative of which it is the sole initiator. Nothing preexists its possibility that it itself institutes by its very occurring: it is pure self-possibilization. Insofar as it is apprehended on the basis of the event and in conformity with its phenomenalization, "possibility" no longer designates the opposite of reality, here, or its complementary concept. The event is not "possible" before being real, its possibility wells up from its realization itself. The possibility of the event is dependent on its reality more real than any possibility. It is an impossible possibility or a possible impossibility. The event is the transformation to the impossibility of the totality of possibilities into which the advenant projects herself and that articulate her world.

This is why the event does not, strictly speaking, occur in a world; it opens up a world by occurring. To be sure, it is never separable from the hermeneutic context in which it takes place, but it exceeds this context by virtue of its very meaning. Incomprehensible in terms of its context, it illuminates that context with a new meaning. This initial incomprehensibility does not mean a zero degree of understanding, but refers to a proper, positive mode of intelligibility: the event is the origin of its own meaning; it is the very opening of a meaning for the one who is to understand it. Consequently, if the world is defined as the horizon of all possible meaning for the advenant, we must at the same time say that the event occurs in a world, in that its meaning is inseparable from that of its context, and that it opens a new world by opening onto a new meaning. Not that the former world would be eliminated, abolished by the event; on the contrary, it is in and by it that the world is revealed. The event occurs neither purely in the world, nor outside the world, but at the unlocalizable location of its openness.

In other words, the event is not a fact on which the advenant would confer a meaning after the fact; it is that whose very sense is to make sense—that is, never to be made[32]; whence its paradoxical temporality. On the one hand, certain events can take place in the instant, suddenly; on the other hand, they can only appear as such retrospectively, according to the temporal gap of their appropriation by the advenant. Their upsetting suddenness is perfectly compatible with their temporalization, that is, with the ripening (*Zeitigung*) of an experience, with the intrinsic duration of a series of alterations—particularly affective ones—nevertheless belonging to its inaugural "sending." The psychiatrist, for example, can try to describe the different "phases" a person goes through who, after an illness or an accident, remains gravely handicapped; the first phase, that of shock, characterized by withdrawal into oneself and apathy, is soon followed by that of denial, in which the new situation and the suffering it causes are hidden as much as possible, then by a phase of effort in which voluntaristic decisions are taken, and finally by a phase of acceptance.[33] All of these phases and their temporal sequence do not ensue from the event as a consequence, but rather belong to it as such and articulate its temporalization: they correspond to various ways in which the advenant can try to face, in a necessarily agonistic relationship, the wound (trauma) inflicted on him; to various postures through which he can attempt to assume and appropriate what remains, for him, to a large extent, impossible to assimilate and to integrate. Here, the magnitude of the event can only appear retrospectively to a necessarily belated consciousness; nonetheless, this after-the-fact character does not suppress the inaugural experience of an unhinged world. That experience is but one with the critical suddenness of the event. For this "suddenness" does not indicate an infinitesimal objective duration. As Erwin Straus remarks, "it is not the suddenness that conditions the shock, but it is rather the magnitude of the transformation within the shock that conditions the experience of suddenness."[34] The suddenness of the event only appears through its temporalization for us—that is to say, after the fact. Experience, according to its twofold modality (affective and hermeneutic), is the temporal articulation of this structural a posteriori: it consists in the multiple behaviors and attitudes through which the advenant is answerable for what happens to it. The event, here, is not temporal, but temporalizing. It does not take place in the instant: it opens itself in the instant as the necessarily retrospective temporal modality of its appropriation by the advenant, that is to say, of its occurrence in and for an experience. This instant is at once always already lost and always still present: it is without possible contemporaneity, and at the same time, I am always contemporary with it as long as the event continues to occur by imposing on me its constraint.

The attempt to describe the event "in itself," as pure appearing, therefore leads to a succession of paradoxes. These paradoxes attempt to articulate apparently opposed determinations, nonetheless belonging to the phenomenon—or rather, they attempt to describe the how of its phenomenalization: (1) The event is a change and it is not a change: this change is "immobile," without change, since nothing changes here but the change itself, its occurrence; (2) The event is new and it is not new: its novelty is without novelty since nothing, here, is new, except the novelty itself; (3) The event is possible and is not possible: indeed nothing is possible here, except the very possibility of the event as self-possibilization; (4) The event happens and does not happen in a world, since nothing happens here in a world except the very opening of meaning in which the appearing of the world is at stake; and (5) The event occurs and does not occur in time, since its taking place in the instant only appears as such retrospectively, according to the constitutive dephasing of its temporalization in and for an experience.

Do not these paradoxes introduce into the phenomenological discourse untenable logical contradictions that suspend all possibility of a phenomenology and lead it to nonsense? How, for example, can we assert that "the event is a change and is not a change" without rejecting the principle of noncontradiction and, along with it, one of the fundamental laws of thought in general? But this kind of objection only makes sense as long as we isolate the aforementioned formulations and analyze them as "propositions" independent from their context. As soon as we pay attention to this context, it becomes on the contrary evident that the assertion "the event is a change and is not a change," for example, does not use the term "change" in both cases in the same sense. The event is not a change in the sense in which something (a "substrate") could be said to "change," to receive opposite determinations. Rather it is a change in the sense that we must say of it that it happens, takes place, or appears. This clarification could, however, occasion a different critique. Is it not simply for reasons of "esthetic preference" that I have chosen these paradoxical formulations, rather than availing myself of formulations not transgressing the principle of noncontradiction? And does not the same arbitrary choice transpire in the adoption of negative turns of phrase? Why that double negation: "nothing changes . . . except . . . ," "nothing is new . . . except . . . ," and so on? Would it not have been just as expedient to use, instead of these negative phrases, corresponding affirmative ones? Of course. And yet, as arbitrary as this choice may seem, it at least has the superiority of conveying something decisive for the understanding of these phenomena, something that belongs in each case to their modality of appearing. The event is nothing other than its pure appearing qua appearing out of the nothing, in the forefront of the nothing, in suspense in the nothing. The nothing and the event are inseparable. If the event did not mean "taking place out of nothing," "change from nothing to something," there would no longer be, strictly speaking, either "event" or "appearing." Or, to borrow Valéry's verse, all that takes place always takes place "between emptiness and the pure event."[35] Emptiness and the event—what does this mean?

A Phenomenology at the Limits: The Problem of the Nothing

In order for the event to be able to manifest itself in the forefront of the nothing, the advenant must participate in nothingness. How? The advenant only participates in the event because he participates in the nothing as in the dawn of its nonobjectifiable "there is." And, conversely, the advenant only participates in the nothing because he participates in the event. But what can be the meaning of that rather vague expression "to have participated in the nothing"?

In order to answer this question we must set out from specific behavior. All expectation, at the same time that it gives itself or pre-gives itself its object, can only expect it against a background of nonexpectable emptiness. Emptiness here is not optional, it is not posited by an "empty intention," it is that without which no expectation of anything—however "indeterminate" it may be—could take place. Everything I can expect can emerge only from the nonexpectable in which all expectation is suspended and setting out from which the out-of-reach of my expectations [*le hors d'attente*] declares itself as what, in the hiatus of surprise, abolishes expectation and cancels it out. This nonobjectifiable nothing is not the Husserlian horizon: the latter is but the constantly reconducted deficit of a structurally incomplete fulfillment that corresponds to the surplus of the empty intentions of consciousness. On the contrary, the void I speak of is prior to all intention as it is to all fulfillment. It is not the result of a deficit, and has no horizon structure, but, uncircumscribed and indivisibly unique, it is the locus—unlocalizable—of all taking-place: its openness. It is close to what Heidegger, breaking with the transcendental approach that is still that of *Sein und Zeit*, called "Region" (*Gegend*) or, borrowing Rilke's expression, the "Open" (*Offene*). The advenant can only expect something if he himself stands in the open, turned toward him, of all "there is." This non-expectable nothing from which the unexpected springs is the world itself. The advenant relates to the world inasmuch as he relates to the unexpectable openness from which the unexpected of all his expectations springs—in keeping with an excess that is the very excess of the nothing over all grasp, apprehension, or objectification. And, similarly, the advenant can only project herself toward possibilities that she herself posits and to which she gives form in her project, if the projection carrying her into them goes to meet the nonprojectable without which this projection would have purchase neither on beings nor meaning. Indeed, no project could configure possibilities if it were not imbued with impossibility, open to the nonanticipatable of what can only come to us peradventure. The nonanticipatable nothing from which all possible events emerge—the world—is, as such, outside the range of projects. But then it follows that neither is there any "project of the world" (*Entwurf von Welt*) whereby *Dasein* could originarily configure the world: "As the respective wholeness of that for the sake of which (*Umwillen*) *Dasein* exists in each case, world is brought before *Dasein* through *Dasein* itself. This bringing of world before itself is the originary projection of the possibilities of *Dasein*, insofar as, in the midst of beings, it is to be able to comport itself toward such beings. . . . This prior casting-over (*Uberwurf*) first makes it possible for beings as such to manifest themselves. This occurrence of a projective casting-over (*entwerfenden Überwurfs*), in which the Being of *Dasein* is temporalized, is Being-in-the-world. '*Dasein* transcends' means: in the essence of its Being it is world-forming (*Weltbildend*)."[36] This project of the world, and this transcendence by which *Dasein* lifts itself above beings and relates to Being as such still belong, to a large extent, to a transcendental style of thought. They make *Dasein* into the operator of the Open and the enthroner of beings within Being. If, on the other hand, the advenant, in order to be able to project herself, must be exposed more originarily to the unprojectable nothing of the world, open in a dehiscence to the impossible "there is," it follows that the world can no longer be thought of as a transcendental determination of the ontologically well-understood concept of the subject, but as the unlocalizable location of all taking-place for this subject: its only meaning is evential. The open of the world is that which is opened in all events as the nothing from which they emerge. The openness of the world and the appearing of the event are but one in the phenomenon. The world is not a prior transcendental structure in which the event would take place; it is not thinkable in terms of "horizon." It is not the horizon of projectual possibles, but the openness—to the impossible—of all eventuality.

If one designates by the term "transcendence" the set of behaviors through which the advenant configures the possible in conformity with his projects, it is therefore necessary to maintain that all transcendence thus understood collides with a dimension it cannot transcend, but that rather transcends it; not a horizon that would continue to delimit the orbit of a potentiality-for-Being, but a break, that is, an opening onto the nothing: the nothing of the unprojectable as such, of the impossible in its eminent sense, which is not the opposite of possibility, but its fullness; the nothing as what conditions all emergence of an event as emergence out of itself. We can try to designate the exposure to the nothing of this openness that results from no project, and by virtue of which all transcendence is originarily transcended, by the term "excendence." Excendence is the relation—prior to all others—that unites the advenant with the open as with the nothing of all there-is. The openness of the world, inasmuch as it makes possible all occurrence of events, precedes and exceeds the projects of *Dasein*: excendence indicates precisely this precession and this excess insofar as they originarily belong to the phenomenon of the world and its evential meaning.

What I designate here with a unique term—excendence—is subjacent to all the modalities of response by which the advenant relates to what happens. Thus, for example, the advenant is exposed to possibilities of which he is not the measure. He is passible of events in that he himself is at stake and in suspense in the nothing of their nonexpectable occurrence. This passibility is prior to all distinction between an "activity" and a "passivity," and is not to be confused with it. The exposure to events presupposes no purely passive attitude toward them: courage or despondency, activism or apathy are different ways of responding to what happens to us, and they all presuppose this passibility equally. Furthermore, passibility is subjacent both to affective and to hermeneutic modalities of appropriation of the event: it is not confined to the sphere of feelings as opposed to that of understanding. Rather, all understanding is always a way of responding to meaning such as it has already come to light for us in addition to any project. And conversely, the "immediate" preconceptual and prelinguistic response of affectivity is already thoroughly of the order of meaning; of a meaning that is, to be sure, implicit and opaque, but that understanding can try, up to a point, to make explicit. Feeling and understanding do not stand opposed to one another, after the manner of facticity versus project, but both pertain to passibility: they are modalities of response to events—eventials.

It is by virtue of his passibility that the advenant is situated in the world in a way that needs to be described. Passibility appears, in this respect, indissociable from what I will call "situationality." To the extent that he is passible to the unforeseen, open in his possibilities to the dehiscence of the future, the advenant is also defined, and by this very fact, by his inherence in a situation and his belonging to a history. But what is the meaning of such a belonging? A situation is, by definition, what I am situated in, and that of which I cannot take an overview, any more than I can take a bird's-eye view of the landscape through which I am moving. Less metaphorically, it is the way the world co-appears in all of my behaviors, as an ever presupposed background that can never become a theme or be made explicit in its entirety. The situation, because it remains unthematizable, is never "objective": its resistance to all objectification is what makes the situation a situation. It is "what I cannot have an overview of from an exterior standpoint, what I cannot 'get out of' in any way" (Jaspers). Indeed, one cannot get out of a situation, but only move within it, and in that way modify it. This is what is meant by being "caught up" in it. To say that I am caught up in a situation is to say, strictly speaking, that it changes, as does my relation to it, and, as a result, my relation to myself. This is why the situational, as Tellenbach writes, "is that . . . in which the individual and that which surrounds him as within the world are still united."[37] It is because I belong to a situation that it escapes me in principle: its nontotalizable totality and unsignifiable significance are what confers on it its latency and "dark clarity." This is why, just as passibility is prior to all projects and grounds their possibility, belonging is prior to all facticity that *Dasein* could "take over" and of which it would have to become master.[38] Indeed, facticity is but the other side of existentiality: it is only to the extent that *Dasein* possibilizes all its possibilities in its resolute projection toward death that it can be thrown back toward its facticity and exist as that facticity as the thrownness (*Geworfenheit*) of its pro-ject (*Entwurf*)[39]—that is to say, make it possible for itself.[40] This possibility, which is that of authentic (*eigentliche*) existence, is but one with "the possibility of acquiring power over *Dasein*'s existence and of basically dispersing all fugitive Self-concealments" in the transparency (*Durchsichtigkeit*) of the instant.[41] But the necessarily latent situationality of the adventure is that which withdraws in principle from any form of transparency and therefore from any form of assumption and mastery. The situationality would be rather precisely what Heidegger asserts it not to be. "Thrownness however, does not lie behind it [*Dasein*] as some event which has happened to *Dasein*."[42] Now it is indeed in such an event that the situational of the adventure is rooted: I belong to a situation, I am inscribed within it, situated, precisely because I come to it by the event of a birth. It is birth that situationally opens the possibility of a world and an adventure—and not the advenant. This is why the notion of thrownness, *Geworfenheit*, with its gnostic connotation,[43] is of little help for the understanding of these phenomena. In order to "be thrown" into the world, it would be necessary either for the world to preexist *Dasein*, which is impossible, since Being-in-the-world is the ontological structure of this being, or for *Dasein* itself to open for itself the world into which it is thrown, just as the Husserlian transcendental ego constitutes its own birth—that is, for it not to be thrown into it at all. In birth, by contrast, the opening of the world is but one with the event of its appearing. The advenant can only come about [*advenir*] to himself or herself from and as this event itself.

The situational of the adventure is therefore defined by the inherence of the advenant in possibilities that transcend any authentic project and any possibility of integral appropriation—making null and void any integral property (*Eigentlichkeit*) of existence to itself and any gathering of its ekstases. While *Dasein* made itself all by itself, its situation is the lot befalling the advenant from the event of a birth. What at once befalls the advenant and is incumbent on it, what he shares with others is not first of all a language, a culture, or a manifold of behaviors and norms, but the adventure itself and its meaning. What falls to his share is the very sharing of his adventure. To the situation qua evential there therefore belongs an interrelatedness that precedes all explicit relation with others and makes it initially possible. I emerge from an originary bond that I did not myself posit but that precedes and grounds all relation to myself. And even, paradoxically, all relation to others! The relation with others, as thematic relation based on a manifold of social or ethical norms, emerges from an anonymous and prepersonal interrelatedness. We may say, in this respect, like Buber, that "in the beginning is the relation,"[44] with this reservation that the relation in question cannot still be thought of as the ethical, personal relation that an I establishes with a Thou. Other cultures and other traditions have attempted to describe this original bond in which the very humanity of man is born. In Japanese, in the two characters that make up the word "man," *ningen*, the first (*nin*), of Chinese origin, means "man," while the second (*gen*) can also be read as *aida* and means the originary between-two, relating them to each other. How is it that an expression that literally means "between human beings" can end up designating man himself? "The only plausible answer," Bin Kimura writes, "seems to be that since time immemorial the Japanese have understood interpersonal social existence, the being-between, life in the *aida* between oneself and the others, as being the essential trait of the human individual. . . . For the Japanese, the individual cannot first be envisaged as an isolated monad establishing a relationship with others after the fact. On the contrary, their view is that the interpersonal *aida* is primary, and it is only subsequently that it is actualized in the form of the self and others."[45] *Aida*, which can be translated literally as the "between," articulates a spatial (or situational) dimension and a relational one. It designates at once a connection and a place: the connection insofar as it is a place, that of the very humanity of man, the place insofar as it is a connection. Now, the emergence of oneself (*ji-ko*) on the basis of such a connection cannot mean a pulling away from the interrelation by an extreme existential isolation, that of the solipsism of anxiety, for example, but on the contrary an entry into the human relatedness, a being-in-relation as the genuine location of existence. Thus, it is only in the forms of failed existence, as Binswanger calls them, and particularly in psychotic existence, that a deep alteration of *aida* takes place in the form of both an invasion of self by others and of an irremediable isolation. "When *aida*, or distance (*ma*) is not established, the self no longer constitutes itself, and 'little by little the others enter me,' 'I can no longer see the others as persons distinct from me,' "[46] in such a way that usurpation by the other and isolation appear not as opposite but as complementary phenomena. Thus, beyond the description of psychoses, the self does not have to "win itself" from a loss, judged pernicious, into the anonymity of the They; it finds its place only in the relatedness, because it is first and foremost as relatedness that the adventure itself takes place, ever since the event of being born.[47]

The excendence of the adventure is therefore articulated in passibility and belonging. Passibility is prior to all projects and designates the exposure to the event as configurator of meaning and possibilities. Belonging is prior to all facticity and is characterized by the inherence in possibilities and in a history of which the advenant is not himself the origin. From the phenomenological standpoint, there is never any pure project, that is to say, any capacity of being capable [*pouvoir de pouvoir*] that is not already dehiscent to itself and traversed by the rays of history, nor any pure facticity that can be taken over through and through, that is to say, exposed to the gaze and offered in a moment of vision to a decision. The dichotomy between facticity and project do not furnish a possible basis for a thinking of freedom. No more, by the way, than the dichotomy of fact and meaning furnished a good basis sufficient for a thinking of events. While facticity and existentiality are structures of Dasein as transcendence, passibility and situationality are modalities of excendence qua originary determination of the advenant.

Excendence, the excess of the nothing of the "there is" over all possible transcendence, the surplus of the possible over all projects and of belonging over all facticity, possesses, by this very fact, a temporal meaning. It is solely because an immemorial having-taken-place precedes and grounds, for the advenant, his or her projects, that the future appears, at the other "extremity" of its adventure, as radically exceeding his possibilities. Precedence and excess are therefore also structures of excendence envisaged from the point of view of temporality. From this viewpoint, excendence signifies the fact for the advenant of being preceded and inscribed in an unassumable past, and of being open, to that very extent, to a nonanticipatable future. It is no longer at the extremity of his project or the peak of his freedom that the advenant temporalizes himself in such a way that its " 'having been' arises, in a certain way, from the future,"[48] but conversely it is his native—and not to be outstripped—inscription in the prepersonal and immemorial possibilities of his having-taken-place that opens up to him a future beyond all projects: belonging and passibility appear inextricable in this regard. Because it is open to the unforeseeable there-is of events and inscribed in the unassumable situationality of a having-taken-place, the adventure is fundamentally characterized by the eccentricity of its meaning. The advenant is not herself the origin of the meaning of her own adventure: this meaning exceeds the advenant and all attempts to understand it. Hence no adventure can gather itself and close back over itself in making its meaning entirely transparent. The both immemorial and ultimately incomprehensible character of the adventure, its nontotalizable finitude, refers back, once more, to excendence as such. The immemorial character of my beginnings is not only the result of a lack of memory but the excess of nonappropriable events over any memory, as memory of meaning. Similarly, the ultimately incomprehensible nature of my own adventure does not mean an incomprehensibility by default, but by excess. Memory as such opens onto the nothing of the immemorial, which is also fullness of meaning and richness. Situated understanding opens onto the nothing of the incomprehensible, that is to say, onto the there-is of an excessive meaning, in excess of and eccentric to the adventure itself.

But is there still room, in such a framework, for a thinking of freedom? No, if by "freedom" we are to understand an autonomous and autarkic potentiality-for-Being, an originary possibilization of the possible, a capacity of being capable: "Freedom alone can let a world prevail and let it world for *Dasein*. . . . Letting world prevail in projectively casting it over us [beings] (*entwerfend-überwerfende Waltenlassen von Welt*) is freedom."[49] In this projection beyond beings that makes *Dasein* a site (*Da*) of the very disclosedness (*Erschlossenheit*) of the world, *Dasein* constrains itself, that is, it both imposes on itself and undergoes an obligation (*Verbindlichkeit*)[50]: that of letting itself be invested by beings, of existing as the thrownness (*jet*) of a project. Now, to obligate oneself is to be autonomous. In that autonomy, *Dasein* only reigns over itself insofar as it is more deeply subjected to itself—according to the constitutive ambivalence of the very concept of "subject." The subject is only subject of itself insofar as it is subjected to itself, subjected in a subjection that it alone imposes on itself. Its very mastery is a servitude. And thus all freedom is all the more radically subject to itself, since it claims to free itself from what makes it possible, to pose itself by itself and for itself outside of all conditionality. In this respect, radical freedom and radical determinism are inseparable. Unbridled freedom is the destiny one inflicts on oneself, as Greek tragedy has repeatedly said and as Hegel condensed it in an admirable phrase: "consciousness of oneself as of an enemy." The alleged "tragic element of freedom" is generally the very forgetting of the tragic truth.

This truth is formulated thus: *to pathei mathos*, wisdom by suffering.[51] Freedom can no longer mean, by this measure, the autonomy of a capacity of being capable that, in positing itself, constrains itself, the exercise of a power that draws on its own finitude, thought of as a "self-projection which closes on itself,"[52] a surplus of power—the "*superior power* [*Übermacht*] of finite freedom."[53] It indicates, for the advenant, the ability to be herself in the face of what happens to her. But in what way is it a question, here, of a capacity—itself acquired—that the advenant would have as her own? Is not every advenant exposed to the event by the passibility of her own adventure? How could that passibility in turn furnish the key to the concept of "freedom" itself?

It does not suffice to be passible to be able to relate personally to events, to be able to relate to them oneself and in the first person. This is indicated by the counterexample of the trauma. A trauma is an incurable wound, a crisis without critical—that is, decisional—import, and consequently impossible to overcome. It is an alteration of the ability of the advenant to be himself: an event has occurred that he cannot make his own, or integrate into an experience—from which he can neither die nor be reborn. This event plunges the adventure itself into an interminable agony. On the contrary, freedom is the capacity to relate personally to what happens to us, to stand open to the critical import of the event. Thus understood, freedom resides mainly in a form of "receptivity," or better yet, of availability, and not chiefly in the exercise of a decision. Freedom is insistence itself within the passibility of the adventure, the availability through which, by standing in the nothing of the world as the openness to the there-is of all event, in forsaking all specific expectations and all projects, the advenant can be available for his situation and eventually act in accordance with it. Freedom in this sense has nothing to perform; it is all the more accomplished as it is without accomplishments. It consists in being. Many—and little heeded—are those who have pointed this out. Ignatius

Loyola, for example: the election that constitutes the peak of the free act is the twofold movement of a choice (*electio*) that I make and of a choice that is made within me (or that God makes: another meaning of *electio*), that is to say, an action that is more profoundly a "motion." To accede to the disposition in which such an action becomes possible requires one to place oneself in a state of perfect availability, at once prior to the order of reasons and to that of affections: "to find myself indifferent, without any inordinate propensity; so that I be not more inclined or disposed to take the thing proposed than to leave it, nor more to leave it than to take it, but find myself as in the middle of a balance."[54] This neutrality of availability has nothing to do with the alleged "indifference of the will [*arbitre*]" with which it was to be identified from Molina on. To make oneself free is first of all to make oneself empty, vacant. The semantic proximity of "free" and "empty" is present at the level of language itself in current expression: a free space, to be in freefall. To make oneself free is to hold oneself suspended in the nothingness of the world as openness to every there-is without configuring it into the prefiguration of a project, freed of all expectation, all will, all care—including that of freedom itself: "But the detached heart does not ask for anything at all, nor has it anything that it would like to be rid of."[55] A lack of concern that is not simply the lack of all care, but a "suspense" and a "forgetting" that are the preliminaries for a livelier and fuller "receptivity." As stance and endurance in the nothing of an immeasurable availability to the excessiveness of the evential, freedom is always freedom for what transcends all possibility of freedom, for the nothing of all taking-place, and therefore freedom for what is beyond all freedom, all project—liberation with respect to freedom itself.

To this extent, freedom is indeed a determination of excendence, of the opening of the adventure to the dehiscence of that which transcends it and makes it possible—to the impossibility of all its powers. Such a freedom must necessarily have its source outside itself, in belonging. For the conditioning of the situation is not the correlate of the project: it is more originarily that which grounds it. If we are conditioned by our situation before any possible project, freedom does not consist in turning away from what conditions us, or even in "choosing one's heroes," but in our appropriating what constitutes us before any possible autonomy. Indeed conditioning is not determinism. While facticity presupposes freedom, conditioning is what frees the advenant—and, more precisely, what frees his freedom toward itself. It is by imitation that the child learns to speak, continuing a signifying sequence that it did not inaugurate, and it is only on this condition—that of a radical heteronomy—that it can learn to say what it alone can say. The same goes for the artist's gesture. A great conductor used to tell his students, "Imitate as much as you like; if there is still something that is yours, that's what you must develop." This transmission is what founds us, and what gives us to transmit, what opens all adventure beyond itself and beyond its own death. For we all have been children; and we still are whenever, opening our own path, seeking the right gesture or word, we draw on an inexhaustible and immemorial reserve—that is to say, whenever by beginning we are recommencing. Our freedom, to this extent, is outside us, in a memory of the immemorial preceding our birth, and giving a meaning to our adventure beyond our own finitude.

The Nothing and Being

At this point the following objection, among many others, may come up: This "nothing" that is not the horizon of a transcendental power of *Dasein* in its configuration of the world, but rather the very openness of the there-is in that it co-appears in every event and is but one with its appearing—this nothing from which, or in the foreground of which, the event occurs—is it not another name for what Heidegger dubs "Being"? Indeed as Heidegger emphasizes repeatedly, "nothingness 'is' not an other than Being, but Being itself (*das Nichts nicht ein anderes zum Sein 'ist,' sondern dieses selbst*)." More precisely, the no-thing (*ne-ens*) is Being itself insofar as the latter is not beings; that is, insofar as it is conceived, in light of the ontological difference, as that which, by its withdrawal, lets beings appear: "The default of Being as such is Being itself. In its default Being veils itself [*verhüllt sich*] with itself. This veil [*Schleier*] that vanishes unto itself, which is the way Being itself essentially occurs in default, is the nothing as Being itself."[56] Therefore, how could we escape the conclusion that the nothingness (*Nichts*) Heidegger is talking about and the "nothing" (*le "rien"*) I am talking about are, after all, one and the same "thing"?

Still, although they correspond to the same problem, that of trying to grasp appearing in its radiant but elusive beginning—absolutely obvious and yet already gone by—they do so in two different ways. In the first place, because the determining experience in the approach to nothingness (from *Sein und Zeit* to "*Was ist Metaphysik*," at least) resides, for Heidegger, in the *Grundstimmung* of anxiety. Anxiety, which in this context plays a role analogous to that of a transcendental reduction, only reveals nothingness as a feature of *Dasein*'s transcendence and of the world as for-the-sake-of-itself. Nothingness is only the fundamental feature of the horizontality of the existence of *Dasein* ensuring its closure on itself and on its meaning, another name for Being as determined by its *Jemeinigkeit*. We have seen what resists this horizontality of existence: birth, the analysis of belonging as a characteristic of adventure, the precession of others over me setting out from an interrelation that in turn makes all selfhood possible; in sum, the eccentricity of meaning itself for the advenant and the impossibility of all totalizing of his or her adventure. But these arguments are only valid for a certain interpretation of nothingness by Heidegger. What about the nothingness understood independently of anxiety as the same as Being? And to start with, what does "Being" mean for Heidegger?

Being is inseparable from the understanding of Being qua *Dasein*'s way of being. Levinas is right, on this score, to maintain that "*Being and Time* has argued perhaps but one sole thesis: Being is inseparable from the understanding of Being (which unfolds as time)."[57] If Being is as inseparable from understanding—and this holds not only for *Sein und Zeit* but throughout Heidegger's work—this is because it "is" itself "the most intelligible": *das Verständlichste*.[58] Only if I have an understanding of Being can I have an understanding of beings. And indeed, the understanding of Being at the same time makes possible the understanding of the mode of being of all beings; therefore, it makes possible all ontology, be it categorial or existential. This is why the meaning of Being can never be entirely detached from that of an essence (*Wesen*), even if essence must be reinterpreted here on the basis of the ontological difference, not as the opposite of the medieval *existentia*, but as the "essencifying" of Being itself: the "*essance*," to adopt Levinas's spelling. In sum, Being is never exclusively for *Dasein* the event of the appearing of the world itself in its unjustification; it is always also what conceals within itself the intelligibility of all its structures (or *existentialia*): the a priori of all a priori. This is what led Heidegger to assert—at least provisionally—that it was possible to think Being without beings, that is, to think it as an "object" of thought, an "object," all the more intelligible in that it conceals and recapitulates within itself all intelligibility: "It belongs to the truth of Being that Being does indeed essencify (*daß das Sein wohl west*) without beings, and that a being never essencifies without Being."[59]

Here we find, certainly in Heidegger's thought, a very subtle and singular form of Platonism that, from the point of view of the problems I have addressed, has the following consequence[60]: Nothingness, if it is another name for Being itself, must as a consequence be not only intelligible, but "what is most intelligible." Incidentally, there is nothing new in this assertion. When Plato approaches the problem of non-being in the *Sophist*, he makes it one of the kinds of being, that is, of the intelligible: the kind Other. To do so, he must exclude the possibility of an absolute non-being as the opposite (ἐναντίον) of being and admit only a relative non-being: alterity, difference. On this point, Heidegger stands at once very far and very close to Plato: very close, in that he does not understand nothingness as "the counterconcept of beings (*Gegenbegriff zum Seiendem*),"[61] that is, as "a null nothing" (*nichtiges Nichts*),"[62] but only as not-a-being (*Nicht-Seiende*) and consequently, as the same as Being: the same as Being, namely the "altogether other than all beings (*schlechthin Andere zu allem Seienden*), the not-a-being"[63]; very far from Plato, in that "Being" is not understood here as an essence—or as the essential in all essence—but as temporality. Despite this radical difference, the fact remains that understandability, intelligibility, is, according to Heidegger, the fundamental feature of Being. Prior to the distinction of the *Daß* and the *Was*, Being signifies at once and inextricably the fundamental event of the appearing of all phenomena (of all beings) and the essencification of their *essance*: what makes possible at the same time their *Daß* and their *Was*. But what exactly does this "at the same time" mean? This is probably the most profound and the most enigmatic aspect of Heidegger's entire project. It is perhaps not excluded, by the way, to think that this same fundamental ambivalence reappears with the adoption, after the *Kehre*, of the key word "*Ereignis*," which must also be understood in conformity with the twofold semantic root of "own" or "proper" (*Eigen*) and event, of *essance* and appearing.

How can Being—that is, the nothing—be at once that on the cusp of which the appearing of the world takes place, the opening of all manifestation, and the source of intelligibility for all beings? Not only does this question, even though it remains implicit, never cease to be the key question of Heidegger's whole thought, but without this twofold determination of Being, nothing like a *Seinsgeschichte* would make sense. Indeed the history of Being, in the sense in which Heidegger understands it, is not a history that starts (*beginnt*) with one event, the event of an understanding of Being, at the dawn of philosophy, by the thinkers generally—and imprecisely—called "pre-Socratic"; it is a history that has its origin (*Anfang*) and thereby also its end and its destiny (*Geschick*) in the original Sending (*Schicken*) of Being. Being, as the thought of thoughts (*pensée des pensées*) of Western history as a whole—that is, of history without qualification, in Heidegger's view—is not *an* event in that history; nor is it the first among them, a beginning among others. Being is the origin of all meaning and all history, and consequently the event that swallows up all other events, since it carries within itself the intelligibility of this entire history and since this history, in turn, is nothing but the drama of the "epochs" or withdrawals of Being. This motif of a fated necessity of history leads Heidegger to an ever more marked forgetting of the finitude of understanding itself, inseparable from its hermeneutic status. The word of the thinker (this thinker: Heidegger!) is not only what responds to, but also what corresponds to the call of Being, and consequently what cannot be considered otherwise than as the pivotal event of this history.[64] Thought frees itself from its finite presuppositions to become the manifestation of Being itself in history, as far as it is the bringing to light of Being's essential forgetfulness.[65]

Such a closed history of which a single thinker could make, as it were, the tour of the property, because his thought would respond to and correspond to the original event (the Sending of Being) that bears within itself all other events, is excluded by principle from a approach of events highlighting their unrepeatable singularity, their irreducible plurality, and their unjustifiability. And this is why the nothingness that is but one with Being, that is to say, with the historical of all history, cannot be the same as that which articulates the manifestation of the event as a springing forth out of itself, an opening in itself of its own meaning. That the event is the origin of its own meaning for a necessarily finite understanding implies, by contrast, that there is no meaning of meaning, no archic event or arch-event, and therefore no fated history of which a single thinker could become the respondent or correspondent. The nothing, insofar as all events are in suspense in it, does not constitute the origin of their meaning—let alone the origin of all possible meaning, the event of all events—but rather that which cannot in any way be conceived of as an origin, and that which signifies, positively, the impossibility of any thinking of an origin. It is not "the most intelligible," but that which imbues all understanding with finitude and exposes it to an incomprehensibility both essential and irreducible. Indeed, the real is what precedes and exceeds all understanding in such a way that this precession and this excess belong to its essence. A truly historical thought must be able to account for its own historicality, that is, for the exceeding of the real over the thinkable, for the exceeding of the to-be-thought over thought, by calling itself into question. This is why the approach of trying to grasp this incomprehensible and in-significant nothing of the openness of the world, at the same time as the irreducible eventialness of all meaning, is an approach that has its source beyond the problematic inaugurated by Parmenides, that of the identity of Being and thought—or rather on the hither side of it.

Was it not this possibility that Heraclitus was already exploring when he conceived of time (αἰὼν) as a game,[66] and even more so when he defined the relation of expectation to what is beyond the scope of expectation, the relation of hope to what is beyond the reach of hope, that is to say, the relation of our faculties to what transcends them, and to what manifests itself out of the nothing of its unforeseeable there-is, with the sudden effraction of lightning, in the form of a series of negations?

"If he does not hope, he will not find the unhoped for; for it is outside of quest and without access."[67]

Notes

Preface

1. *"An sich früheres Sein"*; Edmund Husserl, *Cartesianische Meditationen*, §8, Husserliana (henceforth abbreviated as Hua) §11, Bd. I (1950; repr. Dordrecht, Boston, and London: Kluwer Academic Publishers, 1991), 61; trans. Dorion Cairns, *Cartesian Meditations* (The Hague: Martinus Nijhoff, 1973), 21.

2. Ibid., Hua I, 65; 26.

3. Martin Heidegger, *Sein und Zeit*, 16th ed. (Tübingen: Niemeyer, 1986), 133; trans. John Macquarrie and Edward Robinson, *Being and Time* (New York: Harper and Row, 1962, 171–72.

4. Heidegger, *Sein und Zeit*, 208; *Being and* Time, 251; see also *Grundprobleme der Phänomenologie*, in *Gesamtausgabe*, henceforth abbreviated as GA (Frankfurt am Main: Klostermann), 24, 238ff.

5. GA 24:103, 308, 425, 427; trans. Albert Hofstadter, *The Basic Problems of Phenomenology* (Bloomington: Indiana University Press, 1982), 73, 216, 300–301.

6. GA 24:29; 21–22.

7. See Hans-Georg Gadamer, "Phänomenologie, Hermeneutik, Metaphysik," in *Gesammelte Werke*, vol. 10, *Hermeneutik im Rückblick* (Tübingen: J. C. B. Mohr [Paul Siebeck]),108: "As long as we question in this way, as long as we question in general, everything remains open. Even the possibility of metaphysics."

8. One of the main representatives of that exegetic tendency, Olivier Boulnois, acknowledges this specifically when he maintains that "the exact meaning" of onto-theology is that of Kant: see Boulnois, *Être et représentation* (Paris: PUF, 1999), 462; see also 515: "Unless it is taken in a very general (and unenlightening) sense . . . the 'onto-theological structure of metaphysics' is not valid for every

form of that science, but only within the limits of that scholastic tradition (extending from Henry of Ghent and Scotus to Suarez and especially Kant)."

9. Heidegger, *Nietzsche II*, GA 6.2:313; trans. David Farrell Krell et al., *Nietzsche*, vols. 3 and 4 (San Francisco: HarperSanFrancisco, 1991), 209–10 (my emphasis); see also Heidegger, *Schelling: Vom Wesen der menschlichen Freiheit*, GA 42:79; trans. Joan Stambaugh, *Schelling's Treatise on the Essence of Human Freedom* (Athens, Ohio: Ohio University Press, 1985), 65–66.

10. See Jean-Luc Marion, *Reduction and Givenness* (Evanston, Ill.: Northwestern University Press, 1998); Jeffrey L. Kosky, *Being Given: Toward a Phenomenology of Givenness* (Stanford, Calif.: Stanford University Press, 2002).

11. To sum up, the disregard for nothingness is based on a certain analysis of change that in turn entails a certain understanding of time. The fact that all change is understood in an Aristotelian way, as that which modifies something already given in presence, forbids conceptualizing the happening or the there-is in the sense I give these terms; thus it precludes the conceptualization of appearing in its originary phenomenological sense; the happening of the present becomes the passage from the future to the present, a simple within-time modification. Time is understood and grasped as itself being something that takes place "in time." At issue here is the condition for time's being able to be attributed to mind (or subjectivity) as to a kind of substratum: see, on this point, Claude Romano, *Event and Time* (New York: Fordham University Press, 2014), Section 1.

12. I have chosen to omit from the present translation "La temporalité de l'événement: Analyse et herméneutique," which corresponds to Chapter 7 of the original French version of *Il y a*.

1. Some Sources and Prolongations of "Evential Hermeneutics"

1. Malcolm Lowry, *Under the Volcano* (New York: HarperPerennial, 2008), 375.

2. Romano, *Event and World*, trans. Shane Mackinlay (New York: Fordham University Press, 2009); Romano, *Event and Time*, trans. Stephen E. Lewis (New York: Fordham University Press, 2014).

3. Husserl, Hua XXV, *Aufsätze und Vorträge, 1911–1921*, 36; trans. Quentin Lauer, "Philosophy as Rigorous Science," in *Phenomenology and the Crisis of Philosophy* (New York: Harper and Row, 1965), 116.

4. Sophocles, *Ajax*, v. 647; trans. Richard Claverhouse Jebb.

5. Karl Reinhardt, *Sophocles*, trans. Hazel Harvey and David Harvey (New York: Barnes and Noble, 1979), 35.

6. Racine, *Phèdre*, act I, sc. I, v. 34–36.

7. Friedrich Wilhelm Joseph von Schelling, "Philosophical Letters on Dogmatism and Criticism (1795)," Tenth Letter, trans. Fritz Marti, in *The Unconditional in Human Knowledge: Four Early Essays (1794–1796)* (Cranbury, N.J.: Associated University Presses, 1980), 192–93.

8. Reinhardt, *Sophocles*, 132.

9. Jean-Pierre Vernant and Pierre Vidal-Naquet, *Myth and Tragedy in Ancient Greece*, trans. Janet Lloyd (New York: Zone Books, 1990), 80.

10. Aristotle, *Poetics* 1452*a*22ff.

11. Aeschylus, *Agamemnon*, v. 187.

12. See André Malraux, preface to the first French translation of *Sanctuary*, and his well-known expression "Sanctuary is the introduction of Greek tragedy into the detective novel"; William Faulkner, *Sanctuaire* (Paris: Gallimard, 1972). Valéry Larbaud had already emphasized that proximity in his preface to Faulkner, *As I Lay Dying* [*Tandis que j'agonise*] (Paris: Gallimard, 1973).

13. Jean-Paul Sartre, "Time in Faulkner: The Sound and the Fury," trans. Martine Darmon, ed. Frederick J. Hoffman and Olga W. Vickery, in *William Faulkner: Three Decades of Criticism* (New York and Burlingame: Harcourt, Brace, and World, 1963), 226–27 [translation modified—Tr.].

14. Sartre, "Time in Faulkner," 228–29 [translation modified—Tr.].

15. William Faulkner, *The Sound and the Fury* (New York: Vintage, 1990), 76.

16. See, for example, Aristotle, *Physics* II.5.196*b*17; *Metaphysics* E.3.1027*b*7.

17. Alexander of Aphrodisias, *De Fato* 2.166.5, 2.166.9.

18. See Carlo Diano, *Forme et événement*, French trans. Paul Grenet and Michel Valensi (Paris: L'Éclat, 1994), 78. [This French translation includes four appendices not included in the original Italian version of 1952. I therefore translate from the French translation quoted by Claude Romano, henceforth abbreviated CR–Tr.].

19. Ibid., 18, 19.

20. Gustave Guillaume, *Temps et Verbe* (Paris: Champion, 1993), 93.

21. Ibid., 95.

22. Ibid.

23. Sextus Empiricus, SVF II.166; A. A. Long and D. N. Sedley, *The Hellenistic Philosophers* (Cambridge: Cambridge University Press, 1987), 33B; Diano, *Forme et événement*, 11.

24. Aristotle, *Eudemian Ethics* 1247*b*4–8.

25. Ibid., 1247*b*12–13; see also Aristotle, *Physics* II.5.197*a*20.

26. Aubenque, *Prudence chez Aristote*, 74–75.

27. Aristotle, *Physics* II.5.197*a*9–10.

28. Ibid., II.5.197*a*10–11.

29. Ibid., II.5.197*a*13–14.

30. Aristotle, *Metaphysics* E.3.1027*b*7–14.

31. Diano, *Forme et événement*, 100–101.

32. Aristotle, *Physics* II.5.197*a*5–8.

33. Ibid., II.5.197*b*1–2.

34. Ibid., II.5.197*a*1ff.

35. Wolfgang Wieland, *Die aristotelische Physik* (Göttingen: Vandenhoeck and Ruprecht, 1970), §16. This expression, however, introduces a Kantian coloration that is not present in Aristotle's text. The "as if" does not arise from a kind

of reflective judgment by the subject. It is inscribed, so to speak, in the order of things. The risk of a confusion is even greater, it seems to me, if we introduce, as does Aubenque, the Bergsonian notion of retrospective illusion: "Chance in this sense is nothing but a retrospective illusion, the projection of a human finality on a causal relation, which is, in itself, entirely foreign to that finality"; Pierre Aubenque, *La prudence chez Aristote*, 76. But Aristotle never speaks of *illusion* on the subject of *tukhē*, let alone of an anthropomorphic projection. There is no anthropomorphism unless a subject detaches itself entirely from the order of things and is therefore able to make the latter into an object. But the Aristotelian agent is always inserted in circumstances, which means that his goals are relative to the possibilities offered to him by the situation. Moreover, Aubenque said rightly, a bit before the passage quoted above, that for Aristotle "man is a being of situation" (65). Now, a situation always presents a *meaning* that is not reducible to a "projection" on the part of the agent.

36. Aristotle, *Nicomachean Ethics* VI.8.1142*a*1.

37. Ibid., VI.8.1141*b*33.

38. Rémi Brague, *Aristote et la question du monde* (Paris: PUF: 1988), 178; Aristotle, *Nicomachean Ethics* VI.5.1140*a*26–32.

39. Aristotle, *Nicomachean Ethics* III.2.1111*a*6–8.

40. Ibid., II.2.1104*a*8ff.

41. "I . . . am overwhelmed with my pain. And I know well what pain I am about to undergo, but my wrath overbears my calculation"; Euripides, *Medea*, v. 1077–79; see R.-A. Gauthier and J.-Y. Jolif, *L'éthique à Nicomaque*, vol. 2, *Commentaire* (Leuven: Publications Universitaires de Louvain, 1970), 177.

42. Vernant and Vidal-Naquet, *Myth and Tragedy*, 60, who refer to D. J. Allan, "The Practical Syllogism," in *Autour d'Aristote: Recueil d'études de philosophie ancienne et médiévale offert à Monseigneur A. Mansion* (Louvain: Publications universitaires de Louvain, 1955), 325–40.

43. On this concept, see Romano, *Event and World*, §16.

44. Aristotle, *Nicomachean Ethics* II.1.1103*b*24–25.

45. Sophocles, *Oedipus Rex*, v. 1381.

46. Ibid., v. 1414–15.

47. See Martha Nussbaum, *The Fragility of Goodness: Luck and Ethics in Greek Tragedy and Philosophy* (Cambridge: Cambridge University Press, 1986).

48. Vernant and Vidal-Naquet, *Myth and Tragedy*, 47.

49. Gadamer, "Autobiographical Reflections," trans. Richard E. Palmer, in *The Gadamer Reader: A Bouquet of the Later Writings* (Evanston, Ill.: Northwestern University Press, 2007), 28.

50. Ibid.

51. Heidegger, *Sein und Zeit*, 199; *Being and Time*, 492nvii.

52. See Heidegger, *Phänomenologische Interpretationen zu Aristoteles* (trans. Richard Rojcewicz, *Phenomenological Interpretations of Aristotle: Initiation into Phenomenological Research* [Bloomington: Indiana University Press, 2009]); Hei-

degger, *Platon: Sophistes*, GA 19 (trans. Richard Rojcewicz and André Schuwer, *Plato's Sophist* [Bloomington, Ind.: Indiana University Press, 1997]); Franco Volpi, *Heidegger e Aristotele* (Padova: Dafne Editrice,1984); and Jacques Taminiaux, *Lectures de l'ontologie fondamentale* (Grenoble, Millon), 1990 (trans. Michael Gendre, *Heidegger and the Project of Fundamental Ontology* [Albany, N.Y.: SUNY Press, 1991]).

53. Heidegger, *Platon: Sophistes*, GA 19, §7(*b*):42–44; trans. Rojcewicz and Schuwer, 29–31.

54. Heidegger, *Sein und Zeit*, 61, 112.

55. See below, "The Possible and the Event," in the present volume.

56. Heidegger, *Sein und Zeit*, 251; *Being and Time*, 295.

57. Ibid., 252–53; 297.

58. Ibid., 254; 298.

59. Ibid., 253; 297.

60. Ibid., 273; 318.

61. Ibid., 379: 431.

62. A critique limited, moreover, since Heidegger continues to see in Husserl's *a priorism* "the method of every scientific philosophy that understands itself"; Heidegger, *Sein und Zeit*, 50n1; *Being and Time*, 490.

63. Heidegger, *Metaphysische Anfangsgründe der Logik*, GA 26:217; trans. Michael Heim, *The Metaphysical Foundations of Logic* (Bloomington: Indiana University Press, 1984), 169.

64. Heidegger, *Sein und Zeit*, 373; *Being and Time*, 425.

65. See Theodore Kisiel, *The Genesis of Heidegger's "Being and Time"* (Berkeley: University of California Press), 27; see also Jean Greisch, *L'arbre de vie et l'arbre de savoir* (Paris: Éditions du Cerf, 2000), 40. An English translation by Philip Anderson, *The Tree of Life and the Tree of Knowledge* (New York: Fordham University Press), is in progress.

66. Indeed there is an Augustinian version of the "cogito" that concludes from the act of doubting that the doubter is *alive*, and from there to his *thinking*: see Augustine, *De Trinitate* X.X.14: *si dubitat, vivit . . . si dubitat, cogitat*. Descartes, on the contrary, refuses to draw the conclusion of life from the premise of doubt, because the former implies the body, and he replaces life with existence (*esse, existentia*).

67. Heidegger, GA 19:49; English trans. 34. The *nous praktikos* therefore plays a role that is formally comparable to that of understanding (*Verstehen*) in *Sein und Zeit*, since understanding never designates a theoretical role of relation to the world, but in all understanding, the *Dasein* is itself co-understood, *mitverstanden*; Heidegger, *Sein und Zeit*, 146.

68. Aristotle, *Nicomachean Ethics* VI.5.1139*b*35.

69. Ibid., VI.5.1140b4–6.

70. Heidegger, GA 19:143; 98.

71. Ibid., 19:29; 20–21.

72. Ibid., 19:54; 38.

73. Søren Kierkegaard, *Either/Or: Part II*, trans. Howard V. Hong and Edna H. Hong (Princeton: Princeton University Press, 1990), 176: "Therefore, the point is still not that of choosing something; the point is not the reality of that which is chosen but the reality of choosing." See also 177: "The Either/Or I have advanced is, therefore, in a certain sense absolute, for it is between choosing and not choosing."

74. Kierkegaard, "The Leap Is the Category of Decision," trans. Howard V. Hong and Edna H. Hong, in *Concluding Unscientific Postscript to Philosophical Fragments* (Princeton: Princeton University Press, 1992), 99.

75. Heidegger, *Sein und Zeit*, 268; *Being and* Time, 313.

76. Heidegger, GA 19:150; 103 [translation modified—Tr.].

77. Ibid., 49; 34.

78. Ibid., 56; 39.

79. Heidegger, *Grundprobleme der Phänomenologie*, GA 24:409; *Basic Problems of Phenomenology*, 288–89. See also and especially the interpretation of Paul's two Epistles to the Thessalonians, in Heidegger, *Phänomenologie des religiösen Lebens*, GA 60:75–115; trans. Matthias Fritsch and Jennifer Anna Gosetti-Ferencei, *The Phenomenology of Religious Life* (Bloomington and Indianapolis: Indiana University Press, 2004), 53–82.

80. Heidegger, *Sein und Zeit*, 355; *Being and Time*, 406–7.

81. Ibid., 310; 358.

82. Ibid., 307; 355.

83. See Aristotle, *Metaphysics* Z.15.1039*b*29.

84. John Duns Scotus, *Ordinatio* I., 2, p. 1, q. 1–2; II, 178, 86: ["I do not here call 'contingent' everything that is not necessary or not eternal; instead I refer to something the opposite of which is possible even at the very moment it actually exists or occurs."]

85. François Jacob, *Le jeu des possibles* (Paris: Fayard, 1981), 58.

86. The Aristotelian concept of freedom (*eleutheria*) is even the polar opposite of the modern conception, as attested by this passage, among others, of *Metaphysics*: "But the arrangement is like that in a household, where the free persons have the least liberty to act at random, and have all or most of their actions preordained for them, whereas the slaves and animals have little common responsibility and act for the most part at random; for the nature of each class is a principle such as we have described" (L.10.1075*a*19–23).

87. Alexander of Aphrodisias, *On Fate* 11.179.10.

88. Alexander of Aphrodisias, *De Anima, liber alter* 169.33; 172.16; 175.32; see also Octave Hamelin, *Le système d'Aristote* (Paris: Vrin, 1985), 391.

89. Aubenque, *La prudence chez Aristote*, 104.

90. Jacob, *Le jeu des possibles*, 108.

91. André Leroi-Gourhan, *Le geste et la parole*, vol. 2, *La mémoire et les rythmes* (Paris: Albin Michel, 1964), 34; trans. Anna Bostock Berger, *Gesture and Speech* (Cambridge, Mass.: MIT Press, 1993), 235.

2. Possibility and Event

1. The version of the text given here has been modified from the original version on several points, particularly thanks to the publication in the interim of volume 60 of Heidegger's *Gesamtausgabe: Phänomenologie des religiösen Lebens*, the content of which was accessible at the time of the publication of my text only through a summary (an excellent one, incidentally) by Thomas Sheehan. Despite the corrections I have made of certain formulations of my article, written almost ten years ago, I have left its sometimes hesitant terminology, which differs on certain essential points from that of *Event and World* and *Event and Time.*

2. Heidegger, *Vom Wesen der menschlichen Freiheit*, GA 31:123–24; trans. Ted Sadler, *The Essence of Human Freedom: An Introduction to Philosophy* (London and New York: Continuum, 2002), 86 [translation modified—Tr.].

3. It could of course be objected that Heidegger most often formulated the problem he took up in rigorously opposite terms: indeed, *Sein und Zeit* and its prolongation, *Die Grundprobleme der Phänomenologie*, are concerned with interpreting Being in the light of temporality, itself determined, after the manner of Plato's ἀγαθόν, as the true ἐπέκεινα τῆς οὐσίας (Heidegger, *Grundprobleme der Phänomenologie*, GA 24:405ff; *Basic Problems of Phenomenology*, 285ff.). But to conceive of time as "beyond Being" is still to conceive of it *starting from Being*; it is still to approach it or to circumvent it within the horizon of an *ontological* questioning.

4. Heidegger, *Sein und Zeit*, 248; *Being and Time*, 292.

5. Heidegger, *Metaphysische Anfangsgründe der Logik*, GA 26:267; *Metaphysical Foundations of Logic*, 207.

6. Heidegger, "Le concept de temps," in *Cahiers de l'Herne: Martin Heidegger* (Paris: Éditions de l'Herne, 1983), 36.

7. Heidegger, Phänomenologie des religiösen Lebens, GA 60; *Phenomenology of Religious Life*, 41.

8. This is indicated by the twofold reference underlying the first courses by Heidegger: both to Dilthey and to his concept of life (see Wilhelm Dilthey, *Briefwechsel zwischen Wilhelm Dilthey and Paul Yorck von Wartenburg, 1877–1897* (Halle: Niemeyer, 1923), letter from Dilthey, end of August–beginning of September 1897: "One must take life as one's starting point. That does not mean that one must analyze it, it means that one must relive it and inwardly draw the *consequences* that lie within it. *Philosophy* is an *action* that raises *life* (that is, the *subject* in his *relations as vitality) to consciousness and thinks it through to the end*)," and to the specifically Pauline concept of life (*zōē*), which refers to the life in Christ (faith) as opposed to life in the flesh (sin or death); see Rudolf Bultmann, *Theologie des Neuen Testaments* (Tübingen: Mohr,1948), vol. 1, part 2, chap. 4, §18:210–11; and Heidegger, *Phänomenologie des religiösen Lebens*, GA 60:100; *Phenomenology of Religious Life*, 70: "Life for Paul is not a mere flow of events; it *is* only insofar as he *has* it."

9. Heidegger, *Phänomenologische Interpretationen zu Aristoteles*, GA 61:86; *Phenomenological Interpretations of Aristotle*, 65.

10. [*Bekümmerung* is Heidegger's translation of Augustine's "*cura*" in *Phänomenologie des religiösen Lebens.*—Tr.]

11. Heidegger, *Interprétations phénoménologiques d'Aristote,* bilingual edition, ed. J.-F. Courtine (Mauvezin: TER, 1990), 23.

12. Heidegger, *Interprétations phénoménologiques d'Aristote,* GA 61:120; *Phenomenological Interpretations of Aristotle,* 89–90.

13. Heidegger, *Phänomenologie des religiösen Lebens,* GA 60:80; *Phenomenology of Religious Life,* 55.

14. Ibid., 117; 83–84 [translation modified—Tr.].

15. Ibid., 102; 71.

16. Rom. 5:1. [I quote Paul's Epistles from the King James Version—Tr.]

17. Gal. 5:5. On this tautness of Christian experience between an "already" and a "not yet," see Bultmann, *Theologie des Neuen Testaments,* vol. 1, part 2, §29 and §33–§35; trans. Kendrick Grobel, *Theology of the New Testament* (New York: Charles Scribner's Sons, 1951), vol. 1, part 2, §29 and §33–§35.

18. Heidegger, *Phänomenologie des religiösen Lebens,* GA 60:93; *Phenomenology of Religious Life,* 65.

19. Ibid., 94; 66 [translation modified—Tr.].

20. Ibid., 100; 70.

21. See Thomas Sheehan, "Heidegger's 'Introduction to the Phenomenology of Religion,'" *Personalist* 60, no. 3(1979): 320.

22. 1 Thess. 1–6.

23. Heidegger, *Phänomenologie des religiösen Lebens,* GA 60:103; *Phenomenology of Religious Life,* 72.

24. Ibid.

25. Ibid., 104; 73.

26. Ibid., 105; 73.

27. Heidegger, *Unterwegs zur Sprache,* GA 12:91; trans. Peter D. Hertz, *On the Way to Language* (New York: Harper and Row, 1971), 10: "Without this theological background I should never have come upon the path of thinking."

28. Bultmann, *Theology of the New Testament,* vol. 1, §34:306.

29. The ambivalence tends to lessen in the Gospel according to John, about which we may speak of a "spiritualizing of the eschatology and of its inwardness"; Bultmann, "The Eschatology of the Gospel of John," in *Faith and Understanding,* trans. Louise Pettibone Smith (New York: Harper and Row, 1969), 1:174ff. In this sense, Heidegger's reading, as we will see, orients eschatology in a Johannine direction.

30. Heidegger, *Prolegomena zur Geschichte des Zeitbegriffs,* GA 20:109–10: "Philosophical research is and remains atheism"; trans. Theodore Kisiel, *History of the Concept of Time* (Bloomington: Indiana University Press, 1985), 80.

31. Heidegger, *Sein und Zeit,* 245; *Being and Time,* 289.

32. Ibid., 236; 280.

33. Jack London, *Martin Eden,* last sentence of the novel.

34. Heidegger, *Sein und Zeit,* 237; *Being and Time,* 281.

35. Ibid. [translation modified—Tr.].

36. Ibid., 239; 282.

37. Ibid., 240; 284.

38. Ibid. [translation modified—Tr.].

39. Heidegger will speak later on—to dismiss it—of the "'empirical' certainty" (*"empirischen" Gewißheit*) of death; *Sein und Zeit*, 257; *Being and Time*, 301.

40. Heidegger, *Sein und Zeit*, 257; *Being and Time*, 301.

41. "As soon as a man comes to life, he is at the same time old enough to die"; quotation from *Der Ackermann aus Bömen* in Heidegger, *Sein und Zeit*, 245; *Being and Time*, 289.

42. Heidegger, *Sein und Zeit*, 251; *Being and Time*, 295.

43. Ibid., 191; 235 [translation modified—Tr.]. For example, fear is fear *in the face of* some entity, and fear *for* myself: in anxiety, these two characteristics coincide, and this is why the existential phenomenon of dying is strictly identical with true anxiety, which is anxiety *in the face of* thrown being (*Geworfenheit*) in death, *for* an entity that is Being-toward-death.

44. Ibid., 266; 310.

45. Ibid., 245; 236: "Death is a way to be, which Dasein takes over as soon as it is."

46. Ibid., 253; 297.

47. Ibid., 254; 298.

48. Ibid., 250; 294.

49. Ibid., 261; 305.

50. Ibid., 262; 251.

51. Ibid., 261; 306.

52. Ibid., 247; 291.

53. Ibid., 257; 301.

54. Ibid., 258; 302.

55. Ibid., 262; 307.

56. Ibid., 264; 309.

57. Ibid., 317; 365.

58. Ibid., 325; 372.

59. Ibid., 326; 311.

60. Ibid., 339; 388.

61. Ibid., 299; 345–46.

62. Ibid., 309; 357.

63. Heidegger, *Grundproblemeder Phänomenologie*, GA 24:407–8; *Basic Problems of Phenomenology*, 287.

64. Heidegger, *Sein und Zeit*, 372; *Being and Time*, 424 [CR's emphasis; translation modified—Tr.].

65. Ibid., 373; 425.

66. Ibid.

67. Ibid.

68. For example: joy, hope, disgust, enthusiasm, sadness, melancholy, despair; see ibid., 310 and 345; 357–58 and 395–96.

69. Ibid., 374; 427.

70. Ibid., 374; 426 [translation modified—Tr.].

71. Furthermore, the phenomenon of birth, in its existential correlation with care and ipseity, determines the meaning of authentic historicity, defined as "the *historizing* of *Dasein*" [das *Geschehen* des Daseins] (ibid., 375; 427). To establish the dependency of the historicity of *Dasein* as "connection between birth and death" with respect to an analytic of birth, it suffices to inquire into the *existential meaning* of assertions such as "Dasein's fateful destiny in and with its 'generation' goes to make up the full authentic historizing of Dasein" (ibid., 384–85; 436). What could such an assertion possibly mean in the absence of a deliberate interpretation of the phenomena of generation and filiation that would remove them from the inadequate horizon of an ontology of life in order to conceptualize them in their properly existential sense?

72. Ibid., 248; 292.

73. Ibid., 251; 295.

74. Ibid., 135; 174.

75. Ibid., 192; 236.

76. Ibid., 135; 174.

77. Ibid., 191; 235.

78. Ibid., 136; 175.

79. Ibid., 374; 426.

80. Ibid., 284; 329–30 [translation modified—Tr.].

81. Ibid., 284; 330.

82. Ibid., 285; 330.

83. Ibid., 285; 330–31.

84. Ibid., 306; 354.

85. Ibid.

86. Ibid.: "Care harbours in itself both death and guilt equiprimordially."

87. Ibid., 135; 174.

88. Heidegger, *Être et temps*, French trans. Emmanuel Martineau (Paris: Authentica, 1985), 121, translator's note: "accueilli, intégré et 'assumé.'"

89. Heidegger, *Sein und Zeit*, 391; *Being and Time*, 443.

90. Ibid., 390–91; 442.

91. Ibid., 383 and 385: "*Die Wiederholung ist die ausdrückliche Überlieferung*"; here I follow the translation of Emmanuel Martineau, *Être et temps*, 290, in that the latter term, whose first meaning is "inheritance," "transmission," becomes, in and through repetition—which is not simply restitution of the past but the free choice of a heritage—*release* with respect to tradition, by which *Dasein* "chooses its heroes."

92. This possibility of a repetition of Thrownness is expressly affirmed by Heidegger: "anxiety brings one back to one's thrownness as something *possible* which *can be repeated*" (*Sein und Zeit*, 343; *Being and Time*, 394). At every moment

Dasein can grasp itself in anxiety as thrown, and thus repeat its thrownness itself; strictly speaking, *Dasein* can therefore repeat its birth understood in the existential sense, since its birth is not a past event, but rather *Dasein* is born continuously and as long as it dies in the sense of Being-towards-death. Husserl, in the margin of his personal copy of this work, highlights his puzzlement about that sentence: "What does that mean?" In Husserl's marginal notes to Heidegger's *Sein und Zeit*, revised translation by Thomas Sheehan, 140; http://religiousstudies.stanford.edu/wp-content/uploads/14–1929-MARGINALIA-TO-SZ.pdf, accessed 1 April 2014.

93. The heteronomy of a "gift" that consequently contravenes the existential "autonomy" of *Dasein* (Heidegger, *Sein und Zeit*, 332).

94. For *Dasein*, every understanding is self-understanding as mortal (finite); and since "meaning" is defined, in *Sein und Zeit*, as "that wherein the understandability of something maintains itself," "the 'upon-which' [*das Woraufhin*] of a primary projection" (324; 370–71), the result is that there is not, for Heidegger, any other meaning than the one *Dasein*, as essentially finite being, projects—and this is why *the meaning of Being itself is finitude, i.e., temporality*: "Only *Dasein* can be meaningful or meaningless" (*Sein und Zeit*, 151; 193). In other words, there is only meaning where understanding is operative, and all understanding is self-understanding in the project of a finite potentiality-for-Being. Hence Sartre paraphrases Heidegger perfectly when he writes, in *Being and Nothingness*, that "a meaning can come [into existence] only from subjectivity" (trans. H. E. Barnes [New York: Washington Square Press, 1966], 689): existence, in its radical "autonomy" and autarchy, can receive its meaning only within that horizon that closes it in upon itself—the horizon of my death, not as event yet to come, but as eminent possibility that opens all my factical possibilities and makes possible the world as "*das Ganze der wesenhaften inneren Möglichkeiten des Daseins*," the totality of the essential intrinsic possibilities of Dasein (*Metaphysische Anfangsgründe der Logik*, GA 26:248; *Metaphysical Foundations of Logic*, 192). Here we see how much *Sein und Zeit* remains dependent on a conceptualization inherited from (Kantian and Husserlian) transcendental idealism: "The objective world, the world that exists for me, that always has and always will exist for me, the only world that can be for me—this world, with all its Objects, I said, derives its whole sense and its existential status, which it has for me, from me myself" (Husserl, *Cartesianische Meditationen*, Hua I, 65; *Cartesian Meditations*, 26).

95. Heidegger, *Sein und Zeit*, 339; *Being and Time*, 388.

96. Ibid., 339; 388–89.

97. Ibid., 393; 445.

98. Heidegger, *Metaphysische Anfangsgründe der Logik*, GA 26:248; *Metaphysical Foundations of Logic*, 192. Heidegger speaks here of the world as "the totality of the essential intrinsic possibilities of *Dasein*."

99. Heidegger, *Vom Wesen des Grundes*, in *Wegmarken*, GA 9:164; trans. William McNeill, "On the Essence of Ground," in *Pathmarks* (Cambridge and New York: Cambridge University Press, 1998), 127: "Letting world prevail in projectively casting it over us is freedom."

100. Not by which this collapse according to which the surrounding world (*Umwelt*) of everydayness gives way, in anxiety, to the "world as such," to the *Welt*. We will see in what follows by what phenomenological mode of givenness—radically distinct from the one brought about by anxiety—such a sinking away is to be thought.

101. Henri Maldiney has analyzed these possibilities of human existence in *Penser l'homme et la folie* (Grenoble: Millon, 1991), for example, 277: "*In psychosis, there are no more events*. The challenge of existence is resolved in a tearing apart: no transformation follows. The becoming-other out ahead of oneself has been replaced by the irruption within the self of a pure alterity." I must express here my indebtedness to this philosophy of the event so deep and perspicuous.

102. The anticipation of death not only has the remarkable privilege of opening *that* ownmost, absolute, not to be outstripped possibility—that of my mortality—but also that of giving access to *possibility in general*, and especially to the factical possibilities that stand on the hither side of the not-to-be-outstripped possibility: "The possibility is disclosed because it is made possible in anticipation" (Heidegger, *Sein und Zeit*, 264; *Being and Time*, 309).

103. [This term translates the French neologism "impouvoir," sometimes used in the sense of a moral "force" (which is not properly speaking force at all); for a more adequate explanation, see Jean-Luc Marion, "L'impouvoir," *Revue de métaphysique et de morale* 4, no. 60 (2008): 439–45, or http://www.cairn.info/revue-de-metaphysique-et-de-morale–2008–4-page–439.htm, accessed 1 May 2014), 10—Tr.]

104. Erwin Straus, *The Primary World of the Senses* (New York: Free Press of Glencoe, 1963), 351.

105. Gilles Deleuze, *The Logic of Sense*, trans. Mark Lester and Charles Stivale (London: Athlone Press, 1990), 152.

106. Marcel Proust, *Time Regained*, trans. Andreas Maylor and Terrence Kilmartin, ed. D. J. Enright (New York: Modern Library, 1993), 515–16: "For I realized that dying was not something new, but that on the contrary since my childhood I had died many times. . . . These successive deaths, so feared by the self which they were destined to annihilate, so painless, so unimportant once they were accomplished and the self that feared them was no longer there to feel them, had taught me by now that it would be the merest folly to be frightened of death."

107. Maurice Blanchot, *The Space of Literature*, trans. Ann Smock (Lincoln: University of Nebraska Press, 1982), 154. Suicide, Blanchot adds, is just an absurd way of pretending to take over in the first person and to master this death, which is impersonal, as is birth, and to forearm oneself before its essential anonymity. It "serves essentially to protect us from what is at stake in this event."

108. Heidegger, *Sein und Zeit*, 390; *Being and Time*, 442.

109. Ibid., 307; 355.

110. Ibid., 391; 443 [translation modified—Tr.].

111. Ibid., 299; 345: "The irresoluteness of the 'they' remains dominant notwithstanding, but it cannot impugn [*anfechten*] resolute existence."

112. Ibid., 322; 369.

113. Ibid., 338; 388 [translation modified—Tr.].

114. Since it is existence altogether that takes on an evential meaning here, we can no longer speak of "*existentialia*," but rather of "eventials," of determined modalities of response in the face of what happens to us; despair playing here a role analogous to that of anxiety, in Heidegger, for the laying-bare of the *evential* meaning of existence.

115. Heidegger, "*Die Unmöglichkeit des Möglichen*," GA 26:248–49; trans. *Metaphysical Foundations of Logic*, 193: "the impossibility of something possible."

116. Gustave Flaubert, *Sentimental Education*, trans. Kathleen Rustum and D. F. Hannigan (New York: Barnes and Noble Classics, 2006), 88.

117. Franz Kafka, Journal, 19 October 1921: "Anyone who cannot come to terms with his life while he is alive needs one hand to ward off a little his despair over his fate . . . for he sees different (and more) things than do the others; after all, dead as he is in his own lifetime, he is the real survivor"; in *The Basic Kafka*, trans. Joseph Kresh and Martin Greenberg (New York: Pocket Books, 1979), 262.

118. This passibility before the event, which Maldiney called "transpassibility," is not primarily a passivity that would be mine, since it is only given after the fact (*dans l'après-coup*) and in reaction (*et le contre-coup*) to an event. I am not the measure of events, for otherwise events could not occur in their joyful or heart-rending novelty, in their incommensurability to myself. If "the reception of the event and the advent and the existent are one" (Maldiney, *Penser l'homme et la folie*, 422), one must conceive of a "pre-subjective" openness that does not make possible the reception of the event, but in which the event makes itself possible at the same time that it declares itself in its supreme actuality—more actual than any possibility.

119. "The event emerges before being possible"; Maldiney, *Penser l'homme et la folie*, 433.

120. Kafka, letter to Milena, 12 June 1920, in *Letters to Milena*, trans. Philip Boehm (New York: Schocken Books, 1990), 43.

121. Claude Simon, *The Grass*, trans. Richard Howard (New York: George Braziller, 1986), 127–28.

122. This impersonality appears in the love separation as described by Claude Simon: indeed, *who* wanted it? Did someone want it? Is he or is she responsible for it? The answer is more difficult than it may appear: for I am responsible for what I *wanted*, hence for the *state of affairs* when the decision *declares itself*; but the true event, the decision such as it was being prepared for a long time, the impersonal reconfiguration of my love possibilities—can I be declared "responsible" for it?

123. Friedrich Nietzsche, *Thus Spoke Zarathustra*, ed. Adrian del Caro and Robert Pippin, (Cambridge: Cambridge University Press, 2006), 117: "Thoughts

that come on the feet of doves steer the world": an expression that applies primarily to events, since "the greatest thoughts are the great events" (*Beyond Good and Evil*, §285).

124. Nietzsche, *Beyond Good and Evil*, §285.

125. F. Scott Fitzgerald, *The Crack-Up* (New York: NDP, 2009), 69.

126. Ibid., 71; see also 80: "a crack-up that he scarcely knew of until long after it occurred."

127. Heidegger, *Sein und Zeit*, 287.

128. "Death is never present," Blanchot writes (*Space of Literature*, 104); "it is the abyss of the present, time without a present, with which I have no relationships; it is that toward which I cannot go forth" (154–55).

129. It seems to me difficult to conceive of the event, as Maldiney invites us to do, as an *existentiale* (Maldeney, *Penser l'homme et la folie*, 294), by defining it, according to the conceptuality of the ontology of *Dasein* as "a transformation of presence as Being-in-the-world-for-one's-own-sake" (272), since, on the contrary, a thinking of the event leads us necessarily to a critique of the main concepts of that ontology.

130. Heidegger, *Die Grundbegriffe der Metaphysik: Welt—Endlichkeit—Einsamkeit*, GA 29–30:519: "Nicht *wir* vollziehen ihn, sondern *er* geschieht *mit uns* als Grundgeschehen unseres Daseins"; trans. William McNeill and Nicholas Walker, *The Fundamental Concepts of Metaphysics: World, Finitude, Solitude* (Bloomington: Indiana University Press, 1995), 357.

3. Bergson as Metaphysician and Critic of Metaphysics

1. See Gérard Lebrun, *Kant et la fin de la métaphysique* (Paris: A. Colin, 1970).

2. Henri Bergson, *The Creative Mind: An Introduction to Metaphysics*, trans. Mabelle L. Andison (Mineola, N.Y.: Dover, 2007), 6; see also 117.

3. Ibid., 5.

4. Ibid., 7.

5. Bergson, *Creative Evolution*, trans. Arthur Mitchell (New York: Henry Holt and Company, 1911), 30.

6. Bergson, *Creative Mind*, 85.

7. Ibid., 86.

8. Ibid., 7–8.

9. Aristotle, *Physics* IV.222*b*9ff; see also 221*a*30ff; *Physics*, trans. R. P. Hardie and R. K. Gaye, in *The Complete Works of Aristotle*, ed. Jonathan Barnes, Rev. Oxford Trans. (Princeton: Princeton University Press, 1991), 1:76; see also 1:73–74.

10. For example, in the doctrine according to which, in the now, nothing begins to move, but rather all movement and all change only take place in their state of perfection—and have as their grammatical tense the perfect: "But that which has reference to the beginning is not existent at all; for there is no such thing as a beginning of change, nor any primary time at which it was changing" (Aristotle, *Physics* VI.236*a*13–15; *Physics*, 103). Therefore we must deny that

there is a first moment of change, a moment in which something *begins* to change; the change only occurs as accomplished, and there is only a first moment of *having-been-changed*: ἐν ᾧ πρώτῳ μεταβέβληκε (VI.236*a*7). For a detailed commentary on these passages, see Romano, *Event and Time*, trans. Stephen E. Lewis (New York: Fordham University Press, 2014), 59–67.

11. See Heidegger, *Sein und Zeit*, 425; *Being and Time*, 478: "Why do we say that time *passes away*, when we do not say with *just as much* emphasis that it arises?"

12. Bergson, *Matter and Memory*, trans. Nancy Margaret Paul and W. Scott Palmer (1911; repr. London: George Allen and Unwin), 74 and 280.

13. Bergson, *Time and Free Will*, trans. F. L. Pogson (London: Allen and Unwin 1913), 232.

14. Ibid., 101.

15. Ibid., 75; see Aristotle, *Metaphysics* Z.13.1039*a*12: ὁ ἀριθμός σύνθεσις μονάδων.

16. Bergson, *Time and Free Will*, 79.

17. Ibid., 68; 102.

18. Heidegger, *Sein und Zeit*, 418; *Being and Time*, 470.

19. Aristotle, *Physics* VI.220*a*21; trans. in *Complete Works of Aristotle*, 72.

20. Ibid., VI.219*a*9; 70.

21. Ibid., VI.221a9ff; 70.

22. On this difference, see Brague, *Du temps chez Platon et Aristote* (Paris: PUF, 1982), 97ff.

23. Immanuel Kant, *Kritik der reinen Vernunft*, Ak. III:60; trans. Norman Kemp Smith *Critique of Pure Reason* (London: Macmillan, 1929), 77.

24. Bergson, *Creative Mind*, 125.

25. Bergson, *Time and Free Will*, 98: "time, conceived under the form of a homogeneous medium, is some spurious [*bâtard*] concept, due to the trespassing of the idea of space upon the field of pure consciousness" (see also, on "endosmosis," 109).

26. Bergson, *Creative Mind*, 4.

27. Heidegger, *Sein und Zeit*, 432n1; *Being and Time*, 500n.xxx: "Bergson merely says the reverse [of Hegel's thesis]: that time is space."

28. Bergson, *Creative Mind*, 125.

29. Bergson, *Time and Free Will*, 108.

30. Ibid., 108–9.

31. Ibid., 114.

32. It is on this confusion between movement as "an indivisible act" and movement as a trajectory in homogeneous space that, in Bergson's view, Zeno's paradoxes rest; see *Time and Free Will*, 112: "It is to this confusion between motion and the space traversed that the paradoxes of the Eleatics are due." But is this interpretation tenable? The paradox of Achilles and the tortoise does seem to rest not so much on the confusion of two concepts of "movement" as on that of two concepts of space: continuous, infinitely divisible space, and a discontinuous

space in which movement is repeatedly stopped. This at least is how Aristotle understands this paradox when he emphasizes that the straight line on which movement unfolds is infinitely divisible *in potential*, while Zeno conceives of it as infinitely divisible *in actu*, that is, as discontinuous, and is led for this reason to envisage this movement as repeatedly interrupted by stops. "But," Aristotle objects, "if divisions are made in this way, neither the distance nor the motion will be continuous" (*Physics* VIII.263*a*26–27; *Complete Works*, 153). Therefore the problem is clearly that of the mathematical continuum and not of the difference between two kinds of movement.

33. Bergson, *Matter and Memory*, 268.

34. Seeing the dead end to which the dualism of *Time and Free Will* was leading, Bergson tried to find a way out by asserting that "The universe *endures*" (Bergson, *Creative Evolution*, 11), that there is a "creation of unforeseeable novelty which seems to be going on *in the universe*" (Bergson, *Creative Mind*, 73), by speaking of a "universal mobility" (125), that is, by conceding "whether it is a question of the internal or the external, of ourselves or of things, reality is mobility itself" (ibid.); last, by thinking the difference between inner duration and the time of things as a difference of rhythm: "There is no one rhythm of duration" (Bergson, *Matter and Memory*, 275). Thus four hundred trillion successive vibrations of light are contracted by consciousness to give rise to the perception of red; "the object and the subject must be, with regard to one another, in a situation analogous to that of the two trains we spoke of at the beginning: it is a certain regulating of mobility on mobility which produces the effect of immobility" (*Creative Mind*, 131 [translation modified—Tr.]).

35. Bergson, *Matter and Memory*, 294.

36. Ibid., 296–97.

37. Bergson, *Creative Mind*, 5.

38. Bergson, *Matter and Memory*, 275.

39. Bergson, *Creative Mind*, 3.

40. Ibid., 2 [translation modified—Tr.].

41. Ibid., 4.

42. Ibid., 32 [translation modified—Tr.].

43. In this respect Bergson appears as the predecessor of contemporary endeavors that, without claiming him as their forerunner, end up with comparable theses; see Jacques Derrida, "White Mythology," in *Margins of Philosophy*, trans. Alan Bass (Chicago, Ill.: University of Chicago Press, 1982), 207ff.

44. Bergson, *Creative Mind*, 55.

45. Ibid., 73.

46. Bergson, *The Two Sources of Morality and Religion*, trans. R. Ashley Audra and Cloudesley Brereton (New York: Henry Holt, 1935), 138.

47. Ibid., 134.

48. K. Koffka, *Principles of Gestalt Psychology* (1935; repr. San Diego: Harcourt, Brace, and World, 1963), 178–79.

49. Bergson, *Mind-Energy: Lectures and Essays*, trans. H. Wilden Carr (New York: Henry Holt, 1920), 11: "*In principle*, consciousness is co-extensive with life."

50. Ibid., 39.

51. Bergson, *Creative Mind*, 73.

52. Ibid., 81.

53. Ibid., 84.

54. Ibid., 85.

55. Bergson, *Matter and Memory*, 241.

56. Bergson, *Creative Mind*, 12.

57. Ibid., 14: the possible is "the mirage, in the indefinite past, of reality that has already appeared"; and 83: "The idea immanent in most philosophies and natural to the human mind, of possibles, which would be realised by an acquisition of existence, is therefore pure illusion" [translation of first quote modified—Tr.].

58. Ibid., 131: "In . . . concrete duration . . . the idea of necessary determination loses all significance."

59. Ibid., 73. Bergson will give three examples of this: the meeting I will attend (ibid.), the act that I will perform (8), the painting that the artist will paint, etc.

60. For an analysis of explanation, see Bergson, *Creative Evolution*, 164.

61. "How can we fail to see that if the event can always be explained afterwards by an arbitrary choice of antecedent events, a completely different event could have been equally well explained in the same circumstances by another choice of antecedents—nay, by the same antecedents otherwise cut out, otherwise distributed, otherwise perceived in short, by our retrospective attention?"; Bergson, *Creative Mind*, 84.

62. Bergson, *Creative Mind*, 123.

63. Bergson, *Mind-Energy*, 157. Deleuze gives a commentary on this text in his *Bergsonism*, trans. Hugh Tomlinson and Barbara Habberjam (New York: Zone, 1990), 59.

64. Bergson, *Creative Mind*, 128.

65. Ibid., 124 [translation modified—Tr.].

66. Augustine, *Confessions* XI.20.26.

67. Romano, *Event and Time*, 67–93.

68. Augustine, *Confessions* XI.14.17.

4. Sartrean Freedom, or Adam's Dream

1. Arthur Schopenhauer, *The World as Will and Representation*, trans. Judith Norman, Alistair Welchman, and Christopher Janaway (New York: Cambridge University Press, 2010), 1:334.

2. I will not distinguish, in the present framework, between natural and revealed theology. From the point of view of Sartre's atheism, there can be no distinction between them.

3. Sartre, *Being and Nothingness*, trans. Hazel E. Barnes (New York: Washington Square Press, 1966), 689. All references given in parentheses in the text refer to the page numbers of this translation and edition.

4. Sartre, "Cartesian Freedom," in *Jean-Paul Sartre: Literary and Philosophical Essays*, trans. Annette Michelson (New York: Collier, 1962), 190–91.

5. Ibid., 190 [translation modified—Tr.].

6. Ibid., 191.

7. Ibid.

8. Ibid., 194.

9. René Descartes, "Reply to Objections VI," in *The Philosophical Works of Descartes*, ed. and trans. Elizabeth Haldane and G. R. T. Ross (Cambridge: Cambridge University Press, 1970), 2:250–51.

10. Ibid.

11. Sartre, "Cartesian Freedom," 195.

12. Epistle to the Romans, 5:12.

13. Kierkegaard, *The Concept of Anxiety: A Simple Psychologically Orienting Deliberation on the Dogmatic Issue of Hereditary Sin*, in *Kierkegaard's Writing*, trans. Reidar Thomte (Princeton: Princeton University Press, 1980), 8:30.

14. Ibid.

15. Ibid., 41.

16. Ibid., 41.

17. Ibid., 115.

18. Ibid., 45.

19. Ibid., 49.

20. Ibid., 56.

21. Kierkegaard, *The Journals and Papers of Søren Kierkegaard*, vol. 1, trans. Howard V. Hong and Edna H. Hong (Bloomington: Indiana University Press, 1967–78), entry 94.

22. Kierkegaard, *Concept of Anxiety*, 61.

23. Ibid.

24. Ibid., 156.

25. Sartre, "Kierkegaard: The Singular Universal," in *Between Existentialism and Marxism*, trans. John Matthews (London and New York: Verso, 2008), 161.

26. Ibid., 158 [translation modified—Tr.].

27. Kierkegaard, *Concept of Anxiety*, 79, 98.

28. Sartre, "Kierkegaard: The Singular Universal," 159 [translation modified—Tr.].

29. Ibid.

30. Ibid., 166.

31. Ibid., 161.

32. See Jacques Colette's remarks in his *Kierkegaard et la non-philosophie* (Paris: Gallimard, coll. "TEL," 1994), 162–63.

33. Kierkegaard, *Concept of Anxiety*, 159.

34. Vladimir Jankélévitch, *Le Je-ne-sais-quoi et le Presque-rien* (Paris: Le Seuil, 1980), 3:50.

35. Sartre, "Existentialism Is a Humanism," trans. Philip Mairet, in *Existentialism from Dostoevsky to Sartre*, ed. Walter Kaufmann (New York: Meridian, 1956), 355.

36. Luigi Pareyson, *Ontologia della libertà* (Turin: Einaudi, 1995), 18.

37. For a logical reconstruction of the Master Argument, see the masterful work by Jules Vuillemin, *Necessity or Contingency: The Master Argument* (Stanford, Calif.: CSLI Publications, 1996).

38. Sartre, "Existentialism Is a Humanism," 359 [translation modified—Tr.]. Sartre gave an analogous example in *Being and Nothingness*, 73; my concrete possibility of smoking a cigarette only springs forth for me by the *act* of a freedom, the very act of lighting it up; and, similarly, "it is by the *very act* of drawing this paper and this pen toward me that I give to myself as my most immediate possibility the act of working on this book."

39. Ibid., 364 [translation modified—Tr.].

40. "'Subsequently' and 'first' are terms created by freedom itself,'"; Sartre, *Being and Nothingness*, 625.

41. Sartre, *Notebooks for an Ethics*, trans. David Pellauer (Chicago and London: University of Chicago Press, 1992, 556.

42. Ibid., 364.

43. Ibid., 366–67. [CR's underlining—Tr.]

44. Ibid., 367; see also the analyses of Jean-Louis Chrétien, "Une morale en suspens," *Critique*, no. 438 (November 1983): 856–71.

45. Ibid., 384.

46. Ibid., 338.

5. The Mirror of Narcissus: On the Phenomenology of the Flesh

1. These exceptions are most often due to authors who no longer subscribe to phenomenology or are situated in its "margins"; see Jean-Luc Nancy, *Corpus*, trans. Richard Rand (New York: Fordham University Press, 2008), and Jacques Derrida, *On Touching—Jean-Luc Nancy*, trans. Christine Irizarry (Stanford, Calif.: Stanford University Press, 2005).

2. [In French, there is no good solution for the translation of these terms. To translate *Leib* as "*corps propre*" [my own body] would be to forget, as Didier Franck stresses, that "in the sphere of the 'ownness' all bodies are 'one's own body,' and [that] the difference is not between two kinds of bodies, but between bodies in general and the *Leib*"; Franck, *Chair et corps* (Paris: Éditions de Minuit, 1981), 94. But the translation of "*chair*" [flesh], as emphasized by Derrida, introduces a confusion with another word in the Husserlian vocabulary, *Fleisch* [flesh or meat]; see Derrida, *On Touching—Jean-Luc Nancy*, trans. Christine Irizarry (Stanford, Calif.: Stanford University Press, 2005, 237–38). Furthermore, that translation is less able to bring out what makes every *Leib* a *Leib*, namely, that it

belongs to a pure ego or is its transcendental property: the *Leib* is "the originarily proper to me and constantly proper to me," that is, "the originarily mine (*das ursprünglischt Meine*)," and thus "the organ and means for appropriation (*Zueignung*) of everything"; Hua XIV, 58. The term "flesh" is usually reserved for Merleau-Ponty's special metaphysical use of the French term "*chair*." As for "*corps propre*," I will translate it as "my own body," or in some contexts "one's own body"—Tr.]

3. Husserl, *Ideen zu einer reinen Phänomenologie*, Zweites Buch, Hua IV, §21, 94; trans. Richard Rojcewicz and André Schuwer, *Ideas Pertaining to a Pure Phenomenology and to a Phenomenological Philosophy*, Second Book, *Studies in the Phenomenology of Constitution* (Dordrecht: Kluwer Academic, 1989), 100.

4. Ibid., 147; 2:155.

5. Ibid., 145; 2:152.

6. Ibid. [translation modified—Tr.].

7. Ibid., 145; 2:153 [translation modified—Tr.].

8. Ibid., 147; 2:155 [translation modified—Tr.].

9. Ibid., 148: "*Mein Leib als getasteter Leib getastetes Tastendes ist*" [translation modified—Tr.].

10. See Xavier Tillette, "Husserl's Concept of Nature (Merleau-Ponty's 1957–58 Lectures)," trans. Drew Leder, in Maurice Merleau-Ponty, *Texts and Dialogues*, ed. Hugh J. Silverman and James Barry Jr. (Amherst, N.Y: Humanities Press, 1992), 164n29.

11. Franck speaks of "the endless exchange between the organ and the object *in that finally organ and object become indistinguishable*"; *Chair et corps*, 97.

12. Hua IV, 145; 153 [the English translation has "then the sensation is *doubled* in the two parts of the Body"—Tr.].

13. Ibid., 150; 157 [the English translation has "for us more" rather than "much more (*bien plus*)"—Tr.].

14. Ibid., 151; 158–59.

15. Ibid., 150; 158.

16. Ibid., 153; 160.

17. Ibid., 153; 160.

18. This is what leads Husserl to acknowledge how difficult it would be to elaborate an "independent, proper somatology," which "presupposes the pure separation of sensation from the apprehensional texture into which it is woven" (*Ideen III*, Hua V, 10; trans. Ted E. Klein and William E. Pohl, *Ideas Pertaining to a Pure Phenomenology and to a Phenomenological Philosophy*, Third Book, *Phenomenology and the Foundations of the Sciences* [Hingham, Mass., and Boston: Kluwer, 2001], 9). But on the other hand, without the possibility of such a distinction, it is hard to see what allows us to distinguish between flesh and body.

19. Manuscript D12 IV (1931); Husserl, "The World of the Living Present and the Constitution of the Surrounding World That Is Outside the Flesh," trans. Bettina Bergo, rev. Leonard Lawlor, in *Husserl at the Limits of Phenomenology* (Evanston, Ill.: Northwestern University Press, 2002), 150.

20. Husserl, *Ideen II*, Hua IV, 75; *Ideas II*, 80 [translation modified—Tr.].

21. Ibid., 212; 223.

22. Ibid., 159; 167.

23. Ibid., 75; 80.

24. Husserl, *Zur Phänomenologie der Intersubjektivität, Zweiter Teil (1921–1928)*, Hua XIV, 453.

25. Dominique Pradelle, *L'archéologie du monde* (Dordrecht: Kluwer, 2000), 262.

26. *Ideen II*, Hua IV, 240; *Ideas II*, 252.

27. *Ideen III*, Hua V, 11; *Phenomenology III*: *Ideas*, 10 [translation modified—Tr.].

28. *Ideen I*, Hua, I, 119; trans. F. Kersten, *Ideas Pertaining to a Pure Phenomenology and to a Phenomenological Philosophy*, First Book, *General Introduction* (Dordrecht: Kluwer, 1983), 127 [translation modified—Tr.]. See also §41 in which Husserl gives a transcendental version of the Cartesian dualism of the *res cogitans* and of the *res extensa*: "The adumbrating is lived experience. But lived experience is possible only as lived experience, and not as something spatial. However, the adumbrated is of essential necessity possible only as something spatial . . . and not possible as lived experience" (Hua I, 86; trans. F. Kersten, *Ideas I*, 88) [translation modified—Tr.].

29. *Ideen II*, Hua IV, 157; *Ideas II*, 165 [translation modified—Tr.].

30. Ibid., 213; 224.

31. Ibid.

32. Ibid., 213; 224 [translation modified—Tr.].

33. Ibid., 214; 226.

34. What is true of the flesh, under the transcendental regime, is also obviously true of the soul: "I *am* not a soul, but I *have* a soul" (*Ideen II*, 94; *Ideas II*, 99).

35. Husserl, *Erste Philosophie, Zweiter Teil*, Hua VIII, 62 [trans. H. Sebastian Luft and Thane M. Naberhaus, forthcoming from Springer Press in the series *Husserliana Collected Works*, "First Philosophy," pagination not yet available—Tr.].

36. Husserl, *Cartesianische Meditationen und Pariser Vorträge*, Hua I (The Hague: Nijhoff, 1950), 124; trans. of *Cartesian Meditations* by Cairns, 92–93.

37. *Ideen II*, Hua IV, 158; *Ideas II*, 166.

38. Hua XV, 659.

39. I will use the following abbreviations for Merleau-Ponty's works: *Phenomenology of Perception*, trans. Colin Smith (London: Routledge and Kegan Paul, 1962): *PP*; *Signs*, trans. Richard C. McCleary (Evanston, Ill.: Northwestern University Press, 1964): *S*; *The Visible and the Invisible* (Evanston, Ill.: Northwestern University Press, 1968): *VI*.

40. In truth, Husserl writes rather incomprehensibly in *Ideen II* that it is the flesh (*Leib*) that is an obstacle to itself: "The same Body which serves me as means for all my perception obstructs me in the perception of itself and is a remarkably imperfectly constituted thing (*merkwürdig unvollkommen konstituiertes Ding*)"

(*Ideen II*, Hua IV, 159; *Ideas II*, 167). But how could the flesh, as hyletic substrate, which doesn't really have spatial limits, be an obstacle to anything whatsoever? Merleau-Ponty does not notice this difficulty, probably because the body, as he understands it, is no longer a "means," but the "subject" of perception.

41. Indeed, the flesh "can be constituted originarily only in tactuality" (*Ideen II*, 150; *Ideas II*, 158). Furthermore, for the other senses, and especially for sight, we have mirrors that allow us to see parts of our bodies that are inaccessible to our tactile apprehension.

42. Merleau-Ponty has often been criticized for the symmetry he establishes between touch and vision and blamed for a lack of logical consistency: it seems that there is nothing analogous to the touching-touched relation at the level of vision. I will revisit this question. But the logical inconsistency may be just as much attributable to Husserl when he would have us believe that I could *see* something such as flesh (for it is on the basis of *visual* perceptions that intersubjectivity is chiefly constituted).

43. See Chapter 2 of Part I of *Phenomenology of Perception*: "The Experience of the Body and Classical Psychology."

44. Jacques Colette, "La réflexivité du sensible," in *Maurice Merleau-Ponty: Le psychique et le corporel* (Paris: Aubier, 1988), 47.

45. *Ideen III*, Hua V, Beilage I, 117; *Ideas III*, 104.

46. On this occasion Merleau-Ponty advances a view that has long prevailed, that of a "second Husserl" *less* transcendental (as if transcendentalism admitted of the more or less) and having redirected his thought in a completely different direction. "[His philosophy] has been sufficiently expanded or transformed to be the match for anything, even for what challenges it" (*S* 177). This assertion is probably untenable. Husserl never abandoned the transcendental horizon of his thought or the doctrine of constitution, even if he explored other paths toward the reduction than the Cartesian one. It is true, as Merleau-Ponty stresses (*S* 180), that everything relating to preconstitution, passive synthesis, and an anonymous intentionality operating inside of me but without me, becomes more and more important within the transcendental edifice—but without ever modifying its *foundations*.

47. Here Merleau-Ponty is very close to Erwin Straus, who defined sensing as "a process of coming to terms with the world" (Straus, *The Primary World of Senses* [New York: Free Press of Glencoe, 1963], 363).

48. ["le propre du sentir, c'est le sentir du propre": this phrase is untranslatable—Tr.]

49. Heidegger, *Identität und Differenz* (Pfullingen: Neske, 1957), 62; trans. Joan Stambaugh, *Identity and Difference* (New York, Evanston, and London: Harper and Row, 1969), 67.

50. There is "a generality of the Sensible in itself" (*VI* 139) by virtue of which "this delimitation of the senses is crude" (*VI* 133): the look "palpates" the visible (*VI* 133, 134); there is "encroachment not only between the touched and the touching, but also between the tangible and the visible" (*VI* 134).

51. "One should not even say . . . that the body is made up of two leaves, of which the one, that of the 'sensible,' is bound up with the rest of the world. There are not in it two leaves or two layers" (*VI* 137).

52. Heidegger, *Grundbegriffe*, GA 51:52.

53. Merleau-Ponty, *The Structure of Behavior*, trans. Alden L. Fisher (Boston: Beacon Press, 1963), 215.

54. The flesh seems to be able to be contrasted with the skin, even in painting; there is a kind of painting that is "without identifiable things, without the *skin* of things, but giving their *flesh*" (*VI* 218).

55. Husserl, *Analysen zur passiven Synthesis*, Hua XI, 379; trans. Anthony J. Steinbock, *Analyses Concerning Passive and Active Synthesis* (Dordrecht: Kluwer Academic, 2001), 469: "Transcendental life and the transcendental ego cannot be born; only the human being in the world can be born. The ego as transcendental ego was eternal: I am now, and belonging to this Now is a horizon of the past that can be unraveled into infinity. And this means precisely, the ego was eternal."

56. Eugène Minkowski, *Vers une cosmologie* (Paris: Aubier-Montaigne, 1936), 182 [my translation—Tr.].

57. Étienne Bonnot de Condillac, *Treatise on Sensations*, in *Philosophical Writings of Étienne Bonnot, Abbé de Condillac* (Hillsdale, N.J.: Erlbaum, 1982), 234.

58. Maurice Pradines, *Philosophie de la Sensation*, vol. 2, *La Sensibilité élémentaire* (Paris: Les Belles Lettres, 1926), 247, note [my translation—Tr.].

59. Ibid., 247.

60. Minkowski, *Vers une cosmologie*, 79.

61. *Ideen II*, Hua IV, 150; *Ideas II*, 158.

62. I borrow this idea from J. J. Gibson: see *The Senses Considered as Perceptual Systems* (Boston: Houghton Mifflin, 1966), 150.

63. See Gibson, *The Ecological Approach to Visual Perception* (Hillsdale, N.J.: Erlbaum, 1986), 183.

64. De Condillac, "Treatise on Sensations," 234 [the author's emphasis].

65. Ibid.

6. The Ecological Phenomenology of J. J. Gibson

1. Merleau-Ponty, "The Film and the New Psychology," in *Sense and Non-Sense*, trans. Hubert L. Dreyfus and Patricia Allen Dreyfus (Evanston, Ill.: Northwestern University Press, 1964), 50.

2. Ibid., 52.

3. Viktor von Weizsäcker, *Der Gestaltkreis*, French trans. Michel Foucault and Daniel Rocher, in *Le cycle de la structure* (Paris: Desclée de Brouwer, 1958), 157. On this conception of perception as encounter, see also 141, 156, 188, and 208.

4. Ibid., 208.

5. Alfred Lord Whitehead, *Nature and Life* (Cambridge: Cambridge University Press, 1934), 16–17.

6. Werner Heisenberg, "The Representation of Nature in Contemporary Physics," *Daedalus* 87, no. 3, *Symbolism in Religion and Literature* (Summer 1958): 107.

7. Johannes Müller, *Zur vergleichenden Physiologie des Gesichtsinns* (Leipzig: 1826); Müller, *Handbuch der Physiologie des Menschen*, vol. 2 (Braunschweig: 1838). For a historical reconstruction of these analyses, see E. G. Boring, *Sensation and Perception in the History of Experimental Psychology* (New York: Appleton, 1942), 68ff.

8. Gerald S. Wasserman, *Colour Vision: An Historical Introduction* (New York: John Wiley and Sons, 1978), 19.

9. Isaac Newton, "The New Theory about Light and Colors" (1671), in *Newton's Philosophy of Nature: Selection from his Writings*, ed. H. S. Thayer (New York and London: Hafner, 1953), 74.

10. Newton, *Optiks* (New York: Dover, 1952), 124–25; see also Evan Thompson, *Colour Vision* (New York and London: Routledge, 1995).

11. Gibson, *Senses Considered*, 150.

12. Edwin H. Land, "The Retinex Theory of Colour Vision," *Scientific American* 237, no. 6 (December 1977): 84–99; see also Thompson's commentary *Colour Vision*, 80ff.

13. P. Gouras and E. Zrenner, "Colour Vision: A Review from a Neurophysiological Perspective," *Progress in Sensory Physiology* 1 (1981): 139–40 (quoted by Evan Thompson, *Colour Vision* London: Routledge, 1995, 111).

14. Gibson, *Senses Considered*, 48.

15. Gibson, *Ecological Approach*, 53.

16. Descartes, *Discourse on Method, Optics, Geometry and Meteorology* (Indianapolis: Bobbs-Merrill, 1965), 106ff; Descartes, *The World and Other Writings*, ed. Stephen Gaukroger (Cambridge: Cambridge University Press, 1998), 133ff.

17. Descartes, *Discourse on Method*, 106. It must be noted, however, that the Cartesian response to the problem of distance perception does not rest solely on the idea of angle calculation and judgment of the mind. "We have yet another way of perceiving distance, which is through the distinctness or indistinctness of the shape seen, together with the strength or weakness of the light" (ibid.). Descartes does not say how these two solutions are to be reconciled; he does not clarify what he means by "natural geometry." What his successors retained of his conception was almost exclusively the idea of a calculation or a judgment; see George Berkeley, *An Essay towards a New Theory of Vision*, 2nd ed. (Dublin: Aaron Rhames, for Jeremy Pepyat, Bookseller in Skinner-Row, 1709), 1ff. Berkeley critiques the Cartesian solution to distance perception by measurement of the optical angle and replaces it with an empiricist thesis resting on the habitual and customary connection between the ideas of vision and touch. But he keeps the essential Cartesian presupposition that "Distance of it self, and immediately cannot be seen" (*Essay towards a New Theory of Vision*, 1).

18. Gibson, *Ecological Approach*, 160.

19. Gibson, "Perception and Judgement of Aerial Space and Distance As Potential Factors in Pilot Selection and Training" (1947), reprinted in *Reasons for Realism: Selected Essays of James J. Gibson*, ed. E. Reed and R. Jones (Hillsdale, N.J.: Erlbaum, 1982), 40.

20. Gibson, *Ecological Approach*, 160. One might make the following objection: The grasp of that invariant is not enough to know the real size of the stake, unless one *knows* that the level of the horizon corresponds to the level of the eyes of the observer and unless one *infers* the size of the object by an approximate calculation. Here we may recognize Descartes's idea of a "natural geometry." But this is not what Gibson means. The important thing for the observer is not the analytic grasp of the relation between the level of the horizon on the stake and his own size, which would enable him to *infer* from it subsequently the size of the objet on the basis of a prior *knowledge* of his own. What counts is that one and the same stake *presents* to the observer a perceptual invariance—that it *looks* to rise to the same height above the horizon from whatever distance—in short, that its size appears *immediately visible and identifiable* as the same. The case of the "texture-perspective" is no different.

21. Gibson, *Ecological Approach*, 253.

22. Gibson, "Perceptual Learning: Differentiation or Enrichment?," in *Reasons for Realism*, 320ff.

23. [Paul Claudel's creative/poetic etymology of "connaissance" (one of the French words for knowledge) from the elements "co" and "naissance" ("with" and "birth"), suggests that we should understand knowledge as a "co-birth."—Tr.]

24. Gibson, *Ecological Approach*, 8.

25. Von Weizsäcker, *Le cycle de la structure*, French trans. Foucault and Rocher, 223.

26. Ibid., 45.

27. Ibid., 47.

28. Here we should take care not to misunderstand the meaning of this comparison. It is not a matter of elevating quantum mechanics to the level of a universal paradigm, which would amount to radically misconstruing its meaning. The revolutionary nature of this theory lies not only in its critique of the traditional concepts of subject and object, or of causality, but precisely in its requirement that all reference to an ultimate paradigm for knowledge of the physical world be abandoned. Heisenberg is explicit on this point. He says that we must give up "the earlier ideal of scientific truth" and restrict ourselves to a pluralism of experiential domains. "In the sphere of the exact science of nature, there have never been any definitive solutions, except in certain limited domains of experience" ("Heisenberg, Representation of Nature," 106 [translation modified—Tr.]). This also holds, obviously, for the quantum theory itself, which is a "closed theory" and not a universal theory of nature. However, we find here a radical critique of all naïve application of the objectivist ideal of physics to the most varied domains—a critique in which thinkers such as Gibson have not failed to find inspiration.

29. Von Weizsäcker, *Le cycle de la structure*, 56.

30. Ibid., 57.

31. Gibson, *Ecological Approach*, 225.

32. Gibson, "Notes on action," in *Reasons for Realism*, 388.

33. Ibid., 386.

34. Ibid., 386ff.

35. Ibid., 387.

36. Analogous objections have been addressed to *Gestaltpsychologie* by authors that Gibson does not quote and seems unaware of: Kurt Goldstein, in *The Organism* (New York: Zone, 1995), and, of course, Merleau-Ponty.

37. Gibson, *Ecological Approach*, 206.

38. The example is from Helmholz. It is cited by Gibson in "The Problem of Event Perception," in *Reasons for Realism*, 213.

39. Gibson, "What Is a Form?," in *Reasons for Realism*, 305.

40. Ibid., 305.

41. In Gibson's distinction between *form* and *shape*, see "What Is a Form?," 314ff.

42. [In English in the text—Tr.]

43. We are not very far from the Cartesian idea of a "natural geometry," except that the latter is not inferred, but *given*.

44. These invariants, although qualitative, can be mathematically analyzed in the framework of a geometry sometimes called "synthetic" (see *Reasons for Realism*, 88); some students of Gibson have tried to develop an apposite mathematical formalism in order to describe the modifications of optical information during locomotion.

45. Gibson, "On the Concept of 'Formless Invariants' in Visual Perception," in *Reasons for Realism*, 287.

46. Gibson, *Ecological Approach*, 127.

47. Ibid., 137 [CR's emphasis—Tr.].

48. Gibson, "Notes on Action," in *Reasons for Realism*, 392.

49. See Gibson, "New Reasons for Realism," in *Reasons for Realism*, 374ff.

50. Ibid., 380.

51. Gibson, "Problem of Event Perception," in *Reasons for Realism*, 207.

52. Gibson, "Concept of the Stimulus in Psychology," in *Reasons for Realism*, 346.

53. Gibson, "New Reasons for Realism," 382.

54. Gibson, "A Reply to Johansson from James J. Gibson," in *Reasons for Realism*, 89.

55. Wolfgang Köhler, footnote to the article "Value and Fact," in *Selected Papers of Wolfgang Köhler* (New York: Liveright, 1971), 363; quoted by Victor Rosenthal and Yves-Marie Visetti, "Sens et temps de la *Gestalt*," *Intellectica* 1, no. 28 (1991): 220.

56. Even if Husserl points out, in *Logical Investigations*, that "in talking of 'acts' on the other hand, we must steer clear of the word's original meaning: *all*

thought of activity must be rigidly excluded" (*Logische Untersuchungen*; trans. Findlay, *Logical Investigations* [New York: Routledge, 1970], 2:102), his distinction between acts and sensible contents remains entirely tributary to classical (and mainly empiricist) psychology, as Husserl will later end up admitting: "My original understanding of the immanent sphere thanks to immanent *data*, which through the passive accomplishment of association eventually come to 'be apprehended'—is it not a remnant of the old psychology and its sensualist empiricism?" (Manuscript B.1.2.8 [my translation of Romano's French version—Tr.]).

57. Husserl, *Ideen I*, §49, quoting the Cartesian definition of substance from *Principes de la philosophie* I, §51; trans. Kersten, *Ideas I* (Dordrecht: Kluwer Academic, 1882), 110, and Descartes, *Principles of Philosophy*, http://www.earlymoderntexts.com/pdfs/descartes1644.pdf), p. 13, accessed 14 January 2014.

58. Von Weizsäcker, *Le cycle de la structure*, 145.

59. Husserl, *Ideen II*, Hua IV, 212; trans. Richard Rojcewicz and André Schuwer, *Ideas II*, 223.

60. Ibid., 159; 167.

61. Ibid., 153; 160–61.

62. Ibid., 157; 165 [translation modified—Tr.].

63. Merleau-Ponty, *Structure of Behavior*, 215.

64. Merleau-Ponty, *Visible and the Invisible*, 135.

65. Gibson, *Ecological Approach*, 139.

7. Is a Phenomenology of Nothingness Possible? The Carnap-Heidegger Controversy

1. Henri Maldiney, *Ouvrir le rien, l'art nu* (Fougères: Encre Marine, 2000), 113 [my translation—Tr.].

2. Heidegger, *Was ist Metaphysik?*, in *Wegmarken*, GA 9:106; trans. David Farrell Krell, in *Basic Writings: From Being and Time (1927) to The Task of Thinking (1964)* (San Francisco: HarperSanFrancisco, 1993), 96.

3. Ibid., 107, 117; 97, 105.

4. Bertrand Russell, *Our Knowledge of the External World as a Field for Scientific Method in Philosophy* (London: Allen and Unwin, 1914), chap. 2.

5. Rudolf Carnap, "The Elimination of Metaphysics through Logical Analysis of Language," trans. Arthur Pap, in *Logical Positivism*, ed. A. J. Ayer (Glencoe, Ill.: Free Press, 1959), 60–81.

6. Heidegger, *Wegmarken*, GA 9:118; *Basic Writings*,106.

7. Ibid., 121–22; 109.

8. See Heidegger, *Kant und das Problem der Metaphysik*, GA 3:231: *"Die Metaphysik ist das Grundgeschehen im Dasein. Sie ist das Dasein selbst."*

9. *Heidegger,* Wegmarken, GA 9:122; *Basic Writings*, 110.

10. Kant's remark is in his letter to Markus Herz [about 11 May 1781], in *Philosophical Correspondence, 1759–99*, ed. and trans. Arnulf Zweig (Chicago: University of Chicago Press, 1967), 95.

11. Heidegger, *Sein und Zeit*, 188; *Being and Time*, 233.

12. Ibid., 186–87; 231.

13. Heidegger, *Wegmarken*, GA 9:114; *Basic Writings*, 103.

14. Ibid., 115; 104 [translation modified—Tr.].

15. Kant, *Kritik der reinen Vernunft*, Ak. III.11; trans. Norman Kemp Smith, *Critique of Pure Reason* (London: Macmillan, 1929), 21.

16. Carnap, "Elimination of Metaphysics," 80.

17. Ibid., 72.

18. "The Scientific World Conception" [translation of Part 2 of the anonymous pamphlet "*Wissenschaftliche* Weltauffassung"], in *Empiricism and Sociology*, by Otto Neurath, ed. Marie Neurath and Robert S. Cohen (Dordrecht: Reidel, 1973), 307.

19. Carnap recognized, moreover, the existence of what he calls the "enigmas of life" (*Lebensrätsel*), but denied them the status of questions; see Carnap, *Der logische Aufbau der Welt* (Berlin: Welkreis-Verlag, 1928), §183.

20. Ludwig Wittgenstein, "A Lecture on Ethics," *Philosophical Review* 74, no. 1 (January 1965): 5, 8, 8, respectively.

21. Ibid., 11, 12.

22. Conversation of 30 December 1929, in the *Philosophical Review* 74 (1965): 3–27. The first sentence (reference to Heidegger) and the last paragraph not included [I have therefore translated those portions from the French, quoted from Antonia Carnap Soulez, ed., *Manifeste du Circle de Vienne et autres écrits* (Paris: PUF, 1985), 250–51—Tr.]. On this comparison, see also Franco Volpi, "Wittgenstein et Heidegger: Le 'dépassement' de la métaphysique entre philosophie analytique et philosophie continentale," in *La métaphysique: Son histoire, sa critique, ses enjeux*, ed. Jean-Marc Narbonne and Luc Langlois (Paris: Vrin-Laval, 1999).

23. "Scientific World Conception," 305.

24. Carnap, "Elimination of Metaphysics," 77.

25. Carnap, "Überwindung der Metaphysik," lecture delivered in Brünn in December 1932, quoted by Michael Friedman, in *A Parting of the Ways: Carnap, Cassirer, and Heidegger* (Chicago: Open Court, 2000), 19.

26. Carnap, "Elimination of Metaphysics," 61.

27. See Maurice Clavelin, "La première doctrine de la signification du Cercle de Vienne," *Études philosophiques* 4 (October–December 1973): 475–504.

28. Carnap, "Elimination of Metaphysics," 63.

29. On reduction as a logical procedure of derivation making it possible to establish whether a word has meaning, see Carnap, *Logische Aufbau der Welt*, §2.

30. For a few significant criticisms, see Russell, "Logical Positivism," in *The Philosophy of Rudolph Carnap*, ed. Paul Arthur Schilpp (La Salle, Ill.: Open Court, 1962). See also, for a more general presentation, Pierre Jacob, *Logical Empiricism* (Paris: Éditions de Minuit, 1980).

31. Carnap, "Elimination of Metaphysics," 62.

32. Ibid., 65–66.

33. The *Bailly* Greek-French dictionary lists the following main meanings: (1) beginning, principle, origin; (2) command, power, authority. The meaning "origin," a typical example of the metaphorical use of the term by philosophy, in Carnap's view, is attested several times in Homer: for example, in the *Iliad* 22.116, ἀρχὴ νείκεος means not "beginning of a quarrel," but "origin of a quarrel"; in the *Odyssey* 21.4, ἀρχὴ φόνου cannot be translated otherwise than as "origin of a murder."

34. Carnap, "Elimination of Metaphysics," 66.

35. Ibid., 75.

36. "Difference of type means difference of syntactical function" (Russell, "Reply to criticism," in *The Philosophy of Bertrand Russell*. ed. Schilpp (New York: Tudor, 1951), 692; quoted by Ali Benmakhlouf, in *Bertrand Russell: L'atomisme logique* (Paris: PUF, 1996).

37. "Scientific World Conception," 308.

38. Carnap, "Elimination of Metaphysics," 69.

39. Ibid., 71.

40. Ibid.

41. Ibid., 70.

42. Ibid., 72.

43. Ibid., 71.

44. Ibid.

45. James Conant, "Two Conceptions of *Die Überwindung der Metaphysik*: Carnap and Early Wittgenstein," in *Wittgenstein in America*, ed. Timothy McCarthy and Sean C. Stidd (Oxford: Clarendon Press, 2001), 34.

46. Carnap, "Elimination of Metaphysics," 71.

47. Ibid.

48. Heidegger, *Nietzsche II*, GA 6.2:41; trans. Frank A. Capuzzi, *Nietzsche*, ed. Martin Heidegger and David Farrell Krell (San Francisco: Harper and Row, 1979), 4:19.

49. Carnap, "Elimination of Metaphysics," 71.

50. Heidegger, *Wegmarken*, GA 9:117; *Basic Writings*, 105.

51. Carnap, "Elimination of Metaphysics," 69.

52. Heidegger made the acquaintance of Carnap in Davos in March–April 1929; thereafter they had philosophical exchanges. On 30 March, Carnap relates in his diary that they took a walk, in the course of which they approached "the new question of existence." On April 3, in a café, they discussed "the possibility of expressing everything, even the questions of intention and meaning, in physical terms" (a question that would occupy the Vienna Circle in the following years, as attested by the divergences, on this point, between Carnap and Neurath); see Michael Friedman, *Parting of the Ways*, 19. Let us recall that the lecture "What Is Metaphysics?" was delivered in Freiburg on 24 July 1929—that is, more than three months after these conversations.

53. Heidegger, *Wegmarken*, GA 9:105, note (a).

54. Heidegger, *Grundbegriffe*, GA 51:81; trans. Gary E. Aylesworth, *Basic Concepts* (Bloomington and Indianapolis: Indiana University Press, 1993), 68.

55. Heidegger, *Frühe Schriften (1912–16)*, GA 1:42–43; trans. Theodore J. Kisiel and Thomas Sheehan, *Becoming Heidegger: On the Trail of His Early Occasional Writings, 1910–1927*, ed. Kisiel and Sheehan (Evanston, Ill: Northwestern University Press, 2007), 44. [I have included the German wording for "does not come out of mathematics at all" in square brackets in order to make it clear that what Heidegger has in mind here has nothing to do with the origin of logistics, but with its failure to disengage itself from and rise above mathematics—Tr.]

56. Heidegger, *Die Frage nach dem Ding* (Tübingen: Niemeyer, 1962), 122; trans. W. B. Barton Jr. and Vera Deutsch, *What Is a Thing?* (South Bend, Ind.: Gateway, 1967), 156.

57. Carnap, "Elimination of Metaphysics," 73.

58. Gottlob Frege, "On the Scientific Justification of a Conceptual Notation," in *Conceptual Notation and Related Articles*, trans. and ed. Terrell Ward Bynum (Oxford: Clarendon Press, 1972), 89.

59. Frege, "Function and Concept," in *The Frege Reader*, ed. Michael Beaney (Malden, Mass.: Blackwell, 1997), 138.

60. Ibid., 140.

61. Ibid., 139, 140.

62. For reasons of convenience, I am replacing Frege's symbolism with Russell's more widely used one.

63. Frege, *Foundations of Arithmetic: A Logico-Mathematical Enquiry into the Concept of Number* (New York: Harper, 1960), 60, §47.

64. Frege, "Dialogue with Pünjer on Existence," in *Posthumous Writings* (Chicago: University of Chicago Press, 1979), 63.

65. Benmakhlouf, *Bertrand Russell*, 84.

66. Frege, "Dialogue with Pünjer on Existence," 66.

67. See Denis Zaslawsky, "La philosophie analytique," in *Histoire de la philosophie*, ed. Yvon Belaval, tome III, vol. 2 (Paris: Gallimard, 1999), 773.

68. Frege, "Dialogue with Pünjer on Existence," 64.

69. Ibid., 54.

70. Frege, *Foundations of Arithmetic*, 59.

71. Ibid., §53, 65.

72. Frege, "Dialogue with Pünjer on Existence," 65–66.

73. Ibid., 64.

74. Russell, *The Philosophy of Logical Atomism* (London and New York: Routledge, 1972), 66.

75. Ibid., 67.

76. Ibid., 68.

77. Heidegger, *Sein und Zeit*, 153; *Being and Time*, 195; see also *Wegmarken*, GA 9:104; *Basic Writings*, 195.

78. This has been emphasized by various authors: in particular, P. F. Strawson, "Is Existence Never a Predicate?," *Critica* (1967); P. T. Geach, "Form and

Existence," *Proceedings of Aristotelian Society* (1954–55); C. J. F. Williams, "On Dying," *Philosophy* 44, no. 169 (July 1969): 217–30; and Ernst Tugendhat, "Existence in Space and Time," *Neue Hefte für Philosophie*, no. 8 (1975).

79. Williams, "On Dying," 229.

80. Tugendhat, "Existence in Space and Time," 33.

81. Ibid., 28.

82. Tugendhat, *Self-Consciousness and Self-Determination*, trans. Paul Stern (Cambridge, Mass.: MIT Press, 1986), 155.

83. Heidegger, "Einleitung zu 'Was ist Metaphysik?,'" GA 9:382; trans. R. F. C. Hull and Alan Crick, in *Existentialism from Dostoevsky to Sartre*, ed. Walter Kaufmann, rev. and enlarged ed. (New York: New American Library, 1975), 278.

84. Thomas Aquinas, *ST* III, q. 13, a. 2. [Every creature is changeable into nothingness.—Tr.]

85. Heidegger, *Nietzsche* II, GA 6.2:43; trans. Frank A. Cauzzi, *Nietzsche*, ed. David Farrell Krell (San Francisco: Harper and Row, 1979), 4:21.

86. Heidegger, GA 9:108; *Basic Writings*, 98.

87. Heidegger, "Zur Seinsfrage," in GA 9:402: *"Das Nichts, das als die Absenz der Praesenz Abbruch tut ('nich-tet')."*

88. Heidegger, "Einleitung zu 'Was ist Metaphysik?,'" 374; trans. in *Existentialism from Dostoevsky to Sartre*, 271.

89. Heidegger, "Nachwort zu 'Was ist Metaphysik ?,'" in *Wegmarken*, GA 9:306; trans. in *Existentialism from Dostoevsky to Sartre*, 88.

90. These are the two main moments of Bergson's critique of the idea of nothingness: see his *Creative Evolution*, trans. Arthur Mitchell (New York: Henry Holt, 1911).

91. Heidegger, *Wegmarken*, GA 9:109; *Basic Writings*, 98.

92. Kant, *Kritik der reinen Vernunft*, B347. Wittgenstein was to say the same thing: "But it is important that the signs '*p*' and '~ *p*' *can* say the same thing. For it shows that nothing in reality corresponds to the sign '~'": Wittgenstein, *Tractatus logico-philosophicus*, 4.0621; trans. D. F. Pears and B. F. McGuinness (New York: Routledge, 1961).

93. Cf. Husserl, *Erfahrung und Urteil* (Hamburg: Claassen und Goverts, 1948); trans. James Spencer Churchill and Karl Ameriks, *Experience and Judgment* (Evanston, Ill.: Northwestern University Press, 1975), §21(a).

94. Paradoxically, even a critique of nothingness like Bergson's is a critique of *the idea* of nothingness; it can only attempt to show that nothingness is impossible, contradictory, because it has reduced it in advance to an "idea entirely fabricated by the mind"; Bergson, *Creative Evolution*, 117 (translation modified), to a mere "representation."

95. David Wiggins, "Sentence Meaning, Negation, and Plato's Problem of Non-Being," in *Plato: A Collection of Critical Essays*, vol. 1, *Metaphysics and Epistemology*, ed. Gregory Vlastos (Notre Dame, Ind.: University of Notre Dame, 1978), 273–74n6.

96. See Stanley Rosen, "Thinking about Nothing," in *Heidegger and Modern Philosophy*, ed. Michael Murray (New Haven: Yale University Press, 1978), 116ff.

97. Heidegger, *Grundbegriffe*, 60; *Basic Concepts*, 51.

98. Plato, *Republic* VII.533*c*.

99. Carnap, "Elimination of Metaphysics," 80.

8. "Between Emptiness and the Pure Event": Phenomenology

1. Aristotle, *Meteorology* 355a13–15. I have drawn inspiration from Roger Munier's remarkable commentary "Le flux, le figé, l'apparaître," placed in the appendix of his *Les fragments d'Héraclite* (Paris: Fata Morgana, 1991). [I quote Heraclitus according to the translation of Charles H. Kahn, *The Art and Thought of Heraclitus* (London and New York: Cambridge University Press, 1979)—Tr.].

2. Heraclitus, frag. DK 91.

3. Ibid., 30.

4. Ibid., 46.

5. Ibid., 123 [translation modified—Tr.].

6. Ibid., 122.

7. Munier, "Le flux, le figé, l'apparaître," 82–83.

8. Heraclitus, frag. 12.

9. Munier, "Le flux, le figé, l'apparaître," 90–91.

10. Heraclitus, frag. 84*a*.

11. Heraclitus, frag. 51: "They do not understand how, while being at variance, it is in agreement with itself. There is a back-turning connection, like that of a bow or a lyre." This is why, of all things, the *logos* unites life (surging forth, blossoming) and death (disappearance). "The bow (βίος) is called life (βιός), but its work is death" (frag. 48).

12. Parmenides, frag. 6, verses 8–9 (quoted by Munier, "Le flux," 91); trans. David Gallop, *Parmenides of Elea, Fragments: A Text and Translation* (Toronto: University of Toronto Press, 1991), 61.

13. Aristotle, *Metaphysics* IV.1010a34–35.

14. Ibid., IV.1010a14–15.

15. Aristotle merely follows the lesson of his master who asserts in *Cratylus* 402*a*: "Heraclitus says somewhere that 'everything gives way and nothing stands fast,' and, likening the things that are to the flowing (*rhoē*) of a river, he says that 'you cannot step into the same river twice.'" [Plato, *Cratylus*, trans. C. D. C. Reeve, in *Complete Works*, ed. John M. Cooper and D. S. Hutchinson (Indianapolis: Hackett, 1997), 120]. "Heraclitus says, you know, that all things move and nothing remains still, and he likens the universe to the current of a river, saying that you cannot step twice into the same stream."

16. See Danielle Montet, *Les traits de l'être* (Grenoble: Millon, 1990), 17: "During the Homeric period, *gignesthai* could unproblematically trade places with *einai*. Inextricably, both terms meant what takes place, what happens. For example, a struggle, a war (*polemos, makhè gignetai*, but just as likely *estin*)." It

was Benveniste who first highlighted this trait in Herodotus; see Émile Benveniste, *Problems in General Linguistics*, trans. Mary Elizabeth Meek (Coral Gables, Fla.: University of Miami Press, 1971), 141.

17. Husserl, *Zur Phänomenologie des inneren Zeitbewußtseins*, Hua X, 100; trans. James S. Churchill, *The Phenomenology of Internal Time-Consciousness* (Bloomington and London: Indiana University Press, 1964), 131.

18. Husserl, Manuscript C21, 22.

19. Husserl, Manuscript C13.II (1934), 9.

20. Husserl, Manuscript C7.I (1932), 30.

21. Heidegger, *Identität und Differenz*, 10th ed. (Stuttgart: Neske, 1996), 56; trans. Joan Stambaugh, *Identity and Difference* (New York: Harper and Row, 1969), 64–65.

22. Heraclitus, frag. 16.

23. Aristotle, *Metaphysics* Z.7.1032a13.

24. Georges Braque, *Le jour et la nuit: Cahiers 1917–1952* (Paris: Gallimard, 1952), 9.

25. See Chap. 6, note 23.

26. See Friedrich Hölderlin, "Verfahrungsweise des poetischen Geistes," trans. Thomas Pfau, "On the Operations of the Poetic Spirit," in *Friedrich Hölderlin: Essays and Letters on Theory*, ed. Pfau (Albany, N.Y.: SUNY Press, 1988), 0.

27. Michael Doran, *Conversations with Cézanne* (Berkeley: University of California Press, 2000), 114.

28. Oskar Becker, "Von der Hinfälligkeit des Schönen und der Abenteuerlichkeit des Künstlers," in *Von der Hinfälligkeit des Schönen und der Abenteuerlichkeit des Künstlers* (Berlin: Alexander, 1994), 8 [My translation—Tr.].

29. Ibid., 26.

30. For a more accurate and complete determination of the advenant, see Romano, *Event and World* and *Event and Time.*

31. Maldiney, *Existence: Crise et création* (Paris: Encre marine, 2001), 93.

32. [Or, "never to be a *fact*." The French avails itself here of the linguistic circumstance that the word "fait" can be taken as the past participle of "faire" (to make or to do) or the word "fact." This reinforces the point in question here, since a "fact" ("fait") is what has been done ("fait") by contrast with the event, which is to be grasped as that which enters into the active "making" of sense/meaning—Tr.]

33. A reference to these different phases and a more general reflection on this question may be found in the work by Kenzaburō Ōe, *A Healing Family*, trans. Stephen Snyder (New York: Kodansha, 1996).

34. Straus, *Geschehnis und Erlebnis* (Berlin: Juilius Springer, 1930), 25.

35. Paul Valéry, "Le cimetière marin," strophe VIII.

36. Heidegger, *Vom Wesen des Grundes*, in *Wegmarken*, GA 9:158; trans. William McNeill, "On the Essence of Ground," in *Pathmarks* (Cambridge: Cambridge University Press, 1998), 122–23 [translation modified—Tr.].

37. Hubertus Tellenbach, *Melancholy: History of the Problem, Endogeneity, Typology, Pathogenesis, Clinical Considerations*, trans. Erling Eng (Pittsburgh: Duquesne University Press, 1980), 132.

38. Heidegger, *Sein und Zeit*, 284; *Being and Time*, 330: "As existing, it [*Dasein*] must take over Being-a-basis."

39. [The French says, "le jet (*Geworfenheit*) de son pro-jet." The play on words is untranslatable—Tr.]

40. Ibid., 300; 347: through its project, *Dasein* "*makes possible for itself its factical existence.*"

41. Ibid., 310; 357.

42. Ibid., 284; 330.

43. See Hans Jonas, *The Phenomenon of Life: Toward a Philosophical Biology* (Evanston, Ill.: Northwestern University Press, 2001), 229–30.

44. Martin Buber, *I and Thou*, trans. Walter Kaufmann (New York: Touchstone, 1996), 69.

45. Bin Kimura, *Écrits de psychopathologie phénoménologique*, French trans. J. Bouderlique (Paris: PUF, 1992), 37 [I translate this and the following text from the French—Tr.].

46. Kimura, *L'Entre: Une approche phénoménologique de la schizophrénie*, French trans. C. Vincent (Grenoble: Jérôme Millon, 2000), 129.

47. On the impossibility for Heidegger to conceive of an authentic relation to others from the point of view of *Eigentlichkeit*, and on the aporias of solicitude in *Sein und Zeit*, see my article "Mourir à autrui," in *Critique*, no. 582 (November 1995).

48. Heidegger, *Sein und Zeit*, 326; *Being and Time*, 373.

49. Heidegger, "Vom Wesen des Grundes," in *Wegmarken*, GA 9:164; trans. William McNeill, "On the Essence of Ground," in *Pathmarks* (New York: Cambridge University Press, 1998) 126–27 [translation modified—Tr.].

50. Ibid., 126.

51. Aeschylus, *Agamemnon*, v. 177.

52. Françoise Dastur, *Heidegger and the Question of Time*, trans. François Raffoul and David Pettigrew (Amherst, N.Y.: Humanity Books, 1999), 65.

53. Heidegger, *Sein und Zeit*, 384; *Being and Time*, 436 [translation modified—Tr.].

54. Ignatius of Loyola, *The Spiritual Exercises of St. Ignatius of Loyola* (New York: P. J. Kenedy and Sons, 1914), 44.

55. Meister Eckhart, *Meister Eckhart, from Whom God Hid Nothing: Sermons, Writings, and Sayings*, ed. David O'Neal (Boston, Mass.: New Seeds, 2005), 120.

56. Heidegger, *Nietzsche II*, GA 6.2:319; trans. David Farrell Krell, *Nietzsche*, vols. 3 and 4 (London: Routledge and Kegan Paul, 1993), 214 [translation slightly modified—Tr.].

57. Emmanuel Levinas, *Totality and Infinity*, trans. Alphonso Lingis (Pittsburgh: Duquesne University Press, 1969), 45.

58. Heidegger, *Grundbegriffe*, GA 51:59; trans. Gary E. Aylesworth, *Basic Concepts* (Bloomington: Indiana University Press, 1998), 50.

59. Heidegger, "Nachwort zu 'Was ist Metaphysik?'"; this text is modified in the 5th editon; see *Wegmarken*, GA 9:306; trans. Kaufmann, "Postscript to 'What Is Metaphysics? [1943],'" in *Pathmarks*, ed. McNeill (Cambridge: Cambridge University Press, 1998), 233 [translation modified—Tr.].

60. Gadamer makes the following commentary on this passage: "It is all the old seduction of the *chorismos*, of which Plato rightly says that it was the seduction of the thought of the Idea and that he was nevertheless unable to avoid, in that Heidegger also becomes involved through his critical enquiry into the grounding of metaphysics"; "Qu'est-ce que la métaphysique?" French trans. in Gademer, *L'art de comprendre: Écrits* (Paris: Aubier, 1991), 2:83 [my translation from French—Tr.].

61. Heidegger, *Wegmarken*, GA 9:115; *Pathmarks*, 91.

62. Heidegger, "Nachwort zu 'Was ist Metaphysik?,'" GA 9:306; trans. Kaufmann, "Postscript to 'What Is Metaphysics?,'" 233.

63. Ibid. [translation modified—Tr.].

64. For example, Heidegger, *Wegmarken*, GA 9:372: *"ein vom Sein selbst ereignetes . . . Denken"*: "A thinking that is an event of Being itself" (*Pathmarks*, 282, translation modified). And Heidegger adds, on the subject of this event of the historical dispensation of Being, that it "is never based exclusively or even primarily on philosophical exegesis" (trans. Gregory Fried and Richard Polt, *Introduction to Metaphysics* [New Haven: Yale University Press, 2000], 211). This is why the forgetfulness of Being that is at the source of metaphysics can be thought of as a "fate" or "doom" (*Verhängnis*)," "the necessary fate of the West" (Heidegger, *Vorträge und Aufsätze* [Pfullingen: Neske, 1954], 77; trans. Joan Stambaugh, *The End of Philosophy* [Chicago: University of Chicago Press, 2003], 90).

65. And since being itself is finite, this forgetfulness of finitude does indeed risk manifesting itself as a surreptitious "ontification" of being.

66. Heraclitus, frag. 52.

67. Heraclitus, frag. 18.

Perspectives in Continental Philosophy

John D. Caputo, series editor

John D. Caputo, ed., *Deconstruction in a Nutshell: A Conversation with Jacques Derrida.*

Michael Strawser, *Both/And: Reading Kierkegaard—From Irony to Edification.*

Michael D. Barber, *Ethical Hermeneutics: Rationality in Enrique Dussel's Philosophy of Liberation.*

James H. Olthuis, ed., *Knowing Other-wise: Philosophy at the Threshold of Spirituality.*

James Swindal, *Reflection Revisited: Jürgen Habermas's Discursive Theory of Truth.*

Richard Kearney, *Poetics of Imagining: Modern and Postmodern.* Second edition.

Thomas W. Busch, *Circulating Being: From Embodiment to Incorporation—Essays on Late Existentialism.*

Edith Wyschogrod, *Emmanuel Levinas: The Problem of Ethical Metaphysics.* Second edition.

Francis J. Ambrosio, ed., *The Question of Christian Philosophy Today.*

Jeffrey Bloechl, ed., *The Face of the Other and the Trace of God: Essays on the Philosophy of Emmanuel Levinas.*

Ilse N. Bulhof and Laurens ten Kate, eds., *Flight of the Gods: Philosophical Perspectives on Negative Theology.*

Trish Glazebrook, *Heidegger's Philosophy of Science.*

Kevin Hart, *The Trespass of the Sign: Deconstruction, Theology, and Philosophy.*

Mark C. Taylor, *Journeys to Selfhood: Hegel and Kierkegaard.* Second edition.

Dominique Janicaud, Jean-François Courtine, Jean-Louis Chrétien, Michel Henry, Jean-Luc Marion, and Paul Ricoeur, *Phenomenology and the "Theological Turn": The French Debate.*

Karl Jaspers, *The Question of German Guilt.* Introduction by Joseph W. Koterski, S.J.

Jean-Luc Marion, *The Idol and Distance: Five Studies.* Translated with an introduction by Thomas A. Carlson.

Jeffrey Dudiak, *The Intrigue of Ethics: A Reading of the Idea of Discourse in the Thought of Emmanuel Levinas.*

Robyn Horner, *Rethinking God as Gift: Marion, Derrida, and the Limits of Phenomenology.*

Mark Dooley, *The Politics of Exodus: Søren Kierkegaard's Ethics of Responsibility.*

Merold Westphal, *Overcoming Onto-Theology: Toward a Postmodern Christian Faith.*

Edith Wyschogrod, Jean-Joseph Goux, and Eric Boynton, eds., *The Enigma of Gift and Sacrifice.*

Stanislas Breton, *The Word and the Cross.* Translated with an introduction by Jacquelyn Porter.

Jean-Luc Marion, *Prolegomena to Charity.* Translated by Stephen E. Lewis.

Peter H. Spader, *Scheler's Ethical Personalism: Its Logic, Development, and Promise.*

Jean-Louis Chrétien, *The Unforgettable and the Unhoped For.* Translated by Jeffrey Bloechl.

Don Cupitt, *Is Nothing Sacred? The Non-Realist Philosophy of Religion: Selected Essays.*

Jean-Luc Marion, *In Excess: Studies of Saturated Phenomena.* Translated by Robyn Horner and Vincent Berraud.

Phillip Goodchild, *Rethinking Philosophy of Religion: Approaches from Continental Philosophy.*

William J. Richardson, S.J., *Heidegger: Through Phenomenology to Thought.*

Jeffrey Andrew Barash, *Martin Heidegger and the Problem of Historical Meaning.*

Jean-Louis Chrétien, *Hand to Hand: Listening to the Work of Art.* Translated by Stephen E. Lewis.

Jean-Louis Chrétien, *The Call and the Response.* Translated with an introduction by Anne Davenport.

D. C. Schindler, *Han Urs von Balthasar and the Dramatic Structure of Truth: A Philosophical Investigation.*

Julian Wolfreys, ed., *Thinking Difference: Critics in Conversation.*

Allen Scult, *Being Jewish/Reading Heidegger: An Ontological Encounter.*

Richard Kearney, *Debates in Continental Philosophy: Conversations with Contemporary Thinkers.*

Jennifer Anna Gosetti-Ferencei, *Heidegger, Hölderlin, and the Subject of Poetic Language: Toward a New Poetics of Dasein.*

Jolita Pons, *Stealing a Gift: Kierkegaard's Pseudonyms and the Bible.*

Jean-Yves Lacoste, *Experience and the Absolute: Disputed Questions on the Humanity of Man.* Translated by Mark Raftery-Skehan.

Charles P. Bigger, *Between* Chora *and the Good: Metaphor's Metaphysical Neighborhood.*

Dominique Janicaud, *Phenomenology "Wide Open": After the French Debate.* Translated by Charles N. Cabral.

Ian Leask and Eoin Cassidy, eds., *Givenness and God: Questions of Jean-Luc Marion.*

Jacques Derrida, *Sovereignties in Question: The Poetics of Paul Celan*. Edited by Thomas Dutoit and Outi Pasanen.

William Desmond, *Is There a Sabbath for Thought? Between Religion and Philosophy.*

Bruce Ellis Benson and Norman Wirzba, eds., *The Phenomenology of Prayer.*

S. Clark Buckner and Matthew Statler, eds., *Styles of Piety: Practicing Philosophy after the Death of God.*

Kevin Hart and Barbara Wall, eds., *The Experience of God: A Postmodern Response.*

John Panteleimon Manoussakis, *After God: Richard Kearney and the Religious Turn in Continental Philosophy.*

John Martis, *Philippe Lacoue-Labarthe: Representation and the Loss of the Subject.*

Jean-Luc Nancy, *The Ground of the Image.*

Edith Wyschogrod, *Crossover Queries: Dwelling with Negatives, Embodying Philosophy's Others.*

Gerald Bruns, *On the Anarchy of Poetry and Philosophy: A Guide for the Unruly.*

Brian Treanor, *Aspects of Alterity: Levinas, Marcel, and the Contemporary Debate.*

Simon Morgan Wortham, *Counter-Institutions: Jacques Derrida and the Question of the University.*

Leonard Lawlor, *The Implications of Immanence: Toward a New Concept of Life.*

Clayton Crockett, *Interstices of the Sublime: Theology and Psychoanalytic Theory.*

Bettina Bergo, Joseph Cohen, and Raphael Zagury-Orly, eds., *Judeities: Questions for Jacques Derrida*. Translated by Bettina Bergo and Michael B. Smith.

Jean-Luc Marion, *On the Ego and on God: Further Cartesian Questions*. Translated by Christina M. Gschwandtner.

Jean-Luc Nancy, *Philosophical Chronicles*. Translated by Franson Manjali.

Jean-Luc Nancy, *Dis-Enclosure: The Deconstruction of Christianity*. Translated by Bettina Bergo, Gabriel Malenfant, and Michael B. Smith.

Andrea Hurst, *Derrida Vis-à-vis Lacan: Interweaving Deconstruction and Psychoanalysis.*

Jean-Luc Nancy, *Noli me tangere: On the Raising of the Body*. Translated by Sarah Clift, Pascale-Anne Brault, and Michael Naas.

Jacques Derrida, *The Animal That Therefore I Am*. Edited by Marie-Louise Mallet, translated by David Wills.

Jean-Luc Marion, *The Visible and the Revealed*. Translated by Christina M. Gschwandtner and others.

Michel Henry, *Material Phenomenology*. Translated by Scott Davidson.

Jean-Luc Nancy, *Corpus*. Translated by Richard A. Rand.

Joshua Kates, *Fielding Derrida.*

Michael Naas, *Derrida From Now On.*

Shannon Sullivan and Dennis J. Schmidt, eds., *Difficulties of Ethical Life.*

Catherine Malabou, *What Should We Do with Our Brain?* Translated by Sebastian Rand, Introduction by Marc Jeannerod.

Claude Romano, *Event and World*. Translated by Shane Mackinlay.

Vanessa Lemm, *Nietzsche's Animal Philosophy: Culture, Politics, and the Animality of the Human Being.*

B. Keith Putt, ed., *Gazing Through a Prism Darkly: Reflections on Merold Westphal's Hermeneutical Epistemology.*

Eric Boynton and Martin Kavka, eds., *Saintly Influence: Edith Wyschogrod and the Possibilities of Philosophy of Religion.*

Shane Mackinlay, *Interpreting Excess: Jean-Luc Marion, Saturated Phenomena, and Hermeneutics.*

Kevin Hart and Michael A. Signer, eds., *The Exorbitant: Emmanuel Levinas Between Jews and Christians.*

Bruce Ellis Benson and Norman Wirzba, eds., *Words of Life: New Theological Turns in French Phenomenology.*

William Robert, *Trials: Of Antigone and Jesus.*

Brian Treanor and Henry Isaac Venema, eds., *A Passion for the Possible: Thinking with Paul Ricoeur.*

Kas Saghafi, *Apparitions—Of Derrida's Other.*

Nick Mansfield, *The God Who Deconstructs Himself: Sovereignty and Subjectivity Between Freud, Bataille, and Derrida.*

Don Ihde, *Heidegger's Technologies: Postphenomenological Perspectives.*

Suzi Adams, *Castoriadis's Ontology: Being and Creation.*

Richard Kearney and Kascha Semonovitch, eds., *Phenomenologies of the Stranger: Between Hostility and Hospitality.*

Michael Naas, *Miracle and Machine: Jacques Derrida and the Two Sources of Religion, Science, and the Media.*

Alena Alexandrova, Ignaas Devisch, Laurens ten Kate, and Aukje van Rooden, *Re-treating Religion: Deconstructing Christianity with Jean-Luc Nancy*. Preamble by Jean-Luc Nancy.

Emmanuel Falque, *The Metamorphosis of Finitude: An Essay on Birth and Resurrection*. Translated by George Hughes.

Scott M. Campbell, *The Early Heidegger's Philosophy of Life: Facticity, Being, and Language.*

Françoise Dastur, *How Are We to Confront Death? An Introduction to Philosophy.* Translated by Robert Vallier. Foreword by David Farrell Krell.

Christina M. Gschwandtner, *Postmodern Apologetics? Arguments for God in Contemporary Philosophy.*

Ben Morgan, *On Becoming God: Late Medieval Mysticism and the Modern Western Self.*

Neal DeRoo, *Futurity in Phenomenology: Promise and Method in Husserl, Levinas, and Derrida.*

Sarah LaChance Adams and Caroline R. Lundquist, eds., *Coming to Life: Philosophies of Pregnancy, Childbirth, and Mothering.*

Thomas Claviez, ed., *The Conditions of Hospitality: Ethics, Politics, and Aesthetics on the Threshold of the Possible.*

Roland Faber and Jeremy Fackenthal, eds., *Theopoetic Folds: Philosophizing Multifariousness.*

Jean-Luc Marion, *The Essential Writings*. Edited by Kevin Hart.

Adam S. Miller, *Speculative Grace: Bruno Latour and Object-Oriented Theology.* Foreword by Levi R. Bryant.

Jean-Luc Nancy, *Corpus II: Writings on Sexuality.*

David Nowell Smith, *Sounding/Silence: Martin Heidegger at the Limits of Poetics.*

Gregory C. Stallings, Manuel Asensi, and Carl Good, eds., *Material Spirit: Religion and Literature Intranscendent.*

Claude Romano, *Event and Time.* Translated by Stephen E. Lewis.

Frank Chouraqui, *Ambiguity and the Absolute: Nietzsche and Merleau-Ponty on the Question of Truth.*

Noëlle Vahanian, *The Rebellious No: Variations on a Secular Theology of Language.*

Michael Naas, *The End of the World and Other Teachable Moments: Jacques Derrida's Final Seminar.*

Jean-Louis Chrétien, *Under the Gaze of the Bible.* Translated by John Marson Dunaway.

Edward Baring and Peter E. Gordon, eds., *The Trace of God: Derrida and Religion.*

Vanessa Lemm, ed., *Nietzsche and the Becoming of Life.*

Aaron T. Looney, *Vladimir Jankélévitch: The Time of Forgiveness.*

Richard Kearney and Brian Treanor, eds., *Carnal Hermeneutic.*

Tarek R. Dika and W. Chris Hackett, *Quiet Powers of the Possible: Interviews in Contemporary French Phenomenology.* Foreword by Richard Kearney.

Jeremy Biles and Kent L. Brintnall, eds., *Negative Ecstasies: Georges Bataille and the Study of Religion.*

Claude Romano, *There Is: The Event and the Finitude of Appearing.* Translated by Michael B. Smith.

Jason M. Wirth, *Commiserating with Devastated Things: Milan Kundera and the Entitlements of Thinking.*